Anthropology beyond Culture

WENNER-GREN INTERNATIONAL SYMPOSIUM SERIES

Series Editor: Richard G. Fox, President, Wenner-Gren Foundation for Anthropological Research, New York.

ISSN: 1475-536X

Since its inception in 1941, the Wenner-Gren Foundation has convened more than 125 international symposia on pressing issues in anthropology. Wenner-Gren International symposia recognize no boundaries—intellectual, national, or subdisciplinary. These symposia affirm the worth of anthropology and its capacity to address the nature of humankind from a great variety of perspectives. They make new links to related disciplines, such as law, history, and ethnomusicology, and revivify old links, as between archaeology and sociocultural anthropology, for example. Each symposium brings together participants from around the world, for a week-long engagement with a specific issue, but only after intensive planning of the topic and format over the previous 18 months.

In fulfilling its mission to build a world community of anthropologists and to support basic research in anthropology, the Foundation now extends its distinctive and productive pattern of pre-symposium planning to the preparation and publication of the resulting volumes. Never before has the Foundation taken responsibility for publishing the papers from its international symposia. By initiating this series, the Foundation wishes to ensure timely publication, wide distribution, and high production standards. The President of the Foundation serves as the series editor, and the symposium organizers edit the individual volumes.

Some landmark volumes from the past are: *Man's Role in Changing the Face of the Earth* in 1956 (William L. Thomas); *Man the Hunter* in 1968 (Irv DeVore and Richard B. Lee); *Cloth and Human Experience* in 1989 (Jane Schneider and Annette Weiner); and *Tools, Language, and Cognition in Human Evolution* in 1993 (Kathleen Gibson and Tim Ingold). Reports on recent symposia can be found on the foundation's website, *www.wennergren.org*, and inquiries should be addressed to *president@wennergren.org*.

Anthropology beyond Culture

Edited by

RICHARD G. FOX AND BARBARA J. KING

Oxford • New York

First published in 2002 by
Berg
Editorial offices:
150 Cowley Road, Oxford, OX4 1JJ, UK
838 Broadway, Third Floor, New York, NY 10003-4812, USA

© Richard G. Fox and Barbara J. King 2002

All rights reserved.
No part of this publication may be reproduced in any form or by any means without the written permission of Berg.

Berg is the imprint of Oxford International Publishers Ltd.

Library of Congress Cataloging-in-Publication Data

A catalogue record for this book is available from the Library of Congress.

British Library Cataloguing-in-Publication Data

A catalogue record for this book is available from the British Library.

ISBN 1 85973 524 X (Cloth)
     1 85973 529 0 (Paper)

Typeset by JS Typesetting, Wellingborough, Northants.
Printed in the United Kingdom by Biddles Ltd, Guildford and King's Lynn.

To Dr. Frank Wadsworth, former Chairman of the Wenner-Gren Board of Trustees.

He sold an old castle in Austria in order to secure the future of a foundation in New York.

Contents

Acknowledgments ix

List of Figures xi

Participants at the 2000 Wenner-Gren Symposium xiii

Foreword
Sydel Silverman xv

Introduction: Beyond Culture Worry
Richard G. Fox and *Barbara J. King* 1

Part 1: Leaving Culture Worry Behind

1 Toward a Richer Description and Analysis of Cultural Phenomena
Fredrik Barth 23

2 Adieu, Culture: A New Duty Arises
Michel-Rolph Trouillot 37

3 Culture and Anthropology in Ethnographic Modernity
Yoshinobu Ota 61

Part 2: Emergent Sociality — Developmentalism & Evol'n

4 On Patterned Interactions and Culture in Great Apes
Barbara J. King 83

5 Anthropology as the Whole Science of What It Is to Be

Human
Christina Toren 105

6 The Broader Implications of Borderline Areas of
Language Research
Stuart Shanker 125

Part 3: Patterns and Continuities

7 Archaeology and Culture: Sites of Power and Process
Rita P. Wright 147

8 Language as a Model for Culture: Lessons from the
Cognitive Sciences
Penelope Brown 169

9 Cultural Variation in Time and Space: The Case for a
Populational Theory of Culture
William H. Durham 193

Part 4: The Politics of Culture

10 The Politics of Culture in Post-apartheid South Africa
Richard A. Wilson 209

11 "Culture" as Stereotype: Public Uses in Ecuador
Xavier Andrade 235

12 All *Kulturvölker* Now? Social Anthropological
Reflections on the German-American Tradition
Christopher M. Hann 259

References 277

Index 307

Acknowledgments

We are most grateful to Sydel Silverman, who, while President of the Wenner-Gren Foundation, provided initial support as we developed this symposium and who was a major contributor at the symposium itself. We are also much in debt to Laurie Obbink, the conference co-coordinator for the foundation, and, Mark Mahoney, the foundation's resources administrator, who made sure the symposium ran smoothly and all creature comforts were provided. Laurie efficiently handled post-symposium communications with participants and prepared the manuscript for copy-editing.

To our copy editor, Jane Kepp, we offer many thanks for the fine editing that clarified our meaning and simplified our prose. Kathryn Earle at Berg Publishers has supported this endeavor in many ways, including suggesting the photo of Carhenge for the cover. We appreciate her efforts on behalf of this volume and in support of the Wenner-Gren International Symposium series.

Judy Fox, Jane Kepp, Molly Mullin, Sydel Silverman, and Willow Powers gently prodded us with good comments and criticisms, which sometimes tempered our statements and always made us better aware of the consequences of what we had to say.

Richard G. Fox
Barbara J. King

List of Figures

4.1	The gorilla infant Kwame in contact with his mother, Mandara	97
4.2	Sequence of interaction between Kwame and Mandara	99
4.3	Sequence of interaction among Kwame, his older brother Ktembe, and Mandara	100
11.1	"Shit digger #1," cartoon by Pancho Jaime	250
11.2	"A little wig-wearing cholito," cartoon by Pancho Jaime	252

Participants at the 2000 Wenner-Gren Symposium

Xavier Andrade, New School for Social Research
Robert Aunger, Cambridge University
Fredrik Barth, University of Oslo/Boston University
Christophe Boesch, Max Planck Institute for Evolutionary Anthropology (Leipzig)
Penelope Brown, Max Planck Institute for Psycholinguistics (Nijmegen)
William H. Durham, Stanford University
Richard G. Fox, Wenner-Gren Foundation
Kathleen R. Gibson, University of Texas (Houston)
Christopher M. Hann, Max Planck Institute for Social Anthropology (Halle)
Barbara J. King, College of William and Mary
Molly Mullin, Albion College
Yoshinobu Ota, University of Kyushu
Anne Russon, York University
Stuart Shanker, York University
Sydel Silverman, Senior Fellow, Wenner-Gren Foundation
Christina Toren, Brunel University
Michel-Rolph Trouillot, University of Chicago
Richard A. Wilson, University of Sussex
Rita Wright, New York University
Susan Wright, University of Birmingham

Foreword

Sydel Silverman

The idea for a Wenner-Gren conference on the culture concept was first suggested to me in January 1987, at the first symposium I participated in as president of the foundation. At that symposium, "Gender Hierarchies," anthropologists from the four fields found a number of common interests, especially around processes of social learning, and it seemed that the beleaguered culture concept might still have a role to play in exploring such cross-field concerns. A conference that would reexamine the concept and ask whether we still need it, and why, seemed timely. The idea was not pursued then, but over the subsequent years I continued to look for potential organizers who might realize it. It was finally in 2000, following upon a proposal from Richard Fox and Barbara King, that a conference on culture came to fruition. It was the last Wenner-Gren symposium initiated under my watch.

In 1987 as in 2000, anthropologists (primarily the American variety) were beset by "culture worry," the theme of this book: the uneasiness, apprehension, or defensiveness felt by many at what they perceived as threats to their core concept, culture. Such threats came from criticisms of the concept from within the discipline as well as from its appropriation and, too often, misuse in other academic fields, in public discourse, and in political contexts. Then as now, anthropologists often carried on debates with colleagues without explicitly defining the concept, under the assumption that they, at least, knew what they intended by it, at the same time they complained that others who adopted the term did not understand the anthropological meaning. Yet every anthropologist knows that there is little agreement within the discipline on exactly what is meant by culture. Why, then, do anthropologists care so much—worry so much—about the fate of a concept whose meaning they do not share?

The history of the culture concept, both prior to its adoption by anthropology and over the twentieth-century course of the discipline, has been documented by numerous scholars and need not be belabored here. Suffice it to consider the status of the concept at the time of the exhaustive inventory of extant definitions carried out by A. L. Kroeber and Clyde Kluckhohn (1952). Their survey made it abundantly clear that no consensus on the concept existed even within anthropology, but it also revealed that the multiple definitions were overlapping, differing in their "emphases": emphasizing social heritage or tradition, rule or way, problem solving or learning, patterning or organization, or other things. Kroeber and Kluckhohn sometimes cited a single author as an exemplar of several of these positions. One might take these emphases as different aspects of a single concept, but their totality did not make for an elegant definition, and Kroeber and Kluckhohn opted to talk *about* culture rather than define it.

The landmark compact between Kroeber and the sociologist Talcott Parsons, published in 1958, did take the step of proposing a particular definition, which fixed on ideas and values. These they assigned to anthropology, leaving the "social" (relations, systems, organization) for the sociologists. The influence of prominent anthropologists at Parsons's own institutional base, the Department of Social Relations at Harvard, and subsequently those at the University of Chicago, carried forward an ideational notion of culture, which came into prominence with the ascendance of interpretive and symbolic anthropology in the 1970s. In view of the diversity of prior uses of the concept, it would have been surprising had this ascendancy brought consensus to the discipline—and it did not. The "traditional" definition cited by the editors of the present volume (which takes culture as representations) may or may not be a majority position. However, a cursory survey of recent textbooks (one of the few contexts in which anthropologists actually commit themselves to a definition) makes it plain that most of the "emphases" identified by Kroeber and Kluckhohn a half-century ago are still invoked.

We may note a number of lines of divergence in current uses of the culture concept. First, there are those who adopt an ideational definition (symbols, values, representation) as against those who take an inclusive approach, including ideas and symbols along with the material products, technology, social organization, and other dimensions of group life that Parsons and Kroeber turned over to other social sciences. Second, there are differences in whether culture is seen to reside in the mind (with behavior and artifacts as outcomes of mental models) or in behavior (e.g., its common definition as learned, socially transmitted behavior).

Third, there are differences with regard to the location of culture: in the individual (who exercises choice-making and manipulation) or in a social entity (a group that "has" a culture). Related to this is the issue of agency, some treating culture as if it is a thing in itself (and capable of doing things), others seeing it as an aspect of group life or as subject to the agency of individuals. Fourth, there are differences in assumptions about integration, between those who regard culture as a "package," moving as a piece, and those who see the question of integration as one to be empirically determined. Those who take the latter position generally prefer to use "cultural" as an adjective rather than "culture" as a noun. Finally, the distinction between the singular "culture" (as a general attribute of humans and as an entity that evolves) and the plural "cultures" (which addresses the diversity of human groups in time and place) is still alive. Other distinctions could be added to this list.

The question, then, is, why the worry? One answer lies perhaps in the fact that culture condenses a number of tenets held by anthropologists, much as did the several "emphases" that Kroeber and Kluckhohn pointed to: the distinction between genetic and social inheritance, the connection among different domains of life, the patterning of cultural content (even when the degree of organization is left an open question), the historicity of such patterns, and their potential adaptedness to specific conditions. In much the same way that Michel-Rolph Trouillot, in this volume, endorses the "conceptual kernel" behind the culture concept even as he advocates abandoning the word, anthropologists agree on what the concept summarizes much more than they do on the term itself.

Other answers to the question are specific to American anthropology. For a discipline committed to the study of both human evolution and the time/space diversity of group life, the concept of culture (in both its singular and plural senses) provides a unifying thread. The American notion of culture did not give rise to the four-field organization, itself the product of specific historical conditions, but it afforded a means of discourse among the fields, a sense of shared problems and purpose. It is not an irony (as might appear at first glance) that the move to abandon the culture concept is most prevalent among cultural anthropologists; for them, anthropology without culture is not only feasible but well established in British and continental traditions. For many biological anthropologists, primatologists, archaeologists, and linguistic anthropologists, however, it is "culture" that cements their placement within anthropology rather than in the sister disciplines that each of these specialists straddles.

In the years between 1987 and 2000, the Wenner-Gren Foundation sponsored more than twenty international symposia on topics that cut across the whole anthropological spectrum. In their totality, they provide a window on the discipline during this period. What is surprising about these symposia, from the perspective of the theme of this book, is how infrequently their participants directly invoked "culture," despite its continued status as a core concept for anthropology. Occasionally, culture in the plural sense was used interchangeably with society or social group. "Cultural" was more common, as in "cultural representations," "cultural categories," or "cultural practices," terms taken, for the most part, as self-evident and nonproblematical.

In these symposia, what any anthropologist would recognize as "cultural" phenomena were discussed in exhaustive detail in the context of numerous problems, but definitions of and arguments for or against culture were seldom needed to pursue the issues at hand. For example, "Amazonian Synthesis" (1989) traced the changing relationships of human organization, ideology, economy, and ecology over twelve thousand years of indigenous occupation of the region, assuming the connectedness of these domains without referring to culture as such. "Tools, Language, and Intelligence" (1990) explored the evolutionary linkages among language, tool use, and cognition; it was more strategic to discuss these separately than to collapse them into "culture." "The Great Apes Revisited" (1994) looked at behavioral diversity and social cognition in apes, seeking evolutionary processes behind them, but participants cautioned that to simply call such patterns "culture" might obscure more than it revealed. "Imperial Designs" (1997), in which archaeologists and historians compared the dynamics of diverse empires, fully incorporated the "kernel" of culture but without the term. It did so in its comparative approach, its interest in the relationship among different domains (economic, political, ideological, social structural), and its concern with the "margins" (both social and geographical) as well as the centers of empires.

The culture concept itself came in for scrutiny in two ways in the symposia. First, a number of them were predicated upon critiques of aspects of the concept in its traditional guise. "AIDS Research in Anthropology" (1990) showed how a focus on marginal groups and stigma challenged normative assumptions about culture. "The Politics of Reproduction" (1991) insisted that cultural practices must be seen not merely as local or as neutral "customs" but in dynamic relationship with global political economy. In a similar vein, "Transnationalism, Nation-State Building, and Culture" (1994) argued that analysis of cultural production requires a theoretical framework that takes account of global capitalism, class, and multiple structures of power. "Amazonia and Melanesia" (1996), which took up issues of anthropological comparison, affirmed that it was not "cultures" as such that should be compared but rather relationalities; this kind of comparison neither assumed bounded units nor excluded history.

The second way in which culture became a focus in some symposia was in its use in drawing a contrast to something else. "Rethinking Linguistic Relativity" (1991), which revisited Whorfian ideas about the relationships of language, thought, and culture, posed questions of cultural variation against prevailing theories of linguistic and cognitive universals. "Theorizing Sexuality" (1993) traced the tension, in the history of sexuality study, between biomedically oriented sexology and the "cultural influence" model; the latter model, in turn, was counterposed to cultural constructivism. "Anthropology in the Age of Genetics" (1999) sought to bring together the biology of genetics with cultural understandings of genetic discourse and practices, both critiquing genetic determinism and demonstrating the interdependency of biology and culture.

That so many of the symposia embodied the tenets condensed by the culture concept and pursued the processes entailed in it—without depending upon the word—supports the contention of the editors of this volume that anthropology can have a life beyond culture. Some of the symposia show, however, that culture (the word) still has work to do in underlining contrasts with competing approaches. They also remind us that the culture concept is an evolving one. Assumptions of an earlier period can be challenged and new uses can be adopted; the choice need not be to accept a particular set of meanings intact or abandon the concept altogether. What remains to be seen is whether the "kernel" in culture can be preserved in the long run and whether the work of culture can go forward without the concept (or the term) itself. The contributors to this book represent a variety of views on that quandary, suggesting that neither the worry nor the debates about culture will be settled anytime soon.

Introduction: Beyond Culture Worry

Richard G. Fox and *Barbara J. King*

> Some years ago, when I published a book on the evolution of culture in animals, I received a furious letter from an anthropologist telling me to keep my dirty hands off their word.
>
> —John Tyler Bonner, in a review of Frans de Waal's
> *The Ape and the Sushi Master*

Anthropologists have never had a single concept of culture upon which they agreed. Perplexity and even anguish over culture have been with us for a long time (British anthropologists, for instance, have always been skeptical of the culture concept). But our disquiet with the concept has increased greatly in recent years. We have become increasingly dissatisfied with the traditional definition of culture within anthropology, by which culture is a highly patterned and consistent set of representations (or beliefs) that constitute a people's perception of reality and that get reproduced relatively intact across generations through enculturation. The homogeneity and continuity that this traditional definition assumes, along with its failure to address social inequality and individual agency, distress many anthropologists (Brumann [1999] reviews the arguments, but also see Abu-Lughod 1991; Bourdieu 1977; Fox 1985, 1995; Kuper 1999; Ortner 1984; Trouillot 1991).

Discontent with the traditional definition of culture, most apparent in cultural anthropology, makes for other worries. Primatologists, for example, have become disturbed by what appears to be a "glass ceiling" hanging over their use of the culture concept. As primatologists become more convinced that culture defined as learned traditions exists among nonhuman primates, they find cultural anthropologists modifying the concept or retreating entirely from its use. As a result, primatologists

1

worry that they have expended immense scholarly effort on a concept now thought by many within anthropology to lack analytic rigor.

Meanwhile, in the public sphere, the culture concept has gained broad acceptance. It has achieved a wide (and vapid) usage in popular expression, as, for example, in common terms such as "classroom culture," "corporate culture," and "the culture wars." It has been appropriated for political purposes, as when politicians use it to justify anti-immigration or antiminority policies or by indigenous activists to legitimate claims to rights and property. Such uses of the culture concept—insipid on the one hand and highly politicized on the other—have increased the misgivings about culture felt by anthropologists (see, for example, Kahn 1989; Spencer 1990; Stolcke 1995; Wright 1998).

All of these recent anxieties have inspired ever more valiant but dubious attempts to fix upon a definition of culture that is universally applicable and can be willingly shared by all anthropologists. We anthropologists persist, at least many of us, in allegiance to the idea that anthropology can arrive at such a concept, and to that end we propose a patch here, a stitch there, a reweaving elsewhere—until we have fabricated an unsatisfying crazy quilt instead of the blanket concept we intended. Out of frustration with such patching up, perhaps, some of us go about our scholarship using the term culture as if it were fully agreed upon—as if, by putting it into print, we thereby prove that such a paradigmatic concept covers the discipline. Meanwhile, our patched-up conceptions of culture or, alternatively, our business-as-usual denial that we have any problem with the concept irks those anthropologists who have quit on it altogether. They regard as unhealthy our addiction to a concept that in their view is essentialist or racist or ahistorical or static, and they want to ban culture from the workplace.

Anthropology without Worry

We believe little good has come to anthropology from this long-standing agitation and continuous turmoil over the concept of culture. We think it is time for anthropologists to go beyond handwringing over the definition of this concept, give up worrying over the attempt to fix a universal meaning for it, and stop fretting over the absence of consensus within the discipline. We need to get on with doing anthropology, and the first step is to reject a "love it or leave it" relationship with the concept of culture. We should be aware, as scholars, of its faults and failures, just as we should intellectually acknowledge its value and successes. We should also be open-minded about the alternatives some anthropologists have proposed.

What we cannot afford is to spend our intellectual energies in programmatic and polemical essays either celebrating or savaging this concept. Marshall Sahlins, for example, set out in a recent article (Sahlins 1999) to annihilate any opposition to the culture concept from those he calls "Afterologists," a "pickup" group composed of postmodernists, poststructuralists, neo-functionalists who speak loosely about anthropology's political conservatism, Foucauldians, those who study the "invention of tradition," reflexivists, and all others whom Sahlins finds delinquent in their allegiance to the culture concept. He insists that "human existence is symbolically constituted, which is to say culturally ordered" (Sahlins 1999: 400). Although an anthropologist presumably could accept the idea of symbolic constitution without believing that it implied cultural ordering, Sahlins asserts that this position is one he will never "give away." This intransigence, this conflation and dismissal of other viewpoints on the part of a great anthropologist, tells us something is wrong in our current intellectual proceedings. Sahlins, we suspect, adopted such a defensive stance out of real anger at some summary dismissals of the culture concept (for example, Herbert 1991), but our point is that counting coup never wins intellectual converts. Neither rallying round the concept of culture nor denouncing and banning it are productive strategies for anthropology today, and it is in this sense that we ask anthropology to move beyond culture.

The chapters in this book—which grew out of an international symposium held by the Wenner-Gren Foundation in Morelia, Mexico, in September 2000—evaluate culture concepts, or alternatives to any such concept, in relation to particular research objectives. In part 1, "Leaving Culture Worry Behind," Fredrik Barth, Michel-Rolph Trouillot, and Yoshinobu Ota respectively survey the successes and failures of the culture concept and propose ways to get beyond our current disquiet. Collectively, they indicate that there need be no single solution to the problems surrounding the culture concept, that anthropology can go on productively with or without such a concept, and that choice by scholars is both possible and necessary. The remaining chapters, arranged in three additional parts, embody the scholarly choices presented by Barth, Trouillot, and Ota, and they illustrate the research strategies for anthropology that these choices provide. Part 2, with chapters by Barbara King, Christina Toren, and Stuart Shanker, focuses on emergent sociality. The chapters by Rita Wright, Penelope Brown, and William Durham in part 3 take patterns and continuities as their research objectives. And in part 4, Richard Wilson, Xavier Andrade, and

Chris Hann show how anthropology can study the politics of culture and cultural nationalisms. Some of these chapters employ concepts of culture that work for the questions about humankind they wish to answer, although the concepts they employ vary. Others use concepts that the authors believe answer their questions better than any culture concept could. This variety of conceptions affirms the value of eschewing "global" prescriptions in favor of indicating what works "locally" for particular research questions.

Our goals in this collection may appear parochial because we disregard the really big question—What *is* culture?—that anthropology supposedly must now confront. We would say, however, that we choose to circumvent and go beyond this question because it has become much too big a deal. Has all the worry about the concept of culture produced a global definition or greater consensus among anthropologists? Has it energized better research? Has it informed more disciplined research proposals? Because we answer "no" to each of these questions, because we feel that "worry over" threatens to become "worrying (anthropology) to death," we believe in this case that circumvention represents progress, not diversion.

Here, then, is the proposition—local, we would say, not parochial—we wish to put forward with this collection: Anthropology can prosper without a global concept of culture or without any concept of culture. Such prosperity will come about only when we focus on research questions and then develop the analytic means to answer them. Rather than trying to shape a culture concept (or an alternative-to-culture concept) that we hope will conform to the behaviors and beliefs we wish to understand, why not start with those behaviors and beliefs and the understanding we wish to attain about them and then see what concept works well to help us do that? Many anthropologists, including some contributors to this book, have proceeded in just this way. But even these writers are affected by the ongoing worry about culture and may feel they have adequately met their task only when they put forward their local analysis as a global concept in the making. At least minimally, then, we must place the definitional exercise, the pursuit of a global concept of culture—and the allegiances and dismissals to which it gives rise—on hold.

But can we put it on hold? This worry about the culture concept and the power it holds over anthropology is not new, although the situation may have worsened as culture was enlisted in the wars over identity, immigration, and national integration of the last quarter of the twentieth century (see Kuper 1999). We fear it will not be easy to set the worry aside and adopt a pragmatic research strategy unless anthropologists acknowledge the power of the culture concept (even when it is dismissed, as, for example, in Kuper 1999). We must recognize that this power over us comes from within anthropology today and over the course of its history, although no doubt it is influenced by conditions in the world beyond. Oddly, at the very moment in which our research commonly champions the agency of the poor, the minority, and the subaltern, we anthropologists take our own condition to be determined by outside forces. Who can deny those external forces, but why cannot we anthropologists, like our subaltern subjects, assert our agency over them?

In what follows, we offer a brief look at two instances of the power of anthropology's own culture concept over its practitioners. The first is the "culture worry" displayed by some exemplary cultural anthropologists, past and present. The second is the power of the culture concept over primatologists' studies in nonhuman sociality.

Worrying Cultural Anthropology

In 1952, Alfred Kroeber and Clyde Kluckhohn surveyed the definitions of culture used in anthropology and related fields. They discovered an embarrassing abundance and, even more aggravating, an easy acceptance of what they regarded as a loose usage of the concept, which they found troubling. They felt that the phrase "in our culture" had come into general use by psychologists, psychiatrists, economists, and lawyers in the same mechanical way that medieval writers employed "God willing." For Kluckhohn and Kroeber, this usage had a good side, however: it was a sign that "the idea of culture, in the technical anthropological sense, is one of the key notions of contemporary American thought" (1952: 5)

Kroeber and Kluckhohn wished that "a precise anthropological concept of culture" could be firmly planted in "the thinking of educated citizens" (1952: 68), and they held anthropology responsible for the existing "lack of clarity and precision." They were worried and perhaps even embarrassed about anthropology's failure to clarify the diffuse and facile usage of the culture concept that had by then developed in the United States. Their explanation was that anthropologists had concentrated on "gathering, ordering, and classifying data" and had only recently come to consider problems of theory and "the logic of science" (1952: 69–70).

They nevertheless had faith that culture was the central concept of anthropology, and they hoped their survey of its many usages would somehow coalesce into a single, precise, anthropological definition (1952: 6). This allegiance to the promise of a unitary concept of culture contrasted sharply with the range of variation their survey documented.

For many anthropologists today, the power of the culture concept remains as strong as it was for Kroeber and Kluckhohn, although there is even greater worry about how suitable the concept is in the world at present. For example, Clifford Geertz stands by culture at the same time that he finds the concept troubling. He writes: "Whatever the infirmities of the concept of 'culture' there is nothing for it but to persist in spite of them" (Geertz 1995: 43). But he quickly admits how grave these infirmities proved to be in his own development as a scholar:

> It did not take [me] . . . long to become aware that they indeed do things differently elsewhere . . . . And it took only a little while longer to realize that a conception of culture as a massive causal force shaping belief and behavior to an abstractable pattern—what has been called the cookie-cutter view—was not very useful . . . . Something a good deal less muscular is needed, something a good deal more reactive, quizzical, watchful, better attuned to hints, uncertainties, contingencies, and incompletions. (Geertz 1995: 45)

Geertz does not say what such a culture concept—neither muscle-bound nor wimpy—would look like. In fact, in spite of his testimony for the culture concept, he goes on to do what we recommend: he presents an analysis of his experiences in Indonesia and Morocco that is informed by the study of local history, local behaviors, and local beliefs. His argument in favor of whatever concept he uses in this analysis—it is not clear that it is some less muscular concept of culture, because Geertz avoids such didacticism—is simply that it works for his purposes. Why, then, is his initial pledge of allegiance to culture necessary a half-century after Kluckhohn and Kroeber similarly worried about it?

Even more than Geertz, Sherry Ortner recognizes these infirmities, especially the difficulties the concept faces in dealing with globalization today. Her desire is neither to banish the concept of culture nor to conserve an unsuitable traditional definition. "Rather, the issue," she writes, "is, once again, one of reconfiguring this enormously productive concept for a changing world, a changing relationship between politics and academic life, and a changing landscape of theoretical possibilities" (Ortner 1999: 8).

Ortner's prescription for the reconfiguration requires changes in the anthropologist's state of awareness and political consciousness. It also obliges anthropologists to study new ethnographic locales such as borderlands and zones of conflict, and it obligates them to "situate" cultural analysis beneath, or subordinated to, social and political processes. How these changes sum up to a reconfigured *concept* of culture is unclear, especially when the last requirement appears to question the analytic power of explanations based on a culture concept. To us, her recommendation looks very much like Adam Kuper's argument (1999) against culture and his assertion that the elements it bundles together—politics, religion, and kinship, among others—must be disaggregated.

Ortner (1999: 11) sums up by saying that "the fate of 'culture' will depend on its uses." We admire the pragmatic attitude built into this comment, and our only reservation is that it seems to start from a commitment to the culture concept rather than to a set of research questions. This same priority informs Ortner's pursuit of reconfiguration. As in Geertz's writing, we see in Ortner's the power of the culture concept and the allegiance it claims from anthropologists even when it worries them most.

Worry Joined: The Case of Primatology

That the culture concept may powerfully direct the course of scholarship can be seen also in primatology, a discipline with strong historical roots in, and vital current linkage to, anthropology. In the last decade or so, primatologists who work to understand patterns of social transmission and behavioral diversity in monkeys and apes have joined sociocultural anthropologists in becoming moored to the culture concept.

To be sure, primatologists vigorously debate the definition of culture. They variously embrace or deny the existence of culture in monkeys and apes, especially the great apes such as chimpanzees. Yet this superficially dynamic engagement with the culture concept masks a deeper conservatism. We see in primatology a growing reluctance to acknowledge that the culture concept might be suited for only some research questions involving social transmission and behavioral diversity, or that it might be explored in ways entirely different from those presently being undertaken.

Might a focus on culture in nonhuman primates be, at times, an obstacle to our understanding rather than a boon? If so, then some primatological studies of sociality, social learning, and social sharing of knowledge, now cast as informing anthropology about the evolution of culture, might fare better without the culture concept. Could a broad look at routine, everyday patterns of sociality in monkey and ape groups enhance explorations of the evolution of behavioral diversity within the primate lineage? If so, then a narrow focus on highly visible traditions—how chimpanzees use tools or groom in one population versus others, for instance— needs to be complemented by studies that fully account for the different ways in which patterns of social interaction develop and are maintained across groups. The culture concept holds too much sway in current primatology to permit much attention to be paid to these types of questions.

Let us briefly characterize the allegiance to the culture concept pledged in recent primatology. As we see it, three questions typify the investigation of nonhuman primate culture today, each meant to be understood within an implicit comparative framework: What is culture (how is nonhuman primate culture different from human culture)? Who has culture and who does not (which species, or which populations, are most humanlike in having culture)? How is culture transmitted (how is it transmitted by nonhuman primates similarly to or differently from the ways humans transmit it)?

Most primatologists adhere to one of two closely related definitions of culture. In the first, culture is flatly equated with social learning. Frans de Waal writes: "Culture simply means that knowledge and habits are *acquired* from others—often, but not always, the older generation—which explains why two groups of the same species may behave differently. Because culture implies learning from others, we need to rule out that each individual has acquired a particular trait by itself before we call it cultural" (2001:6). This focus on culture as social learning is traceable to early claims for the cultural transmission of foraging techniques by Japanese macaques—the famous cases of potato washing and wheat mining noted by Japanese scientists (e.g., Kawai 1965; Kawamura 1959).

The second definition requires evidence for "group-specific behavior that is acquired, at least in part, from social influences" (McGrew 1998: 305). In this view, cross-group (but within-species) variation is a necessary requirement for, not just an outcome of, culture. The logic for this definition has been fueled especially by comparative research on chimpanzees (Whiten et al. 1999).

As they work to relate field data and definitions, primatologists grapple with criteria for, and properties of, culture. William McGrew (1992, 1998) has applied Kroeber's criteria for culture (1928), seminal in anthropology, to nonhuman primate behavioral diversity. Primatologists are careful to point out that cross-group differences in social learning occur not only in cases of subsistence (as in macaque potato washing and chimpanzee termite fishing) but also in nonsubsistence behaviors (as in the less famous cases of Japanese macaque stone handling [Huffman 1996] and egg-louse grooming [Tanaka 1995]). Debate has ensued about whether any primate other than humans accumulates modifications in traditions across generations and thus is capable of the "ratchet effect" and true cultural learning (e.g., McGrew 1998; Tomasello 1999). An even greater controversy exists over whether monkeys and apes are capable of imitation and teaching or only of so-called weaker forms of knowledge sharing (see Whiten 2001).

When all is said and done, who ends up in the culture club? For some (de Waal 2001), almost everyone: birds, bats, and whales are as good candidates as monkeys and apes. For others, only some primates make the grade. Chimpanzees, with their material culture, are the agreed-upon best case, but Japanese monkeys, too, are sometimes seen to "fulfill the criteria for culture" (McGrew 1998: 314). Some nonhuman primates are culturally problematic even to those who embrace the notion of nonhuman culture. Gorillas, writes McGrew, "present a unique challenge for cultural primatology" because, for example, "however striking the differences in diet across or within populations, all could be explained by ecological factors" (1998: 316).

Others take care to note that if the award of "culture" is made to chimpanzees, it must be of a type qualitatively different from human culture. Between 1.0 and 0.3 million years ago, a "genetic event" occurred, writes Michael Tomasello (1999: 526), that "involved understanding other persons as intentional agents." It led to "a series of cascading sociological and psychological events in historical time" that essentially defined human culture and burned the bridge between it and nonhuman primate culture. Still other primatologists exclude all nonhumans from the domain of culture. David Premack and Ann James Premack explain that "non-human animals lack culture not only because they do not propagate their traditions by imitation or pedagogy, but also because they are without the foundations on which cultural belief depends . . . they lack the categorical distinctions that are the principal prerequisites for theory-building" (1994: 362).

At one end of the definitional continuum, then, any creature that learns from a social companion has culture, whereas at the other, any creature that lacks theory-building lacks culture.

Primatologists did not always focus as intensively as they do now on compiling spreadsheet answers to the "who, what, and how" questions regarding culture. Many postwar primate field studies, especially those fostered by Sherwood Washburn and Louis Leakey in the United States and Britain, respectively, and by Kinji Imanishi in Japan (Takasaki 2000), were intimately tied to anthropological questions about the origins of human behavior and society. Yet these questions, it seems to us, were broadly conceived and inclusive of data about sociality. Imanishi's concept of "species society," introduced to English readers in a 1960 article in *Current Anthropology,* reflects this continuity of thought, as Pamela Asquith makes clear:

> The study of the species society was a study of social relations among the members of the group, and among other groups of the same species. The concept was developed to fill the lacuna that Imanishi perceived between the study of whole communities of species and that of the individual animal. To that end, the researchers gathered details on intraspecific variation in behavior and group structure, historical change in groups, individual life histories, and so forth. They believed that all the variability over time and place of these cultural, individualistic animals must be identified before one could understand the overall structure—hence, their long-term studies of thirty and more years. (Asquith 2000: 167)

Culture was seamlessly part of a larger sociality, in this view: if cultural differences were assumed, they were assumed no more than the existence of a basic monkey society. We make no claim that this view was peculiarly Eastern. Indeed, Jane Goodall, at a 1962 conference, noted a "fashion" among chimpanzees for building nests in palm trees, indicating an early interest on the part of Western scholars in the possibility of learned cultural behavior (Jolly 2000; see van Lawick-Goodall 1973), and perhaps a willingness to integrate the cultural and the social.

Gradually, as field studies increased in number and time depth, it became clear to primatologists that cross-group behavioral variation in nonhuman primates could occur for purely social reasons. Ironically, given the emergence of the cultural from the social, it was at this point that the momentum slowly began to shift away from a sociality-culture continuum to an intense focus on seeking examples of culture, considered apart. Even when these examples were fleshed out with social details (who did what to whom at a given moment in time, who learned what from whom over some years), the result was an essentially nondynamic presentation of "Gombe chimpanzee culture" or "Mahale chimpanzee culture." This presentation of nonhuman primate culture is reminiscent of the way anthropologists of the past constructed, say, "Navajo culture" and set it apart from "Hopi culture" or "Swedish culture."

We advocate neither a return to postwar primatology nor an approach in which nonhuman primate culture is assumed. We know that years of rigorous data collection, including rich data on social interactions, preceded the confident claim that cultural diversity characterizes the chimpanzee populations of Africa (Whiten et al. 1999). What concerns us is precisely *what gets left behind* when culture is extracted analytically as a thing apart in order to construct trait lists of cultural diversity. Lost is the daily stuff of life, originally recorded in many of the very studies that allowed culture to be discussed in the first place. We see no need to tie these social patterns *necessarily* to culture, but if they are so linked, surely we end up in a realm well beyond culture as trait list—a welcome location. We note that ape "ethnographies," full of rich social detail, continue to be published (e.g., Boesch and Boesch-Achermann 2000; Goodall 1990), but summaries of chimpanzee "cultures" are what appear prominently in *Nature* (Whiten et al. 1999).

In short, we see an ever-increasing canalization and, even more, a stratification related to the culture concept in primatology. What has been deemed important is finding and characterizing examples of culture, at once considered the highest expression of sociality and set apart from sociality. This version of culture, exalted yet presented in collapsed form, has now taken center stage in primatology.

That culture worry should become so central to one area of inquiry within primatology, a discipline that after all draws its scholars from psychology and biology as well as anthropology, attests to its long reach. We ourselves gained experience of the culture concept's power during the symposium that provided the impetus for this volume.

The Wenner-Gren International Symposium on Culture

This worry about the culture concept—which we now wish to put on hold—was the initial motivation for our organizing the symposium that took place in Morelia, Mexico. The two of us, with the active encouragement and involvement of Sydel Silverman, felt it was time to put these worries on the table to see what role, if any, the culture concept might play in the anthropology of the twenty-first century. The resulting symposium brought together eighteen anthropologists from Europe, the United States, Canada, and Japan, all chosen to maximize diversity—

in terms of subdiscipline, professional training, and seniority. We particularly wanted biological anthropologists and primatologists to take part. That way, we thought, the cultural anthropologists could not ignore research on nonhuman primate sociality and what it said about the culture concept. We also wanted the cultural anthropologists to face up to the reservations about the culture concept advanced by British social anthropologists. Archaeologists and linguists, we suspected, might have had different experiences with the culture concept, and those experiences, too, we wanted to put on the table. Our desire from the outset was to take a pragmatic stance in the symposium by addressing whether the concept of culture could help with the scholarly tasks anthropology might confront in the coming century. Nevertheless, the worry over the culture concept today and in the future provided the symposium's central focus.

It almost proved to be its undoing. Throughout the symposium, some participants felt an obligation to present a definition of culture that others could accept. Each attempt at definition obliged others to weigh in heavily against the proposed concept. These critiques convinced no one who valued the culture concept to give it up, sometimes because of firm convictions about culture, sometimes only because the scholar claimed not to know what to use in place of it. Participants repeatedly expressed dread about the way the culture concept was being used in the public sphere, yet they strongly disagreed about anthropology's historical responsibility for these "misuses" and offered very different prescriptions for what anthropology could do about them. By the end of the symposium, three things stood out: it was good to put the arguments for and against the culture concept on the table; the arguments in favor notwithstanding, no global conception of culture would endure intense scrutiny or achieve consensus; and therefore, it was time to move beyond such arguments and get on with doing anthropology. "Doing anthropology" might mean using incommensurate conceptions of culture or altogether different notions; it did not matter so long as anthropological questions got asked and investigated. From these experiences with the symposium, as we have reflected on them afterward, comes our desire to put what we now call "culture worry" on hold. The power of the culture concept over anthropology is difficult to move beyond, however, and this volume is not fully liberated from it. Some contributors remain wedded to a global definition of culture and use their chapters to illustrate its worth. Others employ concepts aside from culture but with the same global presumptions. Still others set aside such overarching claims to get on with their research objectives. Despite this diversity, we are content that whenever a chapter argues for global concepts, the justification rests on specific questions the concept is said to answer. The starting point, in other words, is a particular research objective, and the global definition is only a spin-off of it. We believe that all of these proposed global definitions work well for the research questions to which they are directed—and that none of them works well as a summary and universal concept for anthropology overall. In short, the chapters in this volume indicate the variety of questions anthropologists ask, the broad range of analytical concepts they find useful to answer them, and therefore the immense difficulty faced by any would-be global concept.

We reached no agreement about the culture concept, then—but a major agreement about the continuing worth of anthropology did emerge from the symposium. This surprised us, considering all the recent pessimism about anthropology's future and regrets about its past. It made us feel that anthropology might be ready to get beyond culture worry. Whether a piece of work was truly anthropological or not never came up during the symposium. The implication was that there was no need for simplistic badges of anthropological authenticity based on the culture concept. The vitality of anthropology, with or without a culture concept, was simply assumed. This unspoken consensus confirmed our feeling that culture worry and the "love it or leave it" allegiances it sometimes inspired had to be set aside, and that the value of a culture concept or any alternative could be measured only by the utility of the answers it supplied in particular research projects undertaken to answer particular questions. We believe the individual chapters in this volume sum to this collective judgment, and we now proceed to show how they do.

Leaving Culture Worry Behind

The book begins with three chapters that identify important research objectives for anthropology to pursue once it gets beyond culture worry. Fredrik Barth presents the study of variation as a central task for anthropology. By "variation," he means the emergence of new and divergent instances of social action out of preexisting ones. Barth's concentration on variation rather than the more common concern with social change directs anthropology to study the processes underlying social action and to create generative models based on these processes. He takes exception to the concept of culture that led anthropologists to suppress variation in favor of configurations and overall patterns. This culture concept, he believes, impeded the development of generative models of social action, which Barth takes as an important research objective. The chapters in part 2, "Emergent Sociality," take up this task, as we shall make clear later.

Michel-Rolph Trouillot hopes to get beyond culture worry and the public and political uses of the culture concept by replacing the term "culture" with another word (he suggests several). Trouillot, however, wishes to conserve certain basic conceptual elements, or "kernels," as he calls them, of culture no matter what alias it goes by. One kernel is anthropology's understanding that behavior and belief are learned and passed down—not genetically inherited—from one generation to the next. Preserving this kernel allows anthropology to counteract racism and biological determinism, although Trouillot also shows the history by which anthropology disengaged from confronting racism. Another kernel, for Trouillot, is anthropology's capacity to find the patterns and continuities that order social life. The chapters in part 3, "Patterns and Continuities," exemplify the significance, to some anthropologists, of research questions about shared social patterns and continuities in pattern over time. There, Wright, Brown, and Durham, unlike Trouillot, willingly use the term "culture" to denote their concern with pattern and continuity, although we will also soon show that they mean rather different things by the concept.

Yoshinobu Ota takes anthropology beyond culture worry by probing one of the major reasons for it today: the way indigenous people self-consciously use their culture for political mobilization and identity. Ota sees no threat to anthropology, no misuse of the culture concept, and certainly no cause for worry in the ability of indigenous people to objectify and deploy cultural beliefs and behaviors. He welcomes the fact that these current practices invalidate an older anthropological understanding that portrayed the people studied as thoroughly enmeshed in their culture, which was supposedly below the level of their consciousness. Ota thinks that anthropology may have aided the subjugation of indigenous people by refusing them this ability "to be in culture and yet to look at it" (a phrase he takes from James Clifford). He recommends that anthropologists study the new cultural politics as a means for seeing how the culture concept is being put to use (and therefore amended) outside of anthropology. He hopes that such redefinition of the culture concept in public might also help liberate anthropologists by illuminating more clearly their discipline's entanglement in power relations and inequality. In part 4, "The Politics of Culture," chapters by Wilson, Andrade, and Hann carry forward Ota's focus on the political uses of the culture concept. But unlike Ota, these contributors see danger, not liberation, for anthropology in these uses—that is, if we remain pledged to our own culture concept.

Emergent Sociality

Barbara King opens part 2 of the book by suggesting that one way for primatologists to move past an engagement with the culture concept is to ask how great ape infants come to negotiate their social worlds. She presents longitudinal data from captive bonobo and gorilla families, showing how the youngest infants increasingly come to use body movements and gestures to enter into transformative social action with their family members. For King, just as for Barth, sociality emerges as individuals interact, communicate, and cope with the daily events of life. By reporting a series of social events that unfold over time in the ape families she studies, King allows for the conclusion that the meaning of bodily-gestural communicative events emerges from great ape sociality. She does not claim ape culture for her subjects but rather envisions a focus on great ape sociality freed from the search for culture as an exercise in typologies.

Christina Toren's emphasis on the role of microhistories in understanding emergent sociality in human societies also links closely to Barth's approach. Toren studies ways in which children communicate about everyday events in order to show how humans make meaning intersubjectively. That is, for Toren, children are not conditioned, socialized, or taught, but come to make sense of the world as they live surrounded and transformed by other humans. Arguing against the separation of nature and culture and of body and mind, Toren works to plot the development over time of the individual as both a biological and a social self. She finds no need for a concept of culture in such a model; indeed, the culture concept would impede her analysis exactly to the degree that it assumes cross-generational continuity. Toren's microhistories chronicle the way variations in behavioral repertoires emerge through social interactions between individuals. She shares this focus on social innovation with Barth and King.

Continuing the theme of "on the ground" discovery of what children really do, Stuart Shanker shows how our understanding of the ontogeny of language has been heavily affected by a clash of paradigms. Children with a disorder known as Specific Language Impairment are considered by some scholars to be genetically rendered unable to use language, whereas other scholars think them to be entirely capable of recovery when guided via ameliorative social interaction. For Shanker, this debate is not an empirical one but rather is about ways of conceptualizing what language is and whether the capacity for language is inherent or emergent. Similarly constructed is the debate about whether or not apes have language. Shanker uses these language debates to urge scholars to embrace the study of the cultural—that is, of emergent social action through ontogeny—quite apart from any debate about the culture concept itself.

Patterns and Continuities

In the first chapter of part 3, Rita Wright, an archaeologist, considers the need for a concept of culture to emerge directly from patterns in material objects. Recognizing patterns in the archaeological record is a viable, vital way to reconstruct past lives, according to Wright, and such recognition proceeds best via the culture concept. Like Trouillot, Wright takes such patterns as one of the "kernels," or guiding ideas, of anthropology expressed in the culture concept. Wright uses the concept and the term "culture" precisely to show how her research questions emerge from and link up with the particular understanding of culture that developed in archaeology over the last century. She notes, as one instance of the culture concept's distinctive history in archaeology, how the study of emerging stratification in early societies led archaeologists to read patterns of power out of the material remains they found. Wright's work on gray-ware pottery from the Indo-Iranian borderlands suggests, for instance, that technological boundaries likely symbolize social identities across cultural boundaries. To give up the term "culture," as Trouillot suggests doing, would be to obscure the way this concept has taken its own course in archaeology over time. Wright shows that the concept of pattern that became one of the essentialist elements of the culture concept in sociocultural anthropology remains a vital analytic resource in archaeology.

Questions of pattern and continuity are equally important to Penelope Brown, for whom culture can be found in public, shared representations. Brown's linguistic research among Mayan Indians in Mexico has uncovered a distinctive style in the way these people think and talk about spatial relations. Their characteristic and widely shared pattern of representing space and spatial relations is passed down through social learning across generations. Like King, Toren, and Shanker, writing in the previous section, Brown incorporates data from children into her study and sees children as constructivists. Unlike these authors but like

Trouillot, she finds the concept of pattern to be an essential kernel for answering her research questions. As for the term "culture," Brown says no good-byes. Quite the contrary: she wants anthropologists to wrest control over both the term and the concept from scholars in cognitive science. For her as much as for Wright in archaeology, the history of the culture concept in linguistics is different from Trouillot's chronicle for cultural anthropology. The histories of archaeology and linguistics apparently produced fewer reasons for apology than did cultural anthropology, and therefore much less culture worry and more continuing analytical value in what Geertz might call a muscular version of culture.

William Durham joins Trouillot in wishing to conserve some elements of the culture concept but to revise its configuration and use. Patterns—particularly patterns over time and evolutionary changes in those patterns—constitute the essential element or kernel of the culture concept that Durham conserves. In writing about culture, he emphasizes changes in the frequencies of cultural variants within populations. In this view, cultures are not coherent, homogeneous wholes but are themselves populations of variable entities. Because ideas and behaviors change over time, cultural systems evolve as changes occur in relative frequencies of the variants. Durham illustrates this model through a case study of the Nuer incest taboo. His notion of "pattern" contrasts with those of Brown and Wright. For Wright, a pattern consists of a widely dispersed item of material culture, such as a ceramic decorative style. For Brown, a pattern is a widely shared cognitive understanding, such as the understanding of spatial designations. Durham sees pattern as a frequency distribution of a particular trait, such as the Nuer incest taboo. It is important to see how their respective definitions of pattern depend on the research questions they wish to answer.

The Politics of Culture

For Richard Wilson, whose chapter launches part 4, anthropology must be rid of the culture concept precisely in order to study the uses of the concept in the world at present. Like Ota, Wilson argues that anthropology's culture concept failed to allow for the objectification and manipulation of culture and for the ideological employment of appeals to culture that can now be found worldwide. Unlike Ota, Wilson does not see these developments as liberating, either for the people themselves or for anthropology. Such cultural arguments, as used by the state in South Africa, buttress nativist claims for an ageless, indigenous African custom of democracy, or they create an artificially separated sphere of the so-called cultural from the political. Both of these usages of culture blunt South Africa's ability to confront the mix-up of race, culture, and politics that it inherited from the apartheid era.

Xavier Andrade, following Ota's lead, provides a case study of the way two politicians and an indigenous intellectual in Ecuador can be in culture and look at it, too. At base is the Ecuadorian belief in machismo and the valuation of male sexuality and genital power built into it. One politician, León Febres Cordero, fortified his image by overt and extravagant claims to macho identity. The other, Jamil Mahuad, projected a nonsexual image based on his study of Buddhist scriptures, perhaps as a way of avoiding machismo altogether—unsuccessfully, it turns out, because his opponents were able to label him effeminate. Pancho Jaime, an opposition journalist, looked at the belief in machismo as enabling political dissent. The ribald, vulgar, and scatological cartoons he published made fools of his political opponents by showing them engaged in unmanly sexual practices. At the same time, at a deeper level, the cartoons made fun of the hypervaluation of maleness on which machismo in Ecuador depended. Because political authority and machismo intertwined so tightly, this deeper attack eroded the very legitimacy of Ecuador's ruling elite.

According to Chris Hann, the genealogy for today's politics of culture stretches back to European nationalism at the turn of the twentieth century and the claims to a shared folk identity that the resulting new nations asserted. Hann traces the historical entanglement of this burgeoning nationalism with what he terms the "totalitarian" idea of culture in the academy. The totalitarian notion starts from the idea of cultures in the plural and asserts a relativist and separatist claim for each culture—in much the same manner that European nationalists justified separate nations for each and every people. Hann contrasts the totalitarian view of "a culture," timeless and primordial, with the reality that each is a concatenation of historical circumstances and with the possibilities for social life to which these circumstances give rise. Through his case study of the Lemkos in Poland, Hann shows the way the politics of culture, based on the totalitarian view, can actively construct identity today, and he also indicates that the complex interplay between nationalism and public concepts of culture is still vital. Like Ota, Hann finds people capable of objectifying their beliefs and thereby developing political identities. But unlike Ota, he sees nothing liberating in this situation, either for world politics or for anthropology.

What to Do about Culture?

Underlying the worries about the culture concept expressed by Geertz and Ortner (among many others) and the anger Sahlins vents on culture's critics, we see an abiding commitment to anthropology as the comprehensive study of humankind (including our near primate relatives). The breadth of anthropology—whether that breadth be measured by its coverage of the world's peoples, its historical depth, or the variety of its ethnographic, comparative, evolutionary, and developmental analyses—is unmatched by other scholarly disciplines. We must be wary, then, of making anthropology synonymous with the concept of culture. By doing so, we inadvertently confirm the critics who think they invalidate anthropology because they find cause to condemn the culture concept. We hope this volume helps wean them from such an undernourished view of anthropology's vitality.

Some chapters in this collection illustrate how anthropological questions can be asked successfully without using the culture concept at all. Others, by the variety of definitions they give to culture, resist any facile equation of anthropology with one concept of culture. To further adapt the phrase that Ota takes from Clifford, we can say that anthropologists today "can be in and look at their field," which means we can objectify and construct or reconstruct its parts in the same way indigenous people can reauthorize their own practices. We need not be locked into one view of anthropology in the same way we once asserted that "the natives" were locked into their cultures. Yet much of the current culture worry seems based on just such a deterministic view. It is time to move beyond the attachment to the culture concept that gives it this coercive power over anthropology.

Note

The opinions expressed in this chapter do not necessarily represent the official policy of the Wenner-Gren Foundation for Anthropological Research.

Part 1

Leaving Culture Worry Behind

one

Toward a Richer Description and Analysis of Cultural Phenomena

Fredrik Barth

To clear the way for taking on new tasks with the concept of culture, we need to review old uses and their weaknesses and then construct an alternative so compelling that people will be forced to adopt it and discontinue their old ways of thinking. Given the currency of the concept in a wide range of disciplines outside of anthropology and in various areas of public discourse, we are left little space to pursue this task within an isolated and protected anthropological discourse. Anthropologists no longer have the influence to determine the "proper" definitions and uses of the term "culture," and any usages practiced by others will continually reinvade our own writing and thinking. Yet if we wish to repair culture as an analytical concept, we have no alternative but to build on our own disciplinary experience and strengths and try to improve its power, rigor, and consistency as best we can.

In this chapter, I focus on the present construction of culture as a category and discuss its complexity and some unfortunate forms of reasoning to which it leads, before moving on to what might be done about it. Clifford Geertz recently commented that because of the way anthropology's concept of culture was taught in the 1940s and 1950s, "we were condemned, it seemed, to working with a logic and a language in which concept, cause, form and outcome had the same name" (Geertz 2000: 13)—echoing his previous critique of this same "theoretical diffusion" (Geertz 1973: 4). I submit that the diffusion is still with us, despite Geertz's efforts to develop a semiotic perspective on culture. Even in his own writings, as in those of others, a holistic template of culture still serves both to represent and to explain human behavior—

it is both a "model of" and a "model for," in the thought of the anthropologist as in our accounts of the natives.

To this critique I wish to add a discussion of two further flaws: the logical errors that the present form of the concept invites and its failure to take variation into account. By these steps I aim to stimulate our rethinking and retooling of anthropology's theoretical position, which might enhance both the clarity of our reasoning and the naturalism of our descriptions of what we regard as culture.

I will not duplicate the received wisdom under which we have labored so long: that what we need is a better objectivist definition of culture. It is our reasoning and our practices that we need to change. I assume, however, that we can agree that recent and contemporary uses of the culture concept have helpfully converged upon an emphasis on the ideational, as in the definition "a picture of the ideational world of a people" (Keesing 1976: 184) or "essentially a matter of ideas and values, a collective cast of mind" (Kuper 1999: 227). We are thus speaking not of "material culture" or "human behavior" but about the *ideas* behind such events and manifestations. This may already have been foreshadowed in E. B. Tylor's famous definition, in which the term embraces "that complex whole which includes knowledge, belief, art, morals, law, custom, and any other capabilities and habits acquired by man as member of society" (Tylor 1871).

The Avoidance of Logical Errors

Unfortunately, the movement from Tylor's concrete list of the institutions and behaviors of human life to an explicit focus on the ideas behind them has not much reduced the omnibus character of what is included in the category of culture. A number of perennial frustrations and confusions arise in anthropology from this inclusiveness. Most painful and perplexing are the paradoxes that appear when one tries to make generalizations or theoretical statements about the "nature of culture" as conceptualized in this omnibus usage. A number of statements appear repeatedly in our introductory lectures and our textbooks—and presumably in our reasoning—that sometimes seem mutually contradictory. For example:

Culture is a received tradition; culture is emergent, constantly innovated and in flux.
Culture is shared within a society; culture is distributed among the members of society.

Distinct cultures are associated with distinct societies or groups; culture shows continuous variation and cannot be empirically partitioned and socially or geographically bounded.
Culture is a complex whole; culture is a thing of shreds and patches formed through borrowing and hybridization.
Culture is a depiction of a lifeway; culture is a directive force on human action.

Such paradoxes are a direct result of the diversity of phenomena that we include in our category of culture. Thus, of the ideas encompassed by the mainstream anthropological concept of culture:

Some are ideas that people validate by tradition; others are embraced because they are new or compelling.
Some ideas are widely embraced in a population; others represent specialized knowledge or values held by only a few.
Some ideas are used as emblems by states and groups to mark their social boundaries; others circulate in wider fields of communication, unconstrained by such boundaries.
Some ideas embody or conform to pervasively accepted premises in a group; others are discrepant and may be actively contrapuntal, or separately and individually validated, or derived from recent, extraneous sources.
Some ideas represent outcomes and states of the world; others motivate and shape the actions of people who embrace them.

What is the trouble? A minimum of reflection suggests that the trouble must spring from a weakness in the present construction of our whole category of culture, as well as from the diversity of tasks for which we employ it. Generalizations about a category are valid only in regard to those features that members of the category have in common. But ideas—the stuff of culture—may share little in common, since they are variably related to the world, to social groups, and to social action. Thus, attempts to make generalized statements about all members of such a category—that is, about culture—will turn out to be true for some cases and untrue for others. We need to reason more carefully, with a clear awareness of just what we can claim our whole category of culture, as currently used in anthropology, predicates.

A glance back at Tylor's definition shows us—more clearly there than in later formulations, but in common with them—that the category of culture is indeed an aggregate construction, covering and combining many diverse phenomena. It thus seems to exemplify what George Lakoff (1987: 145–148) called a "complex category." In agreement with prototype theory, a complex category may well lack any single distinguishing common property or distinctive feature (as would be required by the classical, Aristotelian theory of categories). To explicate a complex category, one must look for a structure of central and peripheral members, or chains of linkage where the linking feature varies throughout the chain, or evocation through mere co-occurrence within a large experiential domain, or even construction as an "other" category of "everything else" (for concrete examples, see Lakoff's analysis of Dyirbal categories, 1987: 92–105).

Tylor's definition, however, does seem to contain one candidate for a "distinctive feature," namely, in the phrase "acquired by man as a member of society." But as in the case of his unmarked singular Culture, there is no indication that he meant the acquisition of culture by a member of any *particular* society: the reference is simply to culture's social acquisition, presumably in contrast to other modes of acquisition, such as biological inheritance. Considering the arbitrariness of our practice in delimiting "a society" (discussed, for example, in Barth 1992), there is every reason to give Tylor the benefit of the doubt on this issue.

The mode-of-acquisition clause recurs in later anthropological definitions in the specification of culture as "learned behavior" or even "ideas transmitted through symbols." There is no doubt that this definition addressed a fundamental issue in our understanding of human evolution. But since we frankly lack procedures by which to identify post hoc how most ideas must have been acquired, this seems to be a sleeping clause in our operational definition for distinguishing culture and not-culture in the empirical world of human ethnography—and we are poorly equipped in the way of any general theory of learning to do much about it. We may thus have legitimate doubts about how much can be achieved, generally and theoretically, in the study of human lifeways by thinking along lines of the question, which distinctive features of ideas might be entailed by the fact that ideas are "learned"?

A first step toward clarifying how the complex category of culture is in fact used as an analytical concept might be to look for a prototype or central member within the category: presumably, when we reason with culture as a concept, we will usually have the prototype in mind. Some of the nebulousness of culture may derive from a situation in which different users of the term envision different prototypes—that is, where the prototype image varies among different speakers and different contexts. For a senior generation of anthropologists, I believe "custom" may often constitute such a prototype—rather too simple and old-fashioned to mention in print nowadays, but supplying a best-example image with which to think. I note, for example, that Meyer Fortes, in his classic article on unilineal descent groups, talked explicitly about culture as "the facts of custom—the standardized ways of doing, knowing, thinking, and feeling—universally obligatory and valued in a given group of people at a given time" (Fortes 1953: 21). In commercial life, on the other hand, what is referred to as the "culture" of a corporation typically is the ambience generated by practices of authority, incentives, and attitudes toward change. In the discourse of multiculturalism, the stress seems to be on claims to traditional wellsprings of culture and on culture's direct significance for—indeed, claim to indelible determination of—social identity. For a younger generation of anthropologists, the stress might be on otherness, producing again a very different order of concept, more akin to that expressed in purely relative (deictic) words such as "there" and "here." Those and probably other prototypes may at various times shape the reasoning and general discourses we read and participate in. As a result, culture not only may mean different things to different authors but may unheedingly refer to different things in the different paragraphs of any *one* author.

Unless these various constructions of culture are clearly distinguished and consistently embraced or avoided during a conversation or in a chain of reasoning, bizarre confusions and conclusions will be produced. More generally stated, complex categories invite the logical error of inappropriate reasoning from particular examples, parts, or features to the category as a whole. I return to Lakoff for a general formulation of the problem: "Metonymy is one of the basic characteristics of cognition. It is extremely common for people to take one well-understood or easy-to-perceive aspect of something and use it to stand for the thing as a whole or for some other aspect or part of it" (Lakoff 1987: 77).

The Importance of Variation

The most insidious and deceptive consequences of our present conceptualization of culture, however, arise from the way in which it affects our data through the methodology it encourages. The ethnographer is exposed during fieldwork to a "blooming, buzzing confusion" of different events: a near chaos of actions and utterances and constellations of circumstances. No two events will be identical: we are surrounded by variation, and we know it. Our concepts help us to grope toward some degree of imagined order and pattern.

Listen to the way A. R. Radcliffe-Brown, teacher of the generation of structural-functionalist anthropologists, spoke: "If in the Australian tribe I observe in a number if instances the behaviour towards one another of mother's brother and sister's son, it is in order that I may be able to record as precisely as possible the general or normal form of this relationship, abstracted from the variations of particular instances, though taking account of these variations" (Radcliffe-Brown 1952: 192). In the rush toward culture (which Radcliffe-Brown preferred to call social structure), the variation that is observed is quietly elided from the account, in favor of stereotyped pattern descriptions such as "sister's son privilege" or "mother-in-law avoidance." These are then claimed to be the *objects* of observation. The particular events that were actually observed might be used as illustrations to enrich the description of the stereotype, but they are otherwise trivialized into irrelevancy.

As a result of such practices, the link between observation and data becomes highly ambiguous: a gap is interposed between the events observed and the "general or normal" feature of the interpreted datum. It is also circular in its imputation of social sharing within a group: if I, a white European, am observed taking advantage of my uncle or avoiding my mother-in-law, the behavior is not noted as an example of a custom (of sister's son privilege or mother-in-law avoidance) as it would if an Australian Aborigine were seen doing the same. And the *cultural* aspect of events, as it is conceived in this construction, seems to be visible only as a "pattern" in a carefully selected aggregate of events. A record of observed variation among those events is somehow made irrelevant. But what is it, then, that we can claim to have observed?

Or to put it differently: a fieldworker attuned to recording culture is encouraged stealthily to introduce, or beg, the fundamental assumption: that an ideal form of custom exists as the primary social fact and that people's acts are merely imperfect performances of it. Only such a Platonic assumption could justify writing the stereotype in as the field datum while writing the observation of variation out.

Is an effective counter to my argument perhaps found in a particular version of the ideational view of culture—a claim that since culture is made up of ideas, then our data on these ideas should come directly from the persons who embrace the culture, and not from (objectivist?) observations of events? If so, then sister's son privilege and mother-in-law avoidance are ideas only—ideas about concepts and rules that are named, identified, and embraced by Australian Aborigines but not necessarily embodied in their physical acts. In that case, observation should not be seen as the source of our data at all. Perhaps only the "new ethnography" procedures of the ethnomethodologists, whereby the ethnographer systematically elicits the words and ideas of informants, provide the means to record (ideational) culture—while participant observation of people acting in the world and vis-à-vis each other becomes irrelevant. Following ethnomethodological procedures, do we obtain our cultural data from people who are more knowledgeable than even the best participant anthropologist about the ideas, and arguably even the practices, of local people?

I think not. If ideas made up a world apart from actions, then we would be living in a bizarre world indeed, and one in which I would be much less interested in people's ideas than challenged to make sense of their having ideas at all. If ideas have effects on people's actions, on the other hand, then we must make ourselves responsible for studying the effects by observing them in people's acts. Eliciting verbal data from informants with a view to recording their culture "directly," we may indeed obtain their ideas *about* knowledge, beliefs, art, morals, law, customs, and other capabilities and habits, ordered in conceptual domains. But we will not arrive at data on how these ideas are made manifest, used, and deployed in the activities and interactions of people acting on the world and creating their experienced world. There is every reason to believe that other people perform the same stereotyping and pattern seeking that we have done with our conventional concept of culture, so that by eliciting the natives' accounts, we will end up with the same gap between our elicited data and the events of action in the world that we find when we perform our own cultural stereotyping. We may obtain an account more closely in accord with local sensibilities, but the theoretical frame remains the same: an extracted summary of pattern without data on events of action and on empirical variations among actions.

But what justifies my concern for a more attentive recording of variation? It is that its elision, as authorized by a selective search for the second-order data of pattern and culture, impoverishes our data and prefigures the theoretical questions that will, and indeed can, be raised. Taking the discovered fact of variation seriously, on the other hand, induces a radical ontological shift: variation is recognized as a pervasive feature and thus a property of human ideas and human actions, and any attempt to understand ideas, actions, or both must acknowledge this fundamental feature of them. And why does variation deserve this position as a fundamental property of ideas and actions? Because, I argue, it appears empirically to be ubiquitous, and it poses a general theoretical challenge to any and every account of meaning and social action.

First to its empirical ubiquity. I know from field experience—see, for example, my trail of monographs from New Guinea (1975, 1987), Oman (1983), and Bali (1993)—that if one allows oneself to take systematic note of variation, then variation becomes an incessant discovery and at some level an analytically obsessive concern. But of course, you might object, no two individuals are identical in their ideas or in anything else, yet surely their cultural institutions, because these are collective social facts, will be shared and identical within a group—for example, in the Balinese villages I describe. The observation that individual persons may hold somewhat different ideas about these collective institutions could be dismissed as quite secondary and would not make the institutions themselves variable in any significant sense.

So, indeed, one could argue for a number of the cultural manifestations one might discover in a Balinese village. For example, the rules governing the *pura desa* (village temple) and the *pura dalem* (death temple) might be identical for the inhabitants of the village. Or at least one might expect to find two or more opposed cultural versions, each perhaps associated with a faction in the community. But this example refers to a single case, not of a person's ideas but of a particular village and its temples. The ethnographer who bothers to pursue variation between cases will quickly find that individual examples of village temples and death temples are different from every other example—despite broadly shared templates of what constitutes a village temple and a death temple. In other words, on neither the individual nor the collective level is there a one-to-one identity between idea and manifestation, between cultural construction and event. And that seems to me to raise the crucial theoretical question, what *is* the connection between idea and event? Or, to anticipate my fuller argument, what are the connections between various kinds of ideas and different kinds of manifestations, acts, and events?

Which brings me to the crux of my critique of the culture concept as it has been consistently used in much of the anthropological tradition: it has served to mask what should have been a major theoretical challenge. Our main theoretical paradigms have consistently developed in a covert symbiosis with the practice of reporting cultural generalizations as primary data. Thus:

Functionalism preempted the problem of what shaped human action by offering a teleological explanation for hypercoherent, homogenized patterns of custom.

The normative representation that undergirded structural-functional accounts provided descriptions of conventions and compliance and generally ignored variation—a variation that otherwise could have been handled only by simplistic procedures of statistics or normatively loaded concepts such as "deviance."
Structuralism, modeling itself on linguistics, trivialized the significance of the behavioral analog of *parole* in favor of *la langue,* and it tended to perform its abstraction from data based either on single examples or on generalized cultural forms.
Marxists, characteristically oriented toward macroschemas, were satisfied to work with generalized accounts of people's conditions and gross institutional features.
And "thick description" was practiced to write narratives of other cultural patterns in the sense of ad hoc accounts of locally associated clusters of customs, rules, and institutions—not of multiple cases or the multiple concerns, constraints, and opportunities of acting persons.

In each of the major theoretical schools of anthropology, then, the empirical evidence for deep, ubiquitous variation was elided or minimized, and the theoretical challenges it posed were concealed and ignored.[1] We should no longer be willing to accept theoretical frameworks that depict and generate only stereotyped patterns and determined results. For if the lives of particular Nuer and Tallensi are diverse histories of nonconformity and improvisation, how could a set of norms describe, much less explain, the forms of those lives? If the actions of knowing, intelligent people are highly contingent, how could one hope to understand them by means of the simple logic of structuralist schemas? If some oppressed working-class persons are depressed or angry, whereas others are content or joyous, how could one understand such lives by means of their shared condition? And how might differences between stories of peace pacts and cockfight arenas be supported in a world understood through the thick description of such cultural institutions—unless, of course, the differences were mere artifacts of imaginative or ill-informed ethnographers?

By all means, let us be prepared—indeed, let us expect—to discover *some* functional imperatives, *some* normative pressures, *some* deep structural patterns, *some* effects of the relations of production on life chances, and *some* shared cultural themes in ranges of local institutions. But let us demand that their presence be demonstrated through a record of extant variation, not asserted by fiat. And let us identify their effects in the sectors of cultural manifestation in which they appear, not use them as magical keys to understanding principles of construction valid for all of culture. Our methodologies for recording variations may presently be weak and unsystematic, but that gives us no license to ignore or deny variation, only to critique and improve our methods. Meanwhile, our theoretical imagination can anticipate the findings that improved methods will provide, and we can take on the challenging task of modeling the processes that generate the forms of human thought and action in the way they seem to be: variable, contingent, pragmatic, imaginative. How should we redesign our old concept of culture so that it can serve us better in such a task?

Rethinking Culture

Let us start from a position of strength. By means of a less theory-bound approach to cultural facts, some contemporary anthropologists are indeed providing sensitive and compelling ethnographic analyses of sectors of culture. We read of the centrality in Meratus thought of an image of travel as a dynamo of wealth production (Tsing 1993); we read of the urgency of ideas of managing emotions in the lives of Balinese (Wikan 1990); we read of the pervasive place of genealogy in the historical imaginations of tribal Jordanians (Shryock 1997). These and many other remarkable studies are presently able to build accounts of cultural facts without prejudging pattern, eliding variation, or stereotyping ideas. How do they achieve this? By not aiming to expound "culture" at all: their accounts are about human actions and human lives and human representations and constructions. Cultural facts enter as one set of factors only, in careful analyses of people thinking and doing things in a complex world. It is precisely by shifting their gaze from generalizing about culture to giving a reasoned account of people that these anthropologists are able to capture the reality of cultural things. What they do is to show how cultural images, knowledge, and representations are deployed, and sometimes created, by situated persons with purposes, acting in complex life situations.

The need for such analyses was indeed prefigured in the intellectual issues raised by that leading "culturalist," Alfred L. Kroeber. His ultimate position is clearly set out in the introduction, written in 1951, to his collection of essays *The Nature of Culture* (1952). First, "it is of the nature of culture to be heavily conditioned by its own cumulative past" (1952: 4), which indicated to Kroeber that a historical approach would be most fruitful. "But I see narrative as incidental rather than as essential to the method of history in the wider sense . . . . The essential quality of the historical approach as a method of science I see as its integration of phenomena into an ever widening phenomenal context, with as much preservation as possible . . . of the qualitative organization of the phenomena dealt with" (1952: 5)—something Kroeber contrasted elsewhere to a hard-science wish "to isolate or extricate valid simplicities, recurrent regularities" (1952: 125). This ideal of preserving the specificity and richness of our materials in our analyses has if anything only been strengthened and embraced more widely in the fifty years since Kroeber wrote these words (cf. Fox 1991).

Kroeber's most fundamental step in his reexamination of culture was to problematize the nature of the phenomenon itself—the ontology and conditions of perpetuation of culture. In a lecture presented in 1949 titled "The Concept of Culture in Science" (1952: 118–135), he reflected on the reproduction of culture, its continuity through time. In this text he retreated from his earlier, triumphal embracing of culture as the "superorganic" (first launched in 1917; see Kroeber 1952: 22–51) and took a carefully reasoned position that seems not to have been widely noted.

> All cultural phenomena are invariably related to certain other cultural phenomena to which they are similar and which precede or succeed them or occur near them contemporaneously; and their fullest understanding can be attained only through cognizance of these relations. While these relations are indisputable, they are relations of form, value, and significance. They are not, directly, relations of cause in the ordinary sense of efficient cause. The efficient causes of cultural phenomena are the actions or behavior of men . . . compared to the immediate efficient causality of men on culture, the causation of culture on culture is indirect, remote, and largely a functional relation of form to form. [But] while human beings are always the *immediate* causes of cultural events, these human causes are themselves the result of antecedent culture situations, having been fitted to the existing cultural forms they encounter. There is thus a continuity of indirect causation from culture event to culture event through the medium of human intermediaries. (Kroeber 1952: 132)

Speaking of "microscopic" dissections of culture, Kroeber saw their value to be "as examples of the close-up mechanisms of the change which culture is always tending to undergo" (1952: 133).

Returning to Kroeber's last statements in his introduction, we find him reflecting on how earlier students "too often violated the natural, actual context of the phenomena they compared" (1952: 6). He emphasized how society and culture always co-occur, so that the phenomena available necessarily have both a social and a cultural aspect.... Since societies comprise individuals and especially since individuals are heavily shaped by their culture, there is also a third aspect or factor immediately involved in the phenomena, that of psychology or personality—apart from more remote considerations such as the biological nature of people and the subhuman environment in which they operate. It is of course possible to try to study the cultural, social, and psychological aspects simultaneously and interwoven, as they occur. (1952: 7)

Yet the course he chose to follow fell short of that goal; it entailed "unraveling, out of the snarl with which actuality presents us, the factors of one level at a time ... before retying them into a web of larger understanding with the other strands" (1952: 7). Knowing that Kroeber lacked the conceptual tools to represent complex dynamic systems, I see this as a tactical and pragmatic choice on his part, an attempt to reduce the task ahead to something more manageable. And we can indeed hear something of his regrets: "It is true that, in the study of culture by deliberate suppression of individuals as individuals, the element of human behavior is also eliminated.... Those who want culture as such have to smelt it out of an ore" (1952: 8).

But we no longer have to work under the constraints that guided Kroeber's choice. With the development of systems thinking, we are now familiar with dynamical systems approaches that should enable analysts to lay out linkages and causal connections *in their particularity*, without stripping away the qualitative richness of the phenomena that we, like Kroeber, wish to preserve. We can construct such representations as partial and yet determined models, depicting causal connections without absolutizing them. And we can attempt to construct these representations as generative models, showing the relations between micro and macro and transcending the "levels" of phenomena that Kroeber saw no alternative but to separate.

How might such constructions look? First, they would need to do as the ethnographies did that provided our hopeful point of departure, namely, represent the human behavior of people acting and interacting, without violating the natural context of the phenomena, particularly the necessary unity of social and cultural aspects of every act.

Can we articulate a general and theoretical framework for this way of illuminating cultural material? Notably, the perspective entails a rather different ontology for much of what anthropologists have been calling culture, and this provides criteria for how the concept might be revised for new tasks. Rather than see culture as a complex whole and indeed a thing in itself, we would wish to incorporate a pared-down ideational notion of culture as one among many elements in a larger, enveloping class or category of phenomena: human action. Ideas, cultural or otherwise, may live a life of their own in the private thoughts of a person and there, through the processes of reflection by that person, articulate and engage each other in a separate realm of pure ideas; but these are hypothetical processes that no ethnographer can observe or study. Ideas are made manifest to other persons, including the anthropologist—made immanent, operative, and, to a degree, intersubjectively accessible—only in a necessary conjunction with other aspects or dimensions of existence that together compose social action: aspects such as social relationships, will and purpose, and material context. It is in this larger context of social action that ideas have their major impact on other ideas (that is, on the ideas of others) and, as harvested experience, provide new materials for internal reflection. And it is in such larger contexts that they will have their *only* impact on the material world and on social relationships. These effects they will always and invariably have in conjunction with the other, nonideational components, factors, or elements that merge in a larger battery and interplay of influences. Rather than trying to grasp ideational culture by imagining a separate world of abstract ideas and then trying to study the logical interrelations of these shadowy figures in abstract space, we would surely do better to study cultural ideas in the sites where they are empirically manifested, in combination with other components, as the events of social action.

It may seem paradoxical that I am now arguing for the merging of cultural material into a large, rather than a narrow, class of phenomena, when my main criticism of the omnibus concept of culture has been that it was too complex, inclusive, and therefore confounding. But "social action" is a very differently constituted class of phenomena from that of anthropology's received "culture." For one thing, social actions make up a class of events, of cases, which thus avoids the problem of claiming pattern as a primary datum. Second, social action is conceptualized as composed of distinguishable components, elements that combine in every event of action but can be disaggregated in analysis and indeed studied component by component, sector by sector, if that proves fruitful. Finally, this image of interacting components allows us to construct generative models of the phenomenon (Barth 1966, 1987). It thus holds a promise of allowing more precise analyses of the processes of interaction among components and therefore, among other things, of the roles played by cultural ideas in the acts and lives of people.

Note

1. Feminist thought has given impetus to a similar critique, but leading to a rather different agenda—see, for example, Abu-Lughod 1991.

two

Adieu, Culture: A New Duty Arises

Michel-Rolph Trouillot

> A new duty arises. No longer can we keep the search for truth the privilege of the scientist.
>
> —Franz Boas

The conceptual kernel behind the word "culture," as deployed in North American anthropology, provides a useful and fundamental lesson about humankind. Yet the word culture today is irretrievably tainted by both the politics of identity and the politics of blame—including the racialization of behavior that it was meant to avoid. Contrary to many of the critics reviewed by Robert Brightman (1995), I do not see the concept as inherently flawed on theoretical grounds. I agree with Richard Shweder (n.d.) that something akin to a culture concept remains necessary to anthropology as a discipline and to social science in general. The distinction between concept and word, however, is central to my argument. So is a related emphasis on the sites and processes in which the word and concept are deployed and on the modes of engagement that mediate between concepts and words. For if concepts are not just words, then the vitality of a conceptual program cannot hinge upon the sole use of a noun.

Culture's popular success is its own theoretical demise. Its academic diffusion has generated new institutional clusters on North American campuses: cultural—and multicultural—studies. Culture has also entered the lexicon of advertisers, politicians, businesspeople, and economic planners, up to the high echelons of the World Bank and the editorial pages of the *New York Times*. Culture now explains everything: from political instability in Haiti to ethnic war in the Balkans, from labor difficulties on the shop floors of Mexican *maquiladoras* to racial tensions in British schools and the difficulties of New York's welfare recipients in the job market. Culture explained both the Asian miracle of the 1980s and the Japanese economic downturn two decades later (Jomo 2001).

As the explanatory power of culture increases, many anthropologists react negatively to what they see as the abuse of one of their favorite categories by the general public, journalists, and, especially, colleagues—reserving their most emotional attacks for practitioners of cultural studies.[1] I confess a triple weakness: the narrative and the solutions sketched here are valid only to the extent that we have both a conceptual problem and a *public*—and therefore political—problem; to the extent that these problems are intertwined and urgent; and to the extent that the massive exportation of essentialized and racialized views of culture(s) from the United States increases both the theoretical and the political urgency.

The massive diffusion of the word "culture" in recent times awaits its ethnographer, but even the trivia are revealing. One Internet search engine found more than five million pages linked to the keyword "culture," after exclusion of most references to cultivation and agriculture. When culture was coupled with anthropology or ethnography, however, the total fell to 61,000 pages. Similarly, whereas the search engine of a major Internet bookseller produced more than 20,000 titles containing the word culture, the list dropped to 1,350 titles when culture was coupled with anthropology or ethnography in the subject index. Culture is out there, and anthropologists have no control over its deployment.

Prominent among the 20,000 titles is *Culture Matters* (Harrison and Huttington 2000), an anthology praised by the *Wall Street Journal, Time* magazine, and political heavyweights such as Patrick Moynihan and the president of the World Bank. The underlying argument of most of the essays, quite explicit in Harrison's introduction, is that culture explains the state of affairs in the world today, especially economic inequalities between countries and even continents. Culture matters, indeed, but in ways few anthropologists would recognize. Yet the success of the word is in part a reflection of the corporate success of anthropology in the United States, and to that extent we may wonder whether the anthropological critique of culture's deployment should not start at home.

Words are not concepts, and concepts are not words. Thus the same word can express various conceptualizations. Similarly, a conceptualization can survive the demise of the word that once encapsulated it. Further, conceptualizations, whether or not encapsulated by a single word, take full significance only in the context of their deployment.

That context is inherently multilayered. It extends beyond the walls of academe. It includes not only other concepts—academic, lay, and political deployments of key words (Williams 1989)—but also the very social milieu that is a condition of possibility for any conceptualization. Theories are built on words and with words, but what ties those words together is always a specific moment in the historical process. In short, conceptualizations are always historically situated.

So historicized, the North American trajectory of the concept of culture seems to offer a contradiction. The kernel of the conceptualization teaches fundamental lessons about humanity that were not as clearly stated before its deployment and that cannot easily be unlearned. Yet the deployment of the word culture today, while evoking this conceptual kernel, carries an essentialist and often racialist agenda outside and especially within the United States.

The connection between these two states of affairs is not the misappropriation of an otherwise "clean" concept by nonanthropologists. Rather, North American anthropology's theoretical disregard for "the very context of inequality—and especially the racism—that allowed the emergence of the conceptualization also doomed its deployment." Thus, the contradiction is apparent only if we take concepts as disembodied truths. If we turn to context as a "condition of possibility" of any conceptualization, a different story emerges, that of a political move in theory that denied the culture concept its very conditions of possibility. The trajectory of culture is that of a concept distancing itself from the context of its practice. As it did so, a concept created in part as a theoretical answer to an American political problem lost both its theoretical bite and its progressive political potential—and in doing so, its universalism.

For purposes of this chapter, I distinguish two contexts: academe and society at large. Within the first, the culture concept appears as an anticoncept, what I call here a *political move in theory,* the benefits of which become increasingly restricted by the status of anthropology as a discipline, by the state-centrism of the human sciences, and by micropractices of reproduction. Within the second, the culture concept appears as a *theoretical move from politics,* that is, a theoretical practice that silences its own conditions of possibility.

A Political Move in Theory

Two substantive propositions are central to the conceptualization of culture as deployed in North American anthropology. First, human behavior is patterned. There exist within historically specific populations recurrences in both thought and behavior that are not contingent but structurally conditioned and that are, in turn, structuring. Second, those patterns are learned. Recurrences cannot be tied to a natural world within or outside the human body but to constant interaction within specific populations. Structuration occurs through social transmission and symbolic coding with some degree of human consciousness.

These two propositions are indispensable to the most influential definitions of culture proposed by anthropologists in the United States. They are likely to be agreed upon, as premises of their practice, by a majority of individuals who have earned anthropological degrees in the United Sates. Yet they are not unique to North American anthropology or even to anthropology as a discipline. The first is necessary to Machiavelli's politics and fundamental to Montesquieu's sociocultural geography. The second echoes European thinkers again from Machiavelli, Montaigne, or Montesquieu to Kant and Vico. Nor do these two propositions exhaust all anthropological definitions of culture.[2]

The conceptual kernel made up of these two propositions does not impose an essentialist reading on either the definition or the use of the word culture. Nor does it predispose the word to racialist interpretations. How culture found itself on the essentialist track with a racialist bent is less about definitional truth than about context, and much less about intellectual history than about the history of power that the concept itself was used to silence. Central to that context is race and racism.

North American anthropologists love to claim with no small pride that Boasian anthropology's answer to American racism was its theoretical drive to separate race, language, and culture. If that claim is true, as I believe it is, then the culture concept is not just an intellectual product remotely connected to society—if indeed such a thing could exist—but an intellectual maneuver against the background of a social, political, and intellectual context. I describe that maneuver as a political move in theory.

In its initial context of deployment, culture was first and foremost an anticoncept. It was inherently tied to race, its nemesis. Culture is race repellent—it is not only what race is not, but it is what prevents race from occupying in anthropological discourse the defining place that it otherwise occupies in the larger American society. Within that privileged space, the culture concept can limit the impact of notions and descriptions linked to biological inheritance.

The consequences of this positioning are far-reaching yet unavoidable. As an anticoncept, the peculiarity of culture in North American anthropological theory stems less from its possible German predecessors or its distance from Malinowski's abstractions than from the peculiarity of North American notions of race and practices of racism. What makes culture unique in the U.S. academic context is not a definitional feature or a combination of such features but its deployment in a society with a peculiar one-drop rule (Harris 1964), a society in which either of the two Alexandre Dumas would have been a "black writer," in which black blood becomes a thing—that is, as Marx would say, an objectified relation—and in which that relation supersedes others. What makes Boasian and post-Boasian "culture" peculiar and necessary is the white American gaze on blackness—the centerpiece of American racial consciousness—that justifies culture's gate-keeping function.

Unfortunately, culture's academic career only reinforced the gatekeeping qualities that made its birth possible and necessary. Launched as the negation of race, culture also became the negation of class and history. Launched as a shield against some of the manifestations of racial power, culture eventually protected anthropology from all conceptual fields and apparatuses that spoke of power and inequality. Culture became what class was not, what evaded power and could deny history. How it became so has much to do again with context. The political move in theory was further restricted by anthropology's position within the human disciplines and its practitioners' temptation to mimic the state-centered social "sciences." Its essentialist potential was also enhanced by micropractices of reproduction within the discipline. "Culture" was part of the price sociocultural anthropology paid to gain a legitimate foothold in North American academe.

The Price of Power

I formulated earlier two propositions that constitute the substantive kernel of the culture concept. But the career of the concept was also tied to a third proposition, epistemological and methodological, that propelled if not required the use of the word and its cognates. One can summarize that proposition as follows: Cultural analysis is a legitimate lens of observation that relates to a distinguishable domain of human activity. Culture, like economics, is a way to look at populations.

So stated, this methodological proposition is no more essentialist than the substantive propositions at the core of the conceptualization. Indeed, one can derive from it very strong positions against both essentialism and philosophical empiricism. At best, the domain of culture as practiced by the analyst does not exist independently in the phenomenal world. That reading is a legitimate interpretation of the work of Franz Boas and his followers up the 1920s. Yet as early as perhaps the 1910s, most certainly by the 1920s, and especially in the four ensuing decades, culture shifted from being a domain of analysis to being something out there (Stocking 1968).

Anthropology's disciplinary emergence was part of the institutionalization of the social sciences that took place from the mid-nineteenth century to the start of World War II. That institutionalization followed closely the rise of nationalism and the consolidation of state power in the North Atlantic countries in which the social science disciplines first solidified. It paralleled the partition of the world mainly by the same countries (Wallerstein et al. 1996). Eurocentric ideas, developed or nurtured successively by the Renaissance, the first wave of colonialism, the Enlightenment, and the practice of plantation slavery in the Americas, had gathered new momentum with colonialism's second wave. By the time the social sciences became standardized in degree-granting departments, non-Western areas and peoples were thought to be fundamentally different both in essence and in practice. They could not be known through the same scientific procedures or submitted to the same rules of management as Western areas and peoples. At the same time, the desire to know and to manage them had increased.

It was in that context that cultural anthropology became, by default, a discipline aimed at exposing the lives and mores of the Other to the people of the North Atlantic. Anthropologists became specialists in the "savage slot" (Trouillot 1991), a necessary position within the geography of imagination that paralleled the self-invention of the "West" in the late Renaissance. Wise or innocent, noble or barbarian, the savage was a condition of possibility of the West, an indispensable alter ego to its universalist pretensions.

In the second half of the nineteenth century, the new discipline brought to the savage slot some of the methodological assumptions shared by fields such as history, sociology, and economics that studied the North Atlantic. One such assumption was that state boundaries provided the natural frameworks within which the processes studied by social scientists occurred (Wallerstein et al. 1996: 80). That assumption, equally shared by literary scholars, ran along the following lines: France was obviously a nation-state. It had, therefore, a single economy, a single history, and a single social life, all of which could be studied by the appropriate discipline, and all of which were also fundamentally circumscribed within the distinct political territory called France.

Anthropology easily avoided that assumption when it turned to ancient times. Yet when it came to the study of contemporary "primitives," anthropology mimicked the state-centrism of the other social sciences, often assuming for these peoples a waterish version of the nation-state, the borders of which were alleged to be as obvious and as impermeable as those of the North Atlantic entities.

Since that watered-down polity was only a copy, and a bad one at that, it could provide neither the methodological stability nor the naturalness of borders that made North Atlantic countries obvious units of analysis. From the 1890s to the 1950s, anthropologists increasingly made up for that fuzziness. In France and Britain, notably, they emphasized the rigidity of such concepts as the "total social fact" and the "social structure," each of which supposedly brought to the observer's mind a closure otherwise hard to demonstrate on the ground. In the United States, "culture" provided an even thicker closure.

The solidity of that closure came less from the methodological proposition sketched above than from the way it was used. Culture as a domain became what North American anthropologists could cling to in contradistinction to, say, sociologists or economists (Cole 1999; Darnell 1997, 1998; Stocking 1968). But the emphasis on the distinction also entailed the acceptance of a model: the production of self-evident units of analysis of the kind produced by these "harder" social sciences, and the implicit acknowledgment of an essence within those boundaries. In short, culture became a *thing*, in the footsteps of thinglike entities such as the market, the economy, the state, and society.

As culture became a thing, it also started doing things. Parodying the market and the model set by economists, culture shifted from being a descriptive conceptual tool to being an explanatory concept. And the more it explained, the more rigid and reified it became, just like the market or the state. In the process, North American anthropologists grafted onto the self-evident units of the savage slot an essentialist notion of culture that reproduced the state-centrism of the other human sciences. Just as France or the United States obviously had one economy, one history, and one social life, the Iroquois, the Samoans, the Dobu, the Zuni, or the Japanese, for that matter, could have only one of each of these. The extent to which their economy or their history mattered depended very much on the interests and benevolence of the observer. The extent to which inequality among them mattered was partly silenced by the liberal aversion toward Marxism and by the preconditions of the savage slot, which made the people without history "classless societies."

Here again, culture functioned as an anticoncept, just as the savage had functioned as an anticoncept in earlier times. For Columbus as for Montaigne, Las Casas, or Rousseau, savages were those who had no state, no religion, no clothes, no shame—because they had nature. For North American anthropologists, primitives became those who had no complexity, no class, no history that really mattered—because they had culture. Better, each group had a single culture whose boundaries were thought to be self-evident. Thus, North American cultural anthropology reconciled the Boasian agenda with both the state-centrism of the strong social sciences and the taxonomic schemes (Silverstein 2000) of the even stronger natural sciences, notably zoology and biology.

Not every anthropologist welcomed the essentialist turn. Some, notably Edward Sapir, rejected it quite loudly (Brightman 1995; Darnell 1997). Many acknowledged outside influences (Stocking 1968). Their deep knowledge of history often led early anthropologists to recognize diffusion and thereby to circumvent at times the borders they had erected around culture. The overemphasis on culture was doubly tactical: it helped to inscribe the discipline within academe, and it provided a response to biological determinism. Yet its noblest goals notwithstanding, as North American anthropology became both more powerful and more popular, cultural centrism—if not determinism—obscured the finer points of the intellectual program for the public and graduate students alike.

First, increased specialization made it impossible for single writers or even a group of writers to maintain the back-and-forth movement between race and culture that characterized the early work of Boas. Specialization facilitated a mind-body dualism. Man the symbol maker was freed from the physical realities of his being and of his world. Culture, in turn, was left on its own even within anthropology. Its boundaries became thicker; its negative reference to race blurrier. Anthropologists such as Ruth Benedict (1938) and Ralph Linton (1955) emphasized the "wholeness" of distinct cultures, a theme later revived in the work of Clifford Geertz (1973).

Slanted as it became toward closure, theory alone would not have sufficed to sustain the notion of cultures as isolated wholes. Extreme isolationist pronouncements such as those of Benedict and Linton did not necessarily gain unanimity within the discipline (Brightman 1995; Darnell 1997). Further, the very practice of fieldwork belied the possibility of a cultural quarantine.

Yet whatever individual doubts emerged from field practice crashed against the corporate wall of institutionalization. Disciplines necessarily impose rites of passage that ensure and confirm professionalization. As anthropology gained in demographic and institutional power, the ethnographic monograph became a major proof of professionalization in France, England, and especially the United States, where support for fieldwork was more available. The production of one such work became the privileged rite of access to the profession. In North America, it became the sole credential unanimously recognized for entry into the guild (Cohn 1987).

The institutionalization of the monographic tradition in turn reinforced what I call the ethnographic trilogy: one observer, one time, one place. Since what is accessible to the gaze of a single observer staying in one place for a limited amount of time is inherently limited, the ethnographic trilogy, inscribed in a rite of passage, invited a practical closure.

Contrary to recent critics, I do not see this closure as inherent in fieldwork. Rather, a naive epistemology, strongly influenced by empiricism, predisposed anthropologists to fetishize fieldwork—first by avoiding the issue of the epistemological status of the native voice, and second by blurring the necessary distinction between the object of study and the object of observation (Trouillot 1992a, 2001). Further, in the first half of the twentieth century, procedures of acceptance within the guild provided additional corporate and individual incentives to fetishize fieldwork. By the middle of the twentieth century, the units of analysis were most often taken, on both sides of the Atlantic, as natural, obvious, and, for all practical purposes, impermeable, and "culture" became, in the United States, the impenetrable boundary of these units.

A Theoretical Refuge

The story described so far is academic in most senses of the word. It happens within academe. Its consequences may seem commonplace both within and outside of that context. The parallel between the deployment of culture and the deployment of terms such as economy, state, and society is evident. Each of the last three words has been as thoroughly reified as has culture. Yet none of these terms today suggests the exact opposite of what it was first intended to question. The paradox of culture, as promoted by North American anthropology, is unique. A word deployed in academe to curb racialist denotations is often used today in and out of academe with racialist connotations. A word intended to promote pluralism often becomes a trope in conservative agendas or in late liberal versions of the civilizing project. The story of how that happened is not merely academic. It is the story of a move away from politics, the story of a conceptualization whose deployment denied its very conditions of possibility.

The political move in theory described earlier was not necessarily fatal, even with the limitations mentioned. Within academe, culture could be read as a step back from politics, but this step backward could have been healthy if the privileged space it created had become one from which to address power, even if indirectly. Unfortunately, the pendulum never swung back. The privileged space became a refuge. Culture never went out to speak to power.

I am not suggesting that sociocultural anthropologists should have become political activists. Nor am I blaming them for avoiding "correct" political positions. Indeed, the American Anthropological Association has taken quite a few positions that can be described as politically progressive. I am willing to concede a lot on mere political grounds. Rather, my contention is that within the terms of its own history of deployment, the culture concept failed to face its context. What I see as a move away from politics inheres in that deployment and the silences it produced. Those on which I insist are not political silences as such. They are silences *in theory* that shielded theory from politics.

Two of them are most telling: first, the benign theoretical treatment of race, and second, the failure to connect race and racism in the United States and elsewhere and the related avoidance of black-white relations in the United States as an ethnographic object.

Race for Boas was a biological fact. It did not need to be conceptualized, but it had to be documented. It was between that careful documentation—in the terms of the times—and the development of a program of cultural research that the race-culture antinomy played out in Boas's work (Darnell 1998; Stocking 1968). Yet as biological determinism seemed to fade out of public discourse with the decline of scientific racism, as nineteenth-century definitions of race became questioned in academe, and as anthropologists themselves subspecialized further within the discipline, culture and race each went each its own way (Baker 1998: 168–187). The result is that today there is more conceptual confusion about race among anthropologists than there was at the beginning of the last century.

After a careful survey of anthropological textbooks, Eugenia Shanklin (2000) argued that "American anthropologists deliver inchoate messages about anthropological understandings of race and racism." Echoing the pioneering work of Leonard Lieberman and his associates (Lieberman, Stevenson, and Reynolds 1989; Lieberman et al. 1992), she documented inconsistencies and lacunas that combine to make anthropology "look ignorant, backward, deluded, or uncaring" about race and racism. Should we be worried? Sociocultural anthropologists have also proposed myriad definitions of culture. That they would not agree on definitions of race should come as no surprise.

Yet this response to Shanklin's judgment makes sense only if we reduce conceptualizations to mere definitions. If we return to the kernel I sketched earlier, the two cases—culture and race—are diametrically opposed. Behind the definitional differences over culture is a core understanding of the notion. Indeed, definitional debates about culture are battles over control of that conceptual core. The very opposite is true of race. Definitional divergences reveal the lack of a conceptual core.

The absence of a conceptual core is verified by numerous entries in the *Anthropology Newsletter* on and after October 1997, when the American Anthropological Association presented its chosen theme for 1997–1998: "Is It 'Race'? Anthropology and Human Diversity." Both the statement that announced this theme and the following debates confirmed what we might already have concluded from Lieberman: something on the order of the kernel sketched earlier for culture is blatantly missing.

Both Lieberman's and Shanklin's research confirms my intuition that few within anthropology want control over a concept of race, except for a few politically naive or conservative biological anthropologists. It is as if North American anthropologists—especially those who see themselves as politically liberal—are worried about stating bluntly what race is, even as a matter of intellectual debate. The consensus is that biological inheritance cannot explain the transmission of patterns of thought and behavior; culture (and/or social practice) does. It even explains the transmission of the belief that biological inheritance plays such a role.

That may seem to be good news, and indeed it is. Still, that statement brings us back to our starting point. For in a way we have gone full circle, as far as the race-culture antinomy is concerned. We have restated our belief in the conceptual kernel. Yet in spite of that kernel, within the antinomy itself, culture is what race is not, and race, in turn, is what culture is not. In other words, we have gained nothing *conceptually* on the race-culture relation. Worse yet, culture has been freed from its original milieu of conception, from the political tension that made its deployment necessary. It can function alone. It has become a theoretical refuge.

Some may object to the apparent harshness of this judgment. Have we not learned that race is a "construction"? Indeed, we may have. Yet this catchword states only that race is a proper object of study for sociocultural anthropologists, like other kinds of constructions such as language, history, marriage, ritual, gender, and class. It says little about how to conceptualize this particular construction, about the specific mechanisms of its production or its special modes of operation. To put it most simply, if race does not exist, racism does, and the mere coining of race as a construction fails to give us much of a handle on racism.

Yet mentions of racism are rarer than mentions of race in North American textbooks. The dominant trend is not divergence but neglect. While disagreeing on what race is, North American anthropologists often overlook practices of racism. That outcome was predictable. Studies of racism by anthropologists in North America are extremely rare. So are works on blacks in the United States.[3]

That anthropologists traditionally study people in faraway places is not enough to explain this avoidance. Native Americans have long been favorite objects of anthropological enquiry. Sidney W. Mintz (1971), who juxtaposed North American anthropology's aversion toward the study of the black victims of white domination with its predilection for the "red" ones, had a number of suggestions to explain this bizarre polarity. Most notably, Indians fitted quite well the savage slot. Black Americans did so less well. The combined reasons are theoretical and political in the way addressed here. Whereas each "Indian culture"— enforced isolation abetting—could be projected as a distinct unit of analysis, it is impossible to describe or analyze patterns of thought and behavior among the people who pass for blacks within the United States without referring to racism and its practices. Without that reference, anthropology will continue to look irrelevant to most blacks.[4] With that reference, the pendulum would swing back. Culture would have to address power.

A Liberal Space of Enlightenment

Why does power seem to provide the stumbling block to anthropological theory at almost each point of this story? I contend that a recurring assumption behind the difficulties and silences we have encountered here regarding both culture and race is the illusion of a liberal space of enlightenment within which words-as-concepts can be evaluated without regard for their context of deployment.

On the same front page of the October 1997 *Anthropology Newsletter* is another headline: "AAA Tells Feds to Eliminate 'Race.'" The Association recommended to the U.S. Office of Management and Budget that race be eliminated from Directive 15, "Race and Ethnic Standards for Federal

Statistics and Administrative Reporting." The rationale was that race and ethnicity are indistinguishable and commonly misunderstood and misused. Thus, the Census Bureau should stop classifying Americans on the basis of race. Restating proposals first made by Ashley Montagu (e.g., 1946), the AAA suggested first coupling race and ethnicity and then phasing out race altogether.

The coupling seems awkward: native informants are likely to feel that one is not African American the way one is Italian American, especially since a reconsolidation of whiteness occurred in the half century between Montagu's writings and our times (Jacobson 1998). Thus, in the United States, as elsewhere, ethnicity and race need to be conceptualized together (Trouillot 1995: 133; Williams 1989), not evened out empirically or theoretically. Shanklin (2000) rightly castigated textbook authors who subsumed race under ethnicity. Yolanda Moses, who drafted the AAA statement, rightly implied that the change of labels might prove meaningless so long as "white" remained an unquestioned category. But can we really erase whiteness by a mere stroke of the pen?

A major contention of the official AAA position in 1997 was that the public was misusing ethnic categories and, especially, the concept of race. Thus, anthropology needed to reclaim race and provide a better concept in order to enlighten the public. But the only way we can accept this solution is to assume a liberal space of enlightenment—a space blind to the world, isolated from the messiness of social life, within which the concept of race would go through its own intellectual cleansing and whence it would emerge with the purity of whiteness to edify a world all too social and political.

Left out of the discussion of Directive 15 were the practices within which these concepts and categories are mobilized and reach full realization. Yet the problem with these concepts is not one of scientific exactitude, their purported referential relation to entities existing out there. The crux of the matter is the uses to which these categories are put, the purposes for which they are mobilized, and the political contests that make this mobilization necessary in the first place. Here the academic, lay, and political lives of concepts (Williams 1989) intertwine. Not to address this overlay is to assume the imperviousness of the privileged space. That is a huge assumption. Yet it is a common one in anthropological practice—indeed, the very one that overlies the deployment of the culture concept itself.

In separating race and culture, Boas consistently noted the "errors" of racialist theories. Unlike many of his followers, he did mention race discrimination in both his academic and his popular writings (e.g., Boas

1945). Yet his fundamental strategy was to disconnect race and culture in anthropology, not to connect race and racism in or out of anthropology.

The evidence is overwhelming that Franz Boas, the individual, wanted to go beyond that space and its rules of engagement (Hyatt 1990), especially at the end of his life. When read chronologically, the essays collected posthumously in *Race and Democratic Society* (Boas 1945) hint at a dual progression. From about 1925 to 1941, their themes—as well as a gradual shift in vocabulary—register a move from the description of politically neutral states of affairs (e.g., race, 1925; race feelings, 1932) to *inherently political categories* (e.g., prejudice, 1937; racial injustice, 1937; racism, 1940 [Boas 1932, 1945]). Equally important, the introduction and the concluding essay interrogate the purported isolation of academic institutions—and thus their role as mere exporters of good concepts. Indeed, Boas wondered to what extent academic knowledge was influenced by "demagogues" and by both the prejudices and the institutional structure of the society at large. If this is not a full agenda, it is the closest anthropology came to the real thing in the first half of the last century.

As a rule, however, theory in sociocultural anthropology never followed that agenda. Perhaps the political will was missing in—or poorly channeled through—the discipline as an institutional site. Perhaps the need to establish anthropology as an objective "science" limited the terms of engagement.[5] At any rate, the study of "race relations," relinquished by anthropology, remained a purview of sociology—often with the unfortunate premise that race is a biological given. Sandwiched between Ruth Benedict and Gene Weltfish's "Races of Mankind" (1943) and Boas's *Race in a Democratic Society* (1945), the publication of Gunnar Myrdal's much more influential *American Dilemma* (1945) signaled both the absorption of culture by race and their twin capture from anthropologists in the public arena. Myrdal saw "American Negro culture" as a pathological distortion of the general (i.e., white) American culture.

The public resonance of Myrdal's thesis only verified an old division of labor within academe rarely acknowledged by historians of anthropology (but see Baker 1998). Anthropology's monopoly over both the word and the concept of culture obtained only when the use of either was restricted to the savage slot. When it came to black savages in the cities, white immigrants, or the majority population, other social scientists, such as political scientists or sociologists—notably of the Chicago school—took the lead. Their varying notions of culture sometimes challenged the Boasian race-culture divide. Further, even when nonanthropologists accepted this divide, the politics of race and assimilation and the belief in American exceptionalism led these scholars to emphasize the "white American culture" that Myrdal assumed.

To say that sociologists coined the wrong concept or distorted the right one for a general public obsessed by race is to miss the point. The political persona and professional career of Clark Wissler illustrate how much these public developments came from anthropology's own theoretical ambiguities. Wissler's writings on culture areas and "American Indian cultures" fit broadly within the Boasian paradigm. When Wissler turned his gaze to "Euro-American culture," however, his conceptual handling reveals the extent to which the conceptual and political ambiguities overlapped. He identified three main characteristics of "our American culture," one of which was the practice of universal suffrage and the belief that the vote is one of the "inalienable and sacred rights of man" (1923: 10). This proposition becomes blatantly suspicious when we recall that, at that time, about forty states had laws against miscegenation, and grandfather, poll, and literacy laws kept most blacks from voting throughout the U.S. South.

Wissler's position becomes both conceptually stranger and politically clearer when he backs his reserve toward miscegenation by evoking this major tenet of "our" American culture, universal suffrage. He writes: "If it can be shown that negroes may under favorable conditions play an equal part *in the culture of whites,* it is yet proper to question the social desirability of such joint participation" (emphasis added). The first issue is amenable to "scientific treatment." The second depends only on "the preferences of a majority of the individuals concerned" (Wissler 1923: 284–287). Thus, miscegenation is not a topic for anthropological study but a political matter best left to voters. It may not be surprising, then, that the same Wissler, a member of the Galton Society, also sat on the executive committee of the Second International Congress of Eugenics in 1921 and on the advisory council of *Eugenics: A Journal of Race Betterment.*[6]

I am not arguing that Wissler was a standard representative of the Boasians—if there was such a being. I am arguing that his positions demonstrate not only the inability to produce from the space carved out by the Boasians a clear *theoretical reply to racist practices* but also the possibility of short-circuiting culture as an anticoncept both from within (Wissler, Benedict) and from without (e.g., Davenport et al. 1930; Myrdal 1962; Murray and Herrnstein 1994). The space Wissler used between politics and "science" was carved out by the two moves described here, which fully isolated culture (best dealt with in academe) from issues of power, including racism, which were relevant only to the

52 Leaving Culture Worry Behind

world around the ivy walls. Wissler's position could be made theoretically consistent with Boasian anthropology, just as racist practices today can very well accommodate the belief that "race" is a construction.[7]

Current reactions among many anthropologists to the misuse of the culture concept rely on the same assumption of a privileged space. Worse, they nurture it. If only culture could get back where it belongs, the world would be edified. But who is to say where culture belongs?

The desire to occupy a privileged space of enlightenment is a frequent feature of both philosophical and political liberalism, though it is not unique to them. It echoes dominant ideologies of North American society, notably the will to power. Liberalism wishes into existence a world of free, willing individual subjects barely encumbered by the structural trappings of power. Hence the dubious proposition that if enlightened individuals could get together within their enlightened space, they could recast "culture" or "race" and, in turn, discharge other free, willing individuals of their collective delusions. But is racism a delusion about race? Or is race made salient by racism? That is the crux of the matter.

Albert Memmi (2000 [1982]: 143) may have been the first scholar to proclaim loudly that "racism is always both a discourse and an action," a structuring activity with political purposes. Semantic content and scientific evidence thus matter less than the denunciation of those purposes. Similarly, Etienne Balibar (1991) asked how we might get rid of some of the practices of power rooted in ambiguous identities when we disagree with the politics of those practices. Balibar argued that we cannot get rid of these practices by repression, that is, by forbidding some kinds of thoughts or some kinds of speech. He went on to say that we cannot eliminate these practices through predication, either, that is, by the mere infusion of new kinds of thoughts and new kinds of speech.

One need not put a low premium on the value of thought and speech to recognize that the primary solution anthropological theory has tended to propose to the problems many anthropologists genuinely want to solve is the infusion of new kinds of words. Worse, from the early Boasian wager to more recent recommendations about either race or culture, the reduction of concepts to words has worsened—hence the fetishization of "culture" to the detriment of its conceptual kernel. The distance between theory and its context of deployment has widened as well, and not only in anthropology.

The last two decades of the twentieth century saw a closing of academic discourse to problems felt by a majority of the world's population. Media claims notwithstanding, the influence of academic research that could be labeled politically "progressive" has decreased—if only because these works are increasingly inaccessible to lay readers. Far beyond the absolute need for a technical vocabulary to which research contributes and without which it cannot be sustained, far beyond the specific need for syntactic structures that express the complexity of thought or the gracefulness of language, academics now bask in "the aestheticization of theory." By that I mean a process through which theory not only acquires a birthright of its own—a legitimate claim, indeed—but spends its life spinning in a proselytical circle, the main purpose of which is to verify its beauty. In short, the pressures are much greater now than in Boas's time to find refuge in a privileged space of enlightenment where words are protected and, in turn, protect their writers.

That space does not exist. Once launched, the concepts we work with take on a life of their own. They follow trajectories that we cannot always predict or correct. We can place them in orbit, design them with a direction in mind, but we know they will be challenged in and out of academe. There is no guarantee that the final meaning will be ours. Yet without prior attention to the wider context of deployment, the words that encapsulate our concepts are most likely to become irretrievable for us. That, I think, is what happened to "culture."

Out of Orbit?

The deployment of the culture concept echoes a voluntarism distinctive of the liberal ideologies that permeate U.S. society. If culture had remained tied to the race-culture antinomy even as circuitously as it was in Boas's early writings (therefore maintaining an engagement with biology and biological anthropologists), or, more importantly, if its anthropological deployment had compelled references to sociohistorical processes such as mechanisms of inequality, it would have been more difficult to displace. Launched on some conceptual path, it still could have been nabbed in orbit. But as set, a self-generating, singularized, and essentialized entity, it was literally up for grabs.

The complexity of the Boasians' private debates (Brightman 1995; Darnell 1997) was not immediately accessible to the general public. Even within the discipline, groups of specialists integrated different parts of an increasingly vast corpus and inherited only portions of an increasingly broad agenda. While some cultural anthropologists successfully questioned biological determinism so far as group behavior was concerned, some biological anthropologists may have reinforced biological determinism as it pertained to individual behavior.[8] Further and more important, the separation of race and culture heralded by Boas, the major public purpose of the culture concept, filtered down quite slowly to parts of the citizenry (Baker 1998). Not only did racism survive the Boasians, but it survived them quite well. Worse, it turned culture into an accessory.

Although the culture concept helped in questioning the theoretical relevance of race in some learned circles, it has not much affected racism in the public space. At best, the racism that evokes biological determinism simply made room for a parallel racism rooted in cultural essentialism. At times, the two forms of racism contradict each other. Most often, they reinforce each other in and out of academe. The biological determinism of a Charles Murray or a Vincent Sarich implies an essentialist notion of culture without which the biological package does not hold up. In turn, many of the chapters in *Culture Matters* imply an essentialist take on racial, religious, or geo-ethnic clusters projected as cultural isolates. Instead of the culture versus race effect that Boas expected, many in American society now espouse a culture qua race ideology that is fast spreading to the rest of the world.

Indeed, culture has become a preferred explanation of socioeconomic inequality within and across countries (Banfield 1990; Harrison and Huntington 2000). It has become an argument for a number of politically conservative positions and been put to uses that quite a few anthropologists would question, from the disapproval of cross-racial adoptions to the need for political representation based on skin color. It has also revived, with much less criticism from anthropologists, versions of the white man's burden.

Both the politically conservative use of culture and the late liberal versions of the white man's burden have theoretical roots in anthropology itself: first, in the unchecked explanatory power with which many anthropologists endowed culture, and second, in the use of culture to delineate ever smaller units of analysis. These delineations ("the culture of science," "the culture of academe," "political culture," etc.) make the concept of society and the entire field of social relations less relevant both analytically and politically to any topic under study. The social order need not be analyzed, let alone acted upon; we need only to change the morally dubious or politically ineffective subcultures. On a different scale but in a similar manner, the burden of the North Atlantic today can be formulated as a duty to bring to the rest of the world the enlightenment of Protestant liberalism (Harrison and Huntington 2000).

Many cultural anthropologists are appalled by these uses, which they tend to discover too late anyway. For indeed, few people outside anthropology now bother to ask anthropologists what they mean by culture. Since the early 1980s, a vibrant discussion has been going on in economics about the relationship between culture and development (e.g., Buchanan 1995; Mayhew 1987), with little participation from anthropologists. In policy circles, we are often left out of the debates about multiculturalism, which we all know are "really" about race. Or when solicited, we reject the engagement, preferring the isolation of our place of enlightenment. Even within academe we are losing ground to cultural studies in the debate over the appropriation of the word culture, a loss that seems to irritate anthropologists more than the political capture of the word in the world outside. We keep telling all sides, "You've got it wrong." But a lot of it they got from us—not only through our epiphany of culture but also through our clinging to a space where we feel conceptually safe. If some Afrocentrists today believe that an inner-city Chicago kid is culturally closer to a Kalahari bushman than to her white counterpart on the North Side of town—and if the inequalities between the two are ascribed to culture, however misdefined—then anthropology has to take part of the blame.

Adieu, Culture

Blame is not enough, nor is it the most effective attitude. Solutions are necessary. They will not come from a single individual or group but from the discipline's collective engagement with the context within which we operate. I do not mean by this a political engagement, which remains a matter of individual choice. Anthropology's primary response as a discipline cannot be a political statement, however tempting or necessary that solution may be in critical circumstances. Yet while the primary context of our practice as professionals remains the academic world, the ultimate context of its relevance is the world outside, starting most likely with the country within which we publish, rather than those we write about.[9] Thus, while not suggesting that anthropologists abandon theory for political discourse, I am arguing for a theory that is aware of its conditions of possibility, which include the politics of its surroundings.

The nineteenth century generated a particular model of the relations between academe and politics premised on an alleged difference of nature between scientific and social practices. Challenged as it has been at times, this model continues to dominate North Atlantic academic life. The most visible alternative emerged in the 1960s and remains alive under various guises, including some trends of identity politics. That alternative model negates the autonomy and specificity of academic life and research. It solves the problem of the relationship between academe and politics by collapsing the two: science is politics and theory is insurgency. One does one's politics in the classroom or in academic journals. There is no need to problematize a relation between academe and its context because the two entities are the same, except that the first is a disguised version of the second.

Neither model is convincing. While the first assumes a liberal space of enlightenment where concepts can be cleansed by academics, the second belittles academe's specific rules of engagement and the relative power of different institutional locations. It perniciously allows academics to claim the social capital of political relevance while comforting them in their privileged space. A major hope behind this chapter is that anthropologists might explore the possibility of a third model of engagement.

Until that collective engagement manifests itself forcefully, what do we do about culture? If the story told here is reasonably accurate, then the word is lost to anthropology for the foreseeable future. To acknowledge this is not to admit defeat. It is to face the reality that there is no privileged space within which anthropologists alone can refashion the word. Culture is now in an orbit where chasing it can be only a conservative enterprise, a rearguard romance with an invented past (when culture truly meant culture—as if culture ever meant culture only). If concepts are not words, then Brightman (1995) is correct that strategies of "relexification" are not useful either. There is a conceptual kernel to defend, but that defense need not be tied to a word that the general public now essentializes on the basis of anthropologists' own fetishization.[10] We need to abandon the word while firmly defending the conceptual kernel it once encapsulated. More important, we need to use the power of ethnographic language to spell out the components of what we used to call culture.

Even more importantly, we need to rethink the terms of sociocultural anthropology's engagement with other disciplines and with the world outside of academe. It is not accidental that our increasingly parochial discussions interest fewer social scientists and even less the public at large at a time when the ethical drive of the discipline is not only unclear but not even open to debate. Nor is it accidental that sociocultural anthropology is slowly turning away from the very same populations that globalization now makes irrelevant to the accumulation of capital

(Trouillot 2001: 128–129). Thus again, the long-term and most crucial issue is that of a collective engagement.

It is only with this caveat in mind that, prompted by this volume's editors, I reluctantly propose a few examples of mid-term solutions. In my current efforts to describe the global flows that characterize our times and their impact on localized populations (e.g., Trouillot 2000, 2001), I find that the word culture often blurs rather than elucidates the facts to be explained—especially since globalization itself has become thinglike much faster than culture. Words such as style, taste, cosmology, ethos, sensibility, desire, ideology, aspirations, and predispositions often better describe the facts to be studied on the ground, because they tend to limit better the range of traits and patterns covered. They actually allow a better deployment of the conceptual kernel to which I hold.

Do we gain or lose by describing clashes between *beur* and white youths in France as clashes between Arab (or Muslim) and French (or Western) culture? How close do we want to get to Harrison and Huttington's clash of civilizations? Is the spread of McDonald's in France or China proof of the globalization of American "culture"—whatever that may be? We may be more precise in exploring how successfully North American capitalists export middle-class American consumer tastes. We may want to investigate how U.S. corporations—often dominated by white males—are selling speech forms, dress codes, and performance styles developed under conditions of segregation in North American cities as "black culture." What are the mechanisms through which these forms and styles are accepted, rejected, or integrated in the U.S. South, in the rest of the anglophone world, in Africa, Brazil, or the Caribbean, or in European neighborhoods with substantial numbers of African or Caribbean immigrants? We may want to look at how the expansion and consolidation of the world market for consumer goods, rather than creating a "global culture," fuels a "global production of desire" (Trouillot 2001). What forces and factors now reproduce the same image of the good life all over the world and push people in very different societies to aspire to the same goods? We may want to ask how the current wave of collective apologies for historical sins is propelled by the production of new sensibilities and subjectivities and the virtual presence of a Greek chorus now naively called "the international community" (Trouillot 2000). The production of these new subjects, the rise of new forces and new sites, make it increasingly perilous to hang our theoretical fate on a single word over whose trajectory we have absolutely no control.

Abandoning the word would actually free practitioners in all the subfields of anthropology. It would enhance the dialogue between sociocultural anthropologists, on the one hand, and archaeologists and—especially—biological anthropologists, on the other. Biological anthropologists would not have to find "culture" in the behavior of humans or other primates. Rather, they would have to specify the role of biology in patterning particular instances of cognition, volition, and activity among the groups—human or otherwise—that they study and the degree to which symbolic constructions inform those patterns. The debate would turn on specifics, not on generalities.

Urging fellow physical anthropologists to abandon the word "race," Ashley Montagu (1964: 27) once wrote that "the meaning of a word is the action it produces," suggesting that the only reasons to deploy racial terms were political. Sociocultural anthropologists need to demonstrate a similar courage. The intellectual and strategic value of "culture" depends now as then on use and historical context (Knauft 1996: 43–45). Today, there is no reason to enclose any segment of the world's population within a single bounded and integrated culture, except for political quarantine. The less culture is allowed to be a shortcut for too many things, the more sociocultural anthropology can thrive within its chosen domain of excellence, documenting how human thought and behavior is patterned and how those patterns are produced, rejected, or acquired. Without culture, we will continue to need ethnography. Without culture, we may even revitalize the Boasian conceptual kernel, for we will have to come to the ground to describe and analyze the changing heads of the hydra that we once singularized.

Notes

This adieu took a long time to say. My uneasiness with the race-culture complex in North American anthropology goes back to graduate school. I first put it into words at the presidential session on race at the annual meeting of the American Anthropological Association in San Francisco in 1991. My arguments were revived for the paper "Exploring the Limits of Liberal Discourse: American Anthropology and U.S. Racism," presented at the symposium "Anthropologists of Color Speak Out: Perspectives on Race and Public Anthropology" at American University on 25 October 1997. This essay itself was first proposed at Ben-Gurion University in Israel in April 2000 and was discussed at the Wenner-Gren symposium from which this book springs. I thank participants in all these venues. Xavier Andrade, Lee D. Baker, Bruce Knauft, Sam Kaplan, Richard A. Shweder, George W. Stocking, Jr., and especially Richard G. Fox provided substantial comments. Clare Sammells provided comments and assistance. Special thanks to Brackette F. Williams, from whom I continue to learn both in print and in talk, and to the students who have taken my "Concepts and Categories" seminar over the last sixteen years at Duke, Johns Hopkins, and Chicago. I claim full and sole responsibility, however, for what some will see as the outrageous conclusions of this chapter.

1. The exaggerated focus on cultural studies, which turns fellow academics into prime political targets, and reactions to earlier versions of this chapter, though obviously different in scope and relevance, include some dominant themes: we do not have a *public* problem, only an academic one that can be solved within academe; we have a public problem, but it can be solved with conceptual adjustment; we have only a North American problem: culture and cultural studies are quite healthy everywhere else.

2. Indeed, as conceptual foundations of North American anthropology, these propositions preceded by a decade at least—notably in Franz Boas's writings—the routine use of the word that came later to embody them.

3. Exceptions include Gregory 1998, Gregory and Sanjek 1994, Sanjek 1998, and classics such as Herskovits's *Myth of the Negro Past* (1958). Yet Herskovits's own move from the proposition that "[Negroes] have absorbed the culture of America" to the celebration of a distinct Afro-American culture (Mintz 1990) poignantly reveals the political dilemma of cultural essentialism and augurs the recapture of culture by race.

4. The relationship between anthropology and black Americans has deteriorated greatly since the first generation of black students Boas attracted to the field. Today the number of Ph.D.s in anthropology climbs much faster than in other fields, with a majority of the diplomas going to women. Yet while we attract increasing numbers of Asians, American Indians, and Latinos (except Puerto Ricans, whose numbers are shamefully small), blacks received merely 3.5 percent of our doctoral degrees in 1999. The national average for that year was 5.9 percent, excluding professional schools. Clearly, in comparison with peer disciplines, anthropology is becoming less attractive to blacks (Sanderon et al. 1999, 2000).

5. Many among the individuals least willing to accept anthropology as refuge—St. Clair Drake, Otto Klineberg, Allison Davis, Eugene King—never became its tenors. Yet it would be futile for us today to divide anthropological ancestors along Manichean lines. Ruth Benedict's pamphlet "Races of Mankind" (1943), coauthored with Gene Weltfish and later a victim of McCarthyism, was

banned by the army as "communist propaganda" (di Leonardo 1998: 196). Yet in spite of her antiracist activism, Benedict rarely questioned the implicit evaluation of white advancement.

6. Wissler was most likely the influence behind the presence of Melville J. Herskovits in the pages of *Eugenics,* where Herskovits provided a rather polite rebuttal to those who saw interracial mixture as a recipe for undesired mutants (Davenport et al. 1930).

7. A political climate that mixed nativism and exceptionalism is also part of the story of culture's road to essentialism. Although North Americans have no monopoly on exceptionalism or essentialism, there is a quite specific mixture of the two in North American social science. Drawing from Dorothy Ross (1991), I read the American particularity as the confluence of three trends: a methodological reliance on natural science models, a political reliance on liberal individualism, and an ideological reliance on American exceptionalism. Liberalism and exceptionalism permeate Benedict's dismissal of racism as an aberration of North American democracy.

8. Lest readers think I am singling out biological anthropology as the fall guy, let me remind them that most biological anthropologists—including a majority of those who believe in the existence of biological races—were trained in four-field departments dominated by culturalists. The real issue is how anthropology connects culture and racism, not the biological boundaries of race.

9. Given the power of the United States, the relative responsibility of those of us privileged to write in the United States is obvious.

10. Powerful arguments for the defense of that kernel—rather than for the defense of culture as a unit of analysis—can be found in Wolf 1999. I disagree, however, with Wolf's implicit equation of word and concept, an equation belied by his own work, including the cases treated in that book.

three

Culture and Anthropology in Ethnographic Modernity

Yoshinobu Ota

Everyone played the appropriation game.

—Ralph Ellison, "The Little Man at Chehaw Station"

As a Japanese learning anthropology in the United States during the 1970s and 1980s, I read, with a sense of liberation fitting for the end of the conservative decade, the following remark by Edward Said (1989: 213): "The most striking thing about 'otherness' and 'difference' is, as with all general terms, how profoundly conditioned they are by their historical and worldly context. To speak about 'the other' in today's United States is, for the contemporary anthropologist here, quite a different thing than say for an Indian and Venezuelan anthropologist."

My sense of liberation came from both Said's perspectivism and his emphasis on worldliness as a characteristic of anthropology. The idea of worldliness compelled me to recognize the anthropological subjectivity embedded in concrete practices in the historically formed geopolitical space. I sensed that there might be a different vision of anthropology for the future—a vision emerging out of historical and locational conjunctures often overlooked in the hegemonic narration of the disciplinary past and present.

This recognition helped me to articulate for the first time a persistent, unsettling feeling I could not shake off, the source of which I had thought stemmed from my experience of being a subject as well as an object of ethnographic investigation—or, to be more precise, being interpellated as such (I use "interpellation" in Louis Althusser's sense of "being hailed" [1971:174]). From my parochial perspective it seems that discussions of the concept of culture as an object of anthropology are inseparable from discussions of anthropology itself as a modern institution. Furthermore, anthropology does not necessarily mean the same thing even among those who identify themselves as anthropologists; such differences are the products of people's deciding where to locate themselves within the discipline's "imagined community," historically and geopolitically constituted. I have often wondered what a category such as "native anthropologist" could possibly mean, and what sort of history an unpacking of this term might disclose?

Having been out of sync with my academic surroundings in the United States—to the extent that one of my graduate advisors once characterized me as "someone working on the margins of the discipline"—I could not help recovering in Said's words a powerful tool for historicizing anthropology as I had learned it so far. I mention a sense of being out of sync not because I want to situate myself in the position of vicitimhood for the purpose of enunciating the (suppressed) voice of authenticity— such a desire is certainly one of the sorry by-products of "multiculturalism." I merely want to bring into the open a discourse of authenticity operative in anthropology, something I have experienced personally. Here I define a discourse of authenticity as that which attributes amalgamations of absolute characteristics to the Other: naturalness, immutable identity, organicism, and sedentariness. Such a discourse immediately implies a mobile, translocal anthropological self. I felt out of sync with this aspect of anthropology; such an experience raised for me the question, what does it mean for me to *become* an anthropologist? Thus, my reflection on the concept of culture proceeds with a critique of a discourse of authenticity from within, as it were.

My return to Japan had not made matters easier. Not having been raised within the Japanese academic tradition, I could not help feeling out of sync with my "native" society, too. The term "native" seemed to have a definite meaning only when I spoke with non-Japanese people; to me the term has been a source of confusion, because my return did not produce the harmonious feeling of unity with an "organic" community that such a term connotes. Questions emerged, although still in inchoate forms. Is it possible to renarrate and reimagine anthropology inclusive of my own experience? How could I conceptualize an object of such an anthropology? These two questions are inseparable.

As I formulated these questions, the so-called postmodern critique in anthropology had, it seemed to me, thoroughly worked over the concept of culture, as wedded to a discourse of authenticity, for its tendency toward being totalizing, essentialistic, and local. The critique had suggested various alternative conceptions of culture in terms of its being fragmentary, hybrid, and translocal. In other words, an image of hermetically sealed local symbolic systems had been replaced by that of porous ("import-export"), translocal practices. Remaining sympathetic to such a critique, I also feel it has left untouched another aspect of a discourse of authenticity, the aspect directly related to a constitution of the anthropological self coded doubly as a subject and an object of investigation.

Now that the postmodern critique has, on the one hand, moved rapidly in the direction of "postethnic" (in David Hollinger's term [1995]) and "postculture" (in Joel Kahn's term [1995])—both terms signaling the obsolescence of the concept of culture—and, on the other hand, contributed to the "natives'" conduct of politics of difference—through which the notion of culture has received new articulations—I find myself hesitating. I still cannot completely say adieu to the concept, as Rolph Trouillot (this volume) has done, unless the other side of a discourse of authenticity is adequately critiqued. For this reason, I want to move a little more slowly than some other participants in the Wenner-Gren symposium in the direction of "saying adieu."

For now, I concur with James Clifford (1988: 19) that the concept of culture is "deeply compromised." Moreover, not only the concept of culture but also a discourse of authenticity that produces the essentialized, organic concept of the "native" needs to be examined closely. This discourse posits a mobile, cosmopolitan anthropological self who examines the "natives," who bear a localized, organic culture. Although the concept has been historicized in various ways, the anthropological subjectivity seems to remain singular, not pluralized enough to respond to Said's comment at the beginning of this chapter. I see the historicization of a discourse of authenticity as an urgent task for the purpose of liberating not just the concept of culture but also the anthropological subjectivity from essentialism. To be more concrete, I want to discuss how this discourse operates as it interpellates me in the contradictory and confusing position of being both an object and a subject of anthropological investigation.

I examine in three locations the ways in which both the culture concept and anthropological subjectivity are problematized: an American anthropology of a Boasian variety, embodied in Japan's encounter with Ruth Benedict in the late 1940s and contrasted with the work of Zora Neale Hurston in the American South; postreversion Okinawan cultural mobilization, through which a new image of the local has been created by a mix-and-match process; and a Guatemalan Mayan movement in the late 1990s that makes visible issues such as accountability and subaltern agency. I also raise the question, how can the relationship between anthropology and the notion of culture be reconfigured? This question leads me to reconsider anthropology's founding narrative as it has responded to a global condition of "ethnographic modernity"— "the state of being in culture and looking at culture" at the same time, as Clifford (1988: 9, 93) defined the term. I would like to use this concept of ethnographic modernity as a counternarrative to a discourse of authenticity; consequently, I want to free myself from being entangled in such a discourse. I have decided to take up a narrative mode of exposition rather than analytic one, since I cannot ignore the need to explicate myself, especially in the context of a Wenner-Gren international symposium.

American Anthropology à la Benedict and Hurston

In 1948, immediately after the Japanese translation of Ruth Benedict's *The Chrysanthemum and the Sword,* a Japanese anthropologist, Eiichiro Ishida, gathered four notable Japanese scholars—a philosopher, a rural sociologist, an economic historian, and a folklorist—to discuss Benedict's book on patterns of Japanese culture. Ishida, who would become in the early 1950s a professor of anthropology at the University of Tokyo, was eager to introduce to Japanese academe the "new" science of anthropology, drawing on the current trend of "internationalizing" American anthropology (Stocking 2000: 203). Considering Ishida's effort in inscribing anthropology as a discipline different from "ethnology"— tainted by its association with Japanese imperialism and colonial expansion—and from "folklore studies"—also downgraded by its ties with nationalism—I thought Benedict's impact on the formation of anthropology in Japan must have been something on the order of an "event." But her thought seems to have been siphoned mainly into fields other than anthropology, leaving hardly any legacy in Japanese anthropology even to this day. The eclipse of her ideas within Japanese anthropology does not, however, alter the fact that she is the best-known anthropologist among the Japanese reading public.

As several letters to the editor in the pages of *Current Anthropology* in 1962 indicate, Ishida (1960) wanted to institutionalize anthropology at the university level, with an emphasis on the "holistic" approach to culture then popular in the United States. Nevertheless, during the 1950s, as different theoretical approaches were imported to Japan from Britain and France, the Boasian legacy of culture as reformulated in the first chapter of Benedict's work on Japan was reduced to a model for "national character" studies. Such a reduction might be appreciated now, after the end of the cold war, because national character studies grew out of the North Atlantic countries' involvement in World War II and consolidated themselves during the early phase of the cold war geopolitical realignment. It seems to me that a Japanese encounter with American anthropology has never taken place, for a serious engagement with the Boasian legacy, which is said to define the "character of American anthropology" (Stocking 1974), has not happened. This is so despite the fact that Benedict's effect on Japanese intellectual circles is still quite visible.

In "The History of Anthropology," originally written in 1904, Boas (1974) employed the metaphor of *kulturbrille,* a term he left untranslated, in reference to the difficulty of becoming aware of one's own tradition. The term might be rendered as "cultural eyeglass." Boas acknowledged his debt to one of his fellow ethnology students at the University of Berlin, Karl von den Steinen, yet the basic idea captured by this metaphor was present in many of Boas's previous works, too. The term clearly points to the idea of the linguistic and cultural mediation that is unavoidable in every human interaction (Boas 1974 [1889]). Anthropology is defined as a discipline that helps uncover the veil of cultural mediation and frees people from the "shackles of tradition" (Boas 1974 [1938]). I am not certain whether for Boas anthropology was part of tradition or the detached tool with which one gained a perspective for unveiling it. I think he located the power of anthropology outside of tradition, believing that its disciplinary authority guaranteed its independence from cultural and historical locations.

In Benedict's work this belief becomes even more obvious. In her most popular work, *Patterns of Culture,* she reinterpreted the Boasian hallmark, the metaphor of *kulturbrille,* in order to emphasize the liberating power of anthropology against tradition and customs. These, I think, she equated with the notion of culture. In a characteristically Boasian fashion, Benedict (1934: 10) called for people to become "culture-conscious" when contacts between civilizations resulted in overt expressions of "nationalism and snobbery." It is ironic that her antipathy toward nationalism coexisted with a notion of "configuration"—an idea consolidated under the New Deal United States that later led to full-fledged national character studies (Hegeman 1999).

Benedict domesticated the metaphor as the "lens" without which humans cannot comprehend reality: "No man ever looks at the world with pristine eyes. He sees it edited by a definite set of customs and institutions and ways of thinking" (1934: 2). This awareness of cultural mediation reaches even deeper into "philosophical probings" (1934: 2) and social scientific thoughts: "Custom did not challenge the attention of social theorists because it was the very stuff of their own thinking: it was the lens without which they could not see at all" (1934: 9). Thus, Benedict conceptualizes culture as that which makes humans cultural yet what makes them at the same time natural, to the extent that they remain unaware of culture's arbitrariness. Born as a response to modernity's cultural dislocation, anthropology as conceived in a Boasian style highlights reflexive awareness of every cultural existence except, perhaps, that of its own foundation. In Benedict's understanding of the concept of culture, anthropology seems not to be affected by the mediation of culture; rather, it is what makes such a mediation visible and thinkable as an object of investigation and critical reflection. To her, an expression such as "the culture of anthropology" would have been an oxymoron. Ethnographic modernity was not, for Benedict, a condition shared by both "the native" and the anthropologist; "being in culture" becomes a property of the former, while "looking at culture" becomes a property of the latter (Rosaldo 1989: 206).

Benedict's privileged vista is troublesome for me as someone obliged to read her text on the patterns of Japanese culture from the perspective of a native but also of an anthropologist. The following statement, for example, confuses me:

> It is hard to be conscious of the eyes through which one looks. Any country takes them for granted.... In any matter of spectacles, we do not expect that man who wears them to know the formula for the lens, and neither can we expect nations to analyze their own outlook upon the world. When we want to know about spectacles, we train an oculist and expect him to be able to write out the formula for any lens we bring him. Someday no doubt we shall recognize that it is the job of the social scientist to do this for the nations of the contemporary world. (Benedict 1946: 14)

Again the lens metaphor functions to guarantee the authority of the outside observer, the "oculist," while the proverbial "man in the street" is the source of native authority insofar as he wears the "lens through which the Japanese sees existence" (Benedict 1946: 17). In the opposing metaphors of the oculist and the lens, excluded is, among other things, the possibility for coming to terms with one's own culture from the inside: for the person with the lens to become an oculist. Today, to push the metaphor a little farther, the persons with the lenses are everywhere aspiring to be oculists; increasingly pervasive is the condition that Clifford (1988: 9) termed "ethnographic modernity."

Clifford (1988: 3, 9) did not limit the meaning of "ethnographic modernity" only to the historical condition of the West or to academic practices. Rather, under that rubric he included the general condition of being "off-centered" and rootless as a future increasingly common for everyone. The state of "being in culture while looking at culture" was precisely the condition Benedict excluded for the purpose of establishing her ethnographic authority. Clifford referred to those who create a culture from the position of participant observer—being in culture while looking at it—as ethnographers. This is a modern condition, thus the term "ethnographic modernity" to acknowledge this global condition. Clifford defamiliarized methodological terms and gave them new functions; consequently, he liberated the condition of ethnographic modernity from the original anthropological inscription of observer and observed.

Despite Benedict's popularity, the Boasian concept of culture did not attain hegemonic status in Japanese anthropology, because competing ideas such as structure and social structure, derived from French and British social anthropologies, dominated during its formative years, the 1950s and 1960s. When the concept gained a measure of popularity in the 1980s, it was always understood as a set of cultural practices alien to the analyzer. Its usage appeared in a very essentialized way, as "my own culture" and "the culture of the other." The awareness of cultural mediation—much less of global ethnographic modernity—did not surface for the analyzer at all.

I do not think it appropriate to recuperate a Benedictian notion of culture now, because historical conjunctures have changed. However, I would like to reinstate another protégée of Boas's, someone for whom the condition of ethnographic modernity must have been real: Zora Neale Hurston. More than Benedict, Hurston was aware of her position in her own fieldwork in Eatonville, Florida. Her awareness is something I would like to recuperate. It is a kind of anthropological awareness that Benedict's theoretical elaboration of the Boasian notion of culture does not supply, yet it is necessary for examining the doubly codified position I occupy. A discussion of Hurston's Eatonville folklore leads me to highlight a discourse of authenticity against which I think Hurston also struggled hard.

Being personally closer to Benedict than to Boas, Hurston employed the metaphor of a "spyglass" in order to theorize the object of her investigation, southern black folklore—something that, according to Hurston, she had learned since her childhood in her native town of Eatonville: "It [African-American folklore] was fitting me like a tight chemise. I could not see it for wearing it. It was only when I was in college, away from my native surroundings, that I could see myself like somebody else and stand off and look at my garment. Then I had to use the spy-glass of Anthropology to look through at that" (Hurston 1990 [1935]: 1).

Here, Hurston applies the Boasian metaphor to anthropology, whereas Boas and Benedict both used it in reference to the customs and traditions from which anthropology promises to liberate us. Hurston clearly understood the importance of cultural mediation, and she questioned the foundation for speaking about that mediation. By changing the referent of the metaphor, Hurston not only indicates an *ironic* stance, which she takes up in relation both to her own tradition and to anthropology, but she also highlights intertextually the question that had remained unarticulated by either Boas or Benedict. Is anthropology subject at all to cultural mediation? What guarantees the privileged position of an anthropologist?

In the preface to Hurston's *Mules and Men,* Boas (1990 [1935]: xiii) attempted to locate Hurston's forte as that of an insider who could penetrate southern black culture, which sometimes remained hidden from the view of white observers. But in reality, Hurston herself had suffered from the uncooperativeness of "race men and women" who had regarded her research on folklore as damaging to black social uplift (Basalla 1997: 64). Moreover, her class position, marked by her clothing and her ownership of a new car, made her realize a distance from the workers in Polk County.

To me, Hurston's difficulty in her fieldwork dampens, if not contradicts, Boas's enthusiastic assessment of her forte. In comparing these two assessments of the field situation—Boas's and Hurston's own—I sense that nothing, neither race, gender, nor class, automatically guarantees one a superior access to cultural reality. To think otherwise, as Boas apparently did, means to succumb to a discourse of authenticity from which Hurston wanted to liberate herself (Hemenway 1980: 299). It might have been Boas, not Hurston, who succumbed to a discourse that constructs a desire for speaking from the "insider's" position—a desire especially significant for a discipline that has been anchored in a search for the "native's point of view." Yet I view Hurston's efforts as combating such a desire. She negotiated—almost in a true Spivakian fashion (see Spivak 1988)—between the empowerment and the entrapment that equally stem from an acceptance of the desire produced by the discourse of authenticity, which posits an organic position within her "native" community. She created, instead, a perspective not derivative of that discourse. She forged out of her rootless experience a sensibility for a "reinterpretation" of the tradition she remembered and encountered. Her anthropological self-fashioning is modern in the sense that she did not simply rediscover the "organic" southern black folklore tradition in order to repatriate herself. She observed the process of the people's re-creating it as she also re-created and redefined herself as a mobile local, a "cosmopolitan native." For this reason, Hurston frequently used the term "lies" in reference to the folklore of the area.

Within anthropology, Hurston's contribution has been overshadowed by those of her mentors, Boas and Benedict. The latter, in particular, published major work during the 1930s, about the same time Hurston published hers; the social climate of the thirties in the United States must have been more conducive to a Benedictian articulation of the culture concept (Hegeman 1999; Susman 1970). Hurston, by remaining not completely in sync with the Boasian tradition, gained a distance from the discourse of authenticity embedded in it. She approached southern black folklore neither as an object of investigation nor as part of an organic tradition recuperable through her belonging to it as an insider. Her approach demonstrates a cultural condition that Clifford might term ethnographic modernity, the condition of being "off-centered among the scattered traditions" (Clifford 1988: 3).

For me, a Japanese anthropologist with an interest in connecting various intellectual traditions instead of recovering a nativistic history of ethnological thinking, it is important to appreciate Hurston's oeuvre as an example of writing under the condition of ethnographic modernity. In contrast, Benedict's writing, hitherto much more influential, seems to show anthropology's limits rather than its possibilities for the future. Hurston's rearticulation of the Boasian concept of culture will not, perhaps, develop into a methodology, but it offers a useful reminder in thinking about the condition of ethnographic modernity as a global phenomenon.

If ethnographic modernity is a pervasive global condition, is it useful to deny a self-conscious reinterpretation of the concept of culture to those whose lives have been the objects of anthropological reflections? A powerful discourse of authenticity sanctions against the natives' aspiring to interpretation by redefining those who attempt it as inauthentic. They become opportunistic nationalists when they voice their opinions, giving the anthropological notion of culture a new function for cultural mobilization. I do not naively applaud this global phenomenon, which sometimes resembles, in form, identity politics. But it does not have to be so, as Frantz Fanon (1963) and W. E. B. DuBois (1986 [1903]) suggested: a cultural mobilization is nothing but one necessary phase in decolonization, whose end would open a path toward a more ecumenical cultural goal. Culture becomes politicized because (neo)colonial structure persists in many places, as one representative of the Hawaiian sovereignty movement commented to Jeffrey Tobin (1994). With this qualification in mind, I turn to two different locations and discuss the kinds of problems that each presented to me, a Japanese anthropologist.

Meeting the Ryukyu Cultural Revival

It was almost taken for granted in the 1970s and 1980s that a Japanese student would do fieldwork in Japan; my case was no exception. It does not really matter whether I actively chose to return or whether external pressures made it difficult for me to choose otherwise. The one thing certain was that even then I thought my decision to return to Japan to do fieldwork was somewhat at odds with my fellow graduate students' departure for various parts of the world other than the United States.

I do not believe my experience was extraordinary; I cite just one other such instance from many years earlier. Requesting an opinion from Booker T. Washington on a student from Gold Coast who wished to enter Columbia University, Franz Boas commented: "It is of course evident that if he [the student] developed into a good scientist, he could do excellent work . . . in Africa, which would be of the greatest service to science" (cited in Williams 1996: 65). Returning to one's "native" land might be called a tradition for many students coming from abroad to Britain and the United States.

I went to the southern Ryukyu Islands, mostly because their cultures appeared markedly different from what I had at least imagined to be Japanese culture. In addition, within the Ryukyu chain, the southern Ryukyus remain the most distant and least accessible. This remoteness explains why many folklorists and anthropologists have worked in the southern Ryukyus in search of the more "authentic" Ryukyuan traditions. The Ryukyu Islands were historically part of an independent kingdom that prospered through its trade relationship with China. In 1879, annexation to Japan began a rapid process of acculturation, which was interrupted from 1945 to 1972 while U.S. military forces governed the islands before returning them to Japan.

Until I left for the United States for my higher education, I had been raised in Hokkaido, an internal colony, the island known for the indigenous Ainu people. I wanted to conduct ethnographic fieldwork—as much as I could—in a Malinowskian fashion: going off to a faraway place, as did many of my friends from graduate school. In 1982 I went to the Ryukyus to begin fieldwork on folk religion. From the first I was bombarded by comments about the islands' long history of exploitation by Japan. Although I was in the southern Ryukyus, where no battle of significance took place in 1945, I could not escape from comments about the Japanese militarization of the area. I was taken aback; I was viewed constantly as a member of Japanese society, which had been marginalizing the Ryukyuans. I was addressed by the term *naichā*, a pan-Ryukyuan expression meaning literally "Japanese main islanders." Nevertheless, I could not help identifying with Ryukyuans who told me about their difficulties at schools where speaking in "standard" Japanese was strictly enforced. I recalled the same kind of experience in southern Hokkaido, where the regional dialect diverges greatly from standard Japanese. Indeed, widely circulated in Hokkaido is the term *naichi*—identical to its Okinawan counterpart—used in reference to the Japanese main islands.

   This name-calling indicates to me that an identity shared among the Ryukyuans and called *uchinā'nchu,* translatable as "Okinawan people" (Okinawa, now a word more popular than Ryukyu, is a literalization of *uchinā*, and *nchu* means "people"), has been developing even in the southern Ryukyus, which historically were marginal to the Ryukyu kingdom's political control. Since the 1980s, as the culture of the Japanese main islands has penetrated into Ryukyuan society, a strong sense of sharing a single Ryukyuan culture has been growing throughout the entire archipelago.

   I mention how I was positioned in my fieldwork because this was the starting point for negotiating my relationships with the people of the Ryukyus. I was forced to assume the identity of someone from the "main islands" of Japan, whose culture is distinct from that of Okinawa and whose historical relations with Okinawa were unsettling to many inhabitants of that prefecture. At the same time, I continually viewed the islanders as bearers of a Ryukyuan folk religion whose secrecy I wanted to penetrate, to the extent that religious changes of recent origin ceased to interest me. I came to realize that my desire to find an authentic Ryukyuan culture met their desire to liberate themselves from the constraint of my desire to see them as nothing but bearers of authenticity. Gradually I began shifting my work toward investigating aspects of cultural creation.

The media in which *uchinā'nchu* express themselves are various, from popular music and popular theater to (a high-culture genre of) literature. In all that they create, they mix and match cultural influences, struggling to subvert stereotypical images of "the Okinawans." The meanings of "culture" have shifted as the Okinawans objectify a part of their lives in order to create a space of difference from the homogenizing influences of the Japanese main islands. This objectification is, again, characteristic of ethnographic modernity as Clifford defines it, the condition in which those mediated by culture can at the same time look at that mediation from "outside." Perhaps such a condition is not necessarily recent; anthropological discourse has not allowed us to problematize this aspect of culture, although more attention has been paid to systematic aspects of cultural mediation.

On the main island of Okinawa, cultural expressions have grown out of the complicated elements with which people have been negotiating their relationships: namely, the Japanese political body and U.S. military forces. A basic metaphor that unites many cultural productions is that of *chanpurū*, the name given to an Okinawan cuisine that mixes vegetables, vermicelli, tofu, canned meat, and whatever else is available. This cuisine became popular when food was scarce shortly after World War II.

The musical and theatrical performances thematized under the rubric of *chanpurū* are subverting the stereotypes held by the Japanese, images popular before the end of the war—for instance, that of contemporary Ryukyuan culture as a representation of ancient Japanese culture. After 1972, when the Ryukyu Islands again became part of Japan, development projects began rapidly changing the Ryukyu landscape; along with such rash development appeared a series of works by Okinawan as well as Japanese writers that lamented the passing of Ryukyuan culture (e.g., Arakawa 1987 [1978]).

In images of timeless Ryukyuan culture as a mirror for ancient Japan and of rapidly decaying Ryukyuan culture, Ryukyuans cannot articulate their cultural present as inventive, as reinterpreting the past for the future. It is precisely against this impossibility that *chanpurū* cultural productions aim to fight. I have been thinking of these cultural productions as "Okinawan modernism," a term I consider not an avant-garde usage of the sort often inimical to popular cultural practices but as signaling the Okinawans' general refusal to communicate through the established socio-semiotic code (Ota 1997a, 1997b, 2001). I want to retain this wider usage for the purpose of understanding a variety of cultural productions characteristic of the ethnographic modernity of the Ryukyuan people. I cannot help seeing *chanpurū* aesthetics as a form of modernism by which distinctive Okinawaness has been created out of appropriations of the stereotypes imposed on the people of Okinawa (cf. Baker 1987).

I want to understand this aesthetics not only as characteristic of the culture but also as the way in which Okinawan intellectuals fashion themselves as they struggle within the discourse of authenticity. Take, for example, Fuyū Ifa (1876–1947). Ifa has been discussed by many other scholars (e.g., Hiyane 1981; Kano 1983, 1993; Kinjō and Takara 1972), mostly as one of the "organic intellectuals" fighting for Okinawa's distinctive culture and history at a time when subjugation to the Japanese state through allegiance to the emperor had started to penetrate Okinawan society. But Ifa's cosmopolitan sensibility was already obvious in 1914 (Ifa 1974), when he made use of Booker T. Washington's *Up From Slavery* (1901) to compare the emancipation of slaves in the United States to the making of Okinawa prefecture within Japan, a political process that at least freed the Ryukyuan people from the dual subservience arising out of historical ties to both China and Japan. Once, writing words of encouragement to an Okinawan writer, he offered as a model W. B. Yeats and his Irish cultural revitalization. Ifa was also inclined toward Marxist ideas through his friendship with the Marxist economics scholar Hajime Kawakami; Ifa's later analyses of Okinawan society disclose the notion of class as one of his key terms. Perhaps his involvement with the Anglican church should also be interpreted as an expression of his desire to transcend the local and reach for more ecumenical human values. I think such a desire was already evident in his youth. Ifa protested bitterly against the principal of his senior high school, someone sent from the main islands of Japan, who had announced that the Okinawan students were no longer to study English because they could not even speak standard Japanese correctly. I interpret his activism not simply as a protest against obvious discrimination in national education but as an action prefigurative of his cosmopolitan aspirations, which were often stifled during his residence in Tokyo.

Ifa fashioned himself by making various connections with what might be termed Okinawan culture and history. In short, he was a hodgepodge of many influences, continually transcending each. He was a modern intellectual in the making: a Marxist, a Christian, a member of the literati, a historian, and a folklorist. He lived very much in the spirit of Okinawan *chanpurū,* defying a facile categorization issued from a discourse of authenticity. It is always easier to see him as a local Okinawan scholar delineating the contours of Okinawan culture for us—those coming from the main islands of Japan, for example—than to contextualize him in the cosmopolitan intellectual tradition from which he drew inspiration.

The manner in which Ifa self-fashioned his being as an intellectual in larger Japanese society has been repeated, I think, by many after him. Engaging in cultural production has become inseparable from a consideration of the question of Okinawan identity—what it means to be Okinawan—because those of us in the main islands of Japan also expect the Okinawan writers, for example, to create in such a way that their efforts fulfill our expectations; they cannot afford to disregard our expectations. But some cultural producers make the existence of our expectations visible and unsettled by subverting the place of Okinawa in the dominant imagination of the Japanese. Baku Yamanokuchi (1999), an Okinawan poet living in Tokyo during the 1930s, wrote against the stereotypical images he encountered there, yet his strategy was not one of substituting the "real Okinawa" for the misrecognized one. He sensed that this "real Okinawa" was already lost, and he attempted to create a space—an ineffable space—that would signal the truth of its existence by a series of negations of the stereotypes.

Instead of negation, another strategy is to complicate the historical narrative of Okinawa's role in the Second World War. Beside the cultural narrative of decaying Okinawan tradition, a discourse of victimhood is also popular: the people of the Ryukyus have been exploited by dominant political forces throughout their history, and the worst was the devastation that took place shortly before the end of the war. In his book *Kakuteru Pāti* (cocktail party), Tatsuhiro Ōshiro (1960) problematized this dominant narrative of the Ryukyuan experience by introducing the Chinese experience of the war. To the Chinese, the Ryukyuans, participants in the Japanese political body, were the oppressors. As one of the most visible intellectuals in Okinawa prefecture, Ōshiro has been explicit about the function of his literary work in Okinawan society: he writes to narrativize the Okinawan past, present, and future. But such narrativization has been always framed by a question about his own identity as an Okinawan man living in Japan (Ōshiro 1992 [1970]).

Becoming sensitive to their own cultural existence from an external perspective, these writers share assumptions similar to those espoused by the producers of Okinawan popular culture. Instead of substituting the "real Okinawa" for the stereotypical one, they make parodic displays on stereotypical images of Okinawa, thereby gaining a perspective on their own culture (cf. North 1994; Ota 1997a). Perhaps it is an overstatement to say that the divide between the literary and the nonliterary, or between the high and the popular, is no longer significant in the domain of Okinawan cultural productions, but I am struck by Ōshiro's comments about the popular theater group Shōchiku Kagekidan. Instead of downgrading the group's performances as inauthentic kitsch, he has found in them a will to innovate and create Okinawan culture for the future, in much the same way he tries to do in his literary endeavors.

Culture and Self-Fashioning in the Guatemala Highlands

Since 1996 I have been spending my summers in a Kaqchikel village in the western highlands of Guatemala, studying the formation of pan-Mayan identity as the country struggles to rebuild itself as a democratic nation-state, a topic many scholars from the United States have also been investigating. What made it possible for me to work there was, in a sense, my return to Japan in 1989, because there a bona fide anthropologist is said to work outside of Japan, a definition believed to separate anthropology from fields such as folklore and rural sociology in Japanese academe. I had to renew my anthropological self-fashioning by conducting research outside of Japan, but this time under circumstances different from those of my days in the United States. New theoretical issues had emerged, and changes in global relations had occurred.

When I first went to the southern Ryukyus, I understood why people I met continually referred to memories of the Second World War. Nonetheless, local historians and priestesses were helpful in talking enthusiastically with me about newly discovered genealogies that linked them with royal families on the main island of Okinawa. In the late 1980s and the early 1990s, during my studies of Okinawan popular culture, I never experienced an act of exclusion due to my being an anthropologist from the main islands of Japan.

Studying in Guatemala looked as if it might provide a different kind of experience. Wanting to learn more about the country, I read *I, Rigoberta Menchú* (Burgos-Dobray 1984). One of the points I remember is Menchú's refrain of the word "secret": "I am still keeping secret what I think no-one should know. Not even anthropologists or intellectuals, no matter how many books they have, can find out all our secrets" (Burgos-Dobray 1984: 247). This is a statement about denying access to Ki'chee' culture to outsiders, those who might come and study a Mayan culture. Consequently, I am one of the unwelcome. From the perspective of the "subalterns"—people suffering oppression because of their race, class, gender, and so forth—anthropology might constitute an unwelcome form of knowledge that at best simply describes something and at worst is complicit in neocolonial domination instead of intervening to assist in causes of the indigenous people. After Gayatri Spivak's critique of Foucault and Delueze, presented in her now famous "Can the Subaltern Speak?" (1988), anthropologists can no longer assume that a stance of "letting the people speak for themselves" is innocent and free of oppression, since this assumption hides the privilege of the intellectual. In light of this critique, Menchú's insistence on secrecy seemed to me, at first sight, a guard against forms of knowledge that inevitably end up in enactments of power relations. Underneath Menchú's entanglement with David Stoll (1998) lies her deep mistrust of anthropology—or perhaps of university-based knowledge in general (see Arias 2001).

But it is also true that in her narration Menchú repeatedly creates herself as a Ki'chee' woman speaking against oppression in front of an international audience by mobilizing diverse ideas borrowed from popular social movements, Christianity, Mayan religion, environmentalism, and feminism. I see in her narration a process of getting out of "subalternity." Her efforts in creating herself as an effective political subject have been conducted in the global arena—not restricted to Guatemala—where a discourse of authenticity, as Stoll (1998: 264) seems to have noticed, inevitably operates. It arises from the desire of the First World to see the Third World victim speak up against oppression. For this reason, Menchú's efforts remain always precarious and prone to misinterpretation.

Besides learning about Menchú—an extraordinary case—I wanted to learn more about the way in which some Mayas fashion themselves as intellectuals and political leaders in Guatemala, where state violence has destroyed communal lifestyles and where a new national unity has barely begun to be imagined as the country responds to the forces of neoliberalism. Pan-Mayanists endeavor to construct leadership in this extremely uncertain moment of nation rebuilding under globalization.

Quickly I learned some things about those engaged in Mayan movements (*Maya' moloj* in Kaqchikel). First, they define the current condition as a form of neocolonialism and prefer to call themselves activists in "anticolonialism" rather than in "Mayan nationalism," a term employed by some North American anthropologists (e.g., Smith 1991). Mayan activists consider that decolonization of internal colonies has not yet begun. It must take place not only in economic terms but also in cultural terms, because in Guatemala, categorical distinctions such as that between ladinos (nonindigenous people) and *indígenas* has been repeatedly stressed, even in more progressive discussions of nation building and ethnic relations. The idea of decolonization is that it will undo distinctions such as this.

Second, they have maintained close ties with their communities even if they keep offices in the capital, a space traditionally conceived of as being ladino. They loathe being told that they are not indigenous but are ladinos masquerading as indigenous because they are nothing but opportunists. According to them, they see no contradiction in enjoying the amenities of urban life while maintaining a Mayan identity. Rural areas have historically been marked as places for *indígenas*, whereas urban areas—mostly the capital—have been associated with ladinos, although this demarcation might not hold since the 1980s, when massive displacements of rural Mayas took place in response to state violence. Yet the frequently taken-for-granted categorization seems to reinforce a discourse of authenticity by which Mayan leaders are often disparaged as "inauthentic"—without representational legitimacy. They need to fight against this categorization, too.

Third, even if they insist on fostering a pan-Mayan identity, something concrete still needs to be articulated. They by no means envision a space separate from Guatemala as it exists today; contrarily, they try to redefine their country politically as a nation not of ladinos but of four different ethnicities (*pueblos* in Spanish, *amaq'* in Kaqchikel): Guatemala as multiethnic, multilingual, multicultural. In other words, in their struggle they try to retain the concept of ethnicity as of paramount importance, refusing to relegate it to second class as many other so-called popular movements in Guatemala have done, while at the same time refusing the lure of separatism.

Many scholars (e.g., Fischer and Brown 1996; Hale 1996; Warren 1998; Watanabe 1995) have reported that pan-Mayanists insist on their distinctive identity in Guatemala, where the national subjects have often been equated with ladinos (defined as nonindigenous Spanish monolinguals). The dominant ideology has been that of *mestizaje*, crucial in the process of nation building in many Latin American countries. For the purpose of clearly articulating their differences from other people in Guatemala, pan-Mayanists construct their culture, language, and religion as distinct from those of the dominant other, the ladino. They often emphasize that their "cosmo-vision" (worldview) is one in which humans are subordinated to nature, rather than one in which humans dominate nature, as in ladino culture. The culture concept (*qak'aslem*, "our lives," in Kaqchikel) is useful for pan-Mayanists. But many Mayan leaders seem to realize that the culture they mobilize is not something they can dig up from the ground, as it were; they repeatedly emphasize that culture is to be constructed for the future. One of them, for example, said to me, "Those in the rural area do not have an identity as Maya. That is something to be made for the future of Guatemala."

The critics of Mayan movements are vocal as well. Employing postmodern literary theories, Roberto Morales (1998), for example, has offered a vision alternative to the model of "multiculturalism" that pan-Mayanists propose. He suggests a vision of the country characterized by "intercultural *mestizaje*," in which the national subject, Guatemala, might resemble the "popular" subject created by the penetration of modern capitalism. Thus, Morales (1998: 146) sees a contradiction in the vision of a multiethnic Guatemala, because unity cannot be achieved from diverse ethnicities when pan-Mayanists are, according to him, asserting fundamental, essential differences. Instead of essentialism, Morales supports nonessentialism, which favors a process of articulation on the level of individual identity. Thus, the proper national subject comes from a model of *mestizaje*.

Morales considers pan-Mayanists' propositions to be of a fundamentalist variety based on a logic of exclusion; however, the pan-Mayanists do not aim to ethnically dominate the ladinos. Although Mayas are in the majority now, they clearly realize that in order to redefine the national political space of Guatemala they need to cooperate with various popular ladino sectors (Ota 2001). The idea of "interculturality" (*interculturalidad*), often heard in tandem with other phrases of multiculturalism, is to bridge the gap among the hitherto separated ethnicities.

Although some scholars concur with Morales, I do not think the pan-Mayanists are fundamentalists or essentialists. One reason they cannot be written off as essentialists is that they consistently attempt to break the categorizations that police the social and political spaces in Guatemala (e.g., Nelson 1999). Because of their overt efforts to break down such categorizations—such as those I mentioned earlier—they are often chastised for being culturally "inauthentic" and thus politically "nonrepresentative."

When pan-Mayanists demand to speak, they are also attempting to nullify another categorization—that Mayas are to remain silent. If they do not, they cease to be Mayas (Menchú, cited in Stoll 1998: 225). A corollary to this demand to voice their opinions is not to be silenced in terms of theoretical sophistication or political legitimacy, but to be listened to (Alcoff 1991; Montejo 1993). Both raising the issue of political legitimacy and questioning the political representativeness of Mayan leaders who have been struggling to make their voices heard deny the existence of the pervasive and profound alienation and disempowerment that originally moved such leaders for action (Beverly 2001: 225) For this reason I consider it fundamentally misplaced to situate pan-Mayanists' enunciations within the discursive field of theoretical merits—evaluating them as either essentialistic or not. Consequently, arguing for the usefulness of "not-so-postmodern" ethnographies to the Mayan cause also misses the point.

Working within a discipline that prides itself on upholding a Malinowskian dictum, "from the native's point of view," I find it important these days to listen to the Mayan leaders' demands to be heard, not simply as informants or even "colleagues" but also as political activists with visions for altering the social relationships that engender oppressive forms of knowledge. Critiques from pan-Mayanists are often radical, pressing upon anthropologists the issue of accountability. Whom does research serve? Why does one conduct such research (Cojtí-Cuxil 1990)? If university-based knowledge is complicit in producing the condition of subalternity, as Spivak's claim logically leads one to conclude, then such knowledge must be used to *unmake* that condition (Beverley 1999: 166). I am not sure yet what sorts of efforts are called for in order to achieve this goal, but I have noticed that Mayan leaders are creating new ways of being "Maya" in post-peace-accord Guatemala, ways that continually redefine the possible interethnic relations as well as international relations beyond Guatemala.

Conclusion

Could anthropology be used to respond to the Mayas' demand for gaining a hearing or for the purpose of unmaking their subalternity? Because culture is discursively constructed by anthropological practices, both notions of culture and anthropological subjectivity need to be rethought. But instead of following the beaten track of postmodern critique, which only redescribes the notion of culture without reconfiguring anthropology and its relation to people for whom anthropology might be another form of knowledge to be held over them, I propose a need—meaningful, in particular, to those working on "the margins of the discipline"—to envision an anthropological future out of the common experience of global ethnographic modernity. By marking a position of being on the margins, I do not endorse any form of identity politics, but I want to suggest a path toward liberating all of us from the discourse of authenticity that produces the desire for formulating identity politics (Eagleton 2000: 81).

I insist that the condition of ethnographic modernity has been pervasive to the extent that it is no longer clear and meaningful to dichotomize the native and the anthropologist, to make them correspond to the dichotomy of the primitive and the modern or that of "being in culture" and "looking at culture." If a recognition of the pervasiveness of this condition had come before the institutionalization of anthropology, then what form might anthropology have taken? This could be an exercise in idle thinking, but I believe it is necessary for reimagining anthropology's path toward the future, a path that does not simply repeat previous trajectories and the concept of culture known today. The concept of culture can be refashioned—not simply borrowed—by many for cultural mobilization. Moreover, could anthropology be used, for example, to unmake subalternity? One of many challenges for the future of anthropology certainly lies there.

Note

As a participant in an international conference, I could not help thinking about my role in it. Being suspended within a network of objectives and expectations for the conference, I wanted to negotiate my role in it consciously. Consequently, I tried to remain alert to what Spivak would have called "sanctioned ignorance," something I have frequently been made aware of but have found hard to convey. Although I do not think I was very successful in achieving that goal, I found in this conference unusually accommodating participants. I am grateful for constructive criticisms from every participant in the conference; they have helped me to think more and harder about the issues raised in this chapter. Among the participants, I particularly thank Richard Fox, Barbara King, Sydel Silverman, Xavier Andrade, Chris Hann, Richard Wilson, and Susan Wright.

Part 2

Emergent Sociality

four

On Patterned Interactions and Culture in Great Apes

Barbara J. King

Daughter: I wanted to find out if I could think two thoughts at the same time. So I thought "It's summer" and I thought "It's winter." And then I tried to think the two thoughts together.
Father: Yes?
D: But I found I wasn't having two thoughts. I was only having one thought *about* having two thoughts.
F: Sure, that's just it. You can't mix thoughts, you can only combine them. And in the end, that means you can't count them. Because counting is really only adding things together. And you mostly can't do that.
D: Then *really* do we only have one big thought which has lots of branches—lots and lots and lots of branches?
F: Yes, I think so. I don't know. Anyhow I think that is a clearer way of saying it. I mean it's clearer than talking about bits of knowledge and trying to count them.

—Gregory Bateson, *Steps to an Ecology of Mind*

During the summer of 1999, worldwide media attention was focused on the question of whether nonhuman animals, particularly nonhuman primates, have culture. The journalistic frenzy was spurred by a report claiming that in free-ranging chimpanzees, "39 different behaviour patterns, including tool usage, grooming and courtship behaviours, are customary or habitual in some communities but are absent in others where ecological explanations have been discounted" (Whiten et al. 1999: 682).

This research report, appearing in the respected scientific journal *Nature* and declaratively titled "Cultures in Chimpanzees," is only the most renowned entry in a long list of articles and books claiming culture for our primate relatives (e.g., Boesch and Boesch-Achermann 2000; Boesch and Tomasello 1998; de Waal 2001; Kawai 1965; Kawamura 1959; McGrew 1992, 1998; van Lawick-Goodall 1973). The details of these claims vary both between intellectual traditions—the West versus Japan, for example—and within single traditions (Fox and King, this volume; Takasaki 2000). Some Western scholars (e.g., de Waal 2001; McGrew 1998) "cast their net wide" via a broad definition of culture in their desire to include monkeys and some nonprimates as culture bearers, whereas others (e.g., Boesch and Boesch-Achermann 2000) say that within the nonhuman world, only chimpanzees truly qualify, judging by present evidence. Yet in Western primatology, at least, it is agreed that the strongest evidence in support of nonhuman primate culture comes from variants in population-specific behaviors that are both (1) unrelated to environmental differences across groups and (2) passed on via social learning. Evaluation of these criteria effectively requires data sharing among teams of researchers. When an instance of cross-populational variance in, say, tool using on a particular type of food can be solidly explained by social learning rather than by ecological or genetic variance, then another example of culture—the Holy Grail of current primatology—is considered to have been found.

Extending the concept of culture in this way, to include nonhuman primates as well as humans in the "culture club," has not gone uncontested within anthropology. In a Wenner-Gren symposium held four years before our own, participants briefly considered the culture concept. The biological anthropologist Craig Stanford began to discuss "chimpanzee culture" with cultural anthropologists:

> I was made to feel the full weight of my ignorance. The cultural anthropologists fairly leaped across the seminar table (at least it felt as if they did), to garrote me verbally for using the words "culture" and "chimpanzee" in the same sentence. I had apparently set off a silent alarm, and the culture-theory guards had come running. How dare you use a term such as "cultural diversity," they screamed in high dudgeon, to describe what chimpanzees do? Say "behavioral variation." Apes are mere animals, their lecture continued; people alone possess culture. (Stanford 2000: 39)

My experience as a biological anthropologist at the Morelia symposium, where we collectively voyaged beyond asking who has culture and who does not, did not mirror Stanford's. Made clear there, however, was that primatologists who "count" examples of cross-populational variances in their monkey and ape subjects may be chasing after a prize—"culture!"— that is no longer valued by the very discipline that venerated it for so long (see Toren, this volume; Trouillot, this volume). My own entry point into this lively debate is to encourage, from within my own subfield, the asking of new questions about what monkey or ape "culture" might be. These questions are meant to acknowledge the concerns of cultural anthropologists about a static, essentialized culture concept and, at the same time, advance exploration of the evolution of complex patterns of sociality.

Current insistence upon fulfilling the criteria for culture by tallying up cross-populational variances in a few types of highly visible behavioral patterns has led, ironically, to a missed chance to link the profound nature of monkey and ape sociality to the exploration of culture. In exploring the roots of human culture, we should rethink our notions about which behavioral patterns are appropriate to record. We should thoroughly explore shared meanings and the expression of shared histories (see Barth, this volume; Toren, this volume) in the routine social interactions that make up everyday life for the monkeys and apes we study. Christophe Boesch (2000) begins to do this when analyzing how the *meaning* of so-called leaf-clipping behavior varies across populations of chimpanzees. His focus is not just on *what* is done or *how* but on the fact that when certain leaves are shredded in the "clipping" behavior, it is understood by the leaf-clipper's social partners in Bossou, Guinea (for example), to be a form of communication about play, whereas in Mahale, Tanzania, it is understood to be about courtship, and in Gombe, Tanzania, chimpanzees do not practice leaf-clipping at all.

Documenting such functional variety in the same behavior across populations—only a starting point for what I have in mind—is rarely attempted. If the definitional questions that undergird the investigation of nonhuman primate culture have been narrowly conceived, so, too, have the analytical questions: By what mechanism (imitation or a "simpler" type of learning such as social facilitation) does social transmission operate among monkeys and apes? Which such mechanisms quality as cultural? What properties characterize nonhuman primate culture as compared with human culture?

My goal in this chapter is to ask new analytical questions about a broader range of behaviors in order to move beyond the unsatisfactory listing (i.e., counting) of behavioral variants and assessing of the (static) properties of nonhuman primate culture. We can move instead toward understanding the patterns by which primate infants—intentionally communicative, problem-solving beings—enter into the social worlds they inhabit. My questions include, how do infant great apes come to participate fully in their family groups? What roles do family members, particularly parents and siblings, play in the emergence of the infants' communicative competence? My research focuses on the use of body movements and gestures made during social communication within great ape families living in captivity, and so I also ask, more specifically, how do infants' increasing abilities to produce and comprehend communicative body movements and gestures help them coordinate their actions with those of their family members?

Dynamic Social Interactions: Rejection of Linearity

At the root of my desire to shift the terms of the culture debate is a shift in my own understanding of the evolution of social information transmission in primates. In earlier work (King 1994), I defined two contrasting processes, social information donation and social information acquisition. In a few primate species, including great apes, hominids, and humans, adults may donate information to infants via directed behavioral intervention and teaching. In contrast, primate infants of all anthropoid species are selected to acquire information from adults by various forms of social attention. This view, I now believe, is too linear.

A linear perspective implies that one animal acts and another animal (or animals) then responds. Signals may be exchanged between individuals; information may be donated to or acquired by another individual, just as it is possible to donate or acquire a material item such as a stone tool or a fig. When Michael Tomasello (1999: 33) explains that teaching proceeds from the top down, whereas social learning proceeds from the bottom up, he is embracing a linear framework: knowledge either flows from the teacher, reaching "down" to the student, or is acquired by the student, reaching "up" to the teacher. Preferable to Tomasello's statement, and to the donation/acquisition opposition as well, is a perspective acknowledging that social actors learn or create meaning together as their interaction unfolds (see Johnson 2001). The learning or communication that occurs does not involve skills or information being transferred from one individual to another; rather, the learning or communication *emerges from the interaction itself*. Social partners may *transform* each other during the interaction.

My rejection of linearity in favor of such dynamic interactionism has been influenced by theories and methods developed in anthropology (e.g., Armstrong, Stokoe, and Wilcox 1995; Bateson 1972; Farnell 1999; Ingold 1996, 1998; Toren 1999a, this volume) and psychology/cognitive science (e.g., Fogel 1993; Hutchins 1995; Johnson 1987; Lave and Wenger 1991; Rogoff 1990; Shanker, this volume). In this work, learning and communication are analyzed in use, as active processes, not as collections of static features and properties. Further, this work views skeptically some distinctions and dichotomies accepted within more traditional scholarship in anthropology and psychology—body/mind, biology/culture, individual/society, even gesture/speech. As Christina Toren (1999a: 4) puts it, "theoretical distinctions continue to be a problem for anthropological analyses. As does the equally well-known 'dialectical relation' that is supposed to resolve that problem. This supposed resolution suggests a reciprocal interaction between biology and culture, individual and society, body and mind—but note that there is no place here for transformation, except as a function of an encounter with external forces." For Toren, it is important to understand that "body and mind, the biological and the cultural, the material and the ideal, are aspects of one another, rather than separate and dialectically related phenomena" (1999a: 4).

What Toren is telling us here (see also Ingold 1998) is key to dynamic interactionism. Replacing linearity (A acts and B responds) with bidirectionality (A's acts and B's acts mutually affect each other) is not enough; we must understand that *the social unit AB creates meaning during its unpredictable, unfolding, minute-by-minute interaction.*

Thus, when trying to find out how infant great apes come to use body movement and gesture communicatively when coordinating their actions with those of their family members, it is not enough simply to count which movements and gestures the infant uses at which ages and in which contexts. It is not even enough to acknowledge through qualitative description that infants are active partners with adults during social exchanges. Rather, the transformative nature of dynamic interaction in dyads and subgroups must be shown through fine-grained longitudinal analyses of patterns in the unfolding interactions. Only then is it clear how much these interactions truly shape the lives of all the animals involved.

Great Ape Gestural Communication: Background and Specific Goals

When applying these theoretical ideas to actual research with great apes, I borrow a concept from Alan Fogel's work with human children and their caretakers. Fogel writes of a process he terms *coregulation,* "the dynamic balancing act by which a smooth social performance is created out of the continuous social adjustments of action between partners. In coregulated communication, information is created between people in such a way that the information changes as the interaction unfolds. Coregulated communication is created as it happens; its process and outcome are partially unpredictable" (Fogel 1993: 19).

When searching for tangible expressions of coregulation in great apes, I look for patterned interactions as mediated through body movement and gesture. Patterned interactions unfold in the same general way in the same general circumstances time after time. Primatologists who prefer heavily quantitative approaches might find such a concept uncomfortably intuitive, but patterned interactions are easy to recognize in the kind of qualitative analysis that I do. Just as human children and their caretakers participate in clearly recognizable interactional routines (e.g., Bruner 1983; Ochs and Schieffelin 1986; Peters and Boggs 1986; see also Briggs 1998) as children learn language or how to walk or how to relate to siblings and parents, so great ape infants and their family members interact similarly over time in similar circumstances, as when an adult guides an infant's walking or when the infant learns to gesture appropriately before approaching an older family member.

Much more is known about the vocal repertoires of the four great apes—chimpanzees, bonobos, gorillas, and orangutans—than about their gestural repertoires (Burling 1999). Only anecdotal data about gesture are available from free-ranging great ape populations (King and Shanker n.d.). Systematic study of captive African great apes, however, has uncovered patterns of complex gestural communication, including iconic gesture (Savage-Rumbaugh, Wilkerson, and Bakeman 1977; Tanner and Byrne 1999; see also Burling 1999), through which apes may indicate to their social partners specific, desired social outcomes.

We know very little about how young apes come to use gestures as they mature. Longitudinal data are available from work on captive chimpanzees by Tomasello and his colleagues (Tomasello et al. 1997 and references within). For Tomasello, chimpanzees "acquire" gestures by a process called ontogenetic ritualization (OR), whereby two apes shape their signals and behaviors through repeated interaction. An infant chimp may, for instance, pull on her mother's nipple when she wants to suck. After many such pulls, the mother may respond when the infant only moves toward, rather than actually touches, the nipple. Eventually a subtle arm movement by the infant may be enough to coordinate the suckling.

That OR and not imitation accounts for young chimpanzees' "acquiring" gesture is Tomasello's main conclusion. In the groups he observed, juvenile chimpanzees used gestures not used by adults, and vice versa; adultlike gestures replaced some juvenile gestures over time; idiosyncratic gestures were seen; and gestures recorded across generations were different. For Tomasello, the important aspect of these results is that only imitation, with its "faithful transmission," and not OR, is linked to culture through cumulative cultural learning.

In the next sections, I outline the results of my own approach, which differs substantially from Tomasello's in both its nonlinearity and its interest in describing the richly coregulated, patterned interactions within great ape families.

Gestural Interactions and Coregulation in Bonobos

In 1997–1998, my students and I observed and filmed the emerging gestural skills of an infant bonobo housed with her family at the Language Research Center at Georgia State University. Elikya (born 28 July 1997) lived in indoor-outdoor caging with her mother, Matata (a multiparous wild-caught female born in approximately 1970); frequently with her older sisters Neema (b. 1992) and Tamuli (b. 1987); occasionally with her adoptive brother, Kanzi (b. 1980); rarely with her oldest sister, Panbanisha (b. 1985); and never with her father, P-Suke.

We defined as gestures those nonlocomotor limb and head movements that occurred when the apes were in proximity and either were engaged in social interaction when the movements took place or were so engaged immediately before or after the movements (Tanner and Byrne 1999: 216). In cases where these criteria were fulfilled, I assumed the gestures were intentionally communicative. Excluded from the definition of gesture, but still of interest in the study, were various body movements including those capable of altering the social partner's position or location. "For example, lightly brushing a hand downward on another's body to indicate a desire for downward movement on another's part would be a *tactile gesture,* as opposed to the directed *action* of forcefully pushing the other down" (Tanner and Byrne 1999: 216). Note that some gestures are purely visual—performed in the absence of body contact—whereas others may involve lightly touching or brushing the social partner.

During the first seventeen months of her life, the time period of the study, the infant Elikya increasingly used body movements and gestures as she participated in social interactions with her family members. In that sense, the data revealed clear behavioral shifts over time. Coregulation could be found in these interactions, however, right from day one. In other words, appropriate usage of gestures develops through ontogeny, whereas coregulation just *is* (though its quality may shift through ontogeny, as is made clear later). Five events that occurred before Elikya's first birthday illustrate ways in which she participated at a young age in social interactions mediated by body movement and gesture.

Event 1. Elikya, two months old, sits with her mother, Matata. Her mother hands her over to her sister Neema sitting nearby. From Elikya's facial pout, we can tell she is distressed by this transfer. Three times in succession, she extends her arm and hand, palm up, back toward her mother. She is near enough to touch her mother but gestures instead. After the third gesture, her mother takes her back. As Elikya relaxes against her mother, her sister pats her gently.

Event 2. Elikya, eight months old, sits in front of her mother, Matata. Matata puts her hand lightly on Elikya's back, then with her arms scoops the infant to her ventrum. Matata carries Elikya ventrally for some distance. When Matata sits again, she touches Elikya's back. Elikya releases her foot-grip on Matata's fur. Elikya again sits in front of her mother, still holding onto her mother's fur. Matata again lightly touches Elikya. Elikya releases her hold on Matata.

Event 3. Elikya, eight months old, moves toward her sister Neema; she may lightly touch Neema's outstretched leg—it is hard to tell. Neema lowers her leg, then begins to stamp her feet on a platform as Elikya stands bipedally facing her. Elikya has a playface and raises her arms. Immediately, Neema moves to Elikya and hugs her, covering her with her whole body, then quickly moves back and resumes her previous position.

Event 4. Elikya, ten months old, sits with her sister Tamuli but watches Kanzi, her adoptive brother, play with her sister Neema. Elikya makes an arm gesture toward Kanzi as he walks by, but Kanzi's head is turned and he does not see. Elikya leaves Tamuli, runs to Kanzi, touches him on the back of his thigh, and returns to Tamuli. Both Kanzi and Neema approach Elikya. Kanzi pushes Neema away, then pulls Elikya up awkwardly onto his shoulders. While Elikya rides dorsally there, Kanzi and Neema resume playing.

Event 5. Eleven-month-old Elikya climbs up a chain-link fence outdoors and approaches Kanzi, who rests on his back in a hanging tire. Elikya stops, then extends one leg and foot to Kanzi. Kanzi "opens" his foot, spreading his big toe apart from the other toes. Only then does Elikya climb over Kanzi's body up to his face. Kanzi wraps his arms around Elikya and pats her.

Elikya's manual request to return to her mother (event 1) at two months of age was her first recorded communicative gesture. Via this request she not only participated in but also altered the course of a triadic social interaction. Similarly, in event 5, Elikya stops her forward motion to make a request to her adoptive brother, and only after Kanzi's own subtle foot movement does she proceed and climb on him. While participating in a play bout with her sister (event 3), Elikya makes facial and arm gestures, after which her sister hugs her. In the most complex sequence of all, also a play bout (event 4), Elikya tries—first gesturally, then with a light touch—to join Kanzi and Neema, and she eventually succeeds. Lightly administered tactile gestures alone also mediate social interaction (event 2).

That Elikya is an active participant in interactions with her mother, adoptive brother, and sisters is easy enough to see. Stating this offers only a limited perspective, however. Going further, we can recognize that the social unit "ElikyaMatata" or the social unit "ElikyaKanzi" creates, by its dynamic interaction, a communicative event. The outcome in each case—whether Elikya is able to join a play bout or to be embraced by a sibling, for instance—unfolds not predictably, by some stereotyped "exchange of signals," but unpredictably, as the interactions unfold by the moment. Outcomes are *contingent*; that is, they might have turned out another way (as we will see, outcomes are not always "successful" in the sense of being fluid and well coordinated). Further, it is impossible to assign one participant the role of "sender" and the other the role of "receiver" in any given event. To the extent that doing so seems possible or even a matter of pure common sense, it is an artifact of accepted methodology, in which fragments of behavior are extracted from a continuous, uninterrupted stream of behavior. We do not know why, for example, Matata chose that moment to transfer Elikya to Neema (event 1). Perhaps Elikya indicated restlessness with a subtle body or muscle shift, and perhaps just before *that*, Matata made a subtle body or muscle shift, and perhaps before *that* . . . .

These gestural interactions themselves have roots in even earlier patterned interactions between Elikya and her mother. Notable in addition to coregulation in this next group of events, observed during the first two weeks of Elikya's life, are single examples of different patterned interactions—routines—that occur between mother and infant. At this age the infant is too young to gesture but still is part of the mother-infant unit that together creates movement and experience (and eventually meaning).

92   Emergent Sociality

Event 6. One day old, Elikya gazes up at Matata. Elikya moves her head down, then again gazes up at Matata, then moves her head down once more. Matata, using her whole hand, moves Elikya's head back up and gazes into her eyes.

Event 7. Three days old, Elikya roots for the nipple; as she does so, Matata pulls Elikya's arms up.

Event 8. Elikya, one week old, suckles on Matata's right breast. The nipple comes out of Elikya's mouth (either it slips out accidentally or Matata slightly shifts, causing it to slip out). Elikya roots at the right nipple but Matata shifts her to the left nipple.

Event 9. Matata shifts her position. Elikya, one week old, reaches with her hand to near Matata's right nipple. Matata lifts Elikya to her right nipple. Elikya's head drops a bit to the left, and Matata reorients Elikya's head to the right nipple.

Event 10. One-week-old Elikya has a pout face and gives a tiny peep vocalization. She reaches out her left hand. Matata looks down, then hoists Elikya up on her body and supports Elikya with one thigh.

In these patterned interactions, Matata establishes mutual contact with her newborn daughter, responds to various shifts and limb movements of Elikya's by changing Elikya's position, and alters the infant's position when she suckles and at other times. From the earliest days, Elikya's own movements are part of a web of movements; she comes to experience her own body and its motion in direct connection with her mother's body and motion. Matata is the more active partner, at times guiding her infant's movement in a qualitatively different way from that in which Elikya is able to guide Matata's. Such asymmetry is fully compatible with coregulation. Writing of asymmetric interactions in humans, Fogel (n.d.) notes that the "resulting pattern in the communication is always jointly maintained, and there is a subtle but observable give and take of changes in attention and body movement on the part of the observing partner that are coregulated with the actions of the performer." Elikya and Matata, too, jointly maintain the pattern of their communication in this way.

Over time, a different pattern of jointly maintained movement begins to emerge in this pair:

Event 11. Matata holds Elikya, six weeks old. Elikya stands, rooting for the nipple. Matata looks at Elikya. Matata gives two up and down head nods and immediately pulls Elikya in closer to her chest.

Event 12. Matata places Elikya, six weeks old, on a blanket. While seated behind Elikya, she touches Elikya's genital area. Apparently aided by the motion of Matata's hand, Elikya lifts her bottom up off the ground. Her head bobs unsteadily.

Event 13. Matata places Elikya, seven weeks old, a few feet away from herself. Elikya holds her head up and begins to push up from the floor with her limbs. Precisely as she moves her head toward her mother, Matata reaches out, touches Elikya's back, and orients Elikya toward her own body.

Event 14. Matata repeatedly—four times in as many minutes—lifts three-month-old Elikya off her own ventrum and dangles her up in the air by her hands.

Event 15. Matata lies on her back, dangling Elikya, fifteen weeks old, from her hands and feet. Elikya's arms are splayed out and her legs extended, so that she is in a full, supported stand on Matata's body. When held in this way, Elikya "walks" in place (Matata dangles Elikya two more times in the next five minutes).

Event 16. Matata removes Elikya, four months old, from her back, and sits against the mesh caging. I think she nods her head. Elikya crawls toward Matata. Matata gets up and walks away, looking back at Elikya. Elikya approaches Matata and after a while reaches for and finally "catches" Matata. Matata pulls Elikya toward herself as she backs up toward the wall to sit down again.

Each of these events occurred repeatedly over time, with variations in specific body positions and movements, and thus are good examples of patterned interactions. Those centered on maternal encouragement of Elikya's limb movements and walking were particularly frequent and at times involved Elikya paired not with her mother but with one of her older sisters, Neema or Tamuli. Through these patterned interactions, as her mother or sister guided her toward increasing independence, Elikya gained some control over her muscles. Cumulatively, these interactions provided Elikya with an opportunity to experience how her own body movements, in tandem with those of her relatives, could create certain outcomes.

But does shared *meaning* emerge from such patterned interactions? Charting the development of one specific skill—I have chosen Elikya's dorsal riding on her mother—helps clarify this question. From birth, great ape infants cling ventrally to their mothers' fur, but they eventually switch to riding mostly jockey-style on their backs. The transition is gradual rather than sharp, with overlap in use of the two methods. Some great ape mothers in the wild demonstrate to their offspring how to climb on their (the mothers') backs by repeatedly assuming certain

94   Emergent Sociality

positions and making certain movements (van de Ritj-Plooij and Plooij 1987: 25). Matata played a mentor role to some extent as her daughter began to ride dorsally, but the change in riding position over time is better described as a change in the quality of the coordination between the two bonobos than as Matata's teaching Elikya.

When a "climb on to ride" event is well coordinated, it can look like this:

> *Event 17.* Matata sits eating ice cubes. Elikya, thirteen months old, stands and holds Matata's back, then sits and holds Matata's side. Matata makes a brief arm movement and moves her eyes. Elikya raises both her hands toward Matata's body. Matata turns her head toward Elikya and Elikya puts her hands on Matata's arm; one hand slips down. Matata rises up, and as she is moving away, Elikya puts her hands on Matata's back and climbs dorsally onto Matata. When Matata sits down again, she leans back and Elikya moves from a dorsal grip to a standing position holding Matata's back.

This interaction, which unfolds quickly and fluidly, is a routine one in Elikya's life, yet it offers real insight into shared meaning within this pair. Elikya notices Matata's arm and eye movements (just at this point, a human observer familiar with Matata can predict that she is about to move) and reacts to them by first raising her own arms toward her mother and then—in coordination with Matata's own head motion—placing her hands on Matata's back. Thus, as Matata begins to shift position to stand, Elikya begins her own motions to enact a dorsal ride. The result is a well-coordinated interaction.

Not all instances of Elikya's riding on her mother—even on this same day—unfold in the same well-coordinated manner, however. As with humans, that shared meanings may exist in apes does not preclude instances in which communication between social partners goes awry (and may require repair):

> *Event 18.* Matata sits near the chain-link fence. Elikya has climbed up Matata's body onto the fence, continuing up quite high. Matata moves away into a narrow tunnel area; Elikya begins to whimper while climbing down toward her. At the first whimper, Matata stops, turns, and walks back toward her daughter, halting directly underneath Elikya with her body positioned for Elikya to jump on. Elikya climbs down, directly onto Matata's back.

Patterned Interactions and Culture in Great Apes   95

Event 19. Elikya mouths Matata's hand. From a sitting position, Matata leans forward slightly. Elikya turns and reaches up to Matata's ventrum, as if to cling ventrally. Matata does not rise up but instead moves her hand toward Elikya's hand (the two hands stop short of touching). Elikya resumes mouthing her mother's hand.

Matata, in event 18, was farther away from her daughter than in event 17, thus altering the dynamics of their joint action. Elikya in this case vocalized to bring about a shift in the social interaction, resulting in a different path to coordinated action. In event 19, Elikya "reads" Matata's lean forward as a cue that her mother is about to stand up and walk away; she, interestingly, moves toward a ventral rather than a dorsal cling, perhaps because of her proximity to Matata's ventrum. Apparently, though, Elikya has "misread" Matata—on the same day as the flawless "reading" of event 17.

Even these common "climb on to ride" events, then, unfold variably and unpredictably according to a web of variables in which Elikya joins. "Failures" of coordination offer us as much insight into this process as do the successes, as we see again here:

Event 20. From a spot near eleven-month-old Elikya, Matata stands and moves away quickly. As Matata starts to stand, Elikya moves to her and tries to climb on her back, but Matata keeps moving. Elikya struggles to climb on but succeeds only in clinging to Matata's side. Matata turns around and walks back to her previous location, with Elikya still clinging to her side. When Matata sits, Elikya is lowered to the ground, still holding onto her mother's back.

In this case, there is no apparent "misreading" of cues, but without Matata's cooperation, Elikya could not ride dorsally.

A social partner, however, may simply be inexperienced as opposed to unwilling:

Event 21. Elikya, thirteen months old, walks past her sister Neema. As she goes by, Neema touches her back. Elikya stops and sits near Neema. Neema stands and touches Elikya, then with one hand, pulls Elikya forward along the ground, by the arm. Neema switches to pulling with two hands, then turns her upper body and bends her knees slightly. Elikya climbs onto Neema's back.

In this case, Neema literally drags Elikya along, then indicates very broadly with her body that Elikya should climb on dorsally. The awkwardness that characterizes this event is not atypical for this pair:

> *Event 22.* Neema takes Elikya, nine months old, from their mother. She carries Elikya upside down in her arms. Elikya does not cling to Neema. Neema walks around the cage holding Elikya in this upside-down position. When Neema climbs the wire mesh of the cage, still holding Elikya in this way, Elikya pulls herself up onto Neema's back and clings dorsally.

Elikya's coming to know when and how to ride dorsally develops out of the coregulated, patterned interactions she has been experiencing all along with her mother and to some extent with her older sisters and adoptive brother. Elikya does not "acquire the skill" of dorsal riding as if such behavior were somehow a thing unto itself at which she steadily gets better over time. Rather, the dorsal riding *and the shared meaning on which this coordination is based* emerge from a web of shared moments, mediated in part by Elikya's size, in part by her motor ability, and in part by her ability to "read" her mother's movements (as opposed to just gripping reflexively when her mother starts to move). In a general way, Elikya's movements coordinate increasingly with those of her mother and older siblings over time, but in fits and starts, marked by both improvements and regressions—a result that is unsurprising given the rich matrix of sociality in which the coordination is embedded (see also Ulland 1999).

During "climb on to ride" events, Elikya herself rarely if ever gestures. We have seen, however, as represented in events 1, 3, 4, and 5, that she does gesture communicatively at a very early age. Her gestural ontogeny is thus a seamless meshing of early, coordinated body movements. Later gestural production and comprehension emerge from this base, and coregulation underlies the entire process.

Unfortunately, my observation of Elikya ended during her seventeenth month, just as she began to incorporate more gestures into her communicative repertoire. In any event, this case study cannot address whether Elikya is somehow atypical in her gestural ontogeny or whether other bonobo infants (or chimpanzee or gorilla infants in similar contexts) would come to use gestures similarly. My long-term goal is to collect data on patterned interactions and gestural ontogeny in a series of great ape families and to catalog various pathways to the social emergence of shared meaning.

Gorilla Body Movement and Gesture: Preliminary Results

My current research documents body movements and gestures in social interactions between a western lowland gorilla (*Gorilla gorilla gorilla*) infant and his family members at the National Zoological Park, Smithsonian Institution, in Washington, D.C. This infant, Kwame (fig. 4.1), born on 20 November 1999, now lives with four other gorillas, all captive-born: Kwame's mother, Mandara (a multiparous hand-reared female born in 1982); his father, Kuja (a silverback male born in 1983); his adoptive brother, Baraka (b. 1992); and his biological brother, Ktembe (b. 1997). Two other females lived with Kwame initially but were later transferred into another cage. An unrelated adult female was transferred out in April 2000, and Kigali, the infant's sister (b. 1994), was relocated in August 2000. Data collection, including filming, began when Kwame turned four weeks old. Definitions and sampling techniques are identical to those in the bonobo study. The gorilla behavior, unlike the bonobo behavior in the earlier project, is being filmed with a digital video camera, thus allowing me to capture still photographic sequences with clarity.

Figure 4.1. The western lowland gorilla infant Kwame, left, sits in contact with his mother, Mandara.

The major conclusions of the bonobo study are mirrored in the preliminary results of the gorilla study: social interactions within the family are coregulated, and through time, Kwame increasingly uses body movements and gestures to coordinate his actions with those of his social partners. Kwame's rearing environment, however, differs significantly from Elikya's in the presence of intrusive siblings, including a young brother and a sister with much interest in the infant. These siblings frequently contact Mandara and Kwame, which often elicits a protective response by Mandara toward Kwame. These points are illustrated in the following two events:

Event 1 (fig. 4.2). As Kwame's brother Ktembe approaches the subadult male Baraka, Baraka picks up Kwame, nearly one year old, and runs away with the infant perched dorsally. As Baraka moves, Kwame falls off to the ground. Kwame crawls across the cage to his mother, Mandara, who grabs his arm and puts him up dorsally on her body. When Mandara moves across the cage, she nears a hanging rope with a ball attached at the end. Kwame slides off her back to the ground and swings on the rope/ball. As Mandara walks past Kwame to the back of the cage, Kwame pats the ball, looks over his shoulder at his mother, and raises his arm in her direction (she is much too far away to touch). Mandara does not respond; she may have been unable to see the gesture. Kwame starts to follow Mandara but becomes distracted by a piece of food that he sits near and inspects.

Event 2 (fig. 4.3). Kwame's brother Ktembe, close to four years old, is sitting in front of their mother, Mandara, who is sitting with Baraka. Ktembe begins to suck at Mandara's breast, as he had done several minutes previously. Kwame, slightly over a year old, comes to Mandara's ventrum and also begins to nurse, so that one brother is on each breast. The brothers then switch breasts. Ktembe stops nursing and moves, sitting back away from Mandara. Kwame continues to nurse until Mandara puts her arm around and touches Kwame's back, at which he ceases suckling.

Like Elikya, then, Kwame makes what seems to be a manual request toward his mother (event 1) before his first birthday. Also like Elikya, he responds to communicative touch from his mother (event 2). As predicted from the bonobo observations, Kwame's earliest interactions with Mandara are coregulated, suggesting a seamless developmental trajectory from younger to older infancy:

Event 3. As Kwame, four weeks old, shifts on his mother's ventrum, Mandara pats him.

Figure 4.2. *a,* Kwame rides on Mandara's back. *b,* He slides down off Mandara's back. *c,* He plays at the rope/ball by himself but visually monitors Mandara's movements. *d,* As Mandara moves away, Kwame raises his arm to her in a manual-request gesture.

>*Event 4.* Mandara sits, eating hay, with her legs crossed. Kwame, seven weeks old, is tucked into her lower ventrum. Debris from the hay falls onto Kwame. As Mandara shuffles sideways a bit, Kwame grips her fur with his hand. Mandara's new position results in a more "open" ventrum. Kwame's right hand and leg shift around now; he pushes up slightly with both legs.

Repeatedly during these early weeks, Mandara either shifted position at the approach of Baraka, Kigali, and Ktembe, or she carried Kwame away entirely from their approach. Many patterned interactions occurred within this protective context, as is illustrated by the following events (two of four similar events recorded within one hour, at the start of Kwame's third month):

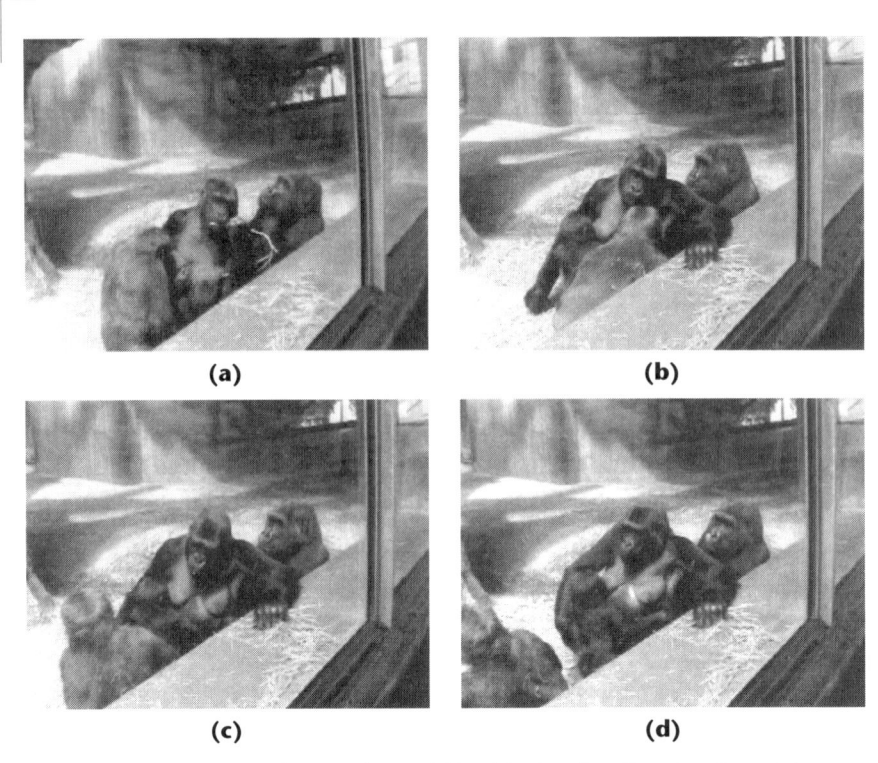

Figure 4.3. *a,* Kwame, front right, and his older brother Ktembe, front left, both nurse from Mandara; Baraka is in back of her. *b,* The brothers switch breasts; Kwame is now on the left. *c,* Ktembe stops suckling on his own. *d,* Mandara brings her arm across Kwame's back and touches him; Kwame stops suckling.

> *Event 5.* Kigali approaches Mandara and Kwame. She touches Kwame and puts her face near him. Immediately Mandara gathers Kwame in and moves away. Kigali follows and touches Mandara from behind. Mandara sits at the front glass window and pulls in Kwame's head with a cupping motion. Kigali approaches them about two minutes later. Immediately Mandara blocks her breasts. Kigali reaches toward Kwame; Mandara blocks this reach with her hand, but Kwame reaches out also so that Kigali and Kwame do touch. Kigali withdraws her hand and, using both hands now, pushes on Mandara's body. Mandara does not visibly react. Kwame leans back with his head and torso. Mandara holds Kwame's arm and hand. Kigali gives another two-handed push to Mandara, then puts her face at Kwame's back and neck. Kigali rolls onto her back and reaches back to Kwame. She pulls on and extends Kwame's arm and reaches near his mouth.

Event 6. Again Kigali approaches Mandara and Kwame. She puts her arm on Mandara's head and, with her feet on a glass window, "walks" first up and then back down the glass. Mandara moves across the cage with her hand on Kwame's head; after a pause, Kigali comes to sit near them. She leans in, touches Kwame, and extends Kwame's hand back toward herself. When Kigali releases him, Kwame touches Mandara's breast. After a pause, Kwame reaches back to Kigali. Kigali reaches and takes Kwame's arm, and Mandara pulls Kwame closer in to her ventrum.

As these events—representatives of patterned interactions—show, Kwame experiences his own body movements in tandem with his mother's through coregulated patterned interactions. Just as Elikya's did, Kwame's behavior becomes increasingly socially oriented—despite his mother's protectiveness:

Event 8. Ktembe sits near Mandara and Kwame. Kwame, twelve weeks old, leans his head back to look at Ktembe, then grasps his brother's foot.

Event 9. Kigali approaches and puts both hands on Kwame, twelve weeks old, as if to pull him to her. Kwame sits up and reaches for Kigali.

Event 10. Ktembe comes to sit with Mandara and Kwame, six months old. Kwame touches his brother on the side of his head twice. The two males begin to play gently.

As Kendra Weber (2001) has documented, Ktembe became Kwame's main play partner in the second half of the infant's first year. Play bouts between the two became more frequent and elaborated over time; they were regulated as much by Kwame as by Ktembe. Yet social interaction between the brothers was not always harmonious:

Event 11. As Mandara and eleven-week-old Kwame sit together, Ktembe approaches and slaps the back of Kwame's head three or four times. At first, Mandara tolerates this behavior, but then she shoves Ktembe away from Kwame. Kwame does not cry or appear distressed by the slaps, but his head wobbles from them!

Although Kwame did not begin to gesture as early as Elikya did, communicative gesture did occur before his first birthday, as we have seen. Just as with Elikya, some of these gestures resulted in coordinated actions, whereas others did not.

Event 12. Kwame, just over eight months, raises both arms above his head. Mandara lifts Kwame up over her own head as the subadult male Baraka runs by.

Event 13. Kwame, nine months old, climbs to Mandara's lap and sits. He pats his mother's right breast, then squeezes the nipple. Mandara swats away Kwame's hand. Kwame continues to pat Mandara's breasts, and Mandara crosses her arms over them. Kwame beats on Mandara's chest. Mandara opens her mouth at him in a mild threat (with no vocalization). Kwame stops his movements.

Event 14. Kwame, nearly ten months old, sits mouthing a branch. Ktembe runs into a recessed area of the cage nearby. Kwame reaches for him with one hand, but the reach falls short. Ktembe sits down. Kwame extends his other arm toward Ktembe, with palm up. Ktembe seems to see neither the reach nor the gesture. Kwame returns his attention to the branch.

At this point, shortly before his first birthday, Kwame began increasingly to reach toward social partners and to make extended-arm gestures, although, as we have just seen, not always in a well-coordinated manner. In this, the trajectory of Kwame's entry into the social world of his family is broadly similar to Elikya's. In sum, both trajectories are marked by patterned interactions in the infants' intensely close association with the mother; communicative gestures such as manual requests before the first birthday; and coregulation with social partners throughout. Certainly, Kwame is more constrained by his mother in his early months than Elikya was by hers. Kwame is just over three months old when Mandara first puts him down, out of contact, whereas Elikya was only about six weeks old when Matata did this. Similarly, Kwame is held by no one but his mother until six weeks of age, whereas Elikya was carried by one of her sisters before one month of age. That Kwame is caged with his father, a large silverback with whom he has not interacted directly as of his eighteen-month birthday, and with persistently rambunctious siblings may alter the pace of his gestural development in comparison with Elikya, who lived almost exclusively with her mother and two sisters. This suspicion is supported by Andrew Whiten's (1999) data showing that gorilla infant development may be greatly accelerated when the infant and mother are caged alone. The meaning of any direct comparison between one bonobo and one gorilla infant, however, is as dubious as that between one apple and one orange. Indeed, my aim is not to compare the infants or even their gestural interactions at aged-matched periods but to describe and understand varying lifeways of apes in different social settings.

Seems pretty feeble

Patterned Interactions and Ape Culture

Do the data I have presented suggest that captive bonobos and gorillas have culture? Using conventional definitions of culture, this question is easy to answer. If culture is equivalent to any form of social learning (de Waal 2001), then yes, these bonobos and gorillas have culture. If group-specific patterns of nongenetic transmission must be demonstrated (McGrew 1998), then an answer awaits more data from a variety of groups in the wild as well as in captivity. Posing this question, though, seriously impoverishes a thorough study of ape social patterns and thus, in turn, of the evolution of complex sociality. If, in the rush to uncover culture, we end up reducing our object of study to some suite of static properties that can be noted as either present or absent in apes, that can be qualified as "intermediate" in apes compared with people (Boesch 2000), or that can be said to be acquired or not acquired by apes during ontogeny, then we have failed to describe the profoundly social and dynamic lives of our ape subjects (and the same is likely true for monkeys). It is precisely because a focus on the questions "who has culture, what is culture, and how is it transmitted?" is so likely to derail the full investigation of ape sociality that I am suspicious of it.

No
Weak
Not sold

Rather than documenting great ape culture, my aim has been to document ways in which great ape infants may enter their social worlds. To this end, I describe how the "lifeway" of an ape family is constructed through dynamic, patterned interactions. A transformative process occurs by which social partners, via highly elaborated patterns reflecting shared histories and shared meanings, shape the world an infant enters *as* that infant also shapes the ongoing interactions with its partners. An exploration of ape "ways of becoming," carried out in the wild and in captivity, is surely a rich area for anthropological research in and of itself, divorced from any concern with the culture concept (see Toren, this volume). Yet I am reluctant to proclaim just now that primatologists who undertake this sort of inquiry should divorce their findings from the realm of culture or abandon the search for the cultural, *so long as the traditional boundaries of what is taken as "culture" and "the cultural" are rethought.* Full evaluation of patterned interactions and shared meanings in monkeys and apes—whether in free-ranging populations or captive groups—will lead us to a much richer understanding of how our closest living relatives construct their social worlds, and thus to an understanding of the evolution of complex sociality in the primate lineage.

okay — ne its sociality

For any of this to be culture, I would argue it should be open-ended + cumulative [this is why diffs from one pop to next are important].

Note

For fruitful sharing of ideas, I thank the Morelia symposium participants, particularly Richard Fox, Stuart Shanker, Sydel Silverman, and Christina Toren. I am grateful to Alan Fogel, Grey Gundaker, Joanne Tanner, and Sherman Wilcox, each of whom helped me understand some aspect of coregulation, nonlinearity, and/or gesture, and to Richard Fox, Willow Powers, and Sydel Silverman for helpful comments on an earlier draft. Thanks also to Sue Savage-Rumbaugh and Duane Rumbaugh and to Lisa Stevens, who enabled me to work at the Language Research Center and the National Zoological Park, respectively. For help in data collection, I thank Dan Rice, Erin Selner, and Heather Bond Poje (bonobo project) and Elizabeth Groneweg and the staff at the Great Ape House, National Zoo, especially Ann Hunter, Laurie Perry, Nicole Meese, Doug Donald, and Melanie Bond (gorilla project). To Kendra Weber, I offer gratitude for skillful help in collecting and analyzing the gorilla data and for endlessly discussing it, and to Curt Moyer, thanks for mentoring in digital-image technology.

five

Anthropology as the Whole Science of What It Is to Be Human

Christina Toren

To claim that anthropology is "the whole science of what it is to be human" is not to be merely provocative. Rather, it seems important to draw attention to anthropology as science at this juncture in the history of the discipline, when it would appear to some to have been eclipsed by the rise of cultural studies, on the one hand, and of cognitive science, on the other. This disciplinary split rests in a distinction between culture and biology that, although once apparently fruitful, now only militates against a holistic understanding of human being and thus of how we become who we are.

For a human scientist, words are analytical tools, so one wants to be able to use words with precision. But like everything else that is human, language is a historical phenomenon—that is, its continuity resides in continuing transformation. It follows that no explanation can be objective in the sense of being immune from history. So how are we to arrive at genuinely explanatory accounts of what it is to be human? The short answer is that we can do so only to the extent that we are able to make our historical nature central to our explanations.

My argument in this chapter rests on one I have made elsewhere: that because mind is the fundamental historical phenomenon—as Husserl, among others, showed us[1]—it makes sense to develop a model of human being that is capable of dealing with the way we "live the world" in terms of our own understanding of it, even while we transform the world we live and, in the process, transform ourselves. An understanding of this process requires a model of mind that allows for reflection on the conditions of mind's own genesis; only thus can it incorporate its own history into the explanation it proposes. I begin, therefore, by arguing briefly for the idea that *mind is a function of the whole person that is constituted over time in intersubjective relations with others in the environing world.*

If there is any conceptual difficulty here, it is not inherent in the idea itself but rather in its doing away with three widely held assumptions: that the body is a container for the mind, which is located in the brain or nervous system; that we can distinguish between biology and culture, such that what is biological in humans forms the real, the universal, substrate of their being, on which the cultural is a malleable overlay; and that mind/brain can be compartmentalized such that, for example, perceptual processes can be distinguished from cognitive processes. These ideas are foundational for the human sciences, including anthropology. The majority of anthropologists, sociologists, and psychologists continue to hold to them, so it is hardly surprising that the public at large is enchanted by, for example, the idea that what is given universally in human beings is "in the genes," and what is variable is "in the culture."

Mind cannot, however, be a function of the nervous system—or, even more narrowly, the brain—because the *kind* of body of which it is an aspect is crucial to its workings. Biologists do not, in trying to understand what makes animals in general behave the way they do, distinguish between their minds and their bodies; they look at the animal as a whole because the animal's physical form provides for certain specific modes of knowing the world—that is, it functions to bring into being the world the animal lives, including its relations with its own kind. And what holds for other animals holds for humans, too. Our entire physical being functions to bring into being the world we live—a process that inevitably implicates those other humans alongside whom we live, whose being in the world contributes to structuring the conditions of our existence. It follows that one's manifest physical form provides in more ways than one for how mind works. If I am born blind or deaf I quite literally do not live the same world as those who are sighted and can hear—I have the world in common with them, but my understanding of it is constituted under different conditions from theirs. Or, to take another example, if I lose a leg, I am likely at first to be severely depressed or immensely angry or alternately both. My subsequent existence will be more or less contented to the extent that I discover satisfactory ways of being who I now am, and this process in turn will have a good deal to do with the other humans alongside whom I live.

Any psychologist would be likely to agree that my imagined examples make sense but would continue nevertheless to conceive of mental states and bodily states as separable and interacting. And if mental states can be recognized and classified independently of their physical manifestations in the embodied nervous system, then we can imagine other beings with minds that function just like human minds—computers, for example, or Martians. From my point of view this cannot make sense. If I try to imagine what it is to live the world as a crocodile, say, or a bird, I know that my physical form is going to make for a very different world from the one I live as a human—and this is about all I *can* sensibly imagine, because I don't have the enormous jaws, huge teeth, and big scaly body of a crocodile or the wings of a bird. And even so, crocodiles and birds are a lot closer to being like humans than a computer can be, simply because, like humans, they bring themselves into being via an embodied engagement in the world. A computer has to be assembled; it does not bring itself into being through differentiation of its own physical substance from single cell to fully mature organism. In other words, the physical form of a computer makes no difference to it, and it is precisely *because* this is so that it is difficult to conceive of it as anything other than a tool.

As an anthropologist, I am continually confronted with the fact that other people conceive of the world differently and live the world as they conceive of it, just as I do. This is because, as humans, we cannot help making meaning of the world—but we never do this in isolation. Rather, we make meaning intersubjectively. Every newborn infant encounters a world that is, as it were, ready-made; this is not a static world but one that in all its aspects is transforming. And because it is filled with other people, it can never be a neutral object of knowledge. The world the infant encounters is the world as understood by those people who care for it and among whom it grows up; the meanings they make of the world inform the child's constitution of ideas over time. These meanings are themselves being transformed even as they are brought into being anew by the developing child. As humans we have the world in common, but, as ethnography demonstrates exhaustively, we live it as if it conforms to our own account of it—an observation that is as true for a Western scientist as it is, say, for a Fijian chief. Our models of mind have to be able to explain how this comes to be so. I argue that sociality is intrinsic to human autopoiesis (self-creation or self-production) and that because this is so, human scientists have to begin with the recognition that mind is *the* fundamental historical phenomenon. Where they fail to do so, one finds at best a partial explanation and at worst a thorough confusion.

The Analytical Confusions of Evolutionary Psychology

The evolutionary psychology of John Tooby and Leda Cosmides provides an example of the thoroughly confused variety of explanation. I single out their work for criticism in part because of its current popularity and in part because of their claim to offer an "integrated causal model" of mind with the potential to unify theory across the human sciences. The main force of my argument here resides in showing that their "integrated causal model" cannot incorporate ethnographic data, precisely because it excludes any possibility of analysis of the conditions of its own production.

Tooby and Cosmides (1992: 65) characterize mind as "an information-processing description of the functioning of an organism's brain." The problem for cognitive psychologists in general, then, is to understand how mind works; as evolutionary psychologists, Tooby and Cosmides want to explain further how mind works as a function of "solutions to the adaptive problems that regularly occurred in the Pleistocene" (1992: 55). The difficulty is that they assume that the information processing mechanism is, in certain key respects, an objective "problem solver" in regard to the environment in which it is programmed to find the information on which it acts. Moreover, *because* they conceive of the brain as an information processing device, they have to suppose that it can function efficiently in accordance with the world only if its abilities (whether manifest at birth or to be developed) are already given (1992: 103). Indeed, this information processing device has to be such that it can make objective, empirically sound judgments about the world, for only thus can it underwrite Tooby and Cosmides' idea of what science is.

Consider the following quotation:

> There is certainly cultural and individual variability in the exact forms of adult mental organization that emerge through development, but these are all expressions of what might be called a single human metaculture. All humans tend to impose on the world a common encompassing conceptual organization, made possible by universal mechanisms operating on the recurrent features of human life. This is a central reality of human life and it is necessary to explain how humans can communicate with each other, learn the culture they are born into, understand the meaning of others' acts, imitate each other, adopt the cultural practices of others, and operate in a coordinated way with others in the social world they

inhabit. By *metaculture,* we mean the system of universally recurring relationships established and constituted by (1) our universal evolved species-typical psychological and physiological architectures, (2) the interaction of these architectures with each other in populations, (3) their interaction with the developmentally relevant recurrent structure of human natural and cultural environments, and (4) their patterned standard impact on human phenomena . . . it is only the existence of this common metacultural structure, which includes universal mechanisms specialized to mesh with the social world, that makes the transmission of variable cultural forms possible. (Tooby and Cosmides 1992: 91)

Up to a point, Tooby and Cosmides have the right idea; they want to be able to explain human variation in terms of the same model they use to explain similarity—an objective with which I am entirely in sympathy. That they are unable to do so is in part a function of their assumption that scientific explanations are historically to be privileged over other explanations. Because they hold this view, they are bound, as in the foregoing excerpt, to retain distinctions between the universal and the particular, the social and the individual, the cultural and the natural. This last distinction is especially important for their view that only a certain subset of human knowledge can be properly described as "social" or "cultural," and this in turn implicitly allows them to isolate from contamination other knowledge processes—especially those they would describe as "perception." In other words, because, in the view of psychologists at large, "culture" and "society" are domains of error, the isolation of the "cultural" from the "natural" allows Tooby and Cosmides to claim that they have objective science to justify their understanding of the world while the rest of us have only folk theories to sustain us.

In this connection it is worth noting an earlier protest by Tooby and Cosmides that "'nothing the organism interacts with in the world is nonbiological to it, and so for humans cultural forces are biological, social forces are biological, physical forces are biological, and so on" (1992: 86). They seem unaware that one might just as well argue that nothing the human organism interacts with in the world is noncultural to it—an argument whose sense resides in our knowledge that biology, too, has a history. An account of human physiology as given by, say, Chinese medicine will differ significantly from that proposed in Western biomedicine and will give rise to significantly different health technologies. Perhaps more telling, however, is that Tooby and Cosmides' idea of a panhuman metaculture as the artifact of a panhuman physiological and psychological architecture can hardly be understood as a successful attempt to get free of the problems posed by the familiar distinction between culture and biology. This is especially the case because, as the careful reader will have noted, we have to suppose an "*interaction* [of that architecture] with the developmentally relevant recurrent structure of human natural and cultural environments" (my italics). Only conceptually separate domains are required to *interact*.

Tooby and Cosmides castigate other psychologists and anthropologists who hold to the "standard social science model (SSSM)," which rests on the Cartesian distinction between body and mind. Apparently they fail to perceive their own distinction between biology and meta-culture as an artifact of a covert version of the SSSM. Ditto for their other misconceived distinctions, which, for example, locate particular forms of mental phenomena (which are themselves conceptual artifacts derived from an analysis of what people say and do) in particular regions of the brain—a proceeding that in their view allows them not only to retain the distinction between so-called levels of analysis but to differentiate, for example, "social knowledge" from, say, "perception." Tooby and Cosmides can pretend to have done away with Cartesian distinctions only by virtue of a sleight of hand that makes what is "cultural" at once synonymous with what is "relative" and the by and large only trivially interesting artifact of a set of "universal evolved psychological mechanisms" located in the heads of "individuals." In other words, they resuscitate in their very analytical vocabulary the distinctions they claim to have done away with.

But what if the human being is not primarily an information processing device with sociality tacked onto it but, as anthropologists have reason to suppose, a social being through and through? I argue that human autopoiesis entails that sociality inform all our cognitions, such that social relations enter into the very structuring of attention, and perception can never be neutral. The challenge, then, is to understand how the history of social relations enters into the cognitive constitution of meaning over time.

Human Nature and History

I referred earlier to a unified model of how we become who we are in which mind and body are aspects of each other (rather than separable systems) and in which, from birth to death, each of us humans makes sense of the world by making meaning out of meanings that others have made and are making—a process in which knowledge is at once maintained and transformed. In this perspective, what we call history

learning as part of mental structuring

is an analytical artifact of the more fundamental embodied history that makes each one of us what we are and in the process provides us with our ideas about the world. Anthropologists have documented extensively the different understandings of the world held by different peoples. In respect of perception, for example, ethnographic studies suggest that what we routinely notice and attend to is a function of what we already know—in other words, what is salient to any one of us has everything to do with the past we have already lived in particular places among particular people. It makes little sense, therefore, to isolate domains of psychological functioning such as perception and maintain that they are immune from social mediation. All humans are fundamentally capable of the same basic discriminations, but the fact that perception is *always* embedded in the complexity of the process we call living means that each person's history enters into what he or she perceives and how he or she understands what is perceived.

In the unified model of human being that I propose, consciousness is that aspect of human self-creation (autopoiesis) that, with time, posits the existence of the thinker and the self-evidentiality of the world as lived by the thinker. Given that human autopoiesis is grounded in sociality—that is, that we humans require other humans in order to become and be human—it makes sense to think of our own personal development and of child development in general as a microhistorical process in and through which mind is constituted over time as an always-emergent function of the whole person (no need here to posit a dialectical relation between mind and body). Moreover, this whole person's moment-to-moment encounters with the material world of objects and other people are always and inevitably mediated by relations with others—that is, by intersubjectivity (no need here to posit a dialectical relation between reified abstractions such as individual and society or biology and culture).

The model rests on two demonstrable propositions: that there are no received meanings,[2] and that the process of making meaning is such that the continuity and transformation of ideas are aspects of each other. Put simply, this is because we make meaning out of meanings that others have made and are making: that is, any neonate, infant, child, young adult, adult, or middle-aged or old person is enmeshed in manifold relations with others who cannot help conveying their own understandings of social relations and of the way the world is. Any given person cannot but assimilate these understandings to his or her own and, in doing so, accommodate—more or less—to the other's ideas both of the world and of their relationship to each other as persons. The relation between any infant and its caretakers is such that the growing child has willy-nilly to come to grips with a world that has already been, and continues to be, rendered meaningful by those caring others. The others structure the conditions of existence that are lived by the child, but even so, they cannot *determine* what the child makes of them. Moreover, however dutiful a child may be to its elders, human autopoiesis entails that the process of making meaning is one in which knowledge is transformed even while it is maintained and in which meaning is always emergent, never fixed.

The emergent properties of mind are thus a function at once of the processes that constitute it and what might be called historical contingency. It often seems to me, for example, that one just goes on and on becoming the person one always was. At the same time, I am aware that there is a definite existential freedom in contingency, because I *know* that had I not by chance met this person and that, taken part in this conversation and that, experienced this and that, I would be a very different person from the person I am now—the problem here being that I cannot even imagine who this person would be if she were not me. Yet I would also argue that greater and lesser degrees of existential freedom reside in the chances life affords one. Certainly, I was fortunate to have many chances afforded me; insofar as I chose what to do or say or think or feel at any given point, however, those choices were foreshadowed in what I was, who I was, when I made them.

It follows from all I have said so far that I know that other people's ideas are as materially warranted by the world as my own. I know this. But I do not quite *believe* it, because I can live the peopled world only as I understand it myself. Nevertheless, it is only to the extent that I see that other people's ideas *are bound to be* as materially warranted by the world as my own that I can, as an anthropologist, recognize the necessity for a theory of human being that explains how this comes to be so. Because this endeavor at explanation addresses the historicity of human being in the world and thus implicates its own historical nature, it may ultimately be impossible. Even so, as a human scientist and an anthropologist I hold that some explanations are demonstrably better than others. From my point of view, a good explanation is one that, without sacrificing any of the data or disallowing their complexity, allows the patterns that are peculiar to those data to emerge—as it were of themselves—such that other analysts are convinced of their material validity. There are various ways of doing this, but they all require an understanding of how complex relations among people enter into their constitution of ideas over time (see, for example, Gow 1989, 2001;

Mimica 1988; Toren 1999a, 1999b). Which brings me to the subject of children and why they are important for anthropology.

What We Can Learn from Studying Children

Children should be central to ethnographic analysis simply because they are bound, over time, to *constitute* a knowledge of adult practices and of the ideas adults use to justify them. They do so not because they are molded, conditioned, socialized, or taught, but because in living the world they are making sense of it intersubjectively: in coming to grips with the peopled world, children cannot but come to grips with the ideas of those others by whom they are surrounded. Obtaining systematic data from children of different ages enables us to understand better the practices and ideas of the people with whom we work because they are bound to reveal what adult informants can neither tell nor show us. As adults, we cannot ourselves recover the processes through which we came to know what we know.

I have long argued that one can gain better access to big ideas such as family, caste, individual, democracy, class, God, hierarchy, and so on by studying how children bring these ideas into being for themselves in a way that *at once* maintains and transforms them. An anthropological approach is required to undertake this study, in large part because anthropological analysis insists on embracing complexity—and whatever is going on in respect of ideas such as God and democracy, one cannot sensibly argue that they can be understood in isolation from the social processes that engage them.

Children should be routinely included in anthropological fieldwork because only they can give us access to what they know about the peopled world, and what they know can provide us with analytical insights that cannot be obtained any other way. The understanding of a nine-year-old is more complex (i.e., more highly differentiated) than that of a four-year-old, so data obtained systematically from children up to age fourteen or so can enable the analyst to uncover systematic transformations in the constitution of ideas over time. This in turn enables us to understand how certain aspects of these same ideas come to be salient to children at different ages and, ultimately, how people come to be "enchanted" (as Bourdieu would say) by ideas they themselves have made.

Consider for a moment the following ideas, each of which is taken for granted as obvious by large numbers of people in the world: "We are all individuals with rights." "Untimely deaths are caused by witchcraft." "Human destiny is preordained by God." "People make of themselves what they choose." "One's personality is given by one's sign of the zodiac." "If a pregnant woman eats foods classified as hot, her baby will be bad-tempered." And perhaps strangest of all: "Virtually everything that humans are is written in their genes, and history is a mere epiphenomenon of genetic predispositions." My argument is that to understand what any of these ideas means, and what its implications are for relations among people in the world, requires that one analyze how those people who hold it to be obvious and given in the nature of things come to be so certain. But how is one to produce this revelation of the constituting process? It is not so difficult as one might think, but it does require that one work systematically with children of different ages, as well as with adults, and that one understand what is good in Piaget.

Piaget's Neglected Legacy

In some respects the widespread contemporary rejection of Piagetian theory is justified. No sensible anthropologist wants to espouse a theory that considers as less developed all those millions of adults in the world who do not respond to Piagetian tests in the same way as middle-class Western schoolchildren. It is easy enough, however, to demonstrate that adults everywhere have at their disposal what Piaget called "concrete operations" (e.g., cognitive operations that give rise to fundamental understandings of quantity, volume, measurement, time, space, etc.). All one has to do is look at what people do, rather than what they say about what they do (see Toren 1990: 14). Moreover, plenty of work shows that children's early cognitive abilities are considerably greater than Piaget was able to detect (see Mehler and Dupoux 1990 for an overview). One might not, therefore, want to hold to a general stage theory that is tied to age, or one might want at least to modify certain aspects of it—as has been done, after all, by numbers of psychologists who have been influenced by Piaget. In certain respects, however, Piaget's work is a very long way from being superseded—most importantly, perhaps, in respect of his idea of genetic epistemology and the cognitive scheme that is its product.

Piaget's idea of the cognitive scheme bears little or no relation to any other. The word "scheme" is much bandied about, but in most usages it denotes a mental representation; thus, in the last fifteen years or so we have seen various elaborations of the idea of the scheme as "cultural model" (see, for example, D'Andrade 1995; Holland and Quinn 1987;

Johnson 1987; Shore 1996). None of these theorists pays any attention to Piaget—indeed, Mark Johnson quite unnecessarily resuscitates Kant's idea of the scheme—and this is a real pity because, despite Piaget's relative indifference to the issues that engage anthropologists, only his scheme is capable of incorporating history.

Piaget's scheme can incorporate history because it is grounded in a biological understanding of living systems. We are not accustomed, perhaps, to giving much thought to our bodily substance, to the actual workings of this bounded entity we call "I." But if you pause to think about it, you realize that what is remarkable about this bounded entity is that, like all other living things, we humans are autopoietic systems—that is to say, self-producing (see Maturana and Varela 1980, 1987).[3]

Autopoiesis means that this living system I call "I" is characterized at once by autonomy and transformation. It started as a single-cell being, and from that moment onward this selfsame system specified what transformations were proper to it: my continuity in time—from conception to death—is the continuity of a system that continuously regulates its own transformation. It is easy enough to see this when we confine ourselves to a consideration of our physical being, to our conception and subsequent development in the womb or to phenomena such as the continual shedding and regrowth of our hair or skin cells, but it seems to be much more difficult to understand when we apply the idea to the psychological aspect of human being—though why this should be so is something of a mystery.

The process Piaget called "genetic epistemology" is the psychological aspect of human autopoiesis. Because Piaget's human subject is the universal epistemic subject or ahistorical individual, the idea of genetic epistemology requires modification: it requires recognition that the process of constituting an understanding of the environing world of objects and other people is always and inevitably embedded in social relations or, in other words, is always a function of intersubjectivity.[4] Nevertheless, because living systems are autopoietic, this process of making meaning is an autonomous one and cannot be otherwise. It is this process that gives rise at once to the differences that reside in our similarity to one another and the similarities that are manifest in our difference.

For Piaget, process and structure were not separable but were aspects of each other. Thus he argued that "only self-regulating transformational systems are structures" (1971: 113) and that such structures are bound to be at once constitutive and continually in process of formation. In Piaget's theory of cognitive development, the newborn child starts off with only a few "reflexlike" behaviors at its disposal—sucking, swallowing, crying, grasping, and so on. The primitive psychological structures that govern these behaviors become differentiated through functioning, giving rise, over time, to cognitive schemes that are at once relatively stable and capable of the most subtle discriminations. To take a simple example: the scheme for sucking rapidly becomes differentiated via the baby's experience of sucking different objects—its own thumb, mother's nipples, the teat of a bottle, a dummy, a piece of cloth. The baby assimilates the oral experience of each new object to its sucking scheme and in doing so accommodates to the what-this-feels-like-in-my-mouth aspect of that particular object. And when the baby manages to grasp an object and get it into its mouth, the assimilation schemes of sucking and grasping are assimilated to one another in such a way as to produce a qualitatively different, more highly differentiated, scheme that provides for a new and more complex accommodation to the world.

Piaget described the functional factors of behavior in terms of assimilation, accommodation, and equilibration. Assimilation refers to the way an action is actively reproduced and comes to incorporate new objects into itself—for example, grasping incorporates someone's finger, a lock of mother's hair, the handle of a rattle, the border of a blanket, the feeding bottle, and so on. Accommodation describes the way in which an assimilation scheme—grasping, for instance—becomes modified in being thus applied to a diversity of objects. Equilibration is the process by which assimilation schemes become mutually coordinated in such a way as to produce a cognitive structure that is relatively stable because the mental operations that inform it are reversible. An example might be the scheme that is constituted at six to eight months via the cross-modal matching of intermodal correspondences in numerosity between sounds and sights (see Smith, Sera, and Gattuso 1988). The structural elements in behavior are order relations (e.g., the order of movements in a habitual act), subordination schemes (e.g., sucking is subordinate to grasping when an infant is able to hold the feeding bottle on its own), and correspondences (e.g., what Piaget calls "recognitory assimilation," an instance of which is the motor recognition a baby evinces when its physical movements mimic those of the person to whom it is attending).[5]

It is because structure and process are inextricable and mutually defining that the process Piaget called "genetic epistemology," although it produces stable and mutually confirming sets of ideas about the peopled world, is never in principle finished but always open to further elaboration. So, meaning is always emergent, never fixed. And this would be true even if each of us acted directly on the world and made meaning in isolation from other persons—as Piaget so often seemed to suggest. When we incorporate intersubjectivity into his model, it becomes plain that the meanings we make of the peopled world are themselves constituted in an encounter with the meanings already made, and still being made, by others.

The idea of the scheme as a self-regulating transformational system in which structure and process are aspects of each other has not been widely understood. It follows that its theoretical usefulness has not been recognized. Piaget's scheme makes it plain that continuity and transformation in the structures of mind have to be considered as aspects of each other. Nor is there any mystery about cognitive schemes being a function of embodied mind. That is to say, the newborn child can engage in the world only by virtue of sucking, grasping, crying, looking, listening, and so on—the world is given to it initially by virtue of the primitive and as yet undifferentiated structures of embodied mind that subserve these behaviors, which become differentiated through functioning because through them the child acts on the world. But because Piaget's child is Everychild (who by definition can have no phenomenological being in the world), it makes sense, in thinking about children's constitution of meaning over time, to have in mind a particular child who comes to consciousness of itself and others in relations that are always historically specific (indeed, always unique).

Irrespective of their disciplinary or subdisciplinary identification, however, theorists of cognition continue, just as Piaget did, to take for granted as their starting point the universal epistemic subject, the ahistorical individual. It follows that to cognitivists of all persuasions it seems obvious that "culture" or "society" is an empirically demonstrable variable rather than an abstract artifact of the analyst's gaze. Its complement is a substrate of innately given, domain-specific, cognitive modules that, taken together, define the mind of the universal epistemic subject. Chomsky's "Language Acquisition Device" is a good example of a cognitive module (see Fodor 1983).

I am not sympathetic to the idea of innate modularity. Given the extraordinary complexity of the human nervous system, the infant's immersion in a world of highly differentiated sensation, and the rapid growth of interneuronal connections, a few months are surely ample time for the autopoietic development of complexly differentiated cognitive schemes out of much more primitive beginnings. Moreover, as a "self-regulating transformational system," a Piagetian scheme, even in its early stages, is going to *look like* what cognitivists call a module.

This is a key point, because one of the main arguments for modularity theories is that the structured properties of mental processes can be a function *only* of an innately given "set of evolved information-processing mechanisms instantiated in the human nervous system ... many of these mechanisms are functionally specialized to produce behaviour that solves particular adaptive problems, such as mate selection, language acquisition, family relations, and cooperation; ... *to be functionally specialized, many of these mechanisms must be richly structured in a content-specific way* [my italics]" (Tooby and Cosmides 1992: 24).

But as Piaget's formulation makes plain, what might look like innate "functional specializations" are just as likely to be artifacts of the process of constituting knowledge—an explanation that not only is more economical and more elegant but also is able to deal *at one and the same time* with continuity and transformation. Thus Piaget points out that "structures—in being constructed—give rise to that necessity which a priorist theories have always thought it necessary to posit at the outset. Necessity, instead of being the prior *condition* for learning, is its *outcome* [italics in the original]" (Piaget 1971: 62).

Genetic Epistemology as a Social Process

Piaget's interest in children arose out of his awareness of the following problem: if what we take to be our most fundamental categories of time, space, number, and so on are not innate and demonstrably not fully understood by a four- or five-year-old, how do they nevertheless finally come to be not only at the disposal of the older child but understood as *necessary*—that is, as self-evident and objectively given dimensions of the world? I have suggested here that asking similar questions of such categories as God, *mana*, democracy, and hierarchy is a fruitful course for anthropologists to pursue in their own way—that is, by supplementing participant-observer studies of people's day-to-day lives with the systematic study of what children of different ages take to be the meaning of the key categories adults use to reflect on and describe the world and their own lives. This systematic study requires the use of diagnostic tasks, which may be quite simple in form—for example, asking children to make a drawing of a particular scene and then talking with them one by one about what they have drawn. This kind of proceeding with children is equivalent to open-ended interviews with adults. There is no point, however, in focusing on children to the exclusion of adults. Moreover, long-term participant-observer study remains absolutely necessary, for without it the anthropologist cannot know where it will be fruitful to focus any more systematic investigations with children.

As an example of the kind of study I am proposing, let me briefly describe one part of my first fieldwork in Fiji (1981–1983). In analyzing the nature of contemporary Fijian hierarchy and how it is constituted in ritual practice, I collected systematic data from sixty-seven children between, roughly, the ages of five and fourteen years. The data consisted of their drawings of people gathered to drink *yaqona* (kava, or the root of the plant *Piper methysticum* pounded and infused in water)—the *yaqona* ceremony being the most important of all Fijian rituals—supplemented by each child's commentary on what he or she had drawn. I also prepared schematic drawings of various ordinary, day-to-day ritualized situations (*yaqona* ceremonies, meals at home, and meetings in the village hall) and asked these same children to tell me who the people represented were and where they were seated. I carried out this work toward the end of my first period of fieldwork of eighteen months—that is, at a point where I was in a position to recognize, first, that the precise nature of Fijian hierarchy is most clearly evinced in people's dispositions relative to one another in space and, second, that gatherings where people drink *yaqona*, meals at home, and meetings in the village hall were all bound to bear on how any given child's understanding of hierarchy was constituted over time and, in this process, transformed. These data revealed how, from its primitive beginnings in the preschool Fijian child, a cognitive scheme becomes differentiated through functioning in such a way as to constitute the idea that hierarchy may be taken for granted as a principle of social relations (see Toren 1990). This analysis of ontogeny had significant theoretical implications: it allowed access to the preoccupations of the people whose manifold relations with one another were the object of inquiry, it incidentally disproved the received views of hierarchy put forward by Marshall Sahlins (1976) and Sherry Ortner (1981), and it provided the basis for a theory of ritual (see Toren 1999a: part 2; Toren n.d.).

The more generalizable finding, and one of particular relevance to the present volume, is that children have to *constitute* so-called cultural categories or cultural schemes: meaning is not received ready-made; it does not reside *in* ritual or *in* myth or *in* various customs and conventions. Perhaps more interesting, however, is that for young children (up to eight and a half or so), practices that adults say are governed by explicit rules cannot properly be described as "symbolic" (see Toren 1999a: 83–127). In other words, for these youngest children, ritualized behavior does not stand for anything; it is simply another facet of children's material existence, part of the way the world is, and they do not seek to interrogate its meaning in the way implied by symbolic analyses. This is not to say that given children do not form specific associations with respect to certain practices. They do, but it is not until around nine years of age that they hold explicitly that the meaning of these practices goes beyond the simple doing of them. Thus, people are *in ritual* and coerced by it long before they come to reflect on its meaning or even to know that it might have meaning, in the sense of standing for something other than itself.

Adults assert that certain practices are expressive because the process by which they constituted that expressive meaning is concealed from them. It is concealed precisely because it involved a shift in cognition, one that was, so to speak, forced upon them as children by the conditions adults created in the world around them. So it is ritualized practice that allows for the appearance of an unchanging status quo. Many anthropologists have recognized this without actually being able to explain precisely how it occurs. In *From Blessing to Violence* (1986), Maurice Bloch showed how the Merina circumcision ritual remained virtually unchanged through the vicissitudes of monarchy, Christian conversion, and the shift to republicanism in Madagascar. The ritual was able to become the vehicle of *any* party seeking legitimacy. Provided that party had sufficient material power, it could always use this ritual to convert its power into authority. Bloch described ritual as being between a statement and an action, and he showed how it makes no sense to analyze ritual for meaning as if all it did were render a cosmology in another form. In effect, ritual works to legitimate the status quo and has to be understood for its political as well as for its cosmological implications.

Here I agree with Bloch, but we part company with respect to our ideas about where meaning lies. Bloch described ritual as only weakly propositional and thus open to use by successive power holders; his analysis made the power of ritual reside *in* ritual practice, as if this power were there by virtue of the ritual format. This seems to me to be a mistaken assumption. Rather, certain practices are powerful to the extent that they inform our childhood experience such that we attribute power to them. In the absence of that experience they can appear arbitrary, even absurd. Even if all that is said about a practice is that "we do this because our ancestors did," its power and its compelling nature are the products of childhood experience, of the process of constituting as meaningful an idea that we *should* do what our ancestors did. We cannot *be* again what we were, nor can we know as adults what we knew as children, so the process by which we came to know the meaning of certain practices is concealed from us. They come to have more meaning than we know—for example, political significance in respect of confirming a particular status quo.

In *Islands of History* (1985), Marshall Sahlins was concerned not with ritual but with "culture." In his analysis, culture is the outcome of the interplay between structure and process. Structure is "the system of relations between categories, without a given subject" (1985: xvi–xvii). Process describes what happens when the human subject, who receives cultural meanings ready-made, risks those meanings by putting them into practice. But here "risk" is a function not even of day-to-day living but of historical contingency. So for Sahlins, change can be induced only from without: the Hawaiians meet Captain Cook. As my foregoing account suggests, however, the meanings made by any given person can never be quite the same as those made by another, and the process of making meaning is inherently transformational. Thus, no matter how apparently homogeneous a group of people may be, historically important shifts in meaning are likely even in the absence of an external push. Sahlins recognized that it was human action that made his cultural system at once reproducible and variable, but even so, he failed to allow a place in his account for historically effective action that was *not* governed by "the system"—which is thus revealed to be an all-encompassing and ahistorical model of possibilities, an artifact of the analyst's gaze (see Kuper 1999: 159–200 for an extended discussion of Sahlins's ideas concerning culture and history).

Sahlins argued that "culture is, by its own nature, an historical object" (1985: 148). But if so, then categories such as "chief," "taboo," and "god" can never be received ready-made; they must be constituted anew by each one of us. This constituting process is crucially informed by ritual practice, for it is only in ritual that ideas such as "chief" and "god" are simultaneously made concrete *and* transformed into those reified abstractions we call "the symbolic." Moreover, it is the ritual process itself that makes the meaning of its product categories appear to be consensual and unchanging rather than negotiable and labile. In other words, because the rules that describe ritual action are explicit—"in *yaqona* ritual, men sit above and women below"—it is possible for everyone to agree on them and indeed to act in accordance with them, such that it appears as if everyone makes the same meaning out of the ritual behavior. In fact, as my own work shows, their meanings may differ profoundly from one another (see Toren 1990: 196–216).

Ritual works to subordinate the concrete and material to symbolic thought. Indeed, if it is to mean anything symbolically, ritual has to make what is material the sign of what is transcendent; it can only work off what is concrete. But insofar as it *is* concrete, it is also inevitably a challenge to collective processes. Only insofar as key rituals continue to be performed can what Sahlins called "the cultural scheme" be constituted anew and, in the process, be at once maintained and transformed. Thus I would argue that it is ritualized behavior—all those actions that are *said* to be governed by explicit rules—that functions as "a synthesis of stability and change, past and present, diachrony and synchrony" (Sahlins 1985: 144). It is because ritualized behavior is understood to be a function of explicit rules that specific rituals work to incorporate the history of particular persons into a transcendent "timelessness." The separation between history and myth is collapsed in ritual, and both can potentially be remade: people can make history happen as myth and vice versa.

Conclusion

In this chapter I have argued for a model of human being that is encapsulated in the following formulation: *Mind is a function of the whole person constituted over time in intersubjective relations with others in the environing world.* This model allows us to make a claim for anthropology as the whole science of what it is to be human, because it offers a means for analyzing ideas as historical products constituted in and through particular forms of social relations in a world that is always dense with meaning. Because the model shows how ideas are transformed in the same process in which they are maintained, it is able to explain how differences reside in our similarity to one another and how sameness is manifest in our differences. Thus we can put aside the existing distinction between biology and culture and avoid the sterile debate concerning what is "in the genes" and what is "transmitted through the environment." More importantly, perhaps, it opens up to us a mode of analyzing our own categories: "culture," for example, or "individuality," or "free will," or "choice." This mode of analysis is capable of revealing the material validity of those categories *and* the limits of their application. By the same token, it allows us access to the preoccupations of the people with whom we work and a means whereby their categories—perhaps very different from our own—can be rendered analyzable.

To arrive at an anthropological understanding of the biological process that is human ontogeny (and remember, we are talking here about a biology in which sociality is given) is to understand how mind as *the* fundamental historical phenomenon imagines the world that warrants its imagination. My proposed model of how the positing consciousness comes into being as the artifact of an embodied microhistorical process is able to show why it is that any one of us, anywhere, at any point in our lives, is convinced that by and large the world conforms to our own description of it (see Toren 1999b). Each of us, over time, from birth to death, constitutes the world anew, but we do so intersubjectively in the course of particular relations with particular others in the peopled world. The autonomy of minds, their integrity, their imaginative potential, their distinctiveness, their authenticity, their openness—in short, their beauty—is a function of the process of a self-making in which others are always and inevitably implicated, such that at any given point our futures are foreshadowed in, while not determined by, our present understandings.

Notes

1. The driving force of Husserl's phenomenology was his concern that "science as a valid systematic theory" must, despite humanity's "historicity," be possible. Historicity gives rise to the relativism that Husserl's phenomenology, his "philosophy as rigorous science" sought to escape. Philosophy should be able to make apparent the underpinnings of science, that is, the workings of human consciousness that makes science possible. This concern required not only that Husserl acknowledge the historical nature of our categories but that he attack the naiveté of the positivist natural science approach to mind (Carr 1970; Husserl 1965: 141).

2. Because there are no received meanings, language acquisition is crucial to the form our understanding takes. Even so, we do not, in learning to speak, simply take on other people's meanings; rather, we constitute anew the concepts and grammar of the language by which we are surrounded and, in doing so, at once maintain and subtly transform that language (see, e.g., Bowerman 1982). The unified model proposed in this chapter also draws on the work of Lev Vygotsky (1986 [1934]) and Maurice Merleau-Ponty (1962 [1945]).

3. Maturana and Varela's idea of autopoiesis should not be confused with Niklas Luhmann's (1990) unwarranted and unnecessary application of it to "social systems."

4. Piaget was not much interested in the neonate's initial engagement with other humans, but it is worth noting that the neonate's orientational bias toward other humans would not necessarily require anything more complex than an innate response to a schematic facial array of eyes and mouth that is just as likely to be given to other primate neonates.

5. The description of Piaget's idea of the scheme is derived from his book *Structuralism*. First published in French in 1968, when he was seventy-two, this book is a succinct statement of Piaget's key ideas as they apply to mathematical and logical structures and also to "structures . . . whose transformations unfold in time: linguistic structures, sociological structures, psychological structures" (Piaget 1971: 15).

six

The Broader Implications of Borderline Areas of Language Research

Stuart Shanker

For those of us who are deeply concerned about the mechanistic trends that dominated psychology in the twentieth century, anthropology has long stood out as one of our most important models, as well as resources, for studying the micro- and macroprocesses involved in the growth of a child's mind. Throughout the last century, the basic conflict in developmental psychology was between the machine model, which assumes that complex behaviors can be broken down into genetically determined subcomponent processes, each of which maturates independently of other aspects of development, and the interactionist approach, which maintains that a child learns—both consciously and unconsciously—through interactions with her caregivers (other adults, siblings, peers, etc.) how to think, act, speak, and even feel like the other members of her community. Whereas the machine model explicitly eschews the relevance of anthropology for its concerns, the interactionist view is vitally dependent on the information that anthropology provides, not just about the processes involved in a child's social development and the cross-cultural variations that have been observed in cognitive, social, emotional, and linguistic development but, further, about the methodological problems that arise in conducting valid and reliable naturalistic studies. Thus it is with some unease, not to mention a foreboding sense of déjà vu, that the interactionist encounters the current debate in anthropology over whether the concept of culture should be formally abandoned in order to inhibit the essentialist and political misuses of the term that have become so prevalent. For the sort of concern one sees in this debate is very familiar to psychologists and in fact can be regarded as one of the main reasons why their field was so drawn to the machine model of development in the first place (Shanker 1998).

The very question "What is culture?"—like such classic philosophical questions as "What is the mind?" "What is cognition?" and "What are intentions?"—frames the issue in such a way that one cannot help getting caught up in essentialist/reductionist disputes. But all the time these metaphysical debates are proceeding, scientists will continue to study the role of cultural factors in a child's development, just as psychologists continued to study the effects of the environment on the growth of a child's mind, or the effects of priming on cognitive processes, or the emergence of intentional behavior in infants. To be sure, such philosophical debates can be of great benefit, insofar as they force us to clarify what we mean when we speak of a "cultural" factor (or a "cognitive" process or an "intentional" behavior). But it is ultimately by surveying these linguistic practices, not by a priori reasoning, that one clarifies what one means when one speaks, in such-and-such a context, of a "cultural" factor (or of the "mind," "cognition," "intentions").

The concern one sees in this debate over the eliminability of the concept of culture is particularly familiar to those working in the area of language acquisition. There, too, scientists have had to consider whether "it may be better to abandon the reifying term 'language,' which tends to connote a closed discrete system, in favor of linguistic practices, which recognize talking as an activity in structural coupling, one with porous borders with other cultural practices, or even, 'languaging'" (Maturana and Varela 1987, quoted in Foley 1997: 27). Indeed, the debate over the eliminability of the term "language" has special relevance for the debate over culture, not simply because language has long constituted one of the paradigms of what the interactionist has in mind when speaking of culture, but also because the formalist definition of language illustrates the manner in which reductionist arguments in the human sciences can seriously constrain research. The formalist definition has proved to be a serious impediment to the study of language development (Barrett 1999) and language pathology (Barwick et al. n.d.).

In this chapter, I hope to show how two fascinating areas of borderline language research—ape language research (ALR) and work done with children suffering from Specific Language Impairment (SLI)—bear on the debate over the eliminability of "language" and thence the elimination of "culture." ALR and SLI push us up against the barriers of the reified concept of language that has dominated psycholinguistics for the past generation: the generativist theory that children are born with innate knowledge of the "essence" of language, as this is defined by generativist theory (Pinker 1994). As we shall see, generativists are forced to question the findings made in these two areas of research on the grounds that the behavior of the subjects involved cannot, according to generativist dictates, be described as linguistic, and hence it can shed no light on what the generativist sees as the mechanical processes involved in language acquisition. From the interactionist perspective, the problem with such an argument is that it denies the relevance of these two important areas of "borderline" language research for our understanding of the various processes involved in language development, precisely because it embraces a formal concept of "language" that cannot permit the very *possibility* of a borderline area of language research.

The generativist sees language acquisition as a matter of the child's (or rather, a particular module of the child's mind/brain) working out the formal properties of a "language system." These formal properties are construed as *facts of language* that a child can discover only if she possesses innate knowledge of the most general principles and parameters of language. The interactionist sees language development not in these epistemological terms but rather as a matter of a child's becoming a skilled participant in culture-specific forms of communicative behavior. Thus, generativists and interactionists are deeply divided, not just over the question of whether the findings obtained in ALR and SLI are relevant to our understanding of the processes involved in language development but, indeed, over our understanding of the very nature of language.

The Generativist View of Language

Language, according to generativist theory, must be formally defined if we are to avoid the problems that arise when the demarcation between language and communication—or, more specifically, between linguistic and nonlinguistic communication—is not strictly observed (for example, the difference between using sign language to communicate some piece of information and waving at a friend). In generativist terms, language is a formal system that uses a finite number of rules to generate infinitely many sentences in order to communicate—that is, "encode" and "decode"—epistemically private thoughts. The generativist view of language thus presupposes, as Chomsky himself emphasized early on, a Cartesian view of the nature of language and its relationship to the mind. In this view, the individual is said to enjoy "privileged access" to her own mental states and uses "language" to communicate her thoughts, desires, intentions, and so forth to another individual (Chomsky 1966; Savage-Rumbaugh, Shanker, and Taylor 1998).

The history of modern linguistics illustrates just how difficult it was for Cartesians to explain how human beings ever came to possess language thus conceived, or how a child acquires the language of her society, or even how two language-speakers can be certain they share the same language and thus understand each other (Taylor 1992). But generativism has a simple answer for all of these problems: at some point in our prehistory, human beings must have acquired, perhaps quite suddenly or perhaps in a well-ordered series of stages, a "language gene" that contains the "information" or "blueprint" for the construction of a Language Acquisition Device (LAD). The LAD is said to contain, in a "neurally embodied form," the general principles and parameters of language that a child must possess if she is to acquire language. A child need only be exposed to a linguistic environment in order for the information that is stored in this LAD to be activated. Thus Chomsky concluded that the child's knowledge of language "develops through the interplay of genetically determined principles and a course of experience. Informally, we speak of this process as 'language learning.' ... I would like to suggest that in certain fundamental respects we do not really learn language; rather, grammar grows in the mind" (Chomsky 1980: 134).

The generativist model of language acquisition has been committed from the start, therefore, to excluding anthropology from the study of language acquisition (see Shanker 2001). According to generativist theory, "language is not a cultural artifact that we learn the way we learn to tell time or how the federal government works. Instead, it is a distinct piece of the biological makeup of our brains. Language is a complex, specialized skill, which develops in the child spontaneously, without conscious effort or formal instruction, is deployed without awareness of its underlying logic, is qualitatively the same in every individual, and is distinct from more general abilities to process information or behave intelligently" (Pinker 1994: 18). Hence, the generativist must also reject any research that suggests that subjects who apparently lack a "language gene" might nonetheless be capable of acquiring language skills—say, by being exposed at an early age to a language-enriched environment, or through instruction and conscious effort.

Herein lies the reason why generativists have responded so forcefully to recent advances in ALR and to the encouraging therapeutic results that have been achieved with children suffering from SLI. In the former area of research, we encounter a species, the bonobo, that was thought to be incapable of acquiring language but has in fact demonstrated linguistic skills comparable to those of a two-and-a-half-year-old child. The latter area of research is concerned with children who are said to have suffered a defect in their "language gene" and therefore must, according to the nativist hypothesis, be incapable of acquiring language—yet anywhere from 20 percent to 50 percent of children diagnosed with SLI recover fully if they are diagnosed early and receive appropriate language therapy. In both cases, the generativist claims that the subjects involved give only a false appearance of possessing normal linguistic skills. That is, the generativist claims that in both cases the subjects' communicative abilities are really the result of enhanced cognitive processes (e.g., their ability to solve complex problems and to memorize a large number of action-symbol pairings). What makes these debates so interesting is that the interactionist cannot prove that, in its own terms, such a skeptical argument is wrong, but rather must show how these two "borderline" areas of research shed important light on the enculturated nature of language development.

Ape Language Research

The first great period of ALR was in the 1960s and 1970s. Alan and Beatrix Gardner's work with Washoe (Gardner and Gardner 1969), David Premack's work with Sarah (Premack 1976), and Duane Rumbaugh's work with Lana (Rumbaugh 1977) suggested that although it was unlikely that apes would ever progress beyond the acquisition of primitive linguistic skills, they were indeed capable of mastering symbols and even of combining those symbols according to simple rules of word order. The publication of H. S. Terrace's *Nim* in 1979, however, created a crisis of such proportions that it seemed unlikely that ALR would ever regain its former luster. Following Terrace's lead, critics of ALR argued that the behavior of the "signing apes" could be explained as the result of imitation, trial-and-error learning, instrumental conditioning, unintentional cueing, or overinterpretation by the researchers. Now, Sue Savage-Rumbaugh's work with Kanzi, a male bonobo who was born and raised at the Language Research Center at Georgia State University, has stimulated renewed interest in the linguistic capacities of nonhuman primates and the possible light that ALR might shed on our understanding of the cognitive, communicative, and socioaffective processes involved in children's language development.

Bonobos (*Pan paniscus*) are congeners of chimpanzees. When he was two and a half years old, Kanzi began using symbols on a lexigram board to request various food items. The use of lexigram symbols as communication tools was first introduced in the Lana project. Lexigrams are colorful, noniconic symbols arranged on a computer keyboard. By pressing them in the proper sequence, Lana, a chimpanzee, could cause food or drinks to be dispensed, turn on music, watch slides, open a window, and invite people into her room to visit and play (Rumbaugh 1977). Kanzi has progressed far beyond these simple routines. He can use close to four hundred lexigram symbols to do such things as refer to objects, people, and locations in his immediate surroundings and in distal locations, comment on events that occurred in the past, ask questions or issue commands, or simply provide information (both requested and unsolicited).

Perhaps even more significant than his use of lexigram symbols is Kanzi's ability to understand spoken English sentences. When he was eight years old, Kanzi was rigorously tested on the same corpus of sentences as Alia, a two-year-old child (Savage-Rumbaugh et al. 1993). The sentences on which they were tested involved requests such as to put something on or in something, to give or show something to someone, to do something to someone, to take something to a distal location, to fetch an object or objects from a distal location, or to engage in some make-believe sequence. Almost all of the sentences were new to Kanzi, and many involved slightly bizarre requests in order to ensure that he was not deriving their meaning solely on the basis of semantic predictability—that is, without really understanding the grammatical relationships involved.

The debate over this research has concerned not the reliability of these findings but their interpretation. The generativist claims that in order to justify the assumption that such behavior is legitimately described in linguistic terms, Kanzi must be shown to possess the same knowledge of the structure of language—as defined by generativist precepts—that a two-and-a-half-year-old child can be assumed to possess. Over the past twenty years we have seen a number of generativist attempts to identify some aspect of linguistic knowledge that will differentiate between ape and child. For example, can apes use symbols for noninstrumental purposes? Can they use symbols intentionally or spontaneously to refer to objects or events that are spatiotemporally removed? Can they use combinations of symbols and grasp the importance of order? Can they master simple syntactical constructions? In each case, ape language researchers have demonstrated that apes can, in fact, master the skill in question (Savage-Rumbaugh, Shanker, and Taylor 1998). The current question concerns whether Kanzi has demonstrated the ability to extract morphological rules for regular inflectional endings "automatically" or "implicitly," as opposed to memorizing particular inflectional forms (without recognizing them as such) on a case-by-case basis (Shanker, Savage-Rumbaugh, and Taylor 1999). As we shall see in the following section, the same question has arisen in the debate over SLI. In both cases the generativist argues that if subjects do not possess such tacit knowledge, then there is no reason to construe their productive behaviors in linguistic terms rather than as (sophisticated) communicational skills that are the result of advanced cognitive abilities.

The question of whether apes can master the use of inflectional endings is certainly interesting, just as were all of the preceding questions. As important as these questions are, however, it is essential to recognize that the debate between the generativist view of language acquisition and the interactionist view of language development is no longer a matter of the latter's continuing to meet a series of increasingly refined challenges set by the former. Ultimately, what this debate is about is the generativist definition of language, which dictates a hard-and-fast distinction between nonlinguistic and linguistic communication: between the communicative acts of the prelinguistic child or apes and the sudden emergence of language skills that can putatively occur only once the LAD has been activated. In other words, the real question we are confronted with in the debate over ALR is whether we *already* have enough evidence to warrant describing an ape's communicative behavior in primitive linguistic terms, and if so, what implications this has for our understanding of the nature of language and of language development.

As opposed to the generativist's "discontinuity" view of language acquisition, the interactionist stresses the emergence of linguistic skills in the context of, and as a way of augmenting and coregulating, nonverbal interactions. From this latter perspective, an essential aspect of Kanzi's remarkable achievements is the events that led up to Savage-Rumbaugh's discovery that, at age two and a half, Kanzi had, without any direct instruction, acquired the use of eight lexigram symbols. In retrospect, we can see how, far from being the result of a sudden "moment of insight," Kanzi's grasp of the function of these symbols was the result of prolonged communicative development. For example, Savage-Rumbaugh tells us that, at the age of six months, Kanzi "became mesmerized by the keyboard, staring at the symbols as they flashed onto the projectors at the top of the keyboard" (Savage-Rumbaugh and Lewin

1994: 129). When he was fourteen months old, Kanzi began "to press keys on the keyboard and then run to the vending machine as though he had grasped the idea that hitting keys produced food" (1994: 130). At eighteen months, Kanzi started "inventing simple iconic gestures, the first of which indicated the direction of travel in which he wished to be carried. He did this not with a finger point, but with an outstretched arm" (1994: 134). He even "added emphasis to his gesture by forcefully turning [Savage-Rumbaugh's] head in the direction he wished to go.... At other times, as he sat on [her] shoulders, he would lean his whole body in the desired direction of travel so that there was no mistaking his intent" (1994: 134). And he often "vocalized while gesturing, which served to catch [her] attention and to convey the emotional affect that accompanied each request" (1994: 134).

Around the age of two, Kanzi began to incorporate lexigrams into his communicative repertoire. For example, he "started deliberately to select the 'chase' symbol. He would look over the board, touch this symbol, then glance about to see if [Savage-Rumbaugh] had noticed and whether [she] would agree to chase him" (Savage-Rumbaugh and Lewin 1994: 134). Interestingly, Kanzi's first recorded use of the lexigram board "was to activate 'apple,' then 'chase.' He then picked up an apple, looked at [Savage-Rumbaugh], and ran away with a play grin on his face" (1994: 135). Throughout that day he repeatedly "hit food keys, and when [Savage-Rumbaugh] took him to the refrigerator, he selected those foods he'd indicated on the keyboard. Kanzi was using specific lexigrams to request and name items, *and* to announce his intention" (1994: 135).

In Savage-Rumbaugh's mind, the most important decision that was made in regard to Kanzi's upbringing was to "abandon any and all plans of [formally] teaching Kanzi and simply to offer him an environment that maximized the opportunity for him to learn as much as possible" (Savage-Rumbaugh and Lewin 1994: 137). This decision demanded that new lexigrams be created for the most important aspects of Kanzi's day-to-day activities: for example, the names of foods, caregivers, other apes, locations in the forest, toys, and games. No symbols were inserted solely for the purpose of ascertaining whether Kanzi could grasp some abstract concept. If anything, we should look at the board in the same way we look at "motherese" (in which a caregiver regulates her prosody according to the child's signals of [non]comprehension and employs tools such as expansion, extension, recasting, reflective and clarifying questions, and repetition to sustain and enhance communication): the board was designed not to test or instruct but to facilitate interactions by providing Kanzi with an artificial communication tool (and a fairly cumbersome one at that). As a result, Savage-Rumbaugh recalled, Kanzi's "communications soon began to revolve around his daily activities, such as where we were going to travel in the forest, what we would eat, the games we wanted to play, the toys Kanzi liked, the items we carried in our backpacks, television shows Kanzi liked to watch, and visits to Sherman and Austin" (1994: 139). Thus, instead of viewing Kanzi's mastery of linguistic skills as the result of a spontaneous mental reorganization or a sudden insight into the representational function of lexigram symbols, we should view his language development as a prolonged process that occurred because he was aware that the keyboard was employed "as a means of communication, and apparently [he] felt keenly motivated to do so as well" (1994: 139).

According to this line of reasoning, the crucial aspect of this research is that Kanzi was raised in much the same way as a human infant. The importance of this point lies not solely in the significance of Kanzi's interactive routines for his socioaffective development but, further, in the fact that Kanzi's use of lexigram symbols and his responses to what others said were constantly being discussed, corrected, evaluated, and embellished, and that he in turn acquired these reflexive abilities. Indeed, according to the interactionist viewpoint, one of the key reasons why Kanzi's communicative behaviors are properly described in linguistic terms is precisely that he acquired these reflexive skills. That is, Kanzi does not simply *respond* to spoken utterances by doing such-and-such, or press a button because he *associates* it with some specific reward. Rather, he can be seen asking someone to clarify what he or she means, or trying to explain what he means, or justifying his uses of various symbols, or trying to clear up misunderstandings. It is the complexity of actions such as these that warrants the description of his behavior in linguistic terms (Shanker and Taylor 2001).

According to the interactionist viewpoint, the research with Kanzi indicates that it is not just exceedingly difficult but is in principle misguided to try to draw a hard-and-fast distinction between a child's (or ape's) communicative and linguistic development. Language does not suddenly appear at some predetermined age in some predetermined form but emerges as a means of coregulating and augmenting such cultural activities as sharing, requesting, imitating, playing, naming, describing, and apologizing. The child or ape is increasingly motivated to use and develop these communicational tools so that he or she may achieve context-dependent, interactional goals—goals which themselves develop as a function of the child's or ape's developing communicational environment and his or her growing abilities and increasingly differentiated affects. By stipulating, on the basis of a technical definition of language, that such research *cannot* reveal anything about the processes involved in language development, the generativist not only denies the relevance of communicative development to language development but also excludes the possibility of learning anything about the enculturated nature of language skills.

Specific Language Impairment

We have become so conditioned to think of language acquisition as a universal human phenomenon that it comes as something of a surprise to learn that approximately 7 percent of all five-year-old children, who are normal in all key respects, nonetheless suffer from a significant language impairment. These children are said to have SLI, a condition in which children have a profound language deficit but no hearing impairment, no neurological damage, no evidence of speech apraxia, and no social or cognitive deficits. In the paradigmatic case, the only thing abnormal about a child with SLI is the fact that he scores significantly below his age-mates on language tests, yet in the normal range on IQ tests.[2] But then, paradigmatic cases are rarely, if ever, encountered; typically, a child presenting a significant language deficit also exhibits some cognitive, affective, communicational, and/or motor problem.

From the beginning, generativists have placed heavy emphasis on the idea that language is "canalized"—that it is a species-typical trait that is strongly buffered from environmental perturbations by a "language gene"—in order to substantiate their claim that children are born with innate knowledge of the fundamental "principles and parameters" of language (Lenneberg 1967). How, then, do they deal with the phenomenon of SLI? The answer, surprisingly, is that as far as generativists are concerned, there could be no more compelling vindication of their modularity thesis than the fact that there is a small minority of cases in which language is selectively impaired (Pinker 1994). This apparent anomaly seems to confirm the generativist view that language is an *autonomous* faculty that matures independently of other cognitive or communicational skills.

Hence the generativist stresses that when a child has SLI, it is only his mastery of syntax that is defective. What such children are said to show us is that "there must be some pattern of genetically guided events in the development in the brain . . . that is specialized for the wiring in of linguistic computation" (Pinker 1994: 324). The generativist regards the child who commonly omits grammatical morphemes when he speaks, or who persistently overgeneralizes regular endings for irregular verbs, in the same way one might view a computer program such as ELIZA, which imitated a Rogerian therapist: each may seem to possess some linguistic skills, but closer inspection reveals that their productive abilities are really the results of very different kinds of processing strategies.

Perhaps the greatest problem of all for the generativist view of SLI is the fact that 20 percent to 50 percent of subjects diagnosed with SLI recover fully, provided they begin intensive speech language therapy early enough. The generativist might, of course, simply argue that these children were wrongly diagnosed as having SLI—that is, that the boundary between slow language development and SLI can be fuzzy in places. Nevertheless, in the vast majority of these cases it is clear that the child's recovery is the direct result of intensive speech-language therapy. And since the generativist is postulating an irremediable genetic defect in SLI, he must convince us that the subjects who recover as a result of speech-language therapy only *appear* to contravene the "language gene" hypothesis.

The generativist solution to this problem is that "although the language-impaired subjects sometimes appear to produce the 'correct' surface form, further analysis of their performance as a whole shows that these forms are produced not by a hierarchically organized system of abstract rules operating on grammatical categories but rather by very specific compensatory strategies, including memorization of inflected forms as unanalyzed lexical items and the conscious application of learned explicit rules" (Gopnik et al. 1997: 115). The justification for this interpretation is said to lie in the fact that the theory accurately predicts certain characteristic kinds of responses (e.g., reaction time latencies in the use of inflectional endings) and morphosyntactic errors (e.g., overregularizations or poor results on novel word tests). In other words, the solution to the problem posed by the apparent recovery experienced by a significant proportion of children with SLI can be found in Pinker's "dual mechanism" hypothesis (Pinker 1991).

According to the dual mechanism hypothesis, in the normal child the acquisition of regular inflectional forms involves the application of an implicit rule that is applied unconsciously, whereas irregular forms are learned (memorized) on a case-by-case basis and applied consciously. The child with SLI, on the other hand, learns all verb forms using the latter cognitive process. The normal child is said to be able automatically to extract morphological rules for regular inflectional endings from the language she hears. The SLI child is said to be unable to construct "implicit" rules for morphological processes on the basis of the input he receives: he must learn *all* inflectional forms on a case-by-case basis. Thus, whereas the normal child acquires these abstract rules without formal instruction and applies them unconsciously and effortlessly, the SLI child can acquire the rules of syntax only laboriously, from formal speech-language therapy, using cognitive skills as a compensating mechanism. That is, the child stores inflected forms as unanalyzed wholes for regular as well as irregular forms.

This use of the dual mechanism hypothesis raises an intriguing problem in regard to Chomsky's famous "poverty of the stimulus" argument, which postulates that a young child *knows* "principles and parameters" of language that could not possibly have been *learned*. For it now turns out that subjects can indeed learn how to speak in a manner that, as far as formal language-testing is concerned, passes as "normal," purely on the basis of explicit rules, memory, and imitation. It follows that "grammaticality tests," which are designed to show that a child knows certain facts about language that she could not possibly have learned, and which have played a prominent role in generativist writings, must in fact be irrelevant as indicators of a child's language competence. But then, the "autonomy of language development" thesis actually dictates such a consequence from the start. For according to the generativist thesis, a child's knowledge of grammar—or lack thereof—is *implicit*, and performance factors can be just as much false indicators of "tacit grammatical knowledge" (in the case of SLI or, for that matter, Kanzi) as they can be false indicators of "grammatical ignorance" (in the case of the normal child).

It is because it is thought to represent a pure case of language impairment that SLI has the appeal that it does for generativists. Yet their very conception of SLI *presupposes* this "pure case" scenario. According to the reading pursued by interactionists, the most important feature of SLI is the way the symptoms can be so markedly different in different children or even in the same child at different times. According to the interactionist, what this tells us is that there is no simple or single process leading up to SLI. Rather, one needs to look at more basic developmental factors, such as the effects that biological challenges can have on a child's early dyadic interactions and thence on the child's development (Owens 1996).

The interactionist stresses that we need a much more comprehensive picture of the kinds of language deficits a child with SLI demonstrates before we can begin to assess the differing causes of his impairment. It is true that the speech of such children is often characterized by the omission of morphological suffixes and function words (grammatical morphemes), that they frequently have trouble with contractions and infinitives, and that their uses of pronouns and verb forms may be far from consistent. But although they may not speak very well, children with SLI can still be seen to have acquired a significant number of language skills. For example, English-speaking children with SLI typically speak in sentences that conform to a subject-verb-object order, they attempt to use pronouns, proper names, adjectives, and even modal operators, and they clearly understand the basic principles of verb tense.

Intensive efforts to identify the underlying causes of SLI have focused on a number of cognitive factors that are involved in mastering the more complex constructions with which these children have difficulty. For example, they may have trouble inhibiting nonsalient information and attending both to their own and to another speaker's use of grammatical inflections. Another factor involved in SLI may be the greater attention that is required to process grammatical elements that occur at the ends of words with a falling pitch (Tallal and Stark 1981). A third important factor concerns the varying complexity of the kinds of constructions a child must master (Leonard 1987). And finally, we need to consider in far greater detail the nature of the environment in which the child masters language—for example, perhaps such errors are a familiar feature of the child's linguistic environment (Owens 1996).

We have, then, two very different pictures, not just of the causes of SLI but indeed of the nature of SLI. It is important to be clear about how the two sides view each other's argument. From the generativist perspective, the interactionist approach trivializes SLI, for it ignores the one feature that makes SLI so fascinating: the putative fact that language can be selectively impaired. Surely what this tells us, according to the generativist, is that SLI is the result of a mutation in the gene that contains the "plan common to the grammars of all languages" (Pinker 1994: 22). The interactionist sees this view of the "paradigm" case of SLI as a generativist oversimplification that will be exposed as such by closer examination of subjects diagnosed as having SLI.

As is generally the case in contentious issues such as this, a significant part of the controversy stems from the radically divergent methodological orientations one finds in the two groups' respective writings. Generativists tend to focus on the presence or absence of syntactic constructions, and at that, they are mostly concerned with inflectional endings. This approach reinforces the picture of SLI as an isolated grammatical disorder. Yet, as I noted earlier, there are substantial indications in the literature that children diagnosed as having SLI invariably experience significant communicative and/or socioaffective challenges at a young age. The generativist regards the latter problems as secondary deficits, the consequences of a language impairment. The interactionist views them as causes rather than effects of SLI and, indeed, sees SLI itself as a secondary phenomenon (Greenspan 1997).

Were this debate between generativists and interactionists over the nature and causes of SLI simply a methodological issue, then it would, in principle, be possible to find a solution that would somehow reconcile each side's central concerns. But this is not simply an empirical issue. What is really at stake here is exactly the same issue we saw in the debate over ALR: whether language as such suddenly appears at some predetermined age in some predetermined form or gradually emerges as a means of coregulating and augmenting the primal activities in which the infant engages with her caregivers. In the latter view, the fact that a significant percentage of children may experience similar difficulties with specific grammatical constructions does not force us to describe all of their linguistic behaviors in nonlinguistic terms. Rather, it compels us to look more closely at the nature of the diverse skills that a child must master in mastering language.

The Nature of Language Skills

As we can see from the foregoing sections, generativists and interactionists are deeply divided over the very existence of borderline areas of language research. The source of this conflict lies in their having adopted such fundamentally differing views of the nature of *language skills*. The generativist treats "language skills" as a physical capacity, which, as such, must be mechanically explained. The interactionist insists that "the learning of linguistic skills crosses into other social and cognitive domains" (Goldstein and Hockenberger 1991: 403) and therefore must be normatively explained. Hence, the debate between the two camps over the findings obtained in ALR and the study of SLI is yet another example of a scientific polemic in which, although they might be using the same terms, neither side is talking about the same thing.

It is because the generativist defines language as a formal system that first emerged and then was genetically encoded at some point in the Pleistocene that he views language acquisition as a maturational rather than a developmental process. What the generativist has in mind here is the idea that certain parts of the neocortex are configured to detect patterned regularities in linguistic input (Marcus et al. 1999). Herein lies the reason why a normal child is said to pick up morphosyntax automatically: the "mind/brain" is said to contain a modular system that is "sensitive to abstract formal distinctions (for example, root versus derived, noun versus verb), more sophisticated than the kinds of "rules" that are explicitly taught, developing on a schedule not timed by environmental input, organized by principles that could not have been learned" (Pinker 1991: 534).

It is puzzling, however, that generativists should persist in describing this preprogrammed behavior as "a complex, specialized skill, which develops in the child spontaneously, without conscious effort or formal instruction, is deployed without awareness of its underlying logic, is qualitatively the same in every individual, and is distinct from more general abilities to process information or behave intelligently" (Pinker 1994: 18). For it is difficult to see in what sense one can refer to a behavior as a "skill" when its development is regarded as "a matter of growth and maturation of relatively fixed capacities, under appropriate external conditions" (Chomsky 1966). We are told that "it is fruitful to consider language as an evolutionary adaptation, like the eye" (Pinker 1994: 24). But the ability to see with 20/20 acuity is not a skill possessed by eyeballs (nor by agents).

In fact, the upshot of the generativist's reductionist argument is that all those concepts that are tied to the development of skills—such as practice, training, volition, and effort—have absolutely no bearing on language acquisition. Clearly, what is involved in the generativist's technical definition of language is a sweeping revision of our understanding of a complex ability. The generativist treats linguistic communication as a mechanical "translation" process (from "mentalese" into a natural language and vice versa) in much the same way that the words that appear on a visual display unit are the end result of a series of "translations" from a computer program's "high-level language" to the "machine language" (as performed by symbolic assemblers that convert the program into machine code). Likewise, when the generativist speaks of a child as "knowing" that a construction is grammatical or ungrammatical, he means this in the same sense that a computer scientist means when speaking of a program as "knowing" that a certain string is well formed or ill formed. Thus, the generativist's use of "knowledge" is not at all the same as that which occurs when one speaks of a child as knowing the rules of a game, which necessarily involves the possibility of being able to say when the child is following and when she is breaking those rules. But then, according to the generativist, this comparison is entirely misplaced, for there are said to be "major and fundamental differences between rules of language and rules of games. The former are biologically determined; the latter are arbitrary" (Lenneberg 1967: 2).

The generativist defends his use of the term "language skill" on the grounds that he is dealing with "rules of language" as conceived on the paradigm of Turing's analysis of calculable functions—that is, "mechanical rules" that are "computed." The ("mind/brain" of a) child learning how to speak is likened to a Turing machine that is formulating the structural rules contained in a text (Pinker 1994). Thus, the generativist is not being metaphorical when he suggests that "in certain fundamental respects we do not really learn language; rather, grammar grows in the mind" (Chomsky 1980: 64). The generativist is committed to the principle that a child cannot *learn* language. If a child—or an ape—does not possess the "abstract principles of language" (as defined by generativist precepts) at birth, then this "knowledge" cannot, despite any amount of strenuous effort by child, caregivers, teachers, or therapists, ever be acquired. And the reason why we are said to be wrong to treat the various skills that Kanzi or a child with SLI masters as demonstrating language proficiency is because these "uttered surface forms provide evidence about the properties of the abstract rules, but do not in themselves constitute language. It is the grammar, the set of abstract rules producing the utterances, that constitutes language, and therefore it is this grammar that must be characterized if we want to understand any language, even impaired language" (Gopnik et al. 1997: 114).

The upshot of the generativist analysis of language skills, therefore, is that we have to qualify what we mean when we describe a child as *trying* or *choosing* to speak like the other members of her community. Generativism requires us to describe a child acquiring language in the same way we would describe the operations of a computer program acquiring language, in all respects: *all* of the normative terms that one uses to talk about language development must be construed as potentially misleading expressions that are grounded in the "ordinary language" concept of language and hence must be abandoned once one has adopted a formal definition of "language." That is, all of the normative terms involved in the description of a child as a *linguistic agent* have to be subjected to reductionist analysis. What one is left with is indeed a computational device whose "linguistic processing" is "automatic, effortless, and uniform"—but only because it makes no sense to speak of a computer in the same way one speaks of a child mastering a skill, as *trying to speak,* or *making mistakes,* or *learning from its errors,* or *understanding an explanation,* or *observing* and *imitating* other people's behavior.

In place of the generativist view that "complex abilities like cognition [or language] are 'inside us' all along, albeit in smaller form, and get passed on to subsequent generations in that form, and just, as it were, 'grow' in individuals" (Richardson 1998: 2), the interactionist stresses that "human abilities are acquired through learning, and this normally involves conscious effort. Learning plays a large role in making people the individual adults they become, as well as equipping people with the skills and abilities they require. As an outcome of engaging in learning activities we gain various kinds of skills, and we also acquire useful knowledge" (Howe 1999: 18). This emphasis on a view of the child as *trying,* even *working* at becoming a member of her linguistic community (Shatz 1994) is an integral aspect of the interactionist argument that the linguistic world into which the child is entering is *enculturated* (Shanker and Taylor 2001).

Thus the debates over ALR and SLI bring to the fore the archetypal problem of how mechanistic reductionism subverts the essentially intentional and normative character of human abilities. That is, they highlight the problems involved in construing the concept of speaking "correctly" or "incorrectly" according to the paradigm of one's being mechanically guided by the construction and inference rules for deriving a well-formed formula in a formal system (Shanker 1998). For the concept of speaking correctly is fundamentally tied to an agent's intentions, to a society's norms, and to the communicative context in which a speech act occurs. Perhaps the greatest irony of all is that the generativist thesis entails that the normal child acquire "language skills" and "know" the "rules of language" in a way that has nothing to do with our ordinary understanding of "skills" and "knowledge." Whereas both Kanzi and the child with SLI acquire certain skills and know certain rules in the way that one normally uses the terms "skill" and "knowledge," their skills and knowledge are said to have nothing to do with language!

The Eliminability of "Language" and "Culture"

The debates over ALR and SLI vividly illustrate the problems that arise when one adopts a formal definition of language that excludes, a priori, the possibility of borderline areas of language research. Why not, then, just abandon the term "language" altogether? Surely what is important in the cases of ALR and SLI is whether or not we can describe Kanzi or a child with SLI as *understanding* a word or an utterance, or as *referring* to objects and people, or as *asking questions* and *explaining* the meaning of a symbol. Why not simply leave the matter at that: why introduce the vexatious question of whether or not Kanzi or the child has acquired *language* when the term is so contentious?

The answer lies in the very issue that is at stake in the debates over ALR and SLI. Generativists are prepared to concede that the behavior of the subjects involved can indeed be described in the terms just mentioned, but they insist that the subjects nonetheless cannot be described as possessing *language,* as defined in generativist terms (Pinker 1994; Wallman 1992). Hence, an eliminativist response to this generativist argument would be self-defeating. From the interactionist perspective, the whole point of this borderline research is that, by describing an ape or a child with SLI as, for example, understanding the meaning of an utterance or using words correctly, one sheds important light on the processes involved in the development of language skills and thence on the nature of language. That is, the reason why these subjects' behavior can be described in linguistic terms is precisely because this research forces us to abandon the formal definition of language proposed by the generativist.

Does a similar point apply to the debate over "culture"? Those who seek to eliminate the concept of culture are certainly aware of the various arguments that have been cited to defend its continuing usage. But they warn that even if the original use of culture was justified, the nature of contemporary society is vastly different from that in which anthropology first adopted culture as its touchstone. They worry that in the present environment, the use of culture has become irrevocably politicized, and thus that any academic endorsement of the term will prove more harmful than beneficial. And why, they ask, should we keep such a problematic concept when we can do all of the work the defenders want simply by limiting ourselves to describing such factors as the "style, taste, cosmology, ethos, sensibility, desire, ideology, aspirations, and predispositions" of the members of a society (Trouillot, this volume) or the "customs, beliefs, and practices" of a society (Hann, this volume). What all of these factors have in common, however, is precisely that they are *cultural,* and not just social traits.

To see the significance of this point, we might consider why the interactionist argues that language development must be seen as an *enculturation,* and not simply as a social process. What the interactionist has in mind is that the concepts of language and culture are internally related and mutually uneliminable. The difference between language and the "hard-wired" communication systems that we see, for example, in ant and bee colonies is not simply a matter of complexity, for to acquire a language is to enter into a community's distinctive way of being-in-the-world (Basso 1988). That is, language development involves a way of thinking, acting, feeling, and communicating that is "distributed across time, space and social networks wider than the one in which we typically live our lives" (Fogel 1993: 161). To develop language skills, therefore, is to learn the ways of behaving that *count*, within a community, as the performance of some culturally conceived act (Shanker and Taylor 2001).

The debate over the eliminability of culture is further complicated by the political dimension of the issue, which raises the troubling question of whether it would be possible to counteract racist misuses of culture by removing anthropology's stamp of approval for the term. An obvious problem here is that it is not clear that the political argument for eliminability is feasible or, for that matter, desirable. One cannot help thinking of the many disturbing precedents in which ideological factors were allowed to intrude on the development of a science. No better example of this phenomenon can be found than the institutionalization of Pavlovian theory and the suppression of Vygotsky's ideas about social interactionism within the Soviet Union. Moreover, one must question whether it is reasonable to expect that the political wrongs we are concerned with can be avoided simply by prohibiting all talk of "culture." The problems encountered with the reification of culture are just as likely to arise with whatever new concept or cluster of concepts is officially sanctioned in anthropological circles.

Perhaps the most effective strategy that anthropology can adopt to counter the growing number of racist misuses of culture is to engage in the sorts of in-depth critiques that Trouillot and Hann present in this volume: for example, surveying the institutional history and early uses of culture and its many different uses in contemporary writings, and contrasting these uses with the dangerous confusions that arise when the concept is reified. The very existence of this volume attests to the importance of such an effort. But then the advocate of the eliminability thesis goes a step further, maintaining that it is possible to reduce culture to some cluster of defining features, each of which can be understood without appealing to or presupposing the concept of culture. But far from eliminating the concept, what Trouillot and Hann really show us is the importance—both political and academic—of clarifying it by showing why culture cannot be reduced to a cluster of "programs" or "modules" that are part of the human genetic makeup. That is, by carefully analyzing culture in all of the foregoing terms, what Trouillot and Hann show us is why these factors *must* be construed in cultural as opposed to biological or mechanical terms—where the "must" here is logical and not political.

To be sure, we are still left with all the problems involved in identifying—let alone understanding—a community in terms of learned thought and behavior patterns that persist over time and can be observed in disparate social groups (Duranti 1997). Yet the tension involved in identifying commonalities and differences in social structures that are constantly shifting is very much one of the dynamics of anthropology. And it is precisely this dynamic that the essentialist definition of culture would remove. As in the debates over ALR and SLI, perhaps the most important point to bear in mind is simply that it must be possible for these borderline disputes to take place: as much in regard to whether some social behavior—such as language!—is a cultural phenomenon as to whether some communicative behavior is a linguistic practice. Far from seeking to constrain these debates, we should be seeking to clarify the reasons why and in what situations anthropologists continue to employ the concept of culture, and above all, what sorts of questions and what sorts of insights are thereby afforded.

Notes

This chapter emerged as the result of the stimulating discussions I enjoyed at the Wenner-Gren meeting in Morelia in 2000; I would like to acknowledge here my debt to all of the participants in this session. I am particularly grateful to Barbara King, whose influence on this chapter extends far beyond the many comments she made on earlier drafts. Finally, I thank Talbot Taylor, with whom I have been working on these problems for several years, and who has done so much to shape my views.

1. I refer here to the behaviorist repudiation of "mind" and all terms "mental." In Pavlov's view, psychology's concern with explaining the operations of the mind should be regarded as the greatest obstacle to its becoming a bona fide science. Not only are mental terms conspicuously missing from his writings, but indeed, the students in his lab were compelled to pay a fine should they slip into using such "barbarisms" in their research.

2. "He" is the apposite pronoun here, because SLI is more likely to be found in males than females. Also, children with SLI are more likely to have parents and siblings with a history of language problems.

Part 3

Patterns and Continuities

seven

Archaeology and Culture: Sites of Power and Process

Rita P. Wright

The concept of culture has a long and privileged history in anthropology. In archaeology, much as in the other subfields, we have grappled with its definition, and some have questioned its usefulness. Articulation of material evidence and its association with patterns has given way to an increasing awareness of both similarities and differences within societies and to research programs designed to disentangle dominant ideologies from more local knowledge.

This chapter begins with a brief discussion of the history of the culture concept in archaeology. Although it is not my purpose to provide a comprehensive review of the culture concept, I do demonstrate similarities and differences between the concept's uses and abuses in archaeology and the wider field of anthropology. The remainder of the chapter consists of examples from feminist archaeology and from studies of social boundaries and technologies that have recently been undertaken by archaeologists. These studies show that even when archaeologists have not directly confronted the culture concept, archaeological scholarship has unfolded in such a way that the concept's usefulness has been implicitly accepted. In that sense, the identification of cultural patterns is a means, not an end (Kohl 1993: 17).

Archaeologists deal with many scales of analysis, and the examples I offer demonstrate how the use of the culture concept can provide a basis from which to articulate patterns in material culture at different scales. An example on the microscale is based on textual evidence from southern Mesopotamia in the third millennium B.C.E. It provides a glimpse into how feminist archaeologists have engaged with the culture concept. A second example, this time at the macroscale, examines crosscutting distributions of material culture and technologies as means of identifying shifting social boundaries. Such boundaries are sites of negotiation that represent aggregate, long-term historical processes involving a wide range of social groups.

Archaeology and Concepts of Culture

The first World Archaeological Congress, held in Southampton, England, in 1986, was a defining moment for many archaeologists with respect to the culture concept. Although the political circumstances surrounding the congress were complex, suffice it to say that a 1984 United Nations economic and cultural boycott against South Africa and a ruling by the Southampton local council prevented South African archaeologists from participating. One result was that the social context of knowledge production emerged as a major issue among scholars in attendance and among others who convened at a separate conference in Brussels, in which South African archaeologists were included. Serious issues came to the fore concerning the potential tyranny of lumping the beliefs of individuals under a single category such as culture. Some questioned whether cultures could actually be considered "entities," given circumstances in which colleagues who might or might not have supported South African nationalist policies were excluded from the meeting.

The discussions also were powerful reminders of the political and practical concerns attendant on the use of the culture concept in scholarly research. Debates covered a variety of issues, but one that emerged as especially germane was how to interpret crosscutting distributions of materials in the archaeological record. On the one hand, as Stephen Shennan explained, archaeologists had not recognized that this "untidiness" (the crosscutting distributions) represented "simply the contingent interrelations of different distributions produced by different factors," rather than "entities" or "cultures" (Shennan 1989: 13). On the other hand, he acknowledged that archaeologists bore responsibility for building on the culture concept, because cultures clearly are not historical actors but are entities constructed by archaeologists, who cannot know whether any group self-consciously identified itself with the materials involved. Archaeological scholarship might be better served by engaging in an active dialogue with culture that recognizes both its political and its practical constraints. Shennan concluded as follows (1989: 14):

> What are we left with at this point? Cultures have been dismissed as imaginary entities which simply confuse an analysis of social and

historical processes. Ethnic identity appears to be an evanescent situational construct.... Is the answer, then, to dismiss all questions relating to such topics as meaningless and irrelevant? This is tempting but unsatisfactory, since the concerns from which they arise are valid even if approaches to them have been misconceived... human practices (and therefore local interpretative principles) *do* vary from place to place and the patterns change over time. Furthermore, the phenomenon of ethnicity plays an important role in the modern world.

In voicing concerns like those expressed by Shennan, many archaeologists draw upon an intellectual tradition that differs in some respects from that of anthropology as a whole. Although there are many family resemblances among anthropologists, there also are differences. Of particular relevance to this review are differences among Old World archaeologists, who, though anthropologists, have been influenced by European prehistory, which developed out of a tradition that emphasized material remains in the context of museum display. Archaeologists in Scandinavia were labeling assemblages of artifacts as representative of cultures or civilizations as early as the 1860s, although the term "culture" was not systematically defined until the 1911 publication of Gustaf Kossinna's *Die Herkunft der Germanen,* which glorified German prehistory as the product of a pure master race. The archaeologist V. Gordon Childe introduced Kossinna's ideas to Great Britain in the 1920s, but like Boas, he rejected racist intents and attempted to free the culture concept of its ethnic implications (Veit 1986). Childe's definition did follow Kossina's emphasis on the recurrence of certain artifact types as representative of individual cultures. Like Boas, he attempted to identify particular cultural groups and to trace out their histories. His observations, however, were based upon changes traced over several thousand years of history. Childe believed that by identifying recurring assemblages, archaeologists could draw social inferences and "reconstruct the behavior pattern that guarantees their association" (1956: 112).

The functionalist interpretation implied by Childe's definition appears to have become part of Americanist archaeology much later in its history than in Europe. For example, although Boas's student Alfred Kroeber (1916) conducted seriation experiments with potsherds found near Zuni Pueblo in the American Southwest and used the term "culture" to describe his findings, it is unclear whether the word had any deeper meaning than that of a simple descriptive term at that time. Still, it was the works of Kroeber and Boas that later inspired the archaeologist W. W. Taylor (1948) to reject the emphasis on classification and description of artifacts and to adopt a definition of culture based on "mental constructs and viewing material remains as products of culture rather than culture itself" (Trigger 1989: 277).

Although there are archaeologists who still find Taylor's and Childe's definitions of culture valid, major changes in theory and method in archaeology during the 1960s emphasized new definitions of culture. Archaeologists drew on a number of theories—for example, Marxist, structuralist, and poststructuralist—but the one that dominated was labeled the "new archaeology." Largely an Americanist phenomenon, it combined concepts from Leslie White's systems theory and Julian Steward's cultural ecology. This ecosystems approach, adopted during the 1960s, 1970s, and 1980s, emphasized the reconstruction of "processes" of cultural evolution, which were expected to follow well-defined courses, though within a multilinear framework, because sociocultural systems took distinctive forms that were the results of adaptations to the environment. Culture, then, was defined as the means by which groups adapted to their environment—an extrasomatic means of adaptation. Lewis Binford, one of the new archaeology's major proponents, was not silent about "cognitive systems" but, rather, dismissive. He believed they were rationalizations and means of enculturation that ensured that individual behaviors fulfilled the functional needs of the ecosystem. In many ways similar to then current practices in cultural anthropology (Wolf 1999: 59), the ecosystems approach resulted in partial views of culture in which behavior was privileged over ideas.

Perhaps the most basic differences between archaeology and cultural anthropology with respect to the culture concept lie in the accumulation of intellectual baggage referred to by many cultural anthropologists and made explicit by Rolph Trouillot (1991 and this volume). First, cultural anthropology became identified with the study of "savages" or non-Western peoples, who "were thought to be fundamentally different both in essence and in practice" from their Western counterparts (Trouillot, this volume). In distinction, Old World archaeology strongly emphasized the study of "civilizations," many of which were interpreted using theories developed in the context of modern, Western societies. Childe, for example, adapted Marxist ideas to his studies of prehistoric states. Second, in cultural anthropology, ethnographic research fostered a view of cultures as self-contained units. Variations among groups were either downplayed or dismissed, thus contributing to the essentialisms that now cast doubt on the concept's usefulness. In archaeology, on the other hand, patterns of artifact distributions kept reminding researchers of the extent of contact among different groups in ancient times. Although I doubt that many cultural anthropologists lost sleep over these data, in archaeology, especially in Old World studies, the development of interpretive models for understanding such distributions occupied major research programs.

In any event, important shifts in the theories and methods employed in archaeology have again taken place since the mid-1980s. Some of them reflect on concepts of culture, although as a topic it has been tangential to more basic theoretical debates. As the two examples provided in this essay show, "encounters" with the culture concept are most apparent in the ways in which scholarship has unfolded, rather than in direct engagements with the concept.[1]

Archaeology at the Microscale: Investigating Culture and Power

Archaeologists typically trace the beginnings of gender analysis to 1984, when scholars, predominantly women, began to question the theory and practice of processual and postprocessual archaeology. In particular, they criticized the almost total emphasis on normative behaviors and claims to "scientific" objectivity that were thought to have been major achievements of processual archaeology. They also raised basic questions germane to both processual and postprocessual approaches concerning the ideologically charged nature of the production of knowledge and the narrow historical reconstructions that privileged the study of past behaviors that, in our contemporary society, are associated with males (Conkey and Spector 1984). Since that time, growth in the literature has been impressive and far-reaching, providing new views of key and lesser-known periods in prehistory worldwide, filling the gaps in some of its unexamined aspects, and developing theories and terms that are gender inclusive.

One major focus of feminist archaeologists has been the negotiation of power and difference in the context of state-level societies. Although few researchers have addressed the culture concept directly, their attempts to identify the ideological and/or organizational means by which states maintain themselves is a tacit acceptance of its usefulness as a means of analysis. For example, Elizabeth Brumfiel (1996) examined imagery in pre-Aztec and Aztec settlements to compare the structure of gender ideologies and look for transformations in the negotiation of gender. Official Aztec imagery depicts a male-dominant ideology in which women are represented as mutilated—in much the same way the state represented the subjugation of its enemies—or as kneeling, suggestive of modesty and industriousness (Brumfiel 1996: 158).[2] In community-level imagery, by contrast, female figurines, which were produced by local specialists, were used in households and embodied a different view of women, one in which they were associated with curing, fertility, and health rituals. Brumfiel interpreted the increased abundance of female figurines in some community-level contexts during middle and later Aztec periods as indicating a preference for local rather than state ideologies. Importantly, the figurines demonstrate the negotiation of gender and resistance to official state ideals. In this example, the culture concept is embedded in the notion of the "state" as the dominant power behind a drive toward coherence. Rather than reifying homogeneity, the concept offers an effective means of analysis to account for difference. As Brumfiel put it: "States have the ability to place certain issues on the popular agenda ... [but] they do not have an unfailing capacity to dictate popular consciousness" (1996: 161).

An example from my own research rests upon written sources from southern Mesopotamia (between the Tigris and Euphrates Rivers and south of Baghdad, Iraq) in the third millennium B.C.E. These official documents clearly convey the narrow perspective of state-run organizations and bureaucratic matters, but when read "against the grain," they offer a rich source of material.[3] They frequently include information about the organization of labor, and they provide a means for reconstructing gendered divisions of labor and the negotiation of kinship, ethnicity, and class. Coming from temple and palace archives, the documents list names, legal statuses, professions, and amounts of compensation to people engaged in labor for those institutions. Though the texts are one-sided and clearly do not represent all members of the society, they yield insights into some of the social categories adopted by temple and palace institutions during the Ur III period (circa 2112–2004 B.C.E.). Although recorded for bookkeeping purposes, they demonstrate how power over men and women was exerted and experienced in the context of a set of legal categories (and thus compensation) imposed by the state. As in the Aztec example, I use the culture concept to tease out the degree to which powerful, bureaucratic states were able to dominate cultural ideals and political economies.

During the Ur III period, the southern part of Mesopotamia was unified by a ruling dynasty. Although a city-state type of government prevailed throughout Mesopotamian history, the Ur III dynasty was the second to unify southern Mesopotamia, an earlier one having collapsed after years of warfare. Throughout its history, whether unified under a single dynasty or divided into independent city-states, southern Mesopotamia was characterized by a cultural overlay that is clearly identifiable in monumental architecture, artistic conventions, uniform material culture, and so on. Religious concepts and myths preserved in documents, though ever changing and modified, leave little doubt that important concepts and worldviews were shared among large segments of society throughout the southern Mesopotamian alluvium.

Until recently, few questions were asked about the degree to which powerful dynasties exerted their will over the Mesopotamian citizenry. An examination of documentary and archaeological evidence by Elizabeth Stone (1999), however, has shown that not all citizens were equally tightly controlled, nor were kings as powerful as scholars once thought. It now appears that local city councils elected leaders and made other important decisions. Many kings were drawn to leadership from ethnic groups other than those that dominated the local population. Much as among the Yoruba, kings served as unifying symbols, but their royal power was restricted. Even during periods of unification, as in the case of the Ur III dynasty, local councils maintained ties to city-centered institutions that most likely remained potential threats to dynastic rule.

Still, individual citizens who were not among the landowning men, who sat on local councils, their families, or the priests and priestesses in temples were situated somewhat differently. One way in which to approach them is through examination of texts that record artisan production. The Mesopotamian documents are a valuable resource for elaborating on the effectiveness of the rulers of early states in imposing their views on local populations. An additional advantage is that they are free of the influence of capitalism and world economies that have made some archaeologists shy away from using ethnographic sources.

My interest in this topic is from the perspective of the organization of labor and the negotiation of power in state-level societies. A basic premise held by many archaeologists, largely derived from modern contexts and the early writings of V. Gordon Childe, has been that leaders in powerful states controlled the production and distribution of specialized products. Childe thought that with the advent of specialization and the social divisions it implied, a kinship form of organization would be replaced by allegiance to and rule by political leaders. Archival sources that record labor arrangements in Mesopotamia are ideally suited to assessing the effectiveness of early states in promoting their political and economic agendas.

Artisans listed in the documents worked in state and temple workshops of varying sizes. A temple might employ 150 to 270 persons, and larger workshops, 500. A government household in one town controlled 2,000 workers, while in another, 6,000 weavers were employed. It has been estimated that the total number of workers in state and temple service during the Ur III period was 300,000 to 500,000 (Waetzoldt 1972, 1987). Accounting records in workshops were highly structured according to a basic debit and credit system. They included information on such things as expected performance against real services, raw materials brought into the workshop, and finished products completed. The debit side comprised lists of total liabilities as against expected and total performance. Some documents include the quality of materials produced and their destinations, as well as the names of workers, their ethnicity (derived from their names), their state-imposed legal designations, and the amount of compensation (see Wright 1998: 64 for specific amounts).

Artisans engaged in a variety of crafts are recorded, but in this chapter I concentrate on two crafts—weaving and forestry—in order to highlight the diversity of legal categories and the potential for negotiating social identities during the Ur III period.[4] Weavers were responsible for the production of cloth, predominantly of wool, and they engaged in a number of activities associated with the craft, from plucking sheep to weaving different grades of cloth. Although no one has ever located the workshops (references are made to repairing them) or housing for the weavers, it is assumed that they lived and worked in the temple or palace "precinct" in which they were employed. Foresters were employed in forests near their homes. In addition to clearing wood in the forest, they made wooden objects such as tools and furniture.

The most dramatic differences between weavers and foresters were based on their gender, ethnicity, and legal status. All weavers were women, and many of them were slaves (as denoted by the designation for slave, *sag*) who were permanently attached to the workshop year-round. Many, perhaps the majority, of weaver slaves had nonlocal names, suggesting that they had been purchased or were prisoners of war, a factor that is well documented for the Ur III period.[5] The term $geme_2$ also appears among the lists of weavers. It applies to semifree women, many of whom were indentured persons who left the workshops upon debt payment. It is unclear whether there were weavers who engaged freely in state employment.

All the foresters listed, on the other hand, were men, which was the case for practically all state workers except weavers and millers. The major differences between weavers and foresters and among the foresters were their legal designations. One group of foresters, listed as $erin_2$, were employed for periods of service on a seasonal basis. For the remainder of the year, while not employed by the state, they were free to practice their craft independent of it. A second legal category, *UN-il*, consisted of workers employed throughout the year.

These texts reveal basic economic and social differences among and between weavers and foresters and provide a gauge against which to assess the state's effectiveness in dominating subordinate classes and maintaining coherence. Economically, foresters in the legal category *erin$_2$* were the only workers with access to their own means of production when not engaged in state service, since only they were regularly allotted plots of land. Compensation for other foresters and weavers included food allotments that were barely at subsistence level and quantities of wool sufficient to produce a single garment per year.

Among foresters, coworkers were related brothers, sons, and grandsons. When more than one worker was recorded in a group, they were listed using patronyms, and younger men were listed as sons of older workers. Moreover, inheritance practices attest to the importance of kinship affiliations among foresters. Supervisors were drawn from men in the various kin groups, and upon a supervisor's death, a junior kinsman, usually a son, inherited the land allotted to his father and took his place in the hierarchy of the work group. Although the texts take us only so far, we can imagine that hierarchies within working units of foresters might have reflected the village organization in which the foresters lived.

Weavers, in distinction, consisted of unrelated adult women, their daughters, and their prepubescent sons. In the accounts, women were not referred to as "wife of," as was customary among high-ranking women. Children of weavers were referred to by their matronym, and their legal status as semifree or slave was the same as their mother's. Unlike foresters, who worked alongside their own kinsmen, women were assigned to specially designated groups, each composed of twenty women comprising diverse ethnic groups.

Read against the grain, these documents also reveal a state strategy of following notions of gender that were already deeply embedded in Mesopotamian society and were widely reflected in popular beliefs. Images of women producing cloth are known from as early as the fourth millennium B.C.E., and in later written poetry, myths, and inheritance records, associations were made between women and weaving. For example, the weaving deity, Uttu, was female; a queen's fertility was referred to as a warp on the loom; the mother of a large family was called "the clothbeam with its finished cloth" (Jacobsen 1987: 85); and a dowry included wool and weaving implements (Postgate 1992: 192).

This gender ideology might account for the dominance of the craft by women in state and temple workshops and for the explicit exclusion of males, who were assigned to other labor groups after pubescence, whereas daughters followed their mothers in the craft. State strategies of employment appear, therefore, to have taken into account popular ideologies that identified women and reproduction with weaving (Wright 1996, 2000).

But what can be concluded about culture and the effectiveness of states in imposing their dominant ideologies and material interests? The Ur III state clearly developed a strategy for imposing its view of economic and political coherence by establishing legal categories that were entangled with kinship, ethnic, and gender ideologies, and it was these legal categories that effectively established the context in which workshop producers negotiated their social identities. Artisans, as a social category and as active agents, were constrained by a rigid bureaucracy in which their skills, though essential to the economy of state and temple institutions, were subject to rigid work rules, output requirements, and compensation amounts, which were governed by the legal designations the artisans were assigned. These designations appear to have outweighed all other considerations.

Within the system of legal designations, however, some individuals were able to maintain other affiliations—namely, extended family ties among foresters—in which, conceivably, loyalty to kin outweighed attachment to official institutional workshops. In such circumstances, sentiments of identity likely conformed to the social categories of a person's village and kinship group, and political alliances and shared concepts might not have conformed to those articulated by state and temple. Among the foresters, therefore, we see the glimmer of a degree of power in a different domain that might have extended to workers in other professions. In distinction, women weavers were diverse and least likely to have had an effective means of promoting their material interests. In only one context—their efforts to escape and return to their ethnic groups—do they emerge as social actors. Their most salient identities, as viewed from the perspective of the documents, were those of slave (a legal status) and member of an ethnic group. As such, they were people who moved outside the fold of Mesopotamian society and had little access to power and prestige.

These examples suggest that although state-based institutional interventions in the name of "culture" were a powerful force in Mesopotamia, some individuals were able to negotiate, modify, and/or maintain their own ideological and material interests. In this there is, as Penelope Brown remarks elsewhere in this volume, something that is "larger than the sum of the individual parts" that is worth identifying. It highlights drives toward coherence amid overlapping webs of difference.

Archaeology at the Macroscale: Making and Using Things

Although the foregoing example demonstrates the processes by which culture is negotiated and "made," it does not speak directly to the way archaeologists work with material culture, the focus of the following case study. What of contexts in which investigation is dependent upon material objects and not words? Are there ways in which people "speak" other than with words? Here I examine this question in the context of material culture, technology, and social processes at the boundaries of cultures.

Material remains originate in social contexts. When archaeologists observe material culture patterns, they are mapping social formations in spatially and temporally specific contexts. These formations are embedded in the everyday happenings and practices in which people engaged, sometimes face-to-face in small communities and sometimes at broader intra- or interregional scales. Embedded in these interactions are symbolic expressions of the aesthetic tastes and needs of certain segments of societies. As items of consumption and exchange, artifacts represent social relationships between producers and consumers. Even the technologies with which objects are produced are embedded in social contexts and patterns of thought that are inseparable from their producers (Dobres 2000).

Research on the mixing of remnants of material culture provides a means of identifying social groups and the construction of new identities and worldviews. The manner in which such research has unfolded suggests that, as in the case of feminist archaeologists, there has been an implicit acceptance of the culture concept. Among topics that have been addressed in this way is culture contact between Europeans and Native Americans. Kent Lightfoot and Antoinette Martinez (1995), for instance, examined the responses of Native American groups to interactions with Russian traders, their *situational* manipulation of identities and political alliances, and the transformation of some segments of the population but not others. The long-term nature of archaeological remains makes it possible to trace a historical sequence from precontact to contact and postcontact periods and to explore changes in ethnic, cultural, and societal interactions. Edward Schortman and Seiichi Nakamura (1991) studied material patterns of interaction between two neighboring groups on the Maya periphery in the Late Classic period (A.D. 600–950). They argued that competing factional groups adopted salient social identities that coalesced around particularly important resources. These identities were discernible in the distribution of material forms such as monumental structures, in intra-site planning, in the utilization of unusual building techniques and construction materials, and in stylistic differences in sculpture and ceramics. In another study along these lines, Gil Stein (1999) conducted research on early "colonization" in northern Mesopotamia at about 4000–3000 B.C.E. He established the complex nature of cultural affiliations, in which two separate nodes of power with different forms of value coexisted in what appears to be one of the first examples of colonization in human history.

These studies and others have shown that cultural groups can be identified through their interactions with individuals and groups from outside their social domains—for example, with artisans, traders, colonizers, or coexisting polities. Interactions at social boundaries are perfect sites in which to observe processes by which culture is reorganized, produced, or reproduced, because objects and information that move among people and networks develop out of the social, political, and economic activities in which they are involved. Such processes are observable because the pattern of activations "is not haphazard but reflects the integration of social groups along its paths" (Trinkaus 1987: 1).

Technology and Culture

One way in which to observe the interaction of social groups is through the study of technology. Recently, some anthropologists have turned to the works of Durkheim and Mauss and to theories of technology as learned cultural practices and forms of communication. The French structuralist archaeologist André Leroi-Gourhan (1943) was interested in the cognitive aspects of technologies and focused on sequences of production (the *chaine operatoire*) that constituted the learned moves in technological processes. His primary interest in terms of the *chaine operatoire* lay in European Paleolithic industries as reflections of changes in cognitive processes in human evolution. Along similar lines, the French anthropologist Pierre Lemmonier (1992: 5) advocated a return to conceiving of a technology as—here he quotes Mauss (1935) in his own translation—"action which is *effective* and *traditional* (and in this it is no different from a magical, religious, or symbolic action) [that is] felt by the [actor to be] . . . mechanical, physical or physico-chemical . . . and . . . pursued with this aim in view." According to this perspective, gestures and actions are learned processes by which individuals habitually perform specific actions on matter, and those actions become identifiers or signatures of social groups.

Closely related, but apparently independently conceived, is the idea of technological style developed by Heather Lechtman (1977) and Arthur Steinberg (Lechtman and Steinberg 1979). Lechtman and Steinberg drew an analogy between technologies and the visual and musical arts, stating that technologies, like the arts, reflect cultural preoccupations. In Lechtman's words (1977: 7), these preoccupations are expressed in "the very style of the technology itself." In that sense, a technological style is a reflection of basic ideologies that go beyond production and are shared by the artisan and his or her culture. The act of making or shaping an object involves putting together component parts in a structural hierarchy that corresponds to an artisan's sensual and imaginative perception.

Using examples from ethnohistoric and materials research on Andean metallurgy, Lechtman reconstructed the way symbolic systems, concepts of the universe, and gilding processes involving gold, silver, and copper came together as essential elements in metal objects created by pre-Columbian Andean artisans. In producing objects, artisans believed it was necessary to make surfaces that were faithful to their inner character. Therefore, instead of simply coating the exteriors of objects with gold in order to achieve the desired color effect, they built up gold, copper, and other metals in layers as part of the metal alloying process in producing the object. This vision was also apparent in textile production, in which designs were incorporated into the structure of the cloth rather than simply sewn onto the exterior. In both instances, the technical process and visual properties of the end products were expressions of cultural ideals. There was no distinction between technology and culture because the material, the social, and the symbolic were manifested in a single process.

These new understandings of technological styles and the *chaine operatoire* demonstrate that material culture provides a strong basis from which to identify stylistic and technological practices with specific groups, but they require modification. The actions they describe appear to be culturally bound, as if they represent a set of values universal to a social group, but in fact, restricting this vision to smaller subgroups may be more compatible with the evidence. The objects discussed by Lechtman clearly fit with this interpretation, since they were produced for an elite class of persons that may have dominated the Moche artisans who produced the objects studied, and they need not refer to the culture as a whole.

Material Culture, Technology, and Social Boundaries

The preceding discussion provides a framework with which to demonstrate how archaeologists use material culture and technologies to identify social groups and map social formations, either in face-to-face communities or in larger intersocietal contexts. Culture is implicated because, given that objects embody actions performed on matter as well as the social relations produced and reproduced in everyday practices, objects represent the signatures of actors making and remaking their worlds.

My understanding of intergroup contact is that it has been a normal part of social and cultural life since at least twelve thousand years ago, when humans began to settle into permanent communities and surround themselves with objects. Ceramics, one of the most durable objects, and other items of material culture were often transported for utilitarian reasons, but they also served as symbols of affiliation for those who produced them and as trophies for those who consumed them, proclaiming contact with worlds beyond the local community. From an exhibition of Asian storage jars curated by Louise Cort at the Smithsonian's Freer Gallery, I recently learned that in seventeenth-century Southeast Asia, people believed imported jars traveled long distances on their own, even to marry and produce offspring!

But if anthropologists are able to define social units on the basis of patterns in material objects, then dare we call those units cultures? Or is it better to label the "conceptual kernel" something like style or ideology, as Trouillot (this volume) suggests, or social organization, technology, custom, as others suggested at the Wenner-Gren symposium? I find culture a more explanatory concept than any of the others proposed, for the reasons discussed earlier. As Fredrik Barth noted during the symposium, but speaking on the other side of this issue, tools do not breed each other (contrary to the seventeenth-century Southeast Asian belief noted earlier). Here, I have tried to show that material culture and technologies are not "out there" but closely represent concepts and actions shared by social groups.

When archaeologists encounter social boundaries, signaled by mixed but patterned assemblages of material remains, they are immediately drawn to the works of Fredrik Barth, especially his *Ethnic Groups and Boundaries* (1969a) and *Cosmologies in the Making* (1987). In my own research I have found Alexander Lesser's "Social Fields and the Evolution of Society" (1961) and Eric Wolf's *Europe and the People without History* (1982) important, and the works of frontier theorists (for example, Lamar and Thompson 1981) useful. These writings remind us of the following:

1. Populations never act in isolation, because external influences are virtually universal. Lesser referred to these as matrices of human association, or social fields. Intersocietal contact is not mere happenstance but a normal part of human social processes (Lesser 1961: 41ff.).
2. Among interacting groups (ethnic, kinship, friendship, etc.), there is agreement on conceptual categories, and these are generally understood by symbols of various kinds.
3. Viewed from a somewhat different perspective, people with similar identities unite to differentiate themselves from those with other identities.
4. Boundaries are places in which individuals, interest groups, and institutions reorganize and regenerate themselves, in which societies are "constructed" or reconstructed (Eisenstadt 1986: 237), and in which "cultural self-reproduction" occurs (Kopytoff 1987: 35).
5. Interactions represent numerous social networks that crosscut a broad scope of activities, which may generate change but also may contribute to the maintenance of stability. Therefore, it is important to take a long-term historical view in which sequences of interaction are observed (Lamar and Thompson 1981).

Fields of Action: Frontiers on the Indo-Iranian Borderlands

In the early twentieth century, the archaeologist Sir Aurel Stein (1929, 1931, 1937) undertook several treks in the Indo-Iranian borderlands and brought to light cultures not previously known. During the same period, the third-millennium-B.C.E. cities of Mohenjo-daro and Harappa in present-day Pakistan were first being excavated and named as parts of the Indus Valley civilization. Stein's research took him to Iranian and (now) Pakistani Baluchistan where he discovered archaeological materials that were not easily placed within the framework of past finds elsewhere. He was able to identify a number of "recurrent assemblages" that were both chronologically and spatially distinct. Of particular relevance to this discussion are two that correspond to a separation between eastern

Iran and western Pakistan, although Stein also found materials suggestive of cultural mixing. In particular, a distinctive painted grey ware was distributed throughout the borderlands. Later scholars suggested that the presence of this artifact in the first half of the third millennium—its distribution extending to the coastal and interior regions of the Arabian peninsula (mainly the present-day United Arab Emirates), although it is now known to be even more extensively distributed (see Méry 2000)—signaled a sphere of interaction among emerging elites and was suggestive of a political hierarchy that preceded the development of more complex societies in the Indus Valley in Pakistan and India and in the Helmand basin from Afghanistan to eastern Iran (Lamberg-Karlovsky and Tosi 1973).

The Indo-Iranian borderlands are marked by great ecological diversity. On the whole, the topography is rugged, consisting of mountainous terrain and desert tracks, and travel today, as in the past, is largely through mountain passes. More hazardous routes run through hill country and the desert to the west, but without camels they are unlikely pathways. The Helmand River cuts a great swath through parts of Afghanistan and may have been traversed along its banks. Between eastern Iran and western Pakistan lies the world's largest mine for lapis lazuli, a precious stone that was highly valued and distributed throughout the greater Near East. The two largest settlements in eastern Iran and western Pakistan show evidence of the manufacture of lapis ornaments. These were not centers devoted to trade, however, for the economy was based primarily on agrarian pursuits, with only limited trading. My principal point is that although third-millennium-B.C.E. settlements appear to have been isolated enclaves, distributions of materials and documented migrations in more recent history clearly indicate that people have been able to travel through these lands with regularity, even with limited transportation.

Settlements appeared in the borderlands very early in prehistory—for example, in western Pakistan (Baluchistan), there is evidence for domestication at 6500 B.C.E.—and they grew in size throughout the third millennium B.C.E. (Jarrige et al. 1995). But contrary to the conclusions reached by Lamberg-Karlovsky and Tosi (1973), wealth and status differences suggestive of an emerging elite are absent. House sizes and contents are fairly uniform, and burials, one of the primary bases on which statements of difference are made—though often replete with precious goods from afar such as turquoise, marine shell, and lapis—exhibit few distinctions. For example, at Shahr-i Sokhta, a site in eastern Iran, the types and quantities of grave goods and the treatment of

Egalitarian

interments in an extensive cemetery are fairly uniform. The only indicators of individual identities appear in the form of artisan tool kits buried with several individuals (Tosi 1983).

But how to account for the widespread distribution of materials in the absence of an exchange system controlled by an emerging hierarchy?[6] One way to approach this question is through an analysis of widely distributed artifacts with the intent of observing small-scale exchanges at the boundaries of social groups. Working with Stein's collections and recently excavated materials from eastern Iran and western Pakistan, I chose a single, distinctive, painted grey-ware ceramic with a broad distribution.[7] My three-part analysis (Wright 1989) began with a typological study designed to define the morphological characteristics of grey wares by identifying clusters of attributes such as vessel form and design elements. Second, I conducted an intensive laboratory analysis in order to reconstruct methods of manufacture as a means of assessing levels of sophistication and uniformity in production methods. Third, neutron activation analyses were designed to identify the chemical fingerprints of clays in order to identify production loci.

Not surprisingly, the results were not straightforward but revealed the complex and nuanced ways in which morphological, manufacturing, and resource signatures reflected different forms of societal interaction. Considering earlier suggestions that grey-ware distributions represented a vast interaction sphere (Lamberg-Karlovsky and Tosi 1973) in which a single dominant group controlled production and distribution, I expected to find a limited number of vessel forms and design clusters, uniform manufacturing procedures, and only one or two clay sources and manufacturing centers. Instead, I discovered significant variability in vessel forms and designs that separated the sherds into distinguishable groups conforming to the cultural divisions between eastern Iran and western Pakistan previously made by Stein, which were based on overall differences in material assemblages in the two regions. Finally, the results of neutron activation analysis identified at least five different clay sources dispersed throughout the region, indicating that the grey wares were produced in several different regions and at a number of settlements.

The technological style of the painted grey wares, based on the reconstruction of the technological sequences of production, did not conform to any of these divisions, however. Overall methods of grey-ware manufacture were relatively uniform throughout the borderlands, and they differed in essential ways from those employed in the manufacture of other contemporary pottery (grey wares were produced on the potter's fast wheel, and two-chambered kilns and reduction firings were unique to this pottery). The widespread use of these techniques emerged as an important shared characteristic throughout the borderlands. Most importantly, it demonstrated that potters throughout the region had developed a sophisticated technology and the ability to manipulate atmospheric conditions and firing temperatures. This technology was developed in western Pakistan, the best evidence being from the site of Mehrgarh (Wright 1987, 1989b), where the technique is known earlier than in any other part of the Indo-Iranian borderlands, suggesting that it spread from there throughout the region.

One way in which to identify the types of interactions represented by my results is to distinguish between technological boundaries and those involving specialist production. First, as I have discussed with respect to technology in general, embedded within technologies are individual actions and choices. The actions performed on matter are deliberate, and the mental processes associated with them represent cognitive deliberations. In that sense, we cannot reasonably separate end products or stylistic measures from manipulations of materials during the production process. In the case of grey wares, the technological processes of production are expressions of broader frameworks situated in the social lives of producers and consumers. Whether the pots were desirable for their unique aesthetic qualities or their durability, embedded within them were social networks or fields of action and influence.

Second, the grey wares were not made everywhere. Their distribution indicates that they were produced in a small number of communities and made for limited consumption. Although produced from locally available clays, they were nonetheless a rare resource available in several identifiable zones that crosscut cultural groups. In view of their unique qualities, their production certainly served as an identifying marker for their makers, and their consumption most likely served as such a marker for those who used them.

Finally, when viewed as a part of long-term historical processes, the painted grey-ware evidence reveals a complex pattern of interaction in which the shifting and realigning of social boundaries can be clearly delineated. In the initial stages of intergroup contact, interaction was between artisan specialists—the most reasonable explanation for the widely dispersed technology. Elsewhere (Wright 1989b), I described this interaction as a "bridge" to later historical contacts, but in light of my discussion of technology as embodied practice and of learned practices as embedded in social contexts, this bridge can be viewed in more dynamic terms as an exchange of information and a process of social construction involving artisans.[8] These interactions were the initial steps that set the stage for an aggregate of human actions; they were followed by limited exchanges of pots on a regional basis and finally, only rarely and late in the sequence, by their exchange to more distant places. Although we can reasonably assume that initial contacts were made among potters, it is impossible to identify precisely who and what sets of relations were at work in the later exchanges, when the painted grey wares produced in western Pakistan were brought to settlements in eastern Iran. Individuals involved in the exchange extended their social networks over a range that cut across social and cultural boundaries, whether through interactions with people en route to eastern Iran or by traveling to distant places themselves.

Although the different pathways discussed here do not make it possible to identify specific groupings (ethnic, kinship, friends, etc.) in all instances, I hope they demonstrate the usefulness of the culture concept. Here, it is used as a unit of analysis (represented by patterned distributions of material culture) against which to identify difference (signaled by the presence of materials that do not fit the patterned distributions). Aspects of material culture—technological styles, production loci, widespread distributions—document interactions among segments of societies and the networks they maintained. When viewed in a historical context, they demonstrate that interactions among social groups extend beyond their face-to-face communities (Welsch and Terrell 1999: 53). They are those specific points in which social construction and reconstruction take place and that, when combined, are larger than the sum of their parts.

Conclusion

In this chapter I have tried to show how the concept of culture has been employed as a means of analysis by some feminist archaeologists and by others involved in social boundary and technology studies. Both instances demonstrate the concept's use as a framework against which to observe those points at which individuals and social groups define and redefine themselves. Such interactions also may set in motion long-term historical processes involving new forms of social interaction. There is a flexibility to the concept that can help identify the patterns I have articulated.

I suspect that archaeologists worry less about culture than do other anthropologists. Perhaps because of the nature of our evidence and our long-term commitment to a particular geographical region or historical sequence, our gaze on the past is always a collective one. We may have a proclivity for taking hard-won concepts such as culture and reconfiguring them, because our sustained familiarity with materials requires shifting and modifying our ideas as new discoveries are made. Constant reassessments of previous analyses are necessary. Entities disappear, coalesce, and are reformed; there is always "noise" and flux, as is observable in the examples I have provided and in all of social life. These differences do not make formulating a common conceptual understanding of culture impossible, just more interesting, if we are willing to accept the challenge.

Can we, should we ignore the culture concept and the power that lies behind it? I seriously doubt that archaeologists *must* hold onto the concept and that we cannot frame our data in other ways. In our work we acknowledge that what might once have appeared as central concepts shared by all fall to dust upon closer examination. Still, I hope the examples provided in this chapter have demonstrated the utility of the concept in specific instances.

Beyond what has been discussed, I find that there are practical reasons to write with the concept of culture. In this I follow the general notions of some feminist archaeologists who have argued that if we abandon foundational concepts rather than building from them, then the power of individual researchers will be the most important consideration or deciding factor in who and what will be heard (Engelstad 1991). An appropriate issue might be to examine the concept of culture and its redefinition in this light. But more than that, I think Eric Wolf was right in asserting that whatever core of meaning lies hidden in the culture concept, there is something to be identified that strives toward coherence, and "assuredly there are people who drive it on, as well as others who are driven" (Wolf 1999: 67). To work in this way goes beyond our disciplinary borders and allows us to observe how human groups in the prehistoric past negotiated their worlds.

Acknowledgments

The Wenner-Gren Conference for which this paper was originally written was among the most stimulating meetings in which I have participated. I want to thank Sydel Silverman, Richard Fox and Barbara King for organizing the seminar and for inviting me, for their feedback on earlier versions of this paper, and for insightful critiques. Other participants at the meeting provided stimulating dialogue and a fund of knowledge against which I was able to compare current archaeological approaches. My special thanks to Laurie Obbink and Mark Mahoney for providing logistical support and a fabulous setting and workplace that lent itself to vigorous, yet collegial discussions. My thanks too to Jane Kepp for her editorial assistance.

Notes

1. This chapter should not be construed as a review of the culture concept in archaeology, a topic that extends beyond its scope. An important source is David Clarke (1968). In the 1960s he advocated more objectively derived interpretations, recognized the "untidiness" of archaeological cultures, and argued for a polythetic definition of cultures in which numerous groups and situations would be recognized. For recent theoretical discussions, readers should investigate the debates between processualists and postprocessualists, the latter being the principal critics of the new archaeology and the archaeological counterparts to postmodernists. For a discussion of some differences between processual and postprocessual archaeology, see Yoffee and Sherratt 1993. See Preucel 1991 for an introduction to the ways in which the culture concept has been employed. For example, although postprocessualists have been critical of archaeological pretensions to science, and the issue might have elicited a debate over "culture," this has not been the case. Although postprocessualists clearly recognize the politically charged nature of concepts like culture, they argue that behavior is "culturally constituted," thus according it a central place. More strongly, they claim that material culture conveys symbolic messages and that explanation involves deciphering the meaning behind material culture. Finally, it has been stated that material culture and culture "just are" (Hodder 1986: 4).

2. According to Brumfiel (1996: 159), these interpretations of Aztec imagery follow verbal statements in which food and cloth are associated with women in texts.

3. In her discussion of technology and gender in late imperial China, Francesca Bray (1997: 46) used the phrase "against the grain" to describe her examination of written sources that recorded gendered divisions of labor and reflect on female status. By reading against the grain, she successfully demonstrated how power over women was exerted and experienced. At the same time, her work provides glimpses of class differences and privilege among women of high status in Chinese society.

4. In the following, I refrain from repeating "Ur III," but my entire analysis is confined to that period. The relationship of the state to its citizens in Mesopotamian history naturally shifted over time.

5. In other periods, weavers may have come predominantly from the local population; this is especially documented for earlier times. See Zagarell 1986.

6. For a recent review of the question of dependency and asymmetry in the interpretation of exchange systems in the ancient past, see Stein (1999). In the early 1980s, when I approached the question of exchange without an overarching hierarchical authority, most archaeologists viewed exchange systems in core/periphery or dominance terms.

7. Newly excavated grey wares from Shahr-i Sokhta and Tepe Yahya comprised the bulk of samples studied from eastern Iran. In Baluchistan, western Pakistan, the majority were from the site of Mehrgarh, where I participated in excavations. At Mehrgarh there were large quantities of grey wares and "wasters" throughout occupation during the first half of the third millennium B.C.E. Mehrgarh is located on the Kacchi Plain at the foot of the Bolan Pass, which leads west into present-day Afghanistan and routes to eastern Iran. Numerous sites with quantities of grey ware have been discovered along the Kacchi Plain and in mountainous zones leading to it.

8. Some researchers have used the term "cultural entanglement" to describe similar instances in other contexts (see several chapters in Cusick 1998, for example). I find the term "social fields" more neutral, in that it implies an active role for the social groups involved. Entanglement brings to mind older views of technology in which societies passively adopted it and relations were asymmetrical.

eight

Language as a Model for Culture: Lessons from the Cognitive Sciences

Penelope Brown

In the anthropological soul-searching of the past couple of decades, a core worry has been over the dismemberment (or "deconstruction") of the traditional anthropological concept of culture (see, for example, Sperber 1996; Kuper 1999; compare Kroeber and Kluckhohn 1952). Still, anthropologists for the most part agree that culture (whatever it is) plays a key role in the development (both phylogenetic and ontogenetic) of humans. While anthropologists have been distracted by their culture wars, the wider scientific community has not been idle: the culture concept has been put to use to argue the *opposite* of the anthropological claim for the dominant role of culture in the development of human beings. Culture is being usurped by cognitive science.

Although anthropology was originally taken to be a contributing member of the cognitive sciences (Gardiner 1989), few sociocultural anthropologists have paid much attention to developments in those fields. Therefore, I have construed my task here as one of characterizing the perspectives toward culture that arise in the cognitive sciences, particularly those that take language, the quintessential cultural phenomenon, as their object of study. To do justice to this assignment would require a serious undertaking in the history of ideas, quite beyond what I can present here. But I will try to sketch the range of presuppositions about culture among this diverse set of theorists and explain why, for some views (including my own), the concept of culture cannot be done away with. Laying my cards on the table at the outset, I see two needs for a concept of culture: we need it in order to talk about comparison (we need the term "cross-cultural"), and we need it in order to talk about thematic and functional links across different domains in the social/semiotic life of a particular group of people. So mine are unfashionably functionalist arguments: we need the culture concept to capture a degree of symbolic unity across the parts and a degree of functional dovetailing of parts across different domains of social life. It is these connections, I argue, that in many detailed ways help children to learn culture.

My interest in addressing cognitive scientists' concepts of culture arises from my preoccupation with a problem at the intersection of the disciplines of anthropology, linguistics, and psychology: how to account for the distinctive cognitive style of a group of Mayan Indians. The specific problem I wrestle with concerns spatial language and cognition across languages and cultures. Space is fundamental to human life, involving much taken-for-granted knowledge and invoked in many everyday activities: reckoning where one is—one's internalized geographical map—navigating and route finding, giving route directions, indicating where to find things one is looking for, tracking locations and travels in a narrative, spatial reasoning, and much more. There is much controversy over the respects in which spatial language and thinking are universal (as most cognitive scientists assume they are), to what extent they can vary cross-linguistically and cross-culturally, and whether variations in spatial language can influence spatial thinking. In short, what are the implications of variability in spatial language for the nature of universals and for the role of language and other aspects of culture in human thinking?

My corner of this problem lies in the Mayan community of Tenejapa, in southern Mexico.[1] There we find a distinctive linguistic repertoire for talking about spatial relations, a distinctive frame of reference for calculating them—based on the uphill-downhill slope of the land—and a distinctive cognitive style associated with these. That cognitive style consists of ways of thinking about, talking about, remembering, and reasoning about space that are, in crucial respects, different from those found in many other societies. Underlying this conclusion are observations on things such as the following:

What people routinely say (in their own language, Tzeltal):
- Someone requests a machete, saying, "Give me the machete uphillward of the door"

What people routinely do and do not do:
- Gesture and pointing are "absolutely" oriented in relation to physical places

- People avoid sleeping with head oriented toward "downhill"
- Ritual life is organized into "uphill" and "downhill" ceremonial sectors

The abstract knowledge that people demonstrate in what they can and cannot do:
- Adults are absolutely oriented at all times (amounting effectively to always knowing where north is)
- There is a complete absence of linguistic left-right distinctions in spatial description
- There is a consonant left-right symmetry in household layout, artifact design, and weaving patterns

How people perform on interactional and cognitive tasks:
- People talk about and remember spatial arrays, whether in large-scale (geographic) or small-scale (tabletop) space, in an absolutely oriented fashion.

In short, members of this community demonstrate an acquired way of thinking and talking about space, a distinctive cognitive style that is evident not only in communicative behavior (speech, gesture) but also in many other aspects of life (weaving styles, house construction, ritual performances). The everyday, taken-for-granted nature of this nonegocentric spatial system flies in the face of claims made in cognitive science that the universal basis for spatial language and thinking lies in our common human egocentric visual system, which strongly constrains how we can think about space. And in many respects, the contexts for learning and using the linguistic system at the heart of this style do not correspond to what has been presumed to be universally necessary for children to learn a language.

I am convinced that I need a notion of culture (including the culture-specific details of the language) in order to talk about how children come to acquire this quintessentially cultural way of thinking. More generally, I believe that culture—despite the current resistance to this idea in the cognitive sciences—has much to do with the processes of language acquisition and the socialization through language of the distinctive cognitive and ideological habits that characterize members of this community. "Culture," in the form of semantic specificity in Tzeltal verbs, in community-specific patterns of verbal interaction, in gesture, and in many other respects, plays a deeper role than most cognitive scientists want to allow.

But culture *in what sense?* And *how* does culture have this effect? I address these questions first by considering the views of culture implicit in different approaches to the study of language, perhaps the preeminent cultural property of humans and a prerequisite for the rest of (human-style) culture. At the same time, language is the property that has been taken by many to be the most self-contained, most dissociable from the rest of culture. Thinking about culture from the perspective of language raises questions distinct from those preoccupying the anthropological critics of the culture concept—those objecting to the idea of culture as shared, integrated, and transmitted intact across generations. Language is a highly integrated symbolic system; as cultural knowledge and behavior it is (usually) part of the automatized, taken-for-granted background of everyday life. In these respects it is quite different from systems of consciously held values and beliefs. The perspective from the language sciences therefore provides a contrast and a foil to the issues central to the culture debates among anthropologists. Later in the chapter, I describe an approach that aims to contribute directly to cognitive science by investigating precisely the relationship between mind, language, and culture.

The View from Linguistics and Cognitive Science

Cognitive scientists are a loose coalition of linguists, psychologists, and computational modelers who share the view that cognition is a set of mental computations. Among many of these theorists, a view of culture has become the publicly dominant view; it has captured the journals and appeared in a number of popularizing books (e.g., Pinker 1994, 1997). The view is of Culture with a capital *C*, a monolithic concept with unspecified content—it is simply that property which distinguishes humans from other animals. Along with this view of culture goes a view of language as a universal property of humans that has a detailed genetic base; it is (in Pinker's words) an "instinct." From this perspective, the idiosyncrasies of specific languages or cultural groups—including my Tzeltal Mayas—can be of no interest whatsoever because they are presumed not to matter.

But if it can be shown that cultural variability is deeper than superficial and can have a fundamental influence on how people think, then the cognitive sciences will have to begin to include *cultural differences* as well as Culture in their understanding of human thinking. This is where anthropologists, with their comparative perspective, are in a position to make an important contribution.

Linguistic scholars, like people everywhere, tend to see the world through the lens of what they know about. Hence, they tend to take language as the model for the way culture is to be construed. Yet they can hold radically different views of culture, and of the role of culture in explanations, depending on which kind of linguistic theory they adhere to. Many linguists, to be sure, ignore culture altogether; it is not considered relevant to their field of operations. For those who do invoke culture, we can identify five broadly characterizable "ideal-type" notions of culture. These are distinguished according to the degree to which, and in what sense, they take culture to be relevant to the object of study and, in particular, according to the views of their proponents concerning the nature of language, of meaning, and of mind.

Stance 1: Culture as Ethnic or Linguistic Group

The first stance, common among linguists, takes culture to be a shorthand way of referring to social groups who share a language. Most of us employ this concept of culture some of the time (talking of culture *X* versus culture *Y*), but for many linguists of a typological or comparative persuasion, it is the only concept of culture at hand. People who share a language are taken to be members of a social group, with social barriers to communication across groups and with boundaries subject to historical change. "Culture" is equated with such groups in an unexamined way. For some, the uniqueness of the language amounts to the same thing as the uniqueness of the culture, which is considered irretrievably lost if the language is lost. For these scholars, languages differ within typologically describable patterns; there are linguistic universals, but by far the majority of these are "conditional" universals of the form, "If a language has feature *X*, then it will have *Y*." Mind is not, for the most part, an explicit focus of interest (except when features of mind are presumed to explain universals). Grammatical meaning is seen as based on a universal repertoire of distinctions (e.g., tense, aspect, person), although lexical meaning is seen as culture specific, varying with the language or the language type.

Besides being politically sensitive, this "culture-equals-language-group" stance—implying, as it does, for example, that an English-speaking Australian Aboriginal is no longer an Aboriginal—is sociolinguistically naive. There simply is no one-to-one mapping of language and social group; instead, social networks, corporate groups, and language interdigitate in very complex ways. Indeed, the concept of language is as problematic as that of culture (in terms of boundedness, holism, etc.). Language typologists do acknowledge certain phenomena that undermine their language-equals-cultural-group stance: for example, they recognize "language areas" where there is structural influence across unrelated languages in an intercommunicating area (as in India or Mesoamerica). To the extent that they try to account for such areal patterns, it is by invoking a "traits" explanation: a set of linguistic traits (e.g., particular grammatical morphemes) diffuses, owing to a particular set of cultural traits (e.g., trade, political dominance, intermarriage).

Stance 2: Culture as Mental Module

A second view of language employs a correspondingly different model for culture. In this stance, founded in Chomsky's generative school of linguistics, culture—if it is considered at all—is construed, by analogy to language, in a very special sense. The distinctive property of language is taken to be syntax, and the abstract core of syntax (Universal Grammar, or UG) is a mental module that is universal and biologically innate. Syntax is taken to be autonomous from meaning, and meaning is seen as being parasitic on a universal human conceptual structure that is also taken to be innate. The innateness argument rests on the problem of how a person can acquire "knowledge of a language," since that knowledge is too abstract to be directly perceived. The answer offered is genetic endowment.

Several theorists have explicitly applied this model to culture. The psycholinguist Steven Pinker, the great popularizer of this stance (Pinker 1994, 1997), states quite bluntly that all the interesting properties of language are universal and are innately specified in our genes, down to the details of UG (phrase structure, nouns and verbs, subjects, case, etc.). Any differences are trivial variations on this fundamental structure (Pinker 1994: 18–19).

He takes the same line toward the rest of culture (1994: 411): "At first glance, the ethnographic record seems to offer a stark contrast [to UG]. Anthropology in this century has taken us through a mind-broadening fairground of human diversity. But might this carnival of taboos, kinship systems, shamanry, and all the rest be as superficial as the difference between *dog* and *hundt* [sic], hiding a universal human nature?"

Pinker points out (with some justice) that the culture of anthropologists themselves gives one cause to worry, because they tend to glorify cultural difference ("Be merchants of astonishment," says Clifford Geertz [Pinker 1994: 411]). The argument for the universality of culture and its genetic basis is developed at length in Pinker's book *How the Mind Works* (1997), which is based essentially on the ideas of evolutionary psychologists such as John Tooby and Leda Cosmides (1992).

Language as Model for Culture   175

In this book, Pinker extends the image of mental modules to include a module for culture (1997: 21). Again, his use of the culture concept is solely to make claims about the set of traits that all humans, or all human subgroups of a certain type (namely, "foragers"), share. For example:

> All human cultures ever documented have words for the elements of space, time, motion, speed, mental states, tools, flora, fauna, and weather, and logical connectives.... They combine the words into sentences and use the underlying propositions to reason about invisible entities like diseases, meteorological forces, and absent animals. Mental maps represent the locations of thousands of noteworthy sites, and mental calendars represent nested cycles of weather, animal migration, and the life histories of plants.... All foraging peoples manufacture cutters, pounders, containers, cordage, nets, baskets, levers, and spears and other weapons. (Pinker 1997: 189)

Here is depicted a kind of generalized forager, characterized by a universal set of traits. The only role for cultural difference is as the historical accretion of expertise: "An information-exploiting lifestyle goes well with living in groups and pooling expertise—that is, with culture. Cultures differ from one another because they pool bodies of expertise fashioned in different times and places" (Pinker 1997: 190).

I have used Pinker to illustrate stance 2 because his claims are so unequivocal that they have received a wide press. But, hard to believe though it may be, this stance is perhaps the mainstream one in cognitive science, taken uncritically from the mainstream linguistics of the past forty years and extended from language to culture by theorists influenced by evolutionary psychologists. Although the view of language as an innately specified mental module has certainly not gone unchallenged,[2] in the work of many other cognitive-science-oriented theorists we can find arguments for what is universal and what is innate in humans along lines very similar to Pinker's. Take, for example, Ray Jackendoff, whose picture of culture focuses on how children learn concepts. Like Pinker, Jackendoff presumes that there is a universal conceptual structure with innately given concepts and rules for restricting possible concepts. In order for children to learn word meanings, Jackendoff (1992) argues, they must have a set of primitives with specific content (e.g., spatial concepts, the concept of possession). Such concepts must be pregiven in the child's "Conceptual Well-formedness Rules," Jackendoff's proposal for a mental module that sets the limits for possible concepts. Thus, not only the ability to form concepts but the content of some concepts—the "primitives" from which concepts are built—must be innately given.

Jackendoff (1992: 69) also argues for "a module or group of modules (a faculty) that is specialized for *social cognition.*" For this there are input-output modules (just like those for, among other things, the language system, the visual system, the motor system, and musical capacity) that provide connections between sensory and motor periphery and central capacities. The social cognition module is what enables children to learn culture. Foreshadowing Pinker (1994), Jackendoff (1992: 74) observed that despite considerable variation both across cultures and within a culture, "following the example of language, perhaps we should be looking for underlying principles that enable a child to learn the culture-specific conventions in which he or she is situated." Many such underlying principles have been proposed in the child development literature, including hypotheses about the necessary cognitive prerequisites for learning language in general and for learning particular aspects of language (e.g., nouns as opposed to verbs).[3] In the grip of the computational metaphor for human thinking, these proposals show a certain lack of imagination about how context and creative inference can fill in the gaps for human learners who (unlike computers) grow up in the matrix of a rich community of practices that inform the use of language.

Jackendoff winds up with an explicit analogy between culture and language in the form of Chomsky's Internal language (I-language), or competence, as opposed to External, or E-language, which is performance: "The hope . . . is that many of the Universals and parameters of human E-[external] social organization can be eventually attributed to the character of I-[internal] social organization, just as many properties of human linguistic communication have been attributed to the mental capacity that constitutes I-[Internal] language" (1992: 76). His detailed proposal for these universals includes some primitives of social cognition: persons, requests versus orders (which rely on a social dominance hierarchy), exchange transactions (which rely on social concepts of agreement and value), and ownership.

What then is left to be learned? Not a lot, according to Jackendoff: "The child only has to learn what parameters govern ownership or property rights in the local culture. The codification of these parameters (and those connected to kinship, etc.) constitutes the basic issues around which a culture constructs its equivalent of a legal system" (1992: 79). And: "'Learning a culture' then consists of fleshing out the particulars of these frames into a culture-particular realization, and creating categories of situations in which to apply the logic of each mode of interaction" (1992: 80). In other words, an innately specified social cognition module provides the underpinnings—including the relevant concepts—for "learning a culture."

In sum, cognitive scientists such as Pinker and Jackendoff insist that one think about culture just as generativists think about language—that is, as a genetically specified set of underlying elements with underlying rules of combination. In their proposals for a Culture module, they seem to be saying, "In the absence of a coherent science of anthropology, we'll make the obvious generalizations from Language and postulate the existence of universal abstract traits of Culture analogous to Language ones, while redirecting attention to the mental underpinnings of Culture. From this perspective the differences between cultures are trivial."

We can give these cognitive scientists credit at least for asking the question that anthropologists have generally failed to ask—How is it that humans can have culture?—and for proposing an answer: Because human minds are different from those of other animals![4] This idea has been irresistibly attractive not only to cognitive and developmental psychologists but also to many cognitive anthropologists. Such proposals, however, fail to recognize that it is by no means straightforward to establish what the cognitive primitives underlying all social life actually are. Everyone would agree that biology places some constraints on human minds, culture, and behavior. But exactly what those constraints are is precisely the issue that should be (and on the whole is not) empirically addressed. Pinker's and Jackendoff's claims for the innate component are entirely too detailed and theory dependent in relation to the evidence assembled. Indeed, all the universalists who take stance 2 are painfully naive about the extent and significance of cultural variation.

As every anthropologist knows, it is not easy to find universals in the cultural domain. Unilinear descent groups, marriage, shamanism, money, the incest taboo—what, on the ground, counts as instances of these categories? Universals are equally problematic in linguistics. Many putative universals are hotly disputed by linguists looking at specific languages: whether languages always have subjects, or distinguish nouns from verbs, or are characterizable in terms of phrase structure. The crux of the problem is that universal traits at a concrete level do not exist. One can find *elements* of putatively universal traits (e.g., marriage) in social life (male-female bonding, maternal child-rearing), as one can in language (e.g., elements contributing to the "nouniness" or "verbiness" of words). But when one looks at particular cases, the elements are not necessarily all present and do not necessarily cohere. The level of universals is in these elements, not in systems or institutions (kinship, marriage) taken as a whole.

In my view, linguists have not yet established exactly what Language is, and so they are hardly in a position to extrapolate to Culture. Turning now to sociological and anthropological approaches to language, we can see that different ideas about the nature of language induce different extrapolations to the nature of culture.

Stance 3: Culture as Knowledge

Closer to home for anthropologists, a third stance treats cultural differences as worthy of investigation but assumes that they are best seen through a language's semantic categories. Language again is the key to culture, but it is language as semantics rather than as Universal Grammar. This is of course the view promulgated in classic ethnoscience, as in Ward Goodenough's famous statement that "a society's culture consists of whatever it is one has to know or believe in order to operate in a manner acceptable to its members, and do so in any role that they accept for any one of themselves. Culture, being what people have to learn as distinct from their biological heritage, must consist of the end product of learning: knowledge, in a most general, if relative, sense of the term" (1964 [1957]: 36).

Like stance 2, this "culture-equals-knowledge" stance is based in a linguistic homology (Duranti 1997: 27). Knowing a culture is like knowing a language—both are mental realities—and describing a culture is like describing a language: one writes "cultural grammars."

Modern proponents of this view range from cognitive linguists (e.g., Langacker 1986) to practitioners of some schools of semantics (e.g., Wierzbicka 1992) and modern descendents of ethnoscience or cognitive anthropology (D'Andrade 1995; Strauss and Quinn 1997). In terms of their views of mind, this group is as cognitivist as the generativists—mind is where the action is—and many advocates of stance 3 are also strongly universalist. Meaning inheres in individual minds but is structured by culturally learned experiences that provide "frames" or "schemata" for organizing and understanding cultural ideas. Culture consists of the contents of such schemata. The cultural notions invoked, however, are often crude, including extreme proposals of modularity. For example, Leonard Talmy's (2000) idea of a cognitive culture module is analogous to Pinker's.

From this perspective, the mind is taken to be rather hodgepodge, for the schemata—the units of culture in the mind—are not necessarily integrated with one another. In fact, "the overall view is one in which culture is seen to be particulate, socially distributed, variably internalized, and variably embodied in external forms" (D'Andrade 1995: 248). This insistence on the heterogeneity and nonintegration of different aspects of cultural knowledge has the virtue of providing an antidote to overholistic views of culture. However, it ignores the fact that some core aspects of cognition (e.g., space) are demonstrably culturally conditioned and yet *crosscut* different mental domains.

Stance 4: Culture as Context

A fourth stance, associated with the ethnography of speaking, takes culture to be the basis for the contextually specific nature of language as it is actually used. Culture is whatever makes us use language differentially in different contexts, with contexts taken to be characterizable in terms of social variables such as gender, age, ethnic group, genre, and social setting. This is a loosely connected family of approaches, crossing disciplinary boundaries from much of linguistic pragmatics to the hyphenated branches of linguistics that are interested in the social setting of language use for adults or for children learning language— sociolinguistics, traditional anthropological linguistics, some developmental psychology. For scholars working from this perspective, analysis centers on activities, the interactions in which activities are embedded, how such activities structure the environment and frameworks for understanding within which language is used and learned, and how this can give rise to miscommunication in cross-cultural interaction. In this stance, it is the cultural contexts that are actually the focus of study. On the whole, the nature of mind is not explicitly of interest. Some universals have been suggested (for example, Dell Hymes's proposal [1974] for the dimensions of context relevant to linguistic variation), but the emphasis is on differences, and this group of scholars studying linguistic behavior is not generally engaged in dialogue with universalists.

Stance 5: Culture as Process

This stance emerged in the last two decades of the twentieth century in the subdisciplines of linguistics, anthropology, and psychology that study actual, naturally occurring interactional behavior in its cultural setting.[5] Here we have the insistence that culture is both knowledge and habits of thinking, on the one hand, and out-there-in-the-world objects, interactions, and communicative behaviors, on the other. In this supraindividual sense it forms the environment—the people, objects, and altered landscapes—into which children are born and which scaffolds their interactions so as to ensure that, within the constraints of their biological endowment, they gradually become enculturated members of the society.

Although there are many differences among theorists who take stance 5, they all stress the emergent nature of mind, meaning, and culture. These emerge in the process of social interaction, relying both on cultural props in the environment and on other minds. Such theorists also share a conviction that to understand this emergent meaning-mind-culture, one must study the emergent process by looking at data drawn from real, situationally embedded social interactions.

Culture, according to this stance, is partly in the mind and partly (re-)created in social interaction. Proponents include practice theorists such as Lucy Suchman (1987) and Jean Lave (1988), who argue that cognition is instantiated in action, in everyday practices, and as such it is "distributed—stretched over, not divided—among mind, body, activity and culturally organized settings (which include other actors)" (Lave 1988: 1). Much cognition occurs *between* individuals, emerging from their interaction (Hutchins 1995). Linguistic anthropologists argue, in addition, that knowledge resides also in the tools people use (Keller and Keller 1996), and so culture as knowledge must include culture as objects.

Other proponents of this approach to culture are the modern interactionist linguistic anthropologists (roughly equivalent to linguistic anthropology minus cognitive anthropology), who ritually cite Pierre Bourdieu as a source of inspiration: for example, Alessandro Duranti (1997), William Foley (1997), John Gumperz (1992), and William Hanks (1995). Work on language socialization (Ochs 1988; Ochs and Schieffelin 1986; Schieffelin 1990) also fits into this perspective.

Another group that takes stance 5 consists of proponents of a newly conceptualized Whorfianism (Gumperz and Levinson 1996; Lucy 1992a, 1992b), who are committed to the comparative study of thought as constrained by language. Rather than treating thought and language as static global entities, they link the language-thought relationship in a particular domain to online processing, habits, and patterns of interaction. These modern studies of linguistic relativity, with their explicitly comparative methodology, are tied to cross-linguistic studies of language acquisition conducted from the perspective of stance 5 (for example, Bowerman 1996; Bowerman and Levinson 2001; Slobin 1996). These have formed a distinct line of research that converges in one respect with that described under stance 3, namely, in the serious attention given to findings in cognitive science about how the human mind works and a commitment to contributing an anthropological, comparative perspective to the cognitive science enterprise. This work reflects a recent swing back in psychology, linguistics, and linguistic anthropology toward a position that views diversity in linguistic and cultural practice *within* what has been learned about universals.

Summary

Cognitive science is the modern setting for the old debate concerning the psychic unity of mankind. The five stances toward culture I have just sketched characterize different positions in the debate, each with its own limitations. Lurking underneath these stances are more fundamental ideological divisions, polar oppositions found in anthropology as much as in linguistics. These are the sources of the chronic cross-talk between universalists and relativists, with their different presuppositions. The three major poles can be characterized as follows.

First, there is the opposition between Culture and cultures. Most cognitive scientists, as just surveyed, deal only with Culture with a capital *C;* humans versus other animals are the focus of interest. A parallel split occurs in linguistics: Language with a capital *L* versus languages. As John Lucy (1996: 39) has pointed out, one's stance toward the importance of variation in language and culture depends greatly on one's view of the significance of having a language at all, as opposed to not having one. The dominant perspective in cognitive science stresses the continuity between humans and other animals and views language as a biological phenomenon that maps in an unproblematical way onto perception, cognition, emotion, and social interaction. Humans, in this view, are unique in occupying the "cognitive niche" (Pinker 1997), to which language is a relatively straightforward addendum. The alternative view holds that despite many continuities, humans differ fundamentally from other animals, because humans alone possess a variable symbolic capacity that adds new levels of organization (self, culture, consciousness, historically developed systems of meaning), all of which depend on human language. This view insists that humans also occupy the "cultural niche," and cultural niches vary (Deacon 1997; Levinson 1998, 2000; Tomasello 1999). Indeed, it is culture's amenability to variation that may be the key to the uniqueness of this human-occupied niche.

Second, one can describe an opposition between concepts of culture as a (partially) integrated whole versus culture as a set of traits. The holistic view of culture insists on common themes, patterns, and structural connections across different domains in a society. Language goes along with a mind-set: the connections are carried in symbolic systems with common themes cross-connecting to different aspects of members' social and cultural lives. This perspective tends to be antitrait and anticomparative, and it is the way many anthropologists (Geertzians, structuralists) have tended to think about culture. The whole has a coherence greater than the sum of its traits.

However, because this notion of culture as the common threads across domains is ineffable, hard to pin down, it remains opaque to virtually all nonanthropologists. The nonanthropologist's view is much easier to grasp: groups who share a culture have particular *traits;* it is irrelevant whether or not one trait is related to another. One can do culture analysis by traits (à la Murdock [1949]), as when one lists a set of traits common to the "culture area" of Mesoamerica. In cognitive science, this traits view of culture reigns.

Third, we have the "culture as mental" versus "culture as material" opposition. Cultural traits may be mental (e.g., Dawkins's [1976] and Dennett's [1991] "memes"), or they may be material (e.g., primatologists' lists of cultural "tools" used by apes). This opposition divides cognitivists, who take culture to be a mental phenomenon, from primate specialists, who look at culture as material, and from archaeologists, who take the material remains of cultures as their starting point. But proponents of stance 5 argue for *both:* culture encompasses the mental and physical environment in which meanings arise in situated interaction with others and in which a child turns into a member of a cultural group (see, e.g., Bowerman and Levinson 2001; Tomasello 1999).

Given these kinds of profound divisions in interests and presuppositions, is there a concept of culture that might usefully feed into cognitive science? The cognitive scientists I have discussed are floundering to include culture in their grand picture while operating with exceedingly primitive concepts of culture. It is time to begin building explicit models and cross-disciplinary research programs for investigating the *interaction* of culture (as socially learned meanings and behavior patterns) with language and with mind. I next describe one such program, coming back to consider my Tenejapan problem of spatial language and cognitive style.

How Can We Study Language-in-Culture Comparatively?

Since about 1990, Stephen Levinson and his collaborators at the Max Planck Institute for Psycholinguistics have developed an empirical comparative program that aims to contribute directly to the cognitive science enterprise. The aim is to establish, against a background of universal constraints (which need to be discovered, not stipulated), dimensions of cognitive variability by looking at particular domains—such as space—that are fundamental to thought while forming part of the taken-for-granted background of everyday life. Culture as "public representations" is both in our minds and in the environment, and it comes into individual minds through social interaction. This notion of culture is more particulate than the anthropologists' "group with its own lifestyle and value system" but less hodgepodge than Roy D'Andrade's (1995) "tidal pool." Cultural ideas are considered within a particular domain, in this case the domain of spatial language and spatial thinking across cultures. They are also considered within a community of practice, as actually used by members, not just as reported by them.

Space was a provocative place to start, because the standard line in philosophy, psychology, and cognitive science has presumed a universal basis for spatial cognition in the biological structures that we derive from our mammalian inheritance. The dominant view is that an egocentric perspective is fundamental to human spatial thinking: three planes through the body provide the basis for thinking in terms of space as in front and behind, to the left and right, and above and below (see, e.g., Clark 1973; Miller and Johnson-Laird 1976). This view seems to be supported, first, by modularity in the brain (distinct "what" versus "where" systems) and, second, by certain linguistic evidence, such as how children acquire spatial prepositions in Indo-European languages. The conclusion was overhastily drawn from these kinds of evidence that the universal basis for spatial language resides in our common human egocentric visual system and that it strongly constrains how we can think about space.

Findings from our large comparative study of spatial language and cognition, however, cast doubt on the universality of egocentric space as the basis for linguistic systems of spatial description. It turns out that spatial linguistic systems around the world are much more variable than has been presumed (Levinson 1996a, 1996b, 1996c). In particular, they differ systematically in their underlying frames of reference—their coordinate systems for reckoning spatial relations. Three major frames of reference are used in languages of the world, and only one of them is egocentric. The *relative* frame of reference uses the speaker's egocentric viewpoint to calculate spatial relations, as in the familiar left-right and front-back systems of European languages. The *absolute* frame uses fixed angles extrinsic to the objects whose spatial relation is being described, as in the cardinal direction systems of many Australian Aboriginal languages. The *intrinsic* frame relies on intrinsic properties of objects being spatially related (e.g., parts and shapes of the ground object or positions of the figure object) in order to reckon spatial relations, as in the body-part systems (top, bottom, side, middle, etc.) of many languages.[6]

These three frames of reference are made use of differently in different societies. First, there are different "default" systems for spatial language across cultures. Western speakers of English, for example, use mainly relative and intrinsic systems, employing the absolute only for large-scale geographic reckoning (between, say, two cities). Speakers of the Australian Aboriginal language Guugu Yimithirr use only one frame of reference, an absolute north-south-east-west system, and Tzeltal speakers use only two—an absolute (uphill-downhill) and an intrinsic (body-part) system. Second, spatial descriptions in different languages and cultural settings may have different default frames of reference for particular purposes (small-scale versus long-distance, for example). Third, cognition is related to the default system. The different frames of reference have different conceptual bases (egocentric, geographically centered, and object centered), resulting in different implications for spatial memory and reasoning.[7] They also differ in cognitive complexity.[8]

Another major finding from the Max Planck project is that there is a clear link between the linguistic system used and nonlinguistic spatial cognition. Results on a range of nonlinguistic tasks carried out by members of social groups representing more than ten unrelated languages show that people think, remember, and reason in the system they use most for speaking (Levinson 1997, 1998; Pederson et al. 1998). This is a prime example of a Whorfian link between language and nonlinguistic cognition.

To illustrate, let me return to the case I started with—the Mayan Tzeltal speakers of Tenejapa in southern Mexico. In this community, set in precipitous mountain terrain, the main spatial frame of reference is in terms of "uphill" and "downhill." Using an abstract conceptual angle based on the overall slope of the land downward from south to north, Tzeltal people routinely describe motion as "ascending," "descending," or "going across" and objects as being "uphill," "downhill," or "acrossways" in relation to another object. They do this on both sloping and completely flat terrain, and in small-scale (e.g., table-top) space as well as over long distances (Brown and Levinson 1993a, 1993b; Levinson and Brown 1994). Correlated with this absolute linguistic system is the fact that on nonlinguistic tasks of memory and reasoning, Tzeltal speakers have a strong tendency to code in absolute terms, in contrast to Dutch speakers, who code in relative left-right, front-back terms (Brown and Levinson 1993a; Levinson 1996b). To achieve this behavioral consistency, Tzeltal speakers must have a cognitive habit of constant background tracking of where abstract "uphill" is. Other cultural features of this Mayan society reflect the absence of left-right distinctions and reinforce the cognitive effects of the absolute frame of reference. For example, there is a strong preference for left-right symmetry in cultural artifacts and activities (weaving, architecture, ritual). There is also evidence that people are to some degree "mirror-image blind,"[9] a result consonant with their speaking a language with no left-right distinction and not (yet) having been forced by literacy or automobiles to attend to left-right distinctions.

How do people come to share a cognitive style with respect to space? How do children learn to think differently depending on what spatial reference system they learn? The mainstream (Piagetian) view is that cognitive development proceeds through universal stages, uninfluenced by the linguistic categories of a particular language; cognitive development precedes, and lays the basis for, linguistic development (Laurendeau and Pinard 1970; Piaget and Inhelder 1967). But a third finding from work at the Max Planck Institute is that children are very early attuned to the particularities of the semantic spatial categories their language uses (e.g., Bowerman 1996). In line with this finding, there appears to be cultural variation in how children learn their spatial linguistic system. Evidence from my longitudinal study of Tzeltal children indicates that they learn the absolute system relatively early, achieving productive mastery of the complex sets of semantic oppositions by age three and a half.[10] They acquire the ability to use the system in novel situations on flat table-top space between ages five and a half and seven and a half.[11] In addition, their linguistic production suggests that they learn the absolute system—the "projective" and therefore cognitively more difficult one—as soon as, or possibly even before, they master their intrinsic "topological" system (Brown 2001; Brown and Levinson 2000).[12]

These findings and others—including that Tzeltal children of eighteen months start talking with verbs, many of them semantically (and culturally) specific verbs—suggest that language itself can influence the concepts children develop during their semantic learning (Brown 1998a). Tzeltal children are also sensitive to the semantic structure of their language, as is revealed in patterns of ellipsis, where speakers can assume that what is elided is recoverable from context (Brown n.d.). More speculatively, certain properties of the language they are learning may influence their cognitive development; it is suggestive that Tzeltal children acquire their absolute linguistic system very early, as soon as or even before the intrinsic system, thus inverting Piaget's claim that topological concepts are always learned before Euclidean ones. It is also of interest that these children very early (from around age three) use and recognize conventional irony, as well as lying, raising the provocative possibility that an early "theory of mind" is induced by culture-specific language practices (Brown 2002).[13]

How do the children do it? Here is where I need a culture concept, in order to capture the coherence of semiotic systems across different domains. The supports afforded to children learning this system apparently so effortlessly include features of the pragmatics of the spatial language system, the characteristics of caregiver speech to small children, the spatial consistency of gestures accompanying speech, and the early engagement of children in the adult world (to fetch things, take messages, take responsibility for child care). I need a culture concept in order to talk about the "limited holism" of symbolic systems linking otherwise disparate activities and realms of social life into coherent patterns. This is not just a random collection of traits; the parts make sense taken together, and the sense they make makes them accessible to the learner.

Some far-reaching conclusions emerge from this research concerning where concepts can come from. Concepts do not have to be innate: linguistic inputs of differing kinds can have demonstrable effects on the process of (semantic) language acquisition. As Stephen Levinson and David Wilkins (n.d.) point out, the abstract nature of the underlying universals means that children have to be constructivists, not just mapping local forms onto preexisting innate concepts but building the concepts as they learn the language. Spatial language is not fully pregiven; the child must construct both domain and range and the mappings between them. Theorists such as Ray Jackendoff (1992), W. V. O. Quine (1960), and Lila Gleitman (1990) have thought this to be logically impossible, and so the concepts must be innate. The Tzeltal findings suggest that there may well be other solutions to the logical problems, solutions derived from some uniquely human abilities—for example, the ability to attribute intentionality to others (Goody 1995) and the ability to understand that others have minds like one's own (Tomasello 1999). These allow humans (unlike computers) to make use of information available in social interaction—that is, in communicative processes—to create culturally specific categories.

A diagram contrasting anthropological and cognitive science perspectives on culture may help to clarify my position. Table 8.1 summarizes anthropologists' views of "culture(s)" and cognitive scientists' views of Culture. The anthropological core of culture is learned, it accumulates over generations, and it is (potentially) different across social groups. (In this core, I see no problem with including apes.) Anthropologists also generally agree about what kinds of content culture has, though they disagree passionately (in both time and space) about which kinds are more important and worthy of study. They also agree for the most part on what culture is *not*. It is not social structure or group identity; it is not well bounded, ahistorical, uniformly shared, or transmitted intact.

But few social or cultural anthropologists ask the questions that are surely crucial to understanding what it is to be human, the questions cognitive scientists are asking: What is the capacity for Culture? What prerequisites allow humans to have Culture at all? Cognitive scientists focus on ingredients of two types (again, with much disagreement about which is the critical ingredient). Set 1 is about *cognitive architecture*—how the brain is wired, which gives humans attentional and representational biases. This architecture provides crucially for symbolic capacity, hierarchic levels of mental organization—the ability to think about our own thoughts, to form sets of sets—and the ability to understand others as intentional agents with minds like our own. Some cognitive scientists also postulate a highly specified innate basis—set 2, the *contents* of the mind—claiming "representational innateness" in specific specialized modules for solving particular evolutionary problems. These include, as we have seen, modules for Universal Grammar and for Culture in the form of modular logic, specified by our genes, for universal cultural and social ideas. They also include word-learning theorists' proposals for word-learning biases, Jackendoff's universal conceptual structure ("Well-Formedness Rules"), conceptual primitives (such as EXIST, spatial concepts such as UP and DOWN, and social concepts such as PERSON and POSSESSION), universals of color terminology, semantic primitives, and "basic concepts."

But what is absurd about the claims for prerequisites for Culture encompassed in set 2 is that they are all made by intuition, with no

Table 8.1. Anthropologists' "culture(s)" versus cognitive scientists' Culture.

Anthropologists' "culture(s)"		Cognitive scientists' prerequisites to Culture	
Learned; accumulated over generations; different in different social groups		Universal, genetically based mental structures	
Shared mental structures:	Semiotic systems, knowledge, ideas, beliefs, values, principles for understanding, emotional habits, cultural models, cognitive styles	Set 1, cognitive architecture:	Symbolic capacity, hierarchic levels, self-reflexivity, ability to understand others as intentional agents
Shared patterns of behavior:	Behavioral styles, interactional "ethos," public rhetoric, etc.	Set 2, content:	Universal Grammar, culture modules, word learning biases (e.g., shape bias), universal conceptual structure, conceptual primitives (e.g., UP/ DOWN, PERSON), "basic concepts"
Shared objects:	Tools, knowledge technologies, etc.		

control over the range of data. They are embarrassingly ethnocentric. The basic problem with such proposals is that they have the *wrong kind of content* in them—far too much content. Constraints on the structure of mind (and language and culture) do exist, but they have to be more like syntax and less like semantics.[14] We have to distinguish the architecture claims (symbolic capacity, hierarchic levels) from the content claims (the concept of "property," for example) and to be skeptical of the latter. I see my Tzeltal child language work as (in part) aimed at testing and challenging these content claims: I drag bits and pieces of what are proposed to be part of the "universal content of mind" over into the "culturally variable" and learnable arena. It is important to ask, What is unique about humans? What is it that allows us to develop the way we do (unlike other animals in important respects)? But it requires redefining the job as a matter of assessing the *interplay* between cognitive preconditions to language and cultural learning, as well as the linguistic preconditions to advanced conceptual development.

The news to cognitive science from this research is that universals of mind are not the whole story in the domain of space. Absolute spatial systems are widespread across the world; they do not necessarily coexist with other systems of spatial reckoning; they clearly can affect everyday cognition, reasoning, and memory; they can affect children's learning of the semantics of their language; and they possibly even influence the children's cognitive development. These results encourage some optimism that we may finally be moving away from universals versus particulars as poles in an argument and toward an awareness that universals and particulars must coexist. Even if there are extensive universal properties of human cognition (as appears to be the case in the domain of space), these may be accompanied by cognition-penetrating cultural specifics (such as the frame of reference used for calculating spatial relations on the horizontal).

What Use Is "Culture"?

I see two distinct needs for the culture concept. Culture$_1$ captures the thematic unity of a symbolic system—the conceptual unity across domains demonstrated, for example, in my findings about early, culture-specific spatial meanings for words supported by semiotically compatible properties of the culturally modified environment (e.g., household and field layout) and properties of social interaction (e.g., gesture). Culture$_2$ captures the functional fit between elements across different domains, as I have argued, for example, in connection with children's initial access to the linguistic system. Elsewhere (Brown 1997, 1998a, 1998b), I have shown that by the time Tzeltal children start to speak at around eighteen months, they have isolated the verb root without the help of prosodic cues or of a special baby-talk register, but with cues provided by an idiosyncrasy of Tzeltal conversational style (dialogic repetition). Retrospectively, it makes sense to structure verbal discourse like this, as an aid to children's language learning. (There may of course be many other reasons, too—redundancy, politeness, or grooming, for example).

My claim is that against a background of universal constraints on what human minds and cultures can be like, children in interaction with the cultural environment come to have distinct cognitive styles in different communities of practice. I agree with Christina Toren (this volume): minds are created in interaction with others and with the culturally shaped environment. I, too, study how children come to have certain kinds of ideas, but unlike Toren, I study ideas that are not (for the most part) consciously accessible. There is a taken-for-granted-way of thinking about spatial relations that is coherent in relation to other ideas also learned along the way. *That* is what I need a notion of culture for. And that is what a pure traits view of culture cannot provide.

What does "culture" buy you? A system greater than the sum of its traits. If you, the learner, grasp one part of the system, you can extrapolate to other parts—for example, pointing, gesture, ritual, and the organization and layout of fields, houses, and schools all help children to grasp the semantics of an absolute spatial system in the language. The presence of these supports, and the absence of contradictory ones (left-right system, asymmetries), means that children become sensitized to an absolute orientation (in terms of the lay of land) quite early, so they can use it to calculate, for example, where a bottle is in relation to a basket on a flat surface. Being embedded in this culturally rich, coherent set of spatial practices is what helps the child "get" one system (absolute) and not another one (relative).

What are the implications for an anthropological concept of culture? Public (shared, semiotic) representations really exist; we need a name for them. And we need a name for the parallels across different aspects of a given "cultural context" that work together to support a particular cognitive style (such as absolute orientation), enabling children to learn it and adults to maintain it. Cultures are overlapping sets of systems that to some extent can be pulled apart; they do not all have to cohere. To the extent that they do cohere into something larger than the sum of the individual parts, we need a concept of culture. We do not, however, need a global theory of culture, but rather the ingredients for understanding human nature and human differences. These will require at least the following: a theory of mind (or mind/body, if you prefer), a theory of how cultural environment interacts with mind, a theory of how culture and mind emerge ontogenetically through social interaction in a community, and a theory of how the capacity for culture could have evolved.

Anthropologists should recognize that cognitive science has taken the ball away from us in our self-styled game of explaining "what it is to be human." The cognitive scientists' answer is, our *minds*. More specifically, for Terrence Deacon (1997) it is our "symbolic capacity," for Steven Pinker (1994) it is our "language instinct," and for Daniel Dennett (1991) it is our "consciousness," all conceived of as parts of the human mind. By presenting these ideas in books designed for a wide readership, these cognitive scientists have had considerable influence on popular views of language and mind. But these views leave a huge hole where culture should be. Perhaps it is time to start filling the hole.

Notes

1. This research was conducted in the Mayan *municipio* of Tenejapa from 1990 to 1998, in collaboration with Stephen Levinson, and was based on my earlier work (1971–1973, 1980) in the same community. The Tzeltal data discussed here are derived from participant observation, videotaped natural social interaction, videotaped interactional "space games" constructed to foster the use of spatial vocabulary, linguistic elicitation, and informal cognitive experiments. See Brown 2001 for details.

2. See, for example, Tomasello's damning review of Pinker's *The Language Instinct* (1994), entitled "Language Is Not an Instinct" (Tomasello 1995), as well as Deacon 1997; Elman et al. 1996; Sampson 1999.

3. See, for example, the "lexical principles" proposed in Golinkoff et al. 1995.

4. An exception to the generalization that anthropologists have failed to ask this question is Michael Carrithers (1992). Biological anthropologists, too, increasingly are asking such questions (see Durham, this volume).

5. The "culture as process" stance rests on pioneering work of the 1960s and 1970s, especially that of ethnomethodologists and conversation analysts, as well as that of interactionist psychologists such as Roger Brown and Jerome Bruner.

6. The terms "figure" and "ground" in discussions of spatial language derive from their counterparts in gestalt psychology and refer to the object being located (the figure) and the object or region in relation to which it is located (the ground). See Talmy 1983.

7. Among such implications are differences in performance on memory tasks. People shown a spatial layout and asked to remember it, then rotated 180 degrees before having to reconstruct it, will perform differently depending on their frame of reference. Relative speakers rotate the spatial scene so that what

was on the left side remains on the left; absolute speakers rotate the remembered array in their heads and reconstruct the array with the same object lying, say, to the north. See Levinson 1996b; Pederson et al. 1998.

8. Complexity clearly is different for the two-place topological relations of an intrinsic system (e.g., "at the house's face"), the three-place egocentric relations of a relative system (e.g., "left of the house"), and the three- or four-place Euclidean grid of an absolute system (e.g., "north of the house"). See Levinson 1996b.

9. For example, on a task requiring discrimination between two otherwise identical but mirror-image-reversed photographs, Tzeltal speakers routinely insist that "they are exactly the same" (Levinson and Brown 1994).

10. The semantic oppositions specialized for this absolute system include those encoded in a set of motion verbs (ascend/descend/go across), some positional verbs (be above/be below), a set of nouns (uphill/downhill/across the slope), and a set of directional adverbials (uphillward/downhillward/acrossways). See Brown and Levinson 1993b, 2000.

11. This compares favorably with Western children's mastery of the left-right distinction, which is not complete until age eleven or twelve (Brown and Levinson 2000).

12. Similar findings are described in de León 1994 for the closely related Mayan language Tzotzil. Related work in Bali (Wassman and Dasen 1998) has also shown early learning of an absolute spatial system, in this case prior to learning of a relative system.

13. These speculations about possible cognitive effects rest to date on linguistic evidence alone. Cognitive tests (of topological/projective reasoning, and "theory of mind" tests) would be required to confirm them.

14. Cognitive scientists' wild proposals for the contents of hard-wiring run up against another objection: there is no possible evolutionary motive for developing a hard-wired concept or representation of something such as "property" (unlike a predator silhouette, for example). There is, however, an evolutionary motive—adaptability—for having the capacity for culture in mental architecture (see Levinson 2000).

nine

Cultural Variation in Time and Space: The Case for a Populational Theory of Culture

William H. Durham

In this chapter I outline a new way of thinking about culture that might help anthropology move beyond its current culture crisis. It is a way of thinking about culture that can be called "populational," for it views cultures not as "complex wholes" or "coherent conceptual structures" but as changing temporary collections of socially transmitted information. I hope to show that there are specific utilities to this conception of culture, particularly for analyzing patterns of human thought and action and their changes over time and space.

Efforts to formulate a populational conception of culture are not entirely new. They date back at least to Edward Sapir's "distributive" theory of culture (Rodseth 1998; see also Shore 1996: 209). What is new, relatively speaking, is recognition that a populational conception highlights three significant features of culture: its transmission, its internal variation, and its mechanisms of selective retention. These features draw attention to the potential for cultural systems to undergo bona fide *evolutionary* change—that is, to "descend with modification from ancestral forms," as Darwin (1859) so succinctly put it in the case of species. In other words, a populational conception of culture emphasizes that cultures are evolutionary systems in their own right, and it paves the way for analyzing cultural change as a kind of evolutionary process. As I hope to show, this way of thinking about culture gives us valuable new tools for thinking about cultural variation in space and time. It is often called "coevolutionary theory" or a "coevolutionary model of culture" (after Durham 1991), for it hypothesizes that cultures are systems of evolutionary change, parallel to and interacting with genes.

Population Thinking about Culture

The starting point for a populational theory of culture is to recognize that cultural systems, for all else that they may or may not be, consist of information that is socially conveyed through space and time within a social group. Culture's defining property, its characteristic feature, from this perspective is its *social transmission.* No matter how small and insignificant the information, at one end of the spectrum, nor how grand and encompassing, at the other end, that which is socially taught and learned is part of culture. "A culture," in this view, is simply the full collection of socially transmitted information within a society. This definition is deliberately ecumenical and open-ended. It is meant to embrace a wide array of informational or "ideational" phenomena, including ideas, values, beliefs, meanings, and so on.

While perhaps not terribly provocative in and of itself, this conception of culture leads to several corollaries that are more controversial. One, for example, is the realization that culture is by no means exclusive to human societies. Many other species of organisms have social groups that harbor collections of socially transmitted information—and not just the great apes or other close phylogenetic kin (for recent examples throughout the animal kingdom, see Dugatkin 2000; for discussion of chimpanzee cultures, which are especially convincing, see Wrangham et al. 1994). If desired, one can add qualifiers to the definition of culture to make it more specific and restrictive. The one that comes immediately to mind is to restrict the "cultural" to the subset of socially conveyed information that is also symbolically encoded (that is, encoded in signifiers arbitrarily ascribed with specific meanings). Though I personally have no objection to adding this qualifier and could well have adopted it in the discussion to follow, I prefer an ecumenical definition of culture that allows models and theories to be tested against a wide range of empirical challenges.

A second corollary to the foregoing definition is the obvious one that culture is a property of social groups of organisms. This raises an important practical question: What do we take to be the relevant social group, and how do we establish its boundaries and membership? On the one hand, a fixed, categorical definition with respect to human populations would risk the essentialist trap, creating the impression that each "ethnolinguistic group," for example, has its own distinctive, characteristic "culture." Such a move would be a big step backward, contributing to the false illusion that there is one uniform culture common to all people who speak a given language, for example, or who occupy a particular geographic or political area. At the other extreme, if one were to insist that the relevant groups must have completely smooth and regular flows of social transmission within them, then one could well end up with tiny groups of two or three individuals, which would also lead nowhere.

A related problem concerns social structure within the pertinent society. All too often, as Joseph Fracchia and Richard C. Lewontin (1999: 69) and I (Durham 1991: ch. 4) have emphasized, power relations and inequalities have not been fully integrated into efforts at building populational models of culture. The question is how to avoid what the former term the "disappearance of the social" in populational models, especially given empirical evidence that power asymmetries have been profoundly important in shaping existing cultural systems. How can we formulate population models without simultaneously "dissolving" social structure?

Answers to these important questions entail drawing boundaries around social groupings. As a general rule, boundaries are probably best drawn at *relative* barriers to social transmission for the specific cultural information under study: natural barriers (rivers, lakes, mountains, etc.), language barriers, social barriers (as may come with various forms of inequality, such as class or caste), and the like. Boundaries will thus depend on the problem under study. The advantage to such procedures is that the relevant population(s) can and should reflect major social "fault lines" of inequality, including race, class, caste, gender, age, and so on. A large and heterogeneous society can thus be subdivided into pertinent "reference groups" within which individuals have similar sociocultural constraints and opportunities (see Durham 1991). This procedure, together with the concept of imposition discussed later, goes a long way toward representing social structure within populational models of culture.

A fourth corollary that follows from the foregoing definition is that cultural transmission may be thought of as particulate and thus as moving between individuals in a social group in more or less discrete chunks of varying size and content. This follows, on the one hand, from the fact that culture has to be learned and stored in minds whose organization, capacities, and limitations impose "cognitively formed units" on culture (as argued, for example, by D'Andrade [1995: 247]).

On the other hand, it also follows from the temporal nature of the transmission process. The full information system of a culture is normally far too vast to be transmitted all at once, in a giant all-or-nothing event. The more usual course is for culture to be transmitted in variable units of different kinds and sizes (on which see, e.g., Williams 1972), units that also vary with the social context of transmission.

It seems reasonable, then, to assume that cultural systems can be broken down into component parts or facets of varying size and content. Just what to call these component parts remains a matter of little consensus (see reviews in Durham 1991: ch. 4 and in Durham and Weingart 1997). Some of the more common ones include "idea," "belief" "concept," and "symbol," whose precedent use in (mostly non-populational) culture theory would seem to recommend them. On the other hand, they also come loaded with connotations from everyday usage, some of which may be troublesome. As a result, the field has spawned a number of fancy-sounding neologisms (also reviewed in Durham 1991). These, too, have problems, including the common one of being tightly associated with specific theories and all that comes with them, for better or worse. For example, "culturgen" has been almost exclusively linked with the theory of epigenetic rules put forward by Charles Lumsden and Edward O. Wilson (1981). "Meme," coined by Richard Dawkins (1976), has become the favorite unit of the "cultural virus" school of culture theory, proponents of which view human beings as plagued by legions of "selfish cultural replicators" (see, e.g., Blackmore 1999; Brodie 1996; Lynch 1996). "Mental representations" has been advocated in Dan Sperber's (1996) epidemiological approach but remains an awkward mouthful even with appropriate precedent usage elsewhere in social and cognitive science.

Perhaps the way easiest forward for now is to use neutral terms such as "cultural unit," "cultural variant," or "cultural item." The key point is that the cultural system in the minds of members of a given group can be thought of as a collection of cultural items in space and time. In other words, culture can itself be represented as a population. It is a population of individual cultural items as they exist in the minds of the culture "carriers."

The next step in the argument is to posit that the "individuals" of this cultural population vary. In other words, we assume that there is *variation* among the individual cultural items, whether in the content, form, or size of their information. For many theorists, this is a completely unproblematic assumption. Sperber (1996: 83), for example, argues that variation is an intrinsic and unavoidable by-product of transmission:

"What human communication achieves in general is merely some degree of resemblance between the communicator's and the audience's thoughts. Strict replication, if it exists at all, should be viewed as just a limiting case of maximal resemblance, rather than as the norm of communication.... A process of communication is basically one of transformation."

Consequently, cultural things are "transformed almost every time they are transmitted" (Sperber 1996: 25), and thus variation is inherent and abundant in the population of cultural units. Other theorists, including a number from archaeology, are not convinced that variation is intrinsically abundant at all times, often citing the million years or so of human history over which Acheulian hand axes remained invariant. While not exactly countering Sperber's claim, these theorists also point out that in human societies there is often substantial peer pressure for conformity, which tends to restrict variation (see, e.g., Boyd and Richerson 1985 on "conformist transmission"). Even so, a growing list of "variation-minded" analysts (Rodseth 1998; see also Barth 1987 and this volume; Borofsky 1994; Vayda 1994) point out that there is always at least *some* variation within populations of cultural "things." For present purposes, that is all we really need to assume. Let me therefore speak of cultural items and their "variants."

Given these assumptions, we are in a position to begin "population thinking" about culture. An expression coined by Ernst Mayr in the context of evolutionary biology (see, e.g., Mayr 1982: 45–47, 1991: ch. 4), population thinking considers a collection of individual items—the usual example in Mayr's field being a collection of members of the same species—in terms of its statistical properties (e.g., means, medians, and modes for some observable feature) while also recognizing the uniqueness of individual members of the set. It assumes that individual members differ, such that the collection embraces substantial variation and no one member or "type" can stand for the whole. In anthropology, we are not used to population thinking. In its place, we have commonly adopted a homogenizing or essentializing way of thinking about culture in which each group has its own characteristic culture. We have sometimes even used the terms "society" and "culture" interchangeably. My point is that anthropology has much to gain if we start population thinking about culture.

To begin with, population thinking about culture opens the door to dealing with variation and complexity. It allows us to stop thinking of culture as "a deeply sedimented essence attaching to or inhering in particular groups of people" (as criticized, for example, by Ortner [1999: 8]).

The new starting point is not to get at uniform "themes" or a uniform "ethos" but to get at variety: for example, to represent the culture of a group by frequency distributions of its internal variants. One can summarize any given cultural belief, say, by the list of variants that have adherents in the pertinent group and by the numbers or percentages of people that adhere to each one. Among other things, this step enables one to describe the features of a cultural system in terms of frequency histograms of variation. It uses distributions to provide a kind of statistical "snapshot" of the cultural variation that exists within the group at a particular time.

In this way, population thinking legitimates variation and its study, allowing us to go beyond reified notions of "characteristic culture." It encourages us to look for novelty in all its forms—to dwell not on the "standard story" but on the range and distribution of stories. Outliers become interesting and informative, not embarrassing and discredited. In short, culture is viewed not as a form but as a *distribution*.

Evolutionary Thinking about Culture

A second advantage to population thinking about culture is that it facilitates the study of cultural change. I think one could fairly say that population thinking *invites* a focus on change, for any given distribution of cultural items and its statistical summary have but short-term value. So many things can cause a distribution to shift—from basic demographic events (migration, births, and deaths) all the way to contagion-like effects of catchy new variants—that what is interesting is to ask, what is causing the changes? Why are some variants increasing in representation over time while others are decreasing? What are the processes behind temporal variations in distribution, and what are the properties of the variants that become more prevalent?

At this juncture, it is helpful to add the third and final feature of cultural systems that are highlighted by populating thinking, namely, what Donald Campbell (1965) termed mechanisms of "selective retention." There exist within cultural systems, and the societies that sustain them, a good number of processes that can cause the differential propagation of variants, favoring the retention of some forms and not others. Such processes are important, Campbell argued, because they are capable of causing systematic, cumulative shifts through time in the frequencies of cultural variants within a society. Campbell offered the first useful tally of these processes, calling them "selective systems." His list included "the selective survival of complete social organizations [or groups]," "selective diffusion or borrowing between social groups," "selective imitation of inter-individual variations," "selective promotion [of individuals] to leadership and educational roles [with differential influence]," and "rational selection," including decision-making processes by individuals or groups.

In the years since the publication of Campbell's list, the number of candidates has increased somewhat, as has the number of subcategories under them (see discussions in Durham 1990; Durham, Boyd, and Richerson 1997), and they have come to be much more fully theorized (see especially Boyd and Richerson 1985 for a list that closely follows Campbell's). But it does look as if Campbell was on the right track: today, the goal remains to elucidate the important mechanisms for the differential propagation of cultural variation and to understand their impact on cultural change over time.

Perhaps the most important of Campbell's arguments, though, and that of a number of authors since him (e.g., Cavalli-Sforza and Feldman 1981; Lewontin 1970), was this: Any system characterized by these elements—the occurrence of variation, a means of transmission, and one or more mechanisms of selective retention—is capable of evolutionary change in the Darwinian sense of "descent with modification." The implication is that cultural systems evolve in their own right: they are transformed through time as products of their repeated social transmission within a group. The process is clearly historical, in the sense of change taking place over time. But it is also a special kind of historical change, being "evolutionary" in the Darwinian sense of change brought about by the dynamics of iterative transmission.

Let me now combine several of the preceding arguments and offer what I hope is a useful *operational* definition of cultural evolution. Cultural evolution can be thought of as any change through time in the distribution of cultural variants in a social group. Thanks to population thinking, it comes down to a relatively simple matter of statistical change in cultural histograms. Let me also emphasize that cultural evolution as defined here does not imply unilinear or even multilinear stage sequences, as have plagued so many theories for so many years in anthropology. It does not imply progress, growth, endurance, or increasing complexity; it implies simply a frequency shift in the course of repeated social transmission. As used here, "cultural evolution" also has none of the problems of so-called genetic determinism or of culture's being merely a "handmaiden" or "delivery system" for the genes, as was often assumed in early works of sociobiology. The potential exists here for culture to operate as a parallel, semiautonomous track of information inheritance—interacting with the genetic track to be sure, but not subordinated to or controlled by the genes.

An Example: Incest Taboos among the Nuer

An example at this juncture will help to illustrate these rather abstract and theoretical arguments. The example I offer concerns an old hobby-horse in anthropology: the incest taboo. Because the defining feature of the incest taboo is the *prohibition* of sexual relations with kin (that is, the rule against such behavior, as contrasted with behaviors of inbreeding avoidance), incest taboos are clearly socially transmitted and are thus good "cultural items" (see also discussion in Durham 1991: ch. 6). More than that, taboos have been shown to vary over space and time within a number of human societies—among them the Nuer cattle herders of Sudan. Let me thus take up the Nuer case as an illustration of population thinking in the cultural domain. My goals are to show that no harm or violence to culture need come from population thinking; to illustrate that such an approach is compatible with, and not antagonistic to, ethnographic richness and other kinds of cultural analysis in the same situation; and to argue that a powerful process of cultural evolutionary change can be seen at work in ongoing Nuer debates over the definition and scope of the incest taboo. The discussion here must be brief and admittedly highly oversimplified (for fuller treatment, see Evans-Pritchard 1940; Hutchinson 1985, 1996). Nevertheless, I hope it will serve to demonstrate a wider potential for the approach outlined here.

In a 1985 paper, the anthropologist Sharon Hutchinson explored the cultural dynamics behind changing concepts of incest in Nuerland. Among other things, Hutchinson found that the scope of the prohibition had been redefined over the previous fifty years in clear association with changes in the Eastern Nuer system of bridewealth, which in turn directly reflected changing power relations in society. Formerly, and still today among Western Nuer, the incest taboo covered all cousins up to and including fifth cousins. Today in the east, the taboo has been rolled back to include only second cousins routinely. What is more, noted Hutchinson, "I documented a case in which two full brothers married two full sisters and a second case in which a man married the natural daughter of his paternal uncle. Both of these marriages would have been inconceivable 50 years ago" (1985: 629).

Attempting to understand this shift, Hutchinson identified and analyzed a crucial social process through which the taboo changed. It was a process that acted upon existing variation among some of the cultural items of Nuer society—namely, existing alternative conceptions of the incest taboo, particularly as concerned its extension beyond the nuclear family. As Hutchinson reported, change in the Eastern Nuer incest taboo resulted from young couples' openly challenging the traditional authority of the courts: "It is not at all uncommon for a couple frustrated in their desire for marriage by official [court] decrees of *rual* [incest] to run off together shortly after the trial. If the union then proves fruitful and the child thrives, the couple can later return to their families, confident that some sort of marriage arrangement will be made. If not, the lovers usually separate voluntarily" (1985: 629).

Couples who eloped were said to have "feuded for each other" in this way, going against public opinion, running off, and eventually bringing back a healthy child. Such "feuding" has three important implications for Nuer culture in light of my arguments here. First, Nuer used the results of feuding to sort among varying extensions of the incest taboo and to show which variants did and did not result in unions with healthy offspring. The process indicates that Nuer were aware of what we Westerners would call the deleterious genetic effects of inbreeding. Writes Hutchinson (1985: 630): "One might say that the limits of incest and exogamy have an experiential correlate in the eyes of the Nuer: 'incest children' are expected to reveal their dangerous origins through illness, abnormality, and early death" (on the "experiential correlates" of inbreeding in other human societies, see Durham 1991: ch. 6). But the important implication for our purposes is that the Nuer used these experiential correlates to weed out alternative extensions of the taboo: "The fecundity of couples who willingly risk possible illness, infertility, infant mortality and other misfortunes in order to challenge received notions of *rual* often proves more powerful in shaping public opinion than official court decrees. It is the fortune or misfortune of such couples, closely watched and commented upon by all, that is later cited as evidence either for or against the validity of a particular [incest] prohibition" (Hutchinson 1985: 630).

In other words, multiple cultural variants existed in the minds of the Nuer in the form of varying extensions of the taboo, and they sorted among them according to their widely noticed and discussed consequences. Public opinion shifted depending on the fortune of the young couple, evidently resulting in a change in the cultural histogram of taboo variants. The example seems a close match to the populational model, at least in regard to this aspect of the Nuer cultural system. There is a discrete, identifiable entity within the socially transmitted cultural information in this society (a prohibition on sex with kin); it varies in at least one perceived feature (the kinship extension of the taboo); and the variations matter to the Nuer in a way that correlates with historical shifts in variant frequencies.

But a second implication of feuding is also noteworthy. Evidence suggests that this process has been influential for a long time—certainly long enough to shape the incest taboo, but also long enough to influence the very meaning of Nuer words and kin terms. Again to quote Hutchinson (1985: 630): "Of course this method of testing the limits of 'divine tolerance' in matters of incest and exogamy is nothing new. The existence and relative severity of different categories of *rual* have long been revealed to Nuer through the experience and interpretation of affliction. *Rual*, as Evans-Pritchard noted, describes not only the incestuous congress itself but also subsequent hardships attributed to it." Indeed, the Nuer reason that incest is morally reprehensible *because* it has these effects. "It is not bad in itself but in its consequences" (Evans-Pritchard 1956: 194).

The third and final implication of the example that I want to mention has to do with the sorting process, the public "weeding" among variants according to their validity. The process is definitely social and has almost a democratic air about it, unless the courts intervene. Feuding is "closely watched and commented upon by all." It is also selective in that not all variants are sustained and granted validity. A judgment or decision process is clearly involved—one that, at least at the time of Hutchinson's fieldwork, was not consistently the product of the imposing authority of the courts. The process has evidently operated over long periods of time, enough to affect the very meaning of the term *rual*. And finally, the process has also been governed or honed by preexisting cultural values. As Hutchinson noted, the outcome of this "pragmatic fecundity testing" rides on an important decision criterion (1985: 630): "The reason why this mode of 'feuding' is so often effective is that most Nuer, Easterners and Westerners alike, regard any union that proves fruitful as divinely blessed, and thus consider it to be in some sense free of *rual*."

Significantly, this decision criterion—that "fruitful" means "divinely blessed"—is itself a cultural item, dependent upon socially transmitted notions of divinity and the power of the gods to reward or punish sexual unions via ensuing offspring. The example thus has a reflexive, self-referential quality about it: preexisting cultural values are brought to bear in the decision process that governs the fate of other cultural variants under scrutiny. In this example, cultural evolution is apparently a self-guiding process.

In short, I believe that changing conceptions of incest among the Nuer illustrate the validity of a populational model of culture and culture change. Again, variable entities clearly exist within the shared ideational "pool" of Nuer culture in regard to the incest taboo. Although the taboo is intimately linked to wider notions of kinship and social structure in Nuer society, as Hutchinson (1985) emphasized, it appears to be semi-independent in its ability to change through the feuding process, even as other parts of the same cultural system remain constant (at least temporarily). Indeed, variation in the taboo is repeatedly introduced by young people who actively challenge the more traditional conceptions defended by the courts. Cultural change shows up as change in the relative frequencies of socially transmitted variants within the pool—in other words, as change by differential social replication, or cultural evolution. [*margin note: No evidence*]

Moreover, the example points to a key process in the dynamics of cultural evolution in the Nuer context, a process that I have elsewhere called "cultural selection" (see, e.g., Durham 1991), inspired by Campbell's (1965) "rational selection." The determination of which taboo variants will be selectively retained in Nuer culture is a value-driven decision process that seems fairly democratic in operation, at least in this one example. Simply put, people choose among the options according to the options' perceived and valued (or devalued) consequences, and they appear to accomplish change through their choices, even in the face of the traditional authority of the courts. If so, then the Nuer example further qualifies as an example of cultural selection *by choice* (that is, by free election among variants), as opposed to cultural selection *by imposition* (in which variants are forced or foisted onto their carriers; for further discussion, see Durham 1991: ch. 4). And finally, the outcome, after much observation and discussion, is governed by a cultural yardstick that guides choice among the variants, namely, the belief that fruitful unions are "divinely blessed."

It is important to note that the outcome is governed neither by innate preferences (or "primary values"), as in some sociobiological theories of culture change, nor by ecological and psychological factors of "attraction" (in the sense of Sperber 1996). It is governed by a simple cultural yardstick, a case of what I call "secondary value selection." In this way, cultural evolution becomes self-directing or "self-selecting": past products of the evolutionary process sometimes go on to serve as values governing the ongoing evolution of culture.

What This Means

What I hope I have accomplished in this essay, then, is to show that there is merit to "population thinking" about culture and that there is no good reason for cultural anthropology to sustain its current fear of evolution, or "evophobia." I have tried to suggest that culture can be thought of as a population of variants—be they representations, meanings, or memes—whose frequencies may change over time as they are iteratively conveyed within a group, and thus evolve. And I have tried to suggest, though arguing only by example in this context, that an important process or mechanism of cultural evolution is cultural selection—that is, decision making according to preexisting cultural values.

In conclusion, let me briefly mention five implications of this coevolutionary perspective for our understanding of cultural variation in space and time. First, coevolutionary models depict culture as socially conveyed information within social groups. On the positive side, this is a very general and inclusive conceptualization of culture; most studies of socially transmitted behavioral patterns in nonhuman primates accordingly qualify as "culture." On the other hand, there remains a gap between this "social information" concept of culture and the more common "symbols and meanings" concept of culture in cultural anthropology. Much socially conveyed information is not symbolically encoded, especially in nonhuman animal contexts. So does this information qualify as culture? The issue is far from resolved, and surely it is not an entirely semantic issue, where one can more or less arbitrarily move the line to be more inclusive or less so. There is increasing evidence that human organic evolution included a specialized cognitive adaptation that made the species especially adept at symbol manipulation (see Tomasello 1999).

Second, coevolutionary models assume some kind of "unit of culture." That is, they assume that a larger cultural system is composed of—and can be broken down into—some sorts of smaller units that cohere long enough to be socially transmitted as intact entities. In this view, a cultural system is not an all-or-nothing thing, socially acquired in one fell swoop. Instead, it is assumed to be socially conveyed in a continuous process, with intermittent transmission of bits and pieces of varying size and content. Moreover, at least *some* variation is assumed to exist among these bits and pieces in every cultural system. In this view, a cultural system is rarely uniform and stable, and it certainly is not an enduring "essence" characteristic of a group of people.

Third, cultures are viewed as changing through time and space as a consequence of the differential social transmission of alternative units among culture carriers. Many different phenomena may cause differential social transmission within a group, including biasing properties of our coevolved psyche, the value-driven decisions of individuals or subgroups, and even the differential physical reproduction of culture carriers, so long as it is coupled with social transmission to offspring (which qualifies as a special case of natural selection, i.e., the natural selection of cultural variation). Although there remains little consensus among contemporary cultural evolutionists about which of these processes are most important, existing evidence (much of it reviewed in Durham 1991) suggests that a likely candidate is cultural selection, or preservation by preference. I therefore hypothesize that cultural variants are most commonly preserved (or not) through the value-based decisions of individuals and groups, whether those decisions are made more or less autonomously (by choice) or through the use of force (imposition). I further hypothesize that cultural selection governed by socially transmitted values—namely, secondary value selection—is the main but not exclusive means of cultural evolutionary change in human societies. I offer this hypothesis as the approximate equivalent, for cultural evolution, of Darwin's original hypothesis about natural selection as the main means of organic evolution.

Fourth, the view of culture outlined here is not only compatible with but a logical extension of recent conceptualizations of culture as a "contested domain" or a "contested process of meaning making." On the matter of contestation, of course, there is no contest: the collections of socially transmitted information discussed here are incessantly buffeted by no less than two kinds or levels of contestation. First, there is the inescapable contest between individuals or groups who are interested, often vested, in the cultural ascendancy of their preferred cultural variant. This contest exists whether the predominant process is cultural selection by choice or by imposition, but it is especially acute in instances of imposition. In that case, one individual or group is able to use some form of power to foist off onto others in the society its preferred cultural variant (see also Durham 1991). The case of the Nuer, although only hinting at the imposing traditional authority of the courts, offers an interesting example of contestation during the process of selection by choice. Young couples who defy public opinion and run off together—to try their hand at what Hutchinson (1985) called "pragmatic fecundity testing"—are appropriately said to have "feuded" for approbation and a change in local culture. Second, there is an even deeper sense of contestation within evolutionary arguments of the kind offered here. Underlying a populational model of culture is the assumption of an inevitable, unrelenting contest among variants for cultural survival in human societies. So long as there is actual or latent variation, there is *always* a contest in cultural evolution.

Finally, let me reemphasize that, in this view, cultures are themselves populations of variable, replicating entities. I have therefore attempted to argue the advantages of population thinking in the realm of culture and to suggest that cultural systems truly do exhibit evolutionary change. Among other things, arguments like those presented here can help to bring into cultural anthropology's analytical tool kit a variety of handy tools of evolutionary thought that are otherwise missing and foreign. A personal favorite, just to give a single example, is the concept of cultural homology, since in a system of "descent with modification" one expects to find many, many similarities among separate, even distant, cultural systems that trace to shared historical origins and are thus features "sprung from a common source." Terms and principles of this kind will surely prove useful as anthropology looks beyond accident and diffusion to understand cultural similarity—and difference, for that matter.

With its focus on cultural variation in space and time, its attention to social processes behind the differential persistence and "cultural life" of ideational phenomena, and its promise of fruitful connection to the wider domain of evolutionary thought, population thinking has much to offer contemporary anthropology, even if it is not for a move "beyond culture." I suggest that coevolutionary approaches in anthropology will eventually prove not just compatible with but useful for the general project of "rethinking and reconfiguring 'culture' in the contemporary moment" (Ortner 1999: 8).

Note

I thank the organizers of this volume for their help in making this a better example of the social transmission of cultural information than it otherwise would have been. I also thank Alison Bidwell, Susan Charnley, Flora Lu, Richard Pocklington, and Amanda Stronza of the Department of Anthropological Sciences, Stanford, for their timely feedback and advice.

Part 4

The Politics of Culture

Query: Relation between Civilization & State? Culture & State?

How to place Rousseau? Rights of Man vs. State as Voice of the People...

ten

The Politics of Culture in Post-apartheid South Africa

Richard A. Wilson

Human rights are universal legal and moral categories of one Enlightenment political tradition, namely, liberalism. During the early modern period, writers such as John Locke and Thomas Hobbes asserted that natural rights were legal entitlements that all humans held by virtue of being human, irrespective of time and place. Human nature and natural law were discoverable through the application of a universal Reason, a view that came from Aristotle through Grotius and was consolidated in Kant and the still-influential neo-Kantian tradition.[1] These ideas then became central in the dissolution of dynastic rule and the establishment of modern nation-states.

Contrary to the view that modernity has always been a single, integrated project, liberal ideals of rationalism and individualism came under immediate attack from the father of German Romanticism, Johann Herder (see Hann, this volume). In the late 1700s, Herder rejected Enlightenment principles and the Rights of Man in favor of a mystical attachment of each individual to his or her community. In the Romantic tradition,[2] human rights are a fiction parading as fact, borne of a wrongly conceived human nature that is undermined by the really existing diversity of cultural practices and beliefs. Over the next three hundred years, this polarity crystallized into the familiar debate between French and Anglo-American Enlightenment universalists and their Romantic relativist opponents. Yet there is something wrong with this "clash-of-ideas" account as it is commonly presented, because it overaccentuates the formal incompatibilities between different political and intellectual traditions. The pervasiveness of this social philosophical dispute has often foreclosed more meaningful discussions about the concrete politics of human rights in democratizing countries, and it has obstructed an analysis of the complex and manifold ways in which human rights talk relates to questions of culture, race, and difference.

As has been argued elsewhere (Cowan, Dembour, and Wilson 2001; Wilson 1997), it is the task of social anthropologists and others to go beyond the decontextualized and discursive contradictions of universalist and relativist thought (which will always be incommensurable) to develop a comparative ethnography of rights. This approach situates rights talk and rights institutions in concrete historical conjunctures and examines their conceptualization and implementation in a legally plural context. The emphasis here is away from becoming mired in the logical contradictions between ideational systems and toward developing strong theories of what happens to human rights when state actors deploy human rights talk to build a "culture of human rights," or when social movements or minority groups articulate their political claims in terms of human rights discourse.

An ethnographic approach to human rights in democratizing countries reveals that political discourses on human rights and on culture are not as opposed as political scientists and political philosophers have assumed. Instead of being diametrically opposed, they present a number of different possibilities existing side by side, from a classic legal blindness toward difference to continuities in form and content. Too little attention has been paid to the ways in which human rights talk has become *the* central language of nation building in democratizing countries such as South Africa and to how state officials can combine elements of both liberalism and communitarianism in their interpretations of human rights.

In redefining the subject matter, the issue becomes less about a clash of cultures and ideas per se and more about the Weberian problematic of the legitimacy of state institutions (such as the judiciary) and bureaucratic power more generally. In the context of nation building in South Africa, human rights talk is deployed by politicians, religious figures, and judges with significant culturalist and Africanist referents in order to legitimate the project of post-apartheid nation building. At the same time, the conceptualization of human rights by more liberal judges may reject any relationship between culture and rights. We see here a fragmentation of elite strategies and a lack of coherence between state institutions, which obstructs attempts to build a single official version of human rights.

The implications of all this for the anthropological conception of "culture" are as follows. Culture as the central analytical concept of the tradition in cultural anthropology that runs from Boas to Kroeber and Benedict and on through Geertz should cease to be used *analytically*, because it is a conception of holism drenched in the Romantic tradition. This view of culture was central to the ideology of ethnonationalist political leaders throughout the twentieth century, and notably so in apartheid South Africa. Even in places where the ethnonationalists have been removed from power, the culture concept continues to be deployed by elite actors to legitimate their project of bureaucratization and nation building. Our focus should therefore shift away from simply deconstructing systematized and totalizing discourses ("culture" versus "human rights") and toward analyzing of the place of rights talk and rights institutions in the consolidation of state power and in mass social regulation.

Due to the exigencies of postauthoritarian conditions, human rights institutions have become significant sites for the legitimation of state institutions that bear many traces of the authoritarian past. This chapter examines the practices, methods, and discourses on culture and race of two main human rights institutions in South Africa, the Constitutional Court and the Truth and Reconciliation Commission (TRC). It focuses on two early episodes in the lives of these institutions—the striking down of the death penalty by the Constitutional Court in 1995 and one application for amnesty heard by the Amnesty Committee of the TRC in 1996. In the legal context of the Constitutional Court, human rights are combined with a romantic image of community, whereas the Amnesty Committee consciously excluded race as a political category. In the context of a fragmented state, different relationships between human rights talk and race or culture may exist simultaneously. Instead of the pure, polarized categories of universalism and romanticism, both expressions are present in the same political order, and they may be combined by a political elite engaged in a nation-building project.

A Brief History of Racism and Rights in South Africa

Before looking in detail at the politics of culture and race in the post-apartheid context, we must first consider briefly the historic place of race, culture, and group rights in apartheid South Africa. During the peace negotiations of 1990–1994, individual human rights emerged as the main alternative to the apartheid model of differential citizenship and group rights.

White settlers in South Africa had practiced racial discrimination against local Africans since Jan van Riebeeck led Dutch colonists to establish a trading post between Europe and Asia at the end of the seventeenth century. Apartheid (Afrikaans for "separateness"), however, as established after the election of the National Party in 1948 under D. F. Malan, was a radically new form of governance insofar as it codified races and institutionalized racially discriminatory practices through constitutional legal means. "Black" Africans and "coloureds" were subjected to pass laws that controlled their movement within the nation-state, as well as to laws that decided which residential areas they could live in, which schools they could attend, which jobs they could take, and which public services they could use. Within President H. F. Verwoerd's grand model of apartheid, pursued in the 1950s, blacks would be denationalized, stripped of their South African citizenship, and made citizens of small, dependent territories called "homelands." This was truly, in the words of Deborah Posel (2001), a "high modernist fantasy" of bureaucratic social engineering and societal regulation in the context of massive post–World War II industrialization and urbanization.

The political discourse of apartheid received close scholarly attention during the 1990s, and writers have drawn our attention to the way the architects of apartheid shifted from primarily biological conceptions of race (discredited because of their association with Nazism in Germany) to more culturalist paradigms. Although metaphors of blood and purity still abounded in popular racial beliefs, state policies mostly took a social constructivist view of racial classification. In the government's definition of race classification, race became an overtly sociolegal category, rather than a scientific-biological one.

In one cornerstone of apartheid policy, the Population Registration Act of 1950, it is clear that the categories "white," "coloured," and "black" were partially constructed through reference to subjective and cultural understandings of identity. White officials of the Department of Native Affairs determined racial classification using some methods of mid-century "scientific racism,"[3] but they also drew from more explicitly cultural criteria such as lifestyle, class status, language(s) spoken, and degree of "general acceptance" of an individual within a particular community. Posel (2001) goes so far as to say that the small number of appeals against racial classification (3,940 appeals by 1964 out of 12 million classifications) was attributable to the fact that the apartheid state's classification was relatively close to people's own subjective classifications, and it meshed with their subjective definitions of racial and class hierarchies.

In the post–World War II context, "culture" and "ethnicity," in the sense of fictive abstractions for organic, bounded, static, and internally homogeneous groups, became euphemisms for race within the dominant South African state discourse.[4] "Culture" became the euphemism for an extension of racialist policy by other means.[5] According to Adam Kuper (1986: 45), culture became the "functional alternative to race in the ideological edifice of South African 'native policy'; that is, it became the thinking bureaucrat's theoretical model of racism."

What was the place of anthropology in all of this, given its historical dedication to the term "culture"? The Afrikaans-speaking and English-speaking universities were divided, the former strongly loyal to Afrikaner nationalism and thus to the apartheid regime, the latter largely eschewing such a collaborative role. As Kuper described it (1986: 47), however, most English-speaking anthropologists "kept their heads down" and did not actively resist apartheid, with some notable exceptions. Social anthropologists such as David Webster of the University of the Witwatersrand rejected the categories of culture and ethnicity and turned instead to a Thompsonian Marxist approach in order to use "ethnography to focus on people made invisible by apartheid" (Gordon and Spiegel 1993: 89).[6]

Cultural models of race classification were reinforced by the Afrikaans ethnological (*volkekunde*) tradition of anthropology, which used a concept of culture markedly similar to that prevalent in the mid-century American cultural anthropology of Kroeber, Sapir, and Benedict.[7] Afrikaner anthropologists played a central role in the intellectual conceptualization and the administration of apartheid, mainly in the Ministry of Bantu Affairs,[8] but there was even an "ethnological unit" in the South African Defence Force. Apartheid theorists were ardent cultural relativists, dividing humanity into separate cultural groups that required "separate development." One such anthropological theorist of apartheid native policy was the University of Pretoria professor P. J. Coertze, whose "ethnos" theory provided a theoretical underpinning to apartheid thinking on race and culture:

> Man [has] his existence in culturally determined, organic social entities, i.e., ethnies (sing. ethnos), whose structures and existential activities are culturally determined. Such units cannot be organized but originate organically as the outcome of the combined actions of the forces controlling and determining human existence. Ontologically speaking, human existence is an existence within the framework of varying ethnical units, each having a separate corporal existence. This is man's normal existence; he cannot survive and lead a happy life any other way. (Quoted in Kuper 1986: 44)

The National Party relied upon cultural understandings of race and ethnicity to foist rights on the designated "population groups" (whites, coloureds, and blacks). Political rights were acceded by the apartheid state on the basis of membership in a racial group, and politicians specifically referred to apartheid as a system of "group rights." Race became entrenched as a sociolegal construct, with drastic effects on the life chances of nonwhites. Not surprisingly, the mainstream of the anti-apartheid movement, a conglomeration of liberals (e.g., in the Progressive Federal Party), socialists, communists, and social democrats (most of whom were in the African National Congress, or ANC), vehemently opposed any conceptual or political use of the terms "race" and "culture." Culture, in the sense of bounded communities with shared beliefs and practices, had no place in the country's anti-apartheid struggle, and it was either reduced to individuals (by liberals) or classes (by Marxists in the ANC and the South African Communist Party). Only black nationalists (such as members of the Pan Africanist Congress, or PAC) made political use of essentialized notions of race and culture in a way that echoed the white supremacists, though obviously they valued "Africanness" above all else.

During the high point of the political and military opposition to apartheid in the 1980s, ideas of human rights were held only by a minority of liberals and some social democrats within the ANC. The bulk of the liberation movement instead supported ideas of popular sovereignty drawn from Soviet-style socialism or black nationalism. Human rights began to command allegiance in the South African political mainstream only during the negotiations phase, after the unbanning of anti-apartheid parties and the release of Nelson Mandela and other political prisoners in 1990.[9] At this point, human rights became *the* paradigmatic discourse of compromise, and constitutionalism came to be the only political blueprint that could unify the various parties in the conflict.

For a short while (1989–1992), the National Party tried to advance a model of power sharing and "minority" rights in order to protect the interests of its constituency. In response, the ANC pushed for majority rule based upon the notion of one person, one vote. The multiparty talks focused on the writing of a new interim Constitution in 1993, including a Bill of Rights drawn directly from international human rights treaties, which outlawed any legislation on the basis of race and a host of other (ambiguously defined) criteria. In Section 9.3, the interim Constitution declared: "The state may not unfairly discriminate directly or indirectly against anyone on one or more grounds, including race, gender, sex, pregnancy, marital status, ethnic or social origin, colour, sexual orientation, age, disability, religion, conscience, belief, culture, language, and birth."

Yet the subsequent weakness of human rights talk after transition was a product of its very success during the negotiations period. During the peace process, human rights talk became the language not of principle but of pragmatic compromise, seemingly able to incorporate any moral or ideological position. The ideological promiscuity of human rights talk meant that it was ill-suited to serve as an immovable bulwark against a new politicization of culture and race.

In the first multiracial elections in South African history, held in 1994, the ANC was elected with a massive majority, and it set about creating the new human rights institutions required by a constitutional state. Of these, none were so important as the Constitutional Court, which had the power to strike down any legislation it deemed contrary to the new Constitution, and the Truth and Reconciliation Commission, which was mandated to document past atrocities and grant amnesty to perpetrators who qualified. It was the task of these institutions to create a new "culture of human rights" in which the individual rights of all, regardless of race, would be protected from violation on the scale seen under apartheid.

South Africa provides a fascinating case of the introduction of human rights talk and institutions into a country where human rights historically had limited ideological appeal. In looking at the implementation of human rights in the immediate post-apartheid years, we can get a sense of the concrete consequences of a universalistic and individualistic political philosophy and whether in practice it is as indifferent to difference as is claimed. My answer to this question is multistranded, insofar as I find evidence of both liberal and difference-blind versions of human rights, as well as continuities with Romantic understandings of race and culture.

Human Rights, *Ubuntu*, and the African Community

> God has given us a great gift, *ubuntu* . . . . *Ubuntu* says I am human only because you are human. If I undermine your humanity, I dehumanize myself. You must do what you can to maintain this great harmony, which is perpetually undermined by resentment, anger, desire for vengeance. That's why African jurisprudence is restorative rather than retributive.
>
> —Truth Commission Chair Desmond Tutu, March 1996[10]

It is appropriate to begin our examination of human rights in South Africa with an account of the supreme legal institution in the new political dispensation, the Constitutional Court. Liberal constitutionalism asserts the neutrality and the transcendence of law above society, but on a number of occasions Constitutional Court judges have sought to link their judgments to what they see as "popular" legal and moral values. This seeming contradiction begins to make sense only when we see law not as an autonomous, value-free process but as a form of domination in the Weberian sense, which is embedded in historically constituted, hierarchical social relations. If we perceive law as an ideological system through which power is mediated and exercised, then in a society where power has historically been exercised though racial/ethnic and national identities, we can expect rights talk to be ensnared by culturalist and nationalist discourses. Constitutionalists hoped that a culturally neutral Bill of Rights would transcend nationalist ideology, but in practice, the reverse has often been the case: rights have been subordinated to nation building.

After the 1994 elections, the connections between human rights and nation building became clear in the discourse of the Constitutional Court on reconciliation, restorative justice, and "African jurisprudence."[11] One African word, *ubuntu,* integrates all these dimensions. *Ubuntu,* a term found in all Bantu languages and championed mainly by former archbishop Desmond Tutu, is an expression of community—a romanticized vision of "the rural African community" based upon reciprocity, respect for human dignity, community cohesion, and solidarity. In the period shortly after the first multiracial elections, the language of reconciliation and rights talk more generally became synonymous with the term *ubuntu,* which became a leitmotif of Tutu's "rainbow" nationalism.

The term *ubuntu* appeared extensively in the first Constitutional Court's judgment on the death penalty—*The State v. T. Makwanyane and M. Mchunu,* 1995 (6) BCLR 605 (CC) (hereafter *State v. Makwanyane*)—particularly in the written opinions of the judges Sachs, Mohamed, Mokgoro, and Langa.[12] In all of these cases, as in the Tutu statement already quoted, *ubuntu* was used to define "justice" proper versus revenge, but the subtext reinforced the view that "justice" in the new culture of human rights would not be driven by a desire for vengeance or even by legally sanctioned retribution.[13] In *State v. Makwanyane,* Judge Langa (224) claimed that *ubuntu* "recognizes a person's status as a human being, entitled to unconditional dignity, value and respect." Langa saw the concept as "a commendable attribute, which the nation should strive for." Judge Mokgoro (307) sought to create a nationally specific South African jurisprudence by referring to *ubuntu* as an indigenous South African value that mitigates against the death penalty and acts as a multicultural unifier—as "a golden thread [that runs] across cultural lines."

Judge Sachs's *State v Makwanyane* opinion relied on the image of a static, ahistorical, and compassionate African community. According to Sachs (375–381), African customary law did not invoke the death penalty except in the case of witchcraft, which Sachs saw as more to do with spontaneous religious emotion than with "customary law." The existence of capital punishment in "African communities," from witch killing to "necklacing" in the 1980s and mob lynchings in the 1990s, was more the product of irrational crowd hysteria than of routine customary court justice, according to Judge Sachs.

This interpretation of capital punishment in African communities resulted from a time-honored tradition in Western jurisprudence in which the jurisdictional boundaries of law are defined by reference to law's opposite. Law excludes from its purview certain categories of persons (children, the mentally ill, and, in colonial contexts, slaves) and actions (violence without due process). Law is cool, rational, and impartial. Therefore, the "wild justice" of political cadres necklacing suspected police informers, of mob burnings of car hijackers, or of customary courts killing "convicted" witches simply is not allowed to be "law."

To see "African law" (itself a rather spurious notion given the dramatic interventions carried out by colonial and apartheid states) as completely excluding violent revenge runs contrary to the historical evidence. Courts administered by Africans have applied the death penalty to certain categories of persons (informers, witches, and, in the 1990s, car hijackers) in numerous and successive historical contexts.[14] South African newspapers regularly report cases of "rough justice" in which suspected criminals are dealt with harshly (or fatally) by vigilantes and impromptu township courts.

Why, then, did the Constitutional Court judges articulate such an implausible view? After 1994, the Constitutional Court was seeking to legitimate its position as the sovereign institution in the land, and the judges faced the difficult task of making an extraordinarily unpopular first ruling. They invoked *ubuntu* to try to demonstrate that the court was sensitive to popular values and to claim that these values were opposed to vengeance (even though every opinion poll showed overwhelming support for the death penalty).[15]

The judges adopted a strategy used by the authors of the interim Constitution's postscript: they sought to express the new "culture of rights" in a popular idiom. In doing so, they reinforced a wider propensity of state officials to connect rights and reconciliation to nation building through an appeal to Africanist ideas of unity and community. As Elsa van Huyssteen (1996: 294) has argued, human rights are the "main site for the reconciliation of constitutionalism with the aims of popular democracy." The concept of human rights, redefined as pan-Africanist reconciliation, is a bridge between an arid constitutionalism with little political purchase in South African society and the idea of popular sovereignty that largely motivated the anti-apartheid struggle.

Although the ANC consciously avoided constitutionalizing race in its first term, it still appealed to a pan-African identity to garner support for its policies, particularly among those who had the highest expectations from the collapse of apartheid. Heribert Adam (1994: 45), for example, acknowledged the dominance of ANC charterists over African nationalists but admitted that "a counter-racism would have great emotional appeal among a frustrated black township youth." The ANC's politicized social base still exerts pressure on the ANC National Executive to adopt an increasingly African definition of the nation. Given the enormous expectations among impoverished black citizens, coupled with the lack of a massive program for the redistribution of wealth and therefore the likelihood of continued material disparity between whites and blacks, the pressure to adopt African political rhetoric has been growing. Robert Price (1997: 171–172) has noted, since 1994, the growing salience of race politics as an important basis for political mobilization, the rise of racially exclusive forms of political association (black management groups, black chambers of commerce, the Black Editor's Forum, etc.), and an "increased reliance on group rather than individually based notions of rights and rewards."

It is tempting to ask, where did *ubuntu* originate? Among the diversity of its uses, which is its "true" meaning? To attempt a definitive etymology of *ubuntu*, particularly one based upon real or imagined African communities, would be to reproduce the language of nation builders. One can only trace the trajectory of its concrete and ideological usage among human rights organizations, religious leaders, Constitutional Court judges, and the general public. In a sense, it does not really matter where and how *ubuntu* originated, since one of the main characteristics of nation-building rhetoric is to historicize and naturalize "cultural" signs.

To draw on a formulation of Althusser's, *ubuntu* is just another "always-already-there" element of pan-Africanist ideology. *Ubuntu* connects human rights, restorative justice, reconciliation, and nation building to the populist language of pan-Africanism. In post-apartheid South Africa, it became the Africanist wrapping used to advertise a reconciliatory version of human rights talk to black South Africans. *Ubuntu* belies the liberal claim that human rights have no culturalist or ethnic dimensions. But from the communitarian understandings of Constitutional Court judges, let me now turn to a diametrically opposed example in which judges on the Amnesty Committee of the Truth and Reconciliation Commission adhered to a liberal individualism antagonistic to invocations of race or culture.

Truth, Reconciliation, and Nation Building

> The Commission of Truth and Reconciliation. It is the creation of a nation.
> —Constitutional Court Judge Albie Sachs[16]

The Truth and Reconciliation Commission (1995–2001) was *the* archetypal transitional statutory body created to promote a "culture of human rights" in South Africa. It was a key mechanism for promoting the new constitutionalist political order and the reformulation of justice in human rights talk as restorative justice (see Wilson 1996, 2001).

Having established in our review of the Constitutional Court's decision on the death penalty that human rights talk has become an integral part of nation-building discourse in South Africa, we must ask, what is this nation building for? It is not only an end in itself but also a means to another end, which is to consolidate a new form of bureaucratic governance. The ANC, when it inherited the battered shell of an authoritarian and illegitimate state, became motivated less by a vision of popular sovereignty than by bureaucratic imperatives. Nation building allows other processes to be carried out, such as the legitimation of the apparatus of justice, which remains tainted by the authoritarian past.[17] Legitimating the state's justice system in turn promotes a process of state building, as the post-apartheid state has embarked upon a project of unifying the diversity of justice institutions in South African society.

Truth commissions are one of the main ways in which new bureaucratic elites in democratizing countries seek to manufacture legitimacy for state institutions, especially the legal system. Along with the Guatemalan "Historical Clarification" Commission, the South African

Truth and Reconciliation Commission was the latest in more than fifteen truth commissions in the world during the last two decades of the twentieth century. (It functioned largely from 1996 through 1998, although amnesty hearings continued throughout 2001.) Truth commissions have become standard institutions in democratizing countries, each set up to investigate certain aspects of human rights violations under authoritarian rule.[18]

In South Africa, the 1995 Promotion of National Unity and Reconciliation Act mandated the TRC to investigate "gross violations of human rights," defined as "the killing, abduction, torture or severe ill treatment of any person" between 1 March 1960 (the Sharpeville massacre) and 5 December 1993.[19] The terms of reference allowed the possibility of including high-ranking intellectual authors of atrocities, for they referred to "any attempt, conspiracy, incitement, instigation, command or procurement to commit an act." This is the widest mandate received by any truth commission to date, but it still received criticism on the grounds that it could not encompass the structural dimensions of apartheid segregation policies (such as forced removals or "Bantu" education policies). The terms limited investigation to those acts that went beyond the wide latitude of abuse permitted by apartheid laws. Detentions without trial, forced removals, and Bantu education policy, all legal under apartheid, were not included under the terms of the act (unless, in extreme cases, the commissioners decided to include specific cases under the rubric of "severe ill treatment").

The work of the TRC was divided among three committees: the Human Rights Violations Committee, the Reparations and Rehabilitation Committee, and the Amnesty Committee. Throughout 1996 and 1997, the Human Rights Violations Committee held eighty hearings in town halls, hospitals, and churches around the country, to which thousands of citizens came and testified about past abuses. This process received wide national media coverage and brought ordinary, mostly black, experiences of the apartheid system into the national public space in a powerful way. The South African TRC took more statements than any previous truth commission in history (more than twenty-one thousand), and the Human Rights Violations Committee faced the daunting task of checking the veracity of each testimony, choosing which would be retold at public hearings and passing along verified cases to the Reparations and Rehabilitation Committee. The TRC also took on a limited investigative role, and by issuing subpoenas and taking evidence in camera, it constructed a fragmented picture of the past. In its final report, published in October 1998, the TRC produced findings on the majority of the 21,298 cases brought before it, and—unlike the Argentine and Chilean commissions—it named four hundred perpetrators of violations. The "truth" of the South African truth commission lay in its officially confirming and bringing into the public space what was already known, rather than discovering hitherto "hidden truths."

The efforts of the Reparations and Rehabilitation Committee to facilitate "reconciliation" represented the weakest of the three committees' activities. Part of the problem lay in the fact that the TRC had no money of its own to disburse to survivors; it could only make non-binding recommendations to the President's Fund. The TRC made it abundantly clear that victims should expect little from the process and only a fraction of what they might have expected had they prosecuted for damages through the courts. In the end, it recommended that those designated "victims" should receive approximately US$3,500 per year over a six-year period. However, reparations were very low on the list of priorities of the ruling ANC, which eventually offered each victim only a one-time payment of a few hundred dollars.

Finally, the South African TRC was unique in bringing the amnesty process into the truth commission, whereas in other countries it had always been a separate judicial mechanism. The final deadline for amnesty applications was 10 May 1996, and the TRC was overwhelmed with more than seven thousand applications. To receive amnesty, the applicant had to fulfil four legal criteria: the violation had to fall within the period of the act (1 March 1960 to 10 May 1994); the violation had to have been committed for a "political objective"—that is, not for personal gain, malice, or spite; the perpetrator had to divulge all he or she knew about the circumstances of the violation, including the chain of command that authored the act; and the violation had to be "proportional" to the intended aims.[20] If amnesty was refused, as it was in the majority of cases, or if it was later found that the applicant had not fully disclosed all material evidence in the case, then individuals were liable to future prosecution.

The amnesty hearings were a theatricalization of the power of the new state, which compelled actors in the previous political conflict to confess when they would rather have maintained their silence. Perpetrators were compelled to speak the new language of human rights and, in doing so, to recognize the new government's power to admonish and punish. This theatricalization of power gives us one clue to why democratizing governments set up truth commissions rather than relying upon the existing legal system: truth commissions are transient political-religious-legal institutions that have much greater symbolic potential than dry, rule-bound, technicality-obsessed courts of law. Truth commissions can, seemingly, transcend not only the banality of the perpetrators but the banality of the law's history-telling capacities.

Human Rights, Race, and Political Motive

Human rights institutions must always distinguish between criminal acts (which are not their concern) and human rights abuses, which are by definition political in character. The boundary between a "political" crime and a "criminal" crime, although essential to the definition of human rights, is blurred and indefinite, because the two categories often overlap. The difficulty that new South African human rights institutions had in distinguishing between political violations and those undertaken for personal gain was most evident when amnesty applicants invoked racism as their political motive.

Given the history of apartheid and the degree to which racism was an ideological mind-set at the center of state policies of racial superiority, segregation, and denationalization of blacks, it would seem fairly obvious that racism in itself constituted a "political motivation." This view was reinforced by the TRC report, which cast racism as a primary component of apartheid. For instance, the chair, Desmond Tutu, used the words apartheid and racism interchangeably in his foreword to the report (TRC 1998, 1: 15–16).

Early on, the Amnesty Committee heard an application from four brothers that would define how the committee subsequently dealt with race and racism. In September 1996, it held hearings in Potchefstroom to decide the case of the van Straaten brothers, who had been convicted of murdering two black security guards, Wanton Matshoba and Sazise Cyprion Qheliso, and stealing a Ford truck from Terblanche Transport in Vereeniging on 17 June 1989. At the time, the brothers were all in the minimum security section of Zonderwater Prison, serving thirteen-year sentences.[21]

The van Straaten brothers—Willem, Adriaan, Gideon, and Dawid—based their appeal for amnesty on the grounds that their actions were racially and therefore politically motivated, and the entire hearings revolved around whether race constituted political motive in and of itself. All four brothers professed to be supporters of the white supremacist Afrikaner Weerstandsbeweging (AWB) organization, led by Eugene Terre'blanche, which was renowned for its neo-Nazi symbolism and swastika-like insignia. They had attended AWB meetings, although they had not formally joined up. Adriaan claimed that he had been approached by an AWB member, Robbie Coetzee, to set up a cell that would engage in terrorist activities, destabilize the National Party regime, and ultimately establish a *volkstaat* for "the Afrikaner people." Coetzee encouraged Adriaan to carry out a preliminary act of violence, which would prepare him for greater acts of terrorism such as planting explosives at government installations. Adriaan claimed that this was the incentive for hatching a plan to tie up two night security watchmen and steal a truck, in order to demonstrate that blacks were incapable of the job and unemployed whites should be hired instead. As Amnesty Committee member Sisi Khampepe dryly commented, the van Straatens presented their actions as just another form of "job creation for whites." On the night of 17 June 1989, the brothers carried out this plan, but the two security men unexpectedly resisted, and the brothers killed them with a chisel and some rocks they found on the premises. They then stole the Ford truck but left it three hundred meters from the gates of the transport depot.

Under cross-examination from the amnesty judges and the TRC evidence leader, Advocate "Cocky" Mpshe, the van Straatens' account began to unravel, and another story emerged. The brothers had come up with their plan only after an all-day drinking session at the National Station Bar. They had not taken any rope to the transport depot, so they could not have been planning to tie up the guards. All had previous criminal convictions, and the eldest, Willem, had been imprisoned for repeatedly driving under the influence of alcohol and for theft of a motor-bike trailer. They admitted that they were not actually members of the AWB and that Willem was a member of the right-wing (but closer to the center than the AWB) Conservative Party. They had no official order or direct instruction from the AWB to commit the act. The AWB dissociated itself from the four men and did not arrange their legal defense; in the end they had to rely upon legal aid. They were defended by a Mrs. Isaks, who, ironically—given the brothers' racist acts—was an Asian woman. In their confessions, taken by police, they pleaded guilty to robbery, thereby acknowledging that the act had a criminal intent. In the eyes of the committee implementing the either/or terms of the act, the murders could not also have had a political intent. In the end, all four amnesty applications were rejected, and the brothers were condemned to serve out the rest of their sentences.

When the judges for the Amnesty Committee determined political motivation, membership in a political organization came to outweigh all other factors. "Political" relied on politics in the narrow liberal sense of formal membership in a political party. The desire to create a separate white nation or to bring about the downfall of apartheid was not enough in itself for the judges; it had to have been accompanied by membership in a political party that had given explicit instructions for the act.

This narrow view of politics forced Amnesty Committee members to take party policies at face value and ignore the more informal, less institutionalized connections between private racism and public ideology. When I suggested to amnesty judge Bernard Ngoepe that racism might be considered "political" insofar as the apartheid state organized society along racial lines and people were killed in the war simply for being white or black, he replied:

> But political parties never recognized this. In fact they denied it, and because of this, racism cannot be included in the act. Even the AWB never accepted this. They said, "We're not against blacks, just communism." When the [National Unity and Reconciliation] Act was drafted, political parties such as the National Party could not have included killing on the grounds of race. If I as a judge were to say that people were killed because of their color and this was politically motivated, then I'd be doing their dirty work for them.

The emphasis on politics' being party defined led to a reductive literalism in which, if the National Party, for example, stated that it was not racist, then racism could not be political, even if in practice (as was the case with the National Party, the Conservative Party, and the AWB) it advocated viciously racialist policies. This line of reasoning relied upon a stark dualism between political racism and private or "pure" racism. In the van Straaten hearings, this legal distinction clashed with the brothers' understandings of their political motivations:[22]

> *TRC Advocate Mpshe:* Do you agree that the fact that you refer in this letter to the fact that it arose from pure racial hatred, that that once again shows that it had nothing to do with politics?
>
> *Mr. van Straaten:* Well, as I understand politics, it was the way I was raised, and in my experience the various races were pitted against each other and these were the consequences.

At one point the Amnesty Committee chair, Judge Hassen Mall, exploded in anger at the brothers' elevation of racism to the status of a political motivation:

Judge Mall: Are you saying to us that you don't distinguish between murder committed through political objectives or motivation, on the one hand, and murder committed as the result of pure racial hatred—you don't distinguish between the two, is that what you are saying to us?

Mr. van Straaten: That is correct, Mr. Chair.

Judge Mall: Are you serious? You are saying that you are motivated, you didn't even say you were motivated by racial hatred, you said by pure racial hatred?

Mr. van Straaten: Because we grew up in this way, I can say that at that time it was difficult to accept the situation.

In defending the Amnesty Committee's ruling, Judge Bernard Ngoepe, when I interviewed him on 17 December 1996, clearly spelled out its logic, which confined and reduced racism to the domain of personal prejudice: "The act says that one should not be motivated by ill will, malice, or spite. My interpretation is that racism is ill will and malice and therefore is not a political motive. The van Straaten case was outrageous. They were saying that if you kill on racial grounds, then it is political. They don't distinguish."

What the brothers did not correctly distinguish between was "political" racism according to the publicly stated policies of political organizations and the "private" racism of their own worldview as individuals. In the classic liberalism of the Amnesty Committee, the two were not linked. The committee's understanding of race was inspired by the combination of human rights talk and the ANC's nonracial constitutionalism discussed earlier, in which race, ethnicity, and culture were not allowed (at least formally) to have any political connotations. Ethnicity was reduced to the level of private belief and could not enter the public political sphere; therefore it was not "political."

Robert Price (1997: 167) described well how the post-apartheid ANC has taken "every opportunity to project its vision of an inclusive nonracial definition of South African national identity." Civic universalism can, however, express some extraordinary blind spots toward the socially embedded aspects of race beliefs. In the transitional period immediately after the 1994 elections, race talk was seen in government circles as belonging to the past. A radical break had to be made with old apartheid thinking, despite the fact that race still played a significant role in the organization of South African politics and society. The amnesty application of the van Straaten brothers, who had always been rather slow on the uptake in life, failed because its language was still caught in an apartheid-era ethnonationalist *mentalité,* and they could not learn to speak the new race-blind language of human rights.

There were clear contradictions between the stances on race and culture of different sections of the commission. The Amnesty Committee adhered much more closely to classic liberal constitutionalism, while the Human Rights Committee pursued a nation-building agenda parallel to that of the Constitutional Court judges—one that combined culture and rights in the language of reconciliation. Using the language of rainbow nation building, TRC officials at Human Rights Violations hearings fused human rights talk to culturalist visions of *ubuntu* and the romantic "African community." The TRC would accept these weakly pan-Africanist expressions of race and nation only from those testifying, and it rejected discourses on race associated with the apartheid era. Amnesty applicants could not dredge up the old political language of racism to explain their past actions, because it clashed with the nation-building vision of the present.

In the legal terms of the Amnesty Committee, racism belonged to the category of the "personal" because no political party ever officially admitted to espousing racism. Its policy was to reject applications made on this basis. In legal terms, this may have been defensible, insofar as it prevented convicted racist murderers from easily securing amnesties by claiming their acts had some grandiose political goal. In postauthoritarian contexts, truth commissions and amnesty processes inevitably have to distinguish between political crimes and criminal crimes. Sociologically, however, the distinction is nonsense, for politics is about the operation of power both in public institutions and between individual members of society. Racism always operates at both levels simultaneously. It is fair to say that the whole thrust of social science studies of racism from the 1960s to the present day has been toward understanding how public and private understandings of race are linked and how political and societal organization of racism rely upon each other.[23] Racism emanates not only from party politics but also from the interaction between policies and everyday societal and cultural assumptions, categories, and ways of talking about racial distinctions, as well as from economic inequalities.

Because of the crossover and overlay of personal and public racism during apartheid, the Amnesty Committee could not always neatly separate the two domains, and this led to inconsistencies in its approach to race and racism. It was perplexing that in the van Straaten case the two murdered night watchmen were included in the final report as victims of gross human rights violations, and their surviving relatives were therefore eligible for reparations. Although their murders were vicious and cruel, Amnesty Committee judges had already excluded them as lying outside the commission's mandate. Since the murders were judged to be common crimes rather than human rights violations, the victims should therefore have been omitted from the list of designated victims, on grounds of consistency. Including them implies that the act was actually "political" all along. Can a person be a political victim if there is no politically motivated perpetrator? It does not seem that the act allowed for this.

The language of nation building came with historical baggage that in the hands of the Amnesty Committee expressed a liberal blindness to issues of race. Constitutionalism, in rejecting race and identity as categories of the "political" and confining them to the realm of the "private," created an environment in which race and ethnicity were dismissed as political motives for committing crimes. The Amnesty Committee showed little awareness of how racial classification and racism actually work in society, and therefore it could not recognize and apprehend the link between private racism and national party politics. In less legally constituted areas of its work, however, the TRC did venture into the culturalist terrain of *ubuntu* and a populist, rainbow Africanism. The TRC emerges as a highly contradictory organization that was overlegalistic in certain contexts (e.g., when it was oblivious to the political aspects of race) and underlegalistic and more moralizing in others (e.g., when it reoriented human rights to the imperatives of a multicultural Africanist nation-building project).

Culture, Nationalism, and the State

Albeit for different reasons, both universalists and relativists conspire to keep the polarity between culture and rights alive, when the examples I have cited from two different court decisions in South Africa show that the relationship between culture and rights is much more complex. Human rights may be combined with symbolic markers of cultural difference as they are subordinated to a strategy of nation building. Conversely, they may be counterposed to categories of culture and race in a literal, legalistic, and procedural liberalism. In South Africa, both strategies are happening simultaneously as different parts of the state seek to realize different programs or to realize the same program in different ways.

Both universalism and relativism rely upon highly systematic and overrepresentational views of both state and society that do injustice to the fragmentation of postauthoritarian states and the context of legal pluralism they often inherit. In democratizing countries of Latin

America, Africa, or Eastern Europe, it is often more useful to look at the concrete forms of connection and disconnection between and within societal and state regulatory practices and concepts of justice. To focus solely on the discursive logic of ideas of culture or liberal renditions of rights does injustice to this complexity. What matters is not the inherent logic of these categories but the concrete political usages that are made of them by social actors such as court judges, religious leaders, and political activists. There is no predetermined place for "culture" in human rights talk, if only because its place is determined not by an inherent discursive logic but by the concrete strategies of bureaucratic elites responding to a context of legitimation crisis.

For South Africa in the 1990s, we have seen three expressions of, or dispositions toward, "culture" in the discourse of state officials: the liberal, the multicultural, and the ethnonationalist.

Classic liberal political visions seek to confine culture, race, and ethnicity to the private domain and exclude them from the public space. One consequence is that in human rights cases, plaintiffs cannot use race, ethnicity, or culture as categories to contextualize their political behavior. Race, racism, and culturalist visions of society disappear as legal evidence—they are rendered immaterial in a court of law. They become vestigial forms of a private and contingent spite or ill will, rather than a public political ideology with real consequences for the behavior of individuals.

Multicultural visions, as expressed by Constitutional Court judges and in the rainbow nationalism of TRC chair Archbishop Desmond Tutu, aim to link liberalism with a weak pan-Africanist reading of community. For purposes of popular legitimation, rights are grounded not only in the liberal sovereign individual (a subject position very thin on the ground within black politics) but also in a romantic notion of the African community. This conjuncture of culture and rights welds together two visions of political sovereignty—the liberal/individual and the popular/collective.

Ethnonationalists assert a bounded and shared Herderian version of culture that is congruent with the Boasian tradition in cultural anthropology. In apartheid South Africa this version was utilized by the ruling Nationalist Party and white-supremacist fellow travelers, including *volkekunde* anthropologists. This version of culture was a vital part of the grand apartheid project to denationalize black citizens and create a whites-only nation in Africa. An essentialized version of culture, also found in mid-twentieth-century cultural anthropology, was central to the doomed delusions of Afrikaner nationalism. In this historical context, one wonders whether culture should ever be used again in an *analytical* capacity. Social and cultural anthropologists have generally rejected the term "race" as an analytical category, after nineteenth-century social Darwinism and twentieth-century Nazi eugenics, and "culture" seems to be in an analogous position in the aftermath of apartheid. As with Paul Gilroy's (2000) theoretical rejection of "race," anthropologists could also benefit from embracing cosmopolitanism and envisaging a theoretical universe that is postcultural.[24]

In addition to the political objection that culture is too heavily implicated in German Romanticism and apartheid state discourse to be in any way redeemable, there are some good epistemological reasons for jettisoning the culture concept. All versions of culture package and bind together beliefs and practices and attribute these shared characteristics to a collective social grouping. Recent reformulations of culture, of course, assert that culture is contested, ever-changing, and emergent, and that cultures are not bounded units, since characteristics can also be shared across a permeable and open group boundary. But this amounts to little more than diluting some attributes while keeping the main holistic features of the concept. Even these recent efforts to revive culture contain an implicit holism where none in fact exists, insofar as they systematize that which is unsystematized and package a set of attributes that they conceive of as shared to a greater or lesser degree within an imagined social grouping.

Not only is the Boasian version of culture epistemologically suspect, it is in all cases normative, for every vision of culture contains within it the impetus and momentum for collective identity building by communitarians. Writing about social behavior as if it is incorporated into a systematized culture has implications in certain circumstances for claims for political autonomy and self-determination. Advocating cultural relativism has clear political consequences for whether one supports or opposes global conceptions of justice and human rights. Culture is never just an analytical category, contained securely within the walls of the academy; it is the bricks and mortar of nation builders and other communitarians. This argument against culture goes back a long way and includes Max Gluckman's (1975) attack on Edmund Leach for overemphasizing cultural difference because of the political implications of this culturological approach in apartheid South Africa.

All this should not, of course, prevent anthropologists and others from studying the uses of culture in political discourse. To the contrary, this is more necessary than ever given the prevailing conjuncture of rights talk and culturalist claims. But such study must always disaggregate the constituent elements of "culture," study them at the level of social action, and assume no inherent relationship between, say, language, religion, and chosen form of political representation. "Culture" is above all a political principle that asserts the congruence between a social group and a set of beliefs and practices in order to legitimate the strategies of social actors. In short, it is an ideology of political contestation that motivates social behavior but provides no independent theoretical insights into actual social behavior. Our main focus should therefore be on an exploration of the contradictions and complexities in the ways power and culture are combined in the language of nation builders, be they liberals, multiculturalists, or ethnonationalists.

All nation-states need myths to live by, and in the 1990s the South African state shifted from a mythology based on ethnonationalism to a position somewhere between procedural liberalism and Africanist multiculturalism—recognizing that at any given moment all three are present in both state and society. Instead of positing an immovable and inherent relationship between rights and culture, we must shift toward a redefinition of the subject matter that provides a long-term historical explanation for the shifting political fortunes of culture within state discourse. The emphasis here is not on culture as a category of explanation, as is commonly found in cultural anthropology, but upon questions of state formation and the legitimation of bureaucratic power.

What is striking about the South African case is that the political use of culture has not gone away within state discourse, even after the ravages of apartheid social engineering. Even Constitutional Court judges with the foremost civic constitutionalist credentials feel compelled to invoke culture, community, and tradition in their decisions on human rights cases. We have to understand this in Ernest Gellner's (1983, 1997) Weberian terms, that is, in terms of a world historical process of industrialization, standardization, and the centralization of a semiautonomous state power. A standardized version of "culture" was not a paradigmatic feature of medieval states but coincided with the advent of modernity. It will be present in nation-building discourse and state formation strategies as long as the social conditions of modern societies require it. This means that versions of culture will be present even where they are least expected—in liberal conceptions of human rights and even while other state institutions try to pursue more ideologically anemic forms of culture-free liberalism.

Gellner's writings approach nationalism as part of the inescapable logic of industrial societies. For Gellner, it is nearly inconceivable for modern societies to function without the realization of the nationalist imperative. Nationalism as a political phenomenon is not merely the result of nationalist doctrine, an aberrant political principle that can be wished away through sheer force of will. Instead, it is embedded in a set of concrete practices, technologies, and social institutions that characterize modernity. A utopian, decultured sense of the nation based upon the "praxis of citizenship" alone—to draw on a phrase coined by Habermas (1992)—seems highly unlikely as long as the conditions that give rise to nationalism prevail: namely, high industry, a capitalist division of labor, modern mass society, geographical and social mobility, and the establishment of science as the dominant idiom of both facticity and technological change.

Although I share Gellner's admittedly rather pessimistic view of the historical inevitability of nationalism, I prefer to emphasize the active role of state officials in cultivating or imposing shared nationalist symbols and loyalties, rather than Gellner's (1983: 39) overreliance on the "objective, inescapable imperative" of industrialization, social mobility, and the division of labor. Modern states with their politicians, lawyers, and intellectuals are the agents of a program of standardization and rely heavily upon overarching unity metaphors. A postauthoritarian context of illegitimate institutions forces state officials to cement collective moralities even further, and they draw upon readily available ideological material to legitimate these moralities. This, ultimately, must be the basis for our explanation of the complex relationship between rights and culture in postcolonial societies of Africa and the new modernities they create.

Notes

1. See Macdonald 1984 on Grotius, reason, and natural rights. See Gewirth 1978 for a neo-Kantian view.

2. The Romantic tradition is one in which cultural anthropology should be included. See Berlin's excellent *The Roots of Romanticism* (2000) for a discussion of Herder and German Romanticism.

3. See Dubow 1995 on scientific racism in South Africa.

4. Boonzaier (1988: 65) wrote: "In South Africa in the early 1960s there was a relatively rapid shift from racial to cultural rhetoric, and from race to ethnicity."

5. I draw here from Dubow's assertion, in his 1994 special issue of the *Journal of Southern African Studies* on "Ethnicity and Identity in Southern Africa," that ethnicity was a euphemism for race.

6. Gordon and Spiegel's excellent article (1993) is still the best overall review of anthropology under apartheid. David Webster was murdered by state security operative Ferdi Barnard outside his Johannesburg home in 1989.

7. See Sharp 1981 on *volkekunde* anthropology. Astonishingly, *volkekunde* anthropologists still found employment in government after 1994 in Valli Moosa's Ministry for Constitutional Development, which dealt with special claims from "indigenous peoples" such as the Griqua and persisted in attempting to define who and what constituted a "tribe."

8. The Ministry of Native Affairs was renamed the Ministry of Bantu Affairs, but in the final death throes of apartheid it became the anodyne Ministry of Plural Relations and Development.

9. At this turning point, an interesting volume evaluating (and often criticizing) constitutionalism in Africa was edited by Issa G. Shivji (1991).

10. Tutu's statement was quoted in the *Mail and Guardian*, 17 March 1996. See Tutu's (1999) account of the TRC for further exposition of his ideas on restorative justice and *ubuntu*.

11. Restorative justice generally eschews criminal prosecution of offenders in favor of material and symbolic reparations for victims and the establishing of a forum for victims to tell their stories. It is generally seen as "victim centered" rather than oriented toward the offender, as is the case with common law. Its stated aims are the restoration of social bonds, the reaffirmation of the dignity of victims, and the rehabilitation of offenders within the community rather than punishment for offenders.

12. For a legal commentary on *ubuntu* in *State v. Makwanyane*, see English 1997.

13. The association between human rights and restorative justice is also found in Latin America. See Benomar 1993; Minow 1998; Roht-Arriaza 1995.

14. See Niehaus 2001 on South African "witch" killings.

15. A *Sunday Times* poll (11 June 1995) reported that more than 80 percent of whites and 50 percent of blacks in urban areas of South Africa (support is usually higher in rural areas) were in favor of the death penalty.

16. Sachs's statement is quoted in Boraine 1994: 146.

17. As Fred Hendricks (1999: 6) has affirmed, "while there have been some crucial institutional changes in South Africa in relation to human rights—the establishment of the constitutional court and the bill of rights—the judiciary itself has not changed in any fundamental way since 1994."

18. See, for starters, Boraine 2000; Ensalaco 1994; Hayner 1994, 2001; Huyse 1995; Wilson 2001.

19. This cutoff date was later shifted to 10 May 1994, due to pressure from the far-right Freedom Front. On the South African TRC, see Jeffery 1999; Krog 1998; Sarkin 1998; Wilson 1996, 2000, 2001; and the 1998 TRC report itself.

20. This last criterion was drawn from the Norgaard principles applied earlier in the Namibian transition, but in practice it was seldom applied by the Amnesty Committee, or it was applied inconsistently.

21. According to the terms of the National Unity and Reconciliation Act, the Amnesty Committee had to deal first with the applications of those serving prison sentences.

22. All text from TRC hearings comes directly from the transcripts on the official TRC Web site CD ROM of November 1998.

23. See, for a start, Boonzaier 1988; Bulmer and Solomos 1999; Donald and Rattansi 1992; Gilroy 1987; Malik 1996; Rex 1982; Rex and Mason 1986.

24. On cosmopolitanism in anthropology, see Kuper 1994.

eleven

"Culture" as Stereotype: Public Uses in Ecuador

Xavier Andrade

This chapter discusses ways in which public uses of the concept of culture contributed to regional tensions in Ecuador during the last two decades of the twentieth century, with a particular focus on the central place acquired by racialized discourses about masculinity within popular and elite conceptualizations of political power. Considering these discourses as elements selected to represent "culture" for public broadcasting, I discuss how diversely situated actors employed them to serve opposing aims.

I use the concept of culture in two senses. First, at the ethnographic level, culture is an object, a discursive construction formulated by the subjects of ethnography that needs to be documented and deconstructed in relation to their differential access to positions of power. Second, given informants' reliance on this concept, the analyst needs to retain a restricted use of culture as an adjective—the "cultural"—inasmuch as it serves to describe commonalities among differentially situated social formations as they are defined by concrete actors. Considering emic versions of this notion, as well as its use as a politically motivated descriptive tool, helps in studying the public uses of the concept of culture in different social contexts.

Readers will probably find echoes of some of the other contributions to this volume in my approach to the subject, especially with regard to their call for moving beyond culture as an analytical tool for anthropological theory (see especially the chapters by Hann, Toren, Trouillot, and Wilson). In contrast to their positions, however, I argue that such a concept is not necessarily exhausted by virtue of its malignant—albeit, I assert, contested—public use. On the contrary, the association of the concept of culture with disciplinary practices and technologies of power across different social contexts calls for paying attention to the processes through which the state, conflicting groups and/or elites, and people in general tend to appropriate "culture" in giving meaning both to various forms of hate and to feelings of commonality and forms of class-based solidarity. For anthropologists to dismiss this concept solely on the grounds of its "perverted" public use would amount to falling into a double entrapment, between, on the one hand, failing to consider what people say and think and how concepts circulate to enable social practices and, on the other, granting an exaggerated importance to the agency of anthropological discourse itself in shaping social life.

Stereotypes constitute omnipresent, if not dominant, conceptualizations about cultural differences. They express a perverted use of the concept of culture, inasmuch as they deny its internal diversity, negate its dynamic and contradictory nature, and freeze its historically situated contents. Typecasting is the result of cataloging culture in static terms, proceeding through a careful selection of traits that are assumed to incarnate one's own and the other's identity, with the intention of producing public understandings of differences among groups, classes, races, and societies. As such, stereotypes distinguish core and peripheral elements and express a synthetic, ready-made, negative anthropological repertoire. The easy classifications make stereotypes particularly suitable for circulation throughout society, from networks of gossip to open broadcasting in the public sphere. Of foremost importance for this chapter, the aim of stereotyping often lies in attempting to debunk the other's self-representation. In other words, typecasting is effective when it is presumed to touch elements central to the perceived "culture" of its targets and therefore of social and emotional importance to them. In this context, stereotypes serve to produce political affiliations that sustain or contest certain forms of power.

In the Ecuadorian case, historically dominant public understandings of culture among the politically hegemonic mestizo population have been phrased in terms of regional stereotypes that are meant to fit populations into distinctive categories of race, class, and gender, broadly following geographic lines.[1] Two basic assumptions justify such distinctions. First, people are perceived to be different as a result of the ecological and climatologic variations between the Pacific coast, *la costa,* and the Andean highlands, *la sierra.* Second, diverse ethnic groups have traditionally populated these geographic areas. The highlands are home to a large Quichua population, and historically speaking, it has been the Quichuas that the state and the media have referenced in efforts to build a sense of national heritage based to some extent upon a heroic Indian past. Although indigenous people do live in Ecuador's coastal regions, they have not been considered by academics and the public at large—or by agencies for international development, for that matter—to be "Indian." The coast is associated with black people. Although they constitute a minority of the population at roughly 5 percent, most blacks live in urban and rural coastal areas.

In economic and political terms, Ecuador is a bipolar society, divided between two major cities—Guayaquil on the coast and Quito in the Andes—each of which represents the main pole of economic development and urbanization in its region. Both cities are inhabited primarily by mestizos, or people of mixed Indian and Spanish descent, and roughly a third of the country's total of twelve million inhabitants live in the two cities together. Massive migration began in the 1940s and 1950s, when booming banana and oil industries and the failure of agrarian reform attracted rural people to the coast. As a result, the urban demographic composition in both regions shifted dramatically. Going back to the nineteenth century, bidirectional migration already existed between Guayaquil, where the most powerful export-oriented industries continue to be based, and Quito, the country's capital and administrative center, promoting a relatively fluid demographic continuum.

These developments, and the resulting similarities between the populations of the two cities, stand at odds with their inhabitants' efforts to sustain racially based stereotypes of each other. Nevertheless, race talk constitutes the basis for representing the other's "culture." Generally speaking, Indianness and blackness are pejorative concepts. In attacking highlanders, coastal people attempt to affirm their supposed biological and cultural distance from that which is indigenous. Highland people, for their part, imply that inhabitants of Guayaquil are somehow contaminated by blackness. This explains their supposed primitiveness—they are even referred to as *monos,* monkeys. It is as if there exist two radically different strands of mestizo Ecuadorianness, a problem that has so far eluded the few scholars who have studied race in Ecuador (see Almeida 1999; Cervone and Rivera 1999; De la Torre 1996; Muratorio 1994; Rahier 1998).

In this context, Ecuador could serve as an example of what Etienne Balibar and Immanuel Wallerstein (1995) identified as "racism without races," inasmuch as racial stereotypes serve primarily to classify, separate, and stigmatize different types of mestizos, opposite political actors, and diverse social classes. The representations created are often inconsistent. As I discuss later in this chapter, Guayaquilian elites tell stories about "Indian" legacies in order to link themselves to a warrior past. Yet the same actors can cite Indianness as the cause of the political backwardness of Quitenian politicians. Quitenian elites, in turn, can deploy a concept of Indianness in their efforts to create a nationalist feeling linked to a concrete historical past. Conversely, they can purposely obliterate any ties to Indianness as a means of distancing themselves from the coastal elites and demonstrating their greater "whiteness" and, hence, greater degree of "civilization." And in yet another case, subordinate groups in Guayaquilian society deploy stereotypes about "blackness" and "Indianness" in order to contest the power of the regional elites.

A set of questions emerges when one ponders this wide range of uses of racial language with political aims. How does mestizo racism relate to stereotypes about *la costa* and *la sierra?* Which perceived "cultural" elements are selected to produce a pointed representation of the other? When are these selected features put forth for political use and public broadcasting?

I assert that racialized concepts of masculinity hold the key to interpreting the regional dimensions of mestizo racism. *Mestizaje,* in this context, refers both to the historical process of racial mixing (i.e., Spaniards and Indians) and to a concrete, political discourse about masculinities. Such language operates in Ecuador as a process not only of differentiation and subjection but also of contestation. The deployment of a language of maleness on the part of regional elites to gain and maintain power, to differentiate among them, and to discriminate against one another coexists with the potential for the subjected populations to contest the hegemony of those elites. In reframing the dominant ideologies of *mestizaje* and maleness, the disempowered reorder perceived cultural principles to reconstitute coherent systems for understanding power relations from below.

The so-called regional question in Ecuador has always alluded to a problematic relationship to political power (see Quintero 1991). At different moments in history, most recently in 1999, claims for autonomy or independence have emerged in Guayaquil as a way to confront the excessive administrative centralism emanating from Quito, the capital. This conflict assumed multiple political forms during the twentieth century, including federalist and separatist attempts, and is evidence of the failure of the Ecuadorian state and the dominant classes to articulate a national project.

Ecuador returned to formal democracy in 1979, after twelve years of military dictatorship. To enforce a smooth transition, the state supported reforms to the party system that were to allow for the inclusion of social sectors that had traditionally been excluded from decision making, particularly the middle class that had emerged after the economic boom of the 1970s. The modernization of political participation through ideologically oriented political parties was meant to overcome two traditional obstacles to electorate mobilization. One of them, commonly known as *caciquismo,* was perceived as a legacy of the hacienda system, with its patronal rule and all-encompassing forms of individual, familial, and communal subjection. The other, according to the democratizing agenda, was the lack of a doctrinaire education, which was most clearly expressed in the emergence of *populismo.* This political phenomenon, dating back to the late 1940s, is characterized in Ecuador, as elsewhere in Latin America, by the potential for authoritarian rule, a highly personal style of government, eclectic political and economic doctrines, and a so-called charismatic influence (for a critical perspective, see De la Torre 2000).

The remainder of this chapter focuses on the cultural language in which the dominant framework of politics has been formulated and reproduced since 1979. Using three cases of study, I show how the languages of location, race, and gender have been conflated in the public sphere to promote regional stereotypes of racialized masculinities as seen from the perspective of both the powerful and their subjects.

Patriarchal Balls

León Febres Cordero (abbreviated here as LFC) has been the dominant political figure of the traditional regional elite in Guayaquil since the return to democracy. A businessman with a supposedly aristocratic lineage going back to the Independence period and an *hacendado* with a passion for imported horses, he became the foremost right-wing representative of the local mestizo oligarchy. He served as president between 1984 and 1988, heading a government characterized by the introduction of neoliberal policies, widespread official corruption, systematic violation of human rights, and the persecution of leftist and political enemies. Deemed an "Andean Margaret Thatcher" because of his aggressive, disrespectful style and his rhetorical defense of neoliberalism, LFC succeeded in dominating the local political scene both before and after his presidency, being elected twice as Guayaquil's mayor for a total of eight years in office (1992–2000).[2] Recently, in 2000, he retired from city hall, only to resume the symbolic position that has won him the admiration of the local electorate and the elite-dominated media for twenty years, namely, as the Guayaquilian patriarch par excellence. He is lauded as a businessman, a landlord, and a macho, all rolled into one tough package. As such, he epitomizes what Ecuadorian sociologists have called "authoritarian culture," a ruling style and a pattern of electoral behavior that take place systematically in Guayaquil and tend to favor aggressive, neopopulist, and undemocratic leaders.

In 1999 I witnessed a crucial event in Guayaquil that illustrates the media's broadcasting of LFC's image as representative of a hegemonic type of masculinity, the racial components in the construction of such an image, and how the collusion of dominant discourses of race and gender are supported but also reinterpreted by subordinated sectors. On 22 March, various political fronts orchestrated a massive public demonstration to contest the central (Quito) government's decision to close the Banco del Progreso, a major Guayaquilian bank whose owner was accused of having stolen from thousands of small and medium-size investors to fund his personal schemes. This measure, which the Guayaquilian elites perceived as another form of state-sponsored regional discrimination, triggered a series of dramatic events, including the collapse of the national financial system and an accelerated devaluation of the currency. Animosity between coast and sierra began to dominate the public debate. In this context, elites broadcast regional stereotypes in order to successfully mobilize public support.

After hours of waiting under a blazing tropical sun, tens of thousands of enraged demonstrators finally got to meet Mayor Febres Cordero when he showed up on the city hall balcony. The scene in the downtown streets was almost surreal: Fernando Aspiazu, the owner of Banco del Progreso, led the march, walking hand in hand with local authorities. Many of the participants were actually customers of his bank. In an amazing exercise of mimesis, Aspiazu, *un guayaquileño de pura cepa,* as the press refers to his "pure blood" and direct ancestry in the old cacao oligarchy, managed to pass literally overnight from his position as a great deceiver to the role of victim of the *serrano* government's persecution. To add to the carnivalesque atmosphere of the mass chanting for an independent Guayaquil, LFC addressed the people with a carefully planned, concise statement delivered in his trademark defiant tone: "Yo no me agüevo jamás!" (I never chicken out; in Spanish this expression refers to the testicles). The response from below was uproarious. People cheered, confident that the old patriarch meant what he said, that he had the courage—the balls—to address this or any problem as only a true man could.

LFC's roar did not come from out of the blue; it was a direct response to what the crowds had been calling out for hours: "León, no te agüeves!" (León, don't chicken out this time). According to local connotations, *agüevarse* means to be without *huevos,* literally "eggs" but popularly meaning testicles, "balls," throughout the Spanish-speaking world. The word can also imply that one's organs are tiny. *Huevo,* pronounced *güevo,* can be singular when referring to the penis or plural, *huevos,* when talking about the testicles. This notion of being potentially *sin huevos*—without balls—applies whenever someone has to confront a set of circumstances or make a decision. *Agüevarse,* therefore, underlines the situational and contextual nature of masculinity and refers simultaneously to a man's lack of character and the flexible physical features of his genitalia. The act of *agüevamiento*—of being without balls— denotes a momentary loss of one of the core aspects of local dominant forms of masculinity, namely, the ability to deal with the toughest conflicts without a second thought. Most important is that in the eyes of the popular classes in Guayaquil, it is not entirely evident that members of the political elites possess such capabilities. LFC's defiant cry enabled him to redeem himself from any doubts his supporters might have had regarding his tricky position as both a macho and a member of the upper class.

Despite the delicacy of LFC's status in the eyes of the populace, he enjoys the adulation of the elite-controlled mass media in Guayaquil. For example, the major newspaper, *El Universo,* described the entry of "el burgomaestre," LFC, to the weekly round table he granted to local journalists in the following terms:

> He appears with his leonine locks and his white *guayabera.* He enters followed by his closest collaborators, as if they were part of his royal retinue. He crosses the room as if he were a bullfighter [*en traje de luces*] or a tenor preparing to perform an aria. With greetings and handshakes for the gentlemen, pleasant smiles and affectionate words for the ladies, he proceeds toward the table at the front and takes a seat in the only chair with the city's emblem, the mayor's chair. (*El Universo,* 16 April 1999, my translation)

To return to the masses, their comments and chanting during the 1999 demonstration serve to situate what Matthew Gutmann (1996), in his ethnography of a workers' colony in Mexico City, termed "the meanings of machismo." Here I refer specifically to the political uses of machismo, an underexplored topic within the current explosion of cross-cultural studies on masculinity in Latin America. The marchers' chanting of "León, no te agüeves" constituted a counterpoint to the adulation of the press. The notion of *agüevamiento* alluded to both character and genital size as flexible, mutable features. In doing so, it revealed a side of hegemonic masculinity that normally should be kept hidden. It implied that maleness, even that of a macho icon such as LFC, has no rock-solid basis and therefore is not beyond questioning in the political arena. It was this that prompted LFC to invest his own masculinity with stability by emphasizing that he would never cave in to adverse circumstances. That "jamás" (I *never* chicken out!) reveals a central paradox of the mestizo elite's masculinity. At issue is the belief that the elite person who projects genital strength as an essential part of his persona needs to declare it publicly, thereby confirming his masculinity in a way that fits the expectations of the masses.

LFC's machista talents have been interpreted by Ecuadorian social scientists as illustrative of an authoritarian political culture from the coast, characterized by temperamental, explosion-prone leaders. The masses' chanting adds an interpretive twist to this analysis. As a member of the local bourgeoisie, LFC is perceived by working-class people as an *aniñado*—a childish and effeminate gentleman whose money, political connections, education, and comfortable lifestyle have taken its toll on his masculinity. Sexual potency is seen as being displaced through excesses of civilization in a way that calls to mind Gail Bederman's (1995) discussion of the effeminate character associated with the new "civilized" man at the end of the nineteenth century in the United States. In Ecuador, only working-class men "naturally" possess real character and physical strength, including the proper size and constitution of genitalia. From this perspective, men from popular sectors tend to perceive themselves as inherently manly, whereas the bourgeoisie must prove their maleness in order to represent them in politics. Men from the regional elites are, therefore, compelled to delineate the dimensions of their penises. The audience in the street that day was not simply boisterous but was in fact establishing the larger framework of a political economy of genitalia.

LFC's next step that sunny afternoon was also aimed at lessening his potential *agüevamiento*. He attempted to imbue his fragile masculinity with a transhistoric character, extending it and projecting it toward "the authentic Huancavilca people, the people from Guayaquil" (*El Extra*, 23 March 1999). This required a double play on his part aimed at negating the cultural features typically cited in stigmatizing the elites. First, as we have already seen, he tried to assert features of his own masculinity as essential and not constructed. Second, he affirmed that the same essential features characterized the Huancavilca people and had been transmitted down the line to him. Therefore his masculinity is something outside of any immediate history; it is an innate characteristic in himself and the people at large. LFC concluded his discourse with an attempt to polish away any differences between himself and the masses: "The people of Guayaquil are waiting [for a response from President Mahuad, who was witnessing the events via satellite from Quito]. The Guayaquilian people are waiting like the cultured people they are, like a gentleman" (*como gente culta, como todo un caballero*). Then he added, "Standing up, with order, with discipline, with peace."

LFC's act constituted a kind of racial transvestism. In one breath he alluded to the ample size of prehispanic, Indian warrior genitals and then declared his people chivalrous and civilized. This is an example of the common way in which mestizo ideology invents for itself a heroic, romantic, Indian past. In addition, another sort of transvestism took place in the case at hand. From LFC's perspective, his genitals were exemplary of his high status as a Guayaquilian oligarch. This class standing is not something that is self-evident but requires public confirmation. It must be conveyed using codes of vulgarity, the language that rules this symbolic economy as constructed by working-class audiences. In the end everyone sang the same song that day, but in different intonations and with different sets of balls in their pants.[3]

LFC's racial and class mestizo ideology was observed not only by the people in attendance at city hall but also by people at home around the country, tuning in to local television and radio stations. By now it was common practice for the Guayaquilian press and regional elites to portray Mahuad as the culprit behind discriminatory practices and a failure of effective decision making and governance. The reasons for his poor performance in office were publicly framed by a largely cultural/racial narrative: Jamil Mahuad is from the sierra and so exemplifies a typically *serrano* style of ruling, which is slow, hypocritical, indecisive, and therefore effeminate. LFC's presence on the balcony at city hall was defiant, whereas Mahuad's decision to stay away from Guayaquil and avoid a personal confrontation about the Banco del Progreso and the larger economic crisis confirmed his absence from real politics. The Guayaquilian press covered the event as if it were a boxing contest between a virile star and a weak opponent unfit to fight. The insistence on the physical presence of Mahuad revealed people's view of politics as an arena of personalities that possess varying degrees of male bravado.[4] In what follows I discuss how Mahuad's public relations group used discourses about racialized masculinity in an attempt to dispel rumors about his sexuality and relocate him as a model of *serrano* manliness.

Prosthetic Maleness

Jamil Mahuad, the most prominent figure in Quitenian politics during the 1990s, serving twice as the capital's mayor, ceaselessly projected himself as the model of a modern, rational, Harvard-educated, neoliberal politician. He was elected president in 1998 but was abruptly removed from office after a coup d'état in early 2000, amid the most dramatic economic crisis in modern Ecuadorian history. To read Mahuad as a rational ruler with a technocratic background would be naive, a mere repetition of the kind of narrative his own apparatus of communication and publicity sold to the media and the electorate alike. The construction of a carefully designed "modern" image—in the words of his collaborators, "the foremost postmodern image" ever attributed to an Ecuadorian politician—was confessedly one of the short-lived president's main concerns. Mahuad's reiterated obsession with his own media image combined rationality with global influences as an alternative to the openly macho style of *costeño* politicians such as LFC. On one hand, he projected a sense of cool detachment and control during the process of decision making. He underlined his political experience and pronounced his skills as a wise political negotiator, an image he successfully exploited as Quito's mayor. On the other hand, he tried to accompany this image with a sense of postmodern sophistication.[5] Mahuad drew from a repertoire of models of consumption that placed selective expenditure, fashion, and the possession of global multicultural influences at the top of the construction of public imagery. The last of these elements was used most frequently in interviews with the press, and it is the most interesting to analyze in terms of race and maleness.

Mahuad's worldly, professional style relied heavily not only on his neat presentation but also on his supposedly vast knowledge of Chinese literature and philosophical treatises, including the I Ching, *feng shui*, Lao-tse, and Sun Tzu on the arts of war and ruling. He was also interested in local witchcraft and all sorts of oracles. The logic for this appropriation, according to himself and his closest collaborators, was twofold. First, in claiming to probe "deep" material, Mahuad hoped to avoid being perceived as a dull or frivolous kind of president. Second, in reinforcing his passion for travel and consumption of the exotic, he hoped to generate an aura of cosmopolitanism that would put him on a par the U.S. president, Bill Clinton, whom he much admired.

This was not pure mestizo sophistication at the end of the twentieth century. There was another, more pragmatic reason to broadcast such profound hobbies. His selection of Chinese and Buddhist books on warfare served to justify a "civilized," nonconfrontational, indeed quite reclusive and isolated approach to politics amid the increasingly fierce public opposition to him, especially from other regional elites. Mahuad preferred to portray himself as a monk, or at least as a quiet, reflective man, who tackled the nation's destiny through table games rather than direct, open debate. Clearly, streets and balconies were not the *mise-en-scène* for his refined performances. Eastern books were displayed for television cameras on Mahuad's desk, carefully arranged amid what was obviously intended to resemble a random selection of bureaucratic papers. With the help of these props, Mahuad could simulate an active participation, if not in the world of financial markets, at least in the market of global images. They conferred a postmodern spiritual aura upon the president, an aura reflecting a balance between morality and consumption. The president, witnessing and simultaneously exacerbating an increasing political isolation that included even his own political party, remained in the intimacy of his office inside the presidential palace, embraced by a privacy that only his rumored gay inner circle could penetrate.

In my fieldwork in Guayaquil and Quito I explored people's perceptions of the former president's image. It became immediately apparent that local readings were fed by regional stereotypes of gender, race, and power. Foremost among people's impressions was the elitism implied in Mahuad's affinity for media images, fashionable clichés, and foreign philosophies and objects. After all, in a country plagued by hyperinflation and a massive devaluation that had prompted the dollarization of the economy, most Ecuadorians experienced globalization exclusively in its negative effects. Second, and more importantly for the present discussion, people perceived Mahuad's politics of style in clear relation to preexisting ideas about masculinity, region, and race.

The secretary of administration, Mahuad's close friend and advisor, provided a concise overview of Mahuad's image, including his fondness for the media (*El Universo*, June 1999). The official, a political marketer with a graduate degree in sociology, referred to the ways in which the president's rationality and cultured, intellectual stance configured a coherent cultural system, "a different culture, and a style." He identified Mahuad's tempered character, formal manners, and knowledge about diverse cultures as the "*serrano* style" for a politician. He contrasted this persona with regional stereotypes of coastal politicians, which appear as natural to the electorate at large as they do to Quitenian intellectuals and elites. Mahuad stood as the polar opposite of the macho, authoritarian, vulgar style exemplified by *costeño* figures such as LFC. In fact, the secretary asserted, Mahuad's image defined the very essence of *serrano* style in its "modern, cultured, cosmopolitan, and refined" dimensions. Betraying his intentions, the secretary was also speaking in the classic language of mestizo ideology, which displaces any trace of Indian or black influence from its supposedly civilized stance.[6]

The paradox of Mahuad's cosmopolitanism is that it merely recycles local, in this case regional, stereotypes about race and maleness that have been present throughout Ecuadorian history. As a result, I prefer to refer to Mahuad's brand of worldliness as "folkloric globalism." My informants interpreted Mahuad's imagery in local and regional terms. His philosophical mannerisms and intellectual poses were taken as a sign of *serrano* effeminacy and, again, *agüevamiento*. This perception seemed all the more accurate when it became clear that Mahuad's civil approach and oriental introspection were allowing the country to fall into greater misfortune. It was at that moment that the president's public relations machine cranked up again, this time relying upon discourses about technology, global cinema, and cyborgs. To their dismay, however, his advisors succeeded only in heightening perceptions of Mahuad's dubious sexuality.

Taking advantage of the local release of the Hollywood blockbuster *Titanic*, Mahuad used the metaphor to describe a sinking country in need of a rational, modern "captain" to overcome the crisis. Naturally, he positioned himself as "El Capitán," in his own words, striving to depict his political movements as if they were calculated and effective. The public was to believe he was cool and dispassionate in confronting the situation. Displaying graphics and computerized images to television audiences, Mahuad explained the many political icebergs through which he had to maneuver and demanded complete confidence in his navigational skills. Since his metaphor left out the fact that the real ship sank and most of its passengers drowned, Mahuad's appropriation of a Hollywood romance seemed all the more absurd.

Informants immediately reinterpreted the metaphor as a desperate recourse to a sort of "prosthetic maleness." In Guayaquil my contacts repeatedly referred to Mahuad and his *Titanic* as a little boy playing with a toy ship. Some of them went further, suggesting that Mahuad would have been better off taking the doomed boat and "shoving it up his ass." In this way they appealed to Latino frameworks that define homosexuality in relation to the passive, or recipient, position occupied during the sexual act (Carrier 1996; Lancaster 1992). Generally speaking, all of my informants emphasized the constructed and hence fake character of the metaphor. As one informant put it, "It is a ship of lies made into a big spectacle." By extension, Mahuad's masculinity was subjected to an alternative reading. It was believed that ultimately the metaphorical ship and its captaincy served only to confer upon Mahuad an air of masculinity that he did not himself possess. In the minds of the people, it was clear what body part the *Titanic* was to stand in for. For them, Mahuad's "estilo serrano" lacked the real penis needed to lead the nation.

Perverted Oligarchs

Racial and gender-based stereotypes are available not only to elites in consolidating their positions. Subordinated sectors of the population also use clichés in confronting those in power. It is standard practice in everyday life in Ecuador to employ concepts of masculinity and race to question the public image of politicians, activating networks of gossip to circulate either factual or imagined knowledge about the private lives of people in public offices. The best example is provided by the publications of Pancho Jaime (1946–1989).[7] Jaime, a.k.a. PJ, was the most popular, outspoken, and controversial political journalist in Ecuador during the 1980s. His mastery of selective elements of popular culture made him legendary in Guayaquil, the country's largest city and, as we have seen, a place renowned in the popular imagination for its extreme machismo and flamboyant politicians.

Between 1984 and his death at the hands of unknown political enemies in 1989, Jaime illegally produced and sold through underground networks of distribution magazines with print runs in the thousands.[8] These magazines totaled nearly a thousand pages and included hundreds of caricatures. Jaime's writing style followed local patterns of speech and embellished upon gossip and rumors about the sexual lives of the mestizo elites. Although he claimed his articles were well documented, his main strategy was to reveal the corruption of politicians by building links between their conduct in public office and their supposedly "deviant" sexuality. Race talk permeated Jaime's textual production in two ways. First, addressing authorities with over-the-top, vulgar language drawn from the poorer sectors of society, he attacked elites' claims to be whiter and less mestizo than the masses. Second, he deployed sexual stereotypes about blacks and Indians to ridicule those in power and sully their public images as straight white men.

Seizing upon particular events involving public figures from key institutions in Ecuador, including Congress and the Catholic Church, Jaime aggressively commented on local and national politics by launching lengthy tirades of heavily charged, obscene language. He presented these texts alongside outrageous, pornographic caricatures of his targets in a variety of heterosexual and homosexual gestures and positions. Portraying enemies as grotesque characters motivated by shameful, "perverted" instincts, Jaime created a carnivalesque representation of political life in order to criticize the establishment. He bestowed elite men with attributes stereotypically associated with subordinated masculinities, such as sexual perversion, impotence, and feminization, and he linked these features to a general inability to manage positions of power. To accomplish his aims, he appealed to the classic repertoire of mestizo ideology. Sometimes he accused his targets of possessing Indian traits. At other times he used illustrations of a symbolic black phallus in order to feminize the powerful and reveal their supposedly real sexual inclinations. Among his strategies was the use of images of and rhetoric about transvestism and cross-naming. As for women, Jaime usually presented them either as the objects of compulsory heterosexuality or as whores. He rarely mentioned lesbianism or other alternative sexualities. In this way his narrative reflected the wider popular concern with specifically male homosexuality, as opposed to many other sexual practices that are still quite invisible in Ecuador.

Part of Jaime's popularity stemmed from the viciously humorous way in which he linked political enemies' private sexual practices, whether real or imagined, with their competence in public office or institutions. A keen observer of political processes and a kind of local ethnographer, he interpreted political episodes as if they were mere tawdry spectacles. Readers appreciated his descriptions because they were painted in colorful and grotesque language with dramatic overtones.[9] His reliance on a topsy-turvy rendition of reality took its cue from the kinds of ironic inversions created, performed, and interpreted by members of the popular sectors in everyday life.

These inversions of the political order, however, raise the issue of the sexual and racial politics asserted by PJ.[10] Activating sexual and racial narratives to portray public life and its principal actors, he confronted official representations of politics made by a submissive mass media and by the politicians themselves. In accomplishing his aims, however, he reproduced an authoritarian political style and reinforced dominant notions of sexuality and race with their accompanying forms of discrimination. The following article, entitled "#1 Shit digger" (*Saca*

"Culture" as Stereotype 249

ñoña #1), is an example of the problematic use of such stereotypes (as well as of Jaime's unconventional punctuation). Note that Lucho is a nickname for Luis.

> In the same way that some whores have acquired fame by eating in bed, some of the ass pushers have acquired merits, which means that they are highly appreciated by the high-class faggots, the same ones that are in the spotlight hugging women in the newspapers but, when they are alone, act just like little butterflies.
>
> The nigger Lucho [Negro Lucho], as black as coal and of disproportionate size, has spent years as a professional ass pusher [for the elites], he was a chauffeur of the old woman Icaza, president of the Red Cross, ex-wife of the multimillionaire . . . Noboa Naranjo, currently she is "la gringa" [Luis] Chiriboga's wife [here PJ inverts the gender of Chiriboga's nickname from "el gringo" to the feminine].
>
> Because he worked as chauffeur for the old woman, he [Negro Lucho] met Lucha Chiriboga [here PJ changes the gender of Lucho, actually a man], and she [Chiriboga] got crazy . . . and there began a romance filled with passion and tenderness, ending with butt fucking, on a pink bed, the nigger Lucho clawed the white-as-milk body and the golden hair of Lucha Chiriboga, it seemed as much a dream as One Thousand and One Nights, but as destiny predicts the unimaginable, one day . . . he [Negro Lucho] ran into the elegant figure of Mrs. Cesarea Carrera [here PJ inverts the gender of Cesareo] and fell in love immediately. [Cesarea] told him to go to hell with the feelings that he had for Chiriboga and in secret they went to [a cabaret] and Cesarea screamed like a steam train. (*Comentarios* 18: 34, my translation)

This excerpt refers, as always in PJ's writings, to actual characters. The love story centers on Negro Lucho, a black chauffeur of Guayaquilian high society, reinvented by Jaime as a top rate "ass pusher." In love with Lucho are Jaime's targets, the politicians Luis Chiriboga and Cesareo Carrera. Chiriboga was a philanthropist and the vice mayor of Guayaquil, fondly called "the gringo" by his friends because of the whiteness of his skin and his aristocratic heritage. Jaime renames Chiriboga, one of his favorite targets, in the feminine as "la gringa," echoing a rumor about his homosexual inclinations. "La gringa" is heartbroken, the story goes, because Negro Lucho has fallen in love with the most powerful man in the Ecuadorian national soccer federation and a former congressman, Cesareo Carrera, and has betrayed "her" (Chiriboga). Jaime also renames the Carrera figure "Cesarea" to reiterate the working-class

250   The Politics of Culture

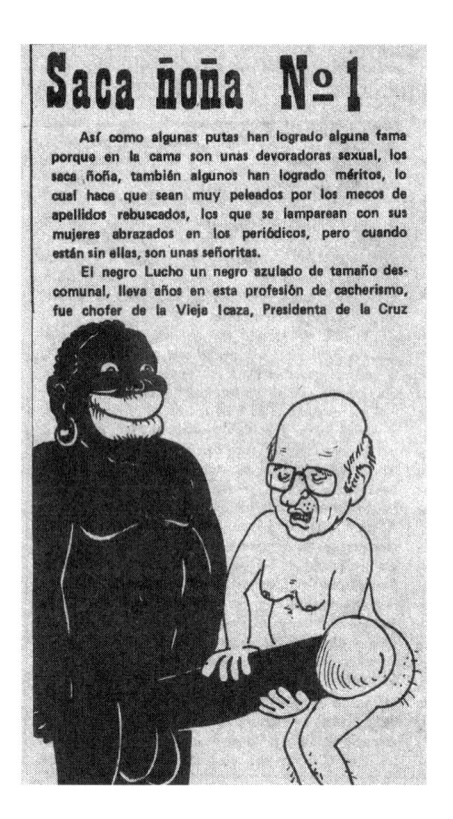

Saca ñoña Nº 1

Así como algunas putas han logrado alguna fama porque en la cama son unas devoradoras sexual, los saca ñoña, también algunos han logrado méritos, lo cual hace que sean muy peleados por los mecos de apellidos rebuscados, los que se lamparean con sus mujeres abrazados en los periódicos, pero cuando están sin ellas, son unas señoritas.

El negro Lucho un negro azulado de tamaño descomunal, lleva años en esta profesión de cacherismo, fue chofer de la Vieja Icaza, Presidenta de la Cruz

Figure 11.1. "Shit digger #1," cartoon accompanying Pancho Jaime's article on homosexuality among the Guayaquilian political elites. Originally published in *Comentarios* 18: 34.

assumption that the elites are "high-class faggots." The article goes on to describe a party where a symbolic marriage between Negro Lucho and Cesarea takes place, an event supposedly attended by the whole homosexual circle, including the archbishop of Guayaquil, another recurring object of Jaime's insinuations.

Negro Lucho is referred to only in terms of his race and of sexual stereotypes surrounding blacks, such as "black as coal and of disproportionate size." The image accompanying the article (fig. 11.1) depicts Lucho as a smiling, naked African primitive with an enormous penis that is embraced by a submissive, somewhat desperate, and also naked Cesarea. Negro Lucho's penis slightly overlaps Cesarea's buttocks, as if to affirm the act of "cacherismo," active penetration or ass pushing. In this way Jaime actualizes the sexual ambiguities of *mestizaje* ideology in Ecuador as broadly expressed by the excessive sexual power of blacks, illustrated this time through the metaphor of the ass pusher. Directing such racist stereotypes against white political power, he reproduced them and simultaneously reinscribed them as political tools for working-class sectors. The exposé of the intimate lives of politicians was perceived as a political practice. Readers linked the image of Negro Lucho and powerless Cesarea to the title of the article, which suggested that Negro Lucho indeed became number one in the end. Although he was only a poor black chauffeur, he was savvy and skillful enough to seduce his wealthy clients and subject them to his sexual power.

Jaime's information about the wild festivities he wrote about came largely from gossip. He took clever advantage of his unique position as the main repository for gossip launched by opposing factions of the Guayaquilian elite. Using his self-conferred poetic license to freely embellish upon this information, he orchestrated a circus by placing in the spotlight of his magazines the freakish bodies of those in power. While other, more respectable political publications aimed to instill in their subscribers a respect for the written word and the intellectual authority of the authors, the repeating images of oligarchs, well-known journalists, and priests dressed as women or engaged in orgies made readers of Jaime's magazines feel more like spectators of an endless parade of debauchery. Male politicians in Ecuador, struggling to keep up "big man" profiles, found crude images of themselves in print for everyone to see. As such, national and local politics became a series of carnivalesque scenes performed by what PJ construed as "perverted" political subjects.

Jaime also used stereotypes about Indians as a political strategy. Generally speaking, his practice of racist naming reproduced the dominant mestizo ideology, within which Indian traits signify degrees of effeminacy. Often PJ launched such attacks in strict regionalist terms. For example, in one extreme case, he represented coastal people with a cartoon of a male figure raping the sierra, shown as a woman dressed in Indian clothes. In that image, however, Jaime referred to coastal identity not as mestizo but rather in terms of the understudied label *cholo*, a term originally applied to rural people from the coast with physical features attributed to pre-Columbian civilizations.[11] The image of the *cholo* is linked to an aggressive male sexuality and a violent nature, characteristics that are appropriated by people in asserting their courage and justifying violent excesses. At other times, Jaime used the concept of "choloness" to attack coastal mestizo elites, implying that their roots were far less than pure. He tried to reveal their true *cholo*

Figure 11.2. "A little wig-wearing cholito," racial transvestism as denounced by Pancho Jaime's magazines. Originally published in *Comentarios* 18: 20.

nature by presenting them as ethnic transvestites whose acts of impersonation were subject to the elite-controlled spectacle of politics (fig. 11.2). An excerpt from Jaime's article "El cholito con aires de pelucón" (A little wig-wearing *cholo*) illustrates this kind of racial stereotyping. In this passage Jaime refers to one of the most influential Guayaquilian lawyers, a defender of corrupt politicians whom Jaime confronted repeatedly in his writings.

> There is a saying that goes: "A united people will never be defeated," knowing about this, the oligarchy or extreme right, searches for a "JUDAS" among the common people, someone to sell out the people of the same [social] class, and for a few nickels defend the enemies of the Ecuadorian people....
>
> This dick-faced *cholo* turned out to be a chameleon. Before, in a book he authored, he denounced the untouchable oligarchy, now he has changed colors to defend them, likes to eat well, and needs more than 50 thousand sucres a week just to pay his bills at the beauty salon, where he gets his *cholo* hair all rolled up and tries hard to cover his purple face with makeup....

> Doing research here and there, I have come to know that this *cholo* is the descendant of the Indians of Santa Elena, way out there [on the peninsula of the same name] . . . .
>
> Nowadays, he appears on TV as a great defense lawyer, he believes he is Petrocheli [referring to a character in a U.S. television series], he uses "Salvador Dali" perfume, with his rolled up hair, and he walks around as if he were a great star like Michael Jackson. (*Comentarios* 18: 20–21, my translation)

Pancho Jaime, having grown up with the same racist discourse that forbade those of Indian heritage access to power, talks about the *cholo*'s makeover as a sign of betrayal to both his race and the working-class people. His anti-oligarchic stance uses both a blatant machismo and racist talk to reinscribe stereotypes about identity within populist understandings of the politics and "culture" of the working classes. His magazines correspond to a politics of masculinity that can be broadly identified with, but not reduced to, populism in Guayaquil. As such, it is important to read these materials in relation to traditions of political rhetoric, print media, and local oral tradition, fields of social production that I have omitted from this chapter owing to space constraints.

Conclusion

Anthropologists are justifiably concerned about the dangerous political implications of the concept of culture, because in different contexts the term can serve to boost fanatic nationalisms and ethnic, religious, and racial hate. This concern, however, should not prevent us from examining the contradictory roles that essentialist assumptions about differences perceived to be of cultural origin play in both the exercise of power and everyday practices of contestation. If one of the main aims of anthropology is to understand how people experience and make sense of their place in life, and if one of the native categories used is "culture," then we still have to trace the historical development of its use, the meanings that compose such a concept, and people's practical and political uses of it.

Ecuador is an example of a country with a fragile state, an exclusive political system, elite-controlled mass media, a corrupt system of justice, and restricted notions of citizenship. At the end of the 1990s, a massive economic crisis, manifested in the bankruptcy of the entire financial system, a chaotic process of dollarization of the economy, hyperinflation, massive layoffs, and urban violence, dramatically eroded the living conditions of most Ecuadorians. The country passed in less than a decade from being a self-declared "island of peace" within the otherwise conflictive Andean region to ranking among the most corrupt countries in the world. Its present economic and social decline cannot be separated from renewed local manifestations of intolerance and prejudice that are formulated in the language of culture. Here I have focused on how culture has been deployed to mobilize regionally based affiliations. An exploration of the local foundations of regional stereotypes shows that discourses about masculinity and race occupy a central place in public representations of culture and politics, a process that became more evident during the last two decades of the twentieth century when, contrary to state-sponsored modernization efforts, the reemergence of personalistic and patron- based forms of leadership came to dominate political representation.

Literature about the state in Africa, such as Achille Mbembe's (1992) discussion of the banality of power and Jean-Francois Bayart's (1993) definition of political culture as the "politics of the belly," shows the importance of notions of obscenity, vulgarity, the grotesque, and the banal in the construction of exclusive political systems and predator states. In the future, such ideas could help us to think about the aesthetics of vulgarity in the Ecuadorian case and might open a window from which to view people's conceptions of society and power. The cases of León Febres Cordero and Jamil Mahuad, two of the most important recent political figures in Guayaquil and Quito, respectively, illustrate opposite styles in typecasting to construct public imagery: the former displays macho bravado, the latter, pretended sobriety. In both cases, the production, circulation, and reception of stereotyped images concerning the regional conflict in Ecuador have produced contradictory interpretations among audiences. Most perspectives, however—no matter how outwardly opposed—depend upon a racist mestizo ideology. Many viewers confront the public images of those in power, and the mestizo and machista notions that frame those images, with irony and symbolic violence in order to reposition themselves as spectators of (and not participants in) political life. The third case discussed here, that of the underground journalist Pancho Jaime, illustrates the humorous and dangerous way in which dispossessed sectors frame the imagery of, and the economic and power struggles among, elites.

To transform the concept of culture from an analytical category into an object of study will help to address what I perceive to be a central issue in the culture debate—namely, that precisely because of its wide circulation and consumption, culture has become, at least in certain social and historical contexts, a "native" category that serves people as a key referent for formulating their own agendas. Fleeing the anthropological vocabulary and being rearticulated in different ways by our own informants, the concept is not only "out there," to use Trouillot's phrase, but is also in permanent process and open to diverse forms of deconstruction by those who broadcast it or try to debunk it in different public spheres. The concept is in an "out there" structured by social differences, hierarchies, complicities, and struggles, a complex terrain for ethnographic inquiry that reminds us, again and again, of the centrality of power for the construction of anthropological theory.

Notes

This chapter makes use of ethnographic materials compiled while I conducted fieldwork for my dissertation in Guayaquil and Quito, Ecuador, between July 1998 and June 1999, a project funded by a Predoctoral Grant from the Wenner-Gren Foundation for Anthropological Research. I would like to acknowledge Shanti Pillai for editing this article, Richard Fox, Sydel Silverman, and Barbara King for their insightful readings, and all the participants in the Morelia symposium. Special thanks to Robert Aunger, Frederick Barth, Yoshinobu Ota, Christina Toren, Richard Wilson, Rita Wright, and Sydel Silverman for their comments and exemplary camaraderie.

1. In politics, "region" is the most meaningful category in common understandings of what constitutes different urban political social formations in Ecuador. I understand a region to be a spatial dimension of heterogeneous social production that results in specific and unequally organized political economies (see Lomnitz-Adler 1992: 59, 66). I concentrate on one aspect of such regional formations, using Poole's concept (1997: 8–10) of "a visual economy" to refer to images as commodities, the products of concrete processes of production, circulation, and consumption that transcend locality and encompass larger national and transnational fluxes. As Poole suggests, defining the concepts of "region" and "visual economy" in this way underscores the inequality in the production of shared, but also contested, symbols and meanings, issues that are central to the public uses of stereotypes about culture.

2. LFC's record of steady service in public office is worth mentioning. Before becoming president, he served in Congress from 1979 to 1984, representing

the interests of the Guayaquilian industrial sector. During those years he led the political opposition against Oswaldo Hurtado's Christian-democrat regime (1980–1984), a task that was tainted with regional claims. As of July 2001, it seems likely that LFC could run for president once again.

3. Many scholars have noted the political ends to which obscenity and vulgarity can be put (among others, Cohen 1995; Hunt 1993). As Mbembe (1992) and some of his critics (Coronil 1992; Olaniyan 1992) have pointed out, vulgarity can function as a discursive technology associated with either the state in its exercise of power or with subaltern sectors in their daily confrontations with the state. Trouillot (1992b: 76) discussed the ways in which vulgarity is subject dependent and socially defined. In the event under examination, different sets of meanings were posed in the languages of race and class.

4. Such political discourses about masculinity are not strictly Guayaquilian products. Simultaneously in Quito, flyers circulated denouncing the so-called Opus Gay. They referred both to the collusion between Mahuad's government and the Catholic Church through a massive charity program and to the rumored homosexuality of the president and some of his close collaborators.

5. This image, however, was not free of internal contradictions, the most obvious of which was his association with the Catholic Church and his humanitarian, religious undertone. In response to growing poverty, Mahuad spearheaded the only state-sponsored charity program directed toward dispossessed sectors, the "poverty bonds." In order to secure assistance, the poor were asked to head to their local church and basically confess their economic woes.

6. In his inaugural address, Mahuad referred to Andean myths, spoke about shamanistic legacies, and even made use of Indian paraphernalia. But this sort of multiculturalism was soon forgotten and replaced by supposedly more cosmopolitan elements that ended up reinscribed within the framework of regional hate talk.

7. Additional biographical information about Pancho Jaime, as well as a more detailed discussion of his magazines and their different audiences, is also available in Andrade 2001. This section draws in part on materials I explored in that article. My dissertation-in-progress explores at length Jaime's importance in the local scene and his relation to wider fields of social production, some of which are briefly mentioned here to highlight his reliance upon local traditions and to provide a more accurate context for my interpretation. My ethnography in Guayaquil combined participant observation with interviews and focus groups using Jaime's texts and images to approach particular readerships and their understandings of masculinity, popular culture, and politics.

8. Estimates of the magazines' circulation by people close to PJ vary between 8,000 and 18,000, remarkable figures for a domestically produced magazine in Ecuador. Additionally, the magazine circulated widely via photocopies and word of mouth.

9. An example of audiences' responses from my field notes follows. Ethnographer: "So, what made you laugh?" Reader 19: "The ways in which he described people [in positions of power] and the things they did. For example, that they had a party at someone's house, and that everybody got drunk and then they got naked. He added who had fucked whom during these orgies. And the drawings were also that way. The funny way in which he described those orgies, it was as if he were directing a satire. For us [the reader and her female college friends] it was a satire about what can go on right in the middle of an orgy. State problems were solved, politics negotiated, and deals accomplished. That is what caught our attention. On one hand, he created doubt in us, he made us question the formality [of politics]. On the other hand, [politics] were shown to be like domestic stuff that is solved among friends, between acquaintances."

10. Following Stallybrass and White's (1986) discussion of Bakhtin's original notion of "carnivalesque," it is important not to construe these inversions as the mere celebration of opposites. At stake is the issue of machista sexual politics, as well as the ugly circumstances surrounding Jaime's death, proof enough that the carnivalesque is also dangerous business when transgressive practices turn out to be excessive for the elites to handle or to appropriate (see also Hall 1993).

11. For example, Whitten's (1999) attempt to map out a wide range of racial typecasting in Ecuadorian society fails to consider native categories such as *cholo* and the similar *montubio*.

twelve

All *Kulturvölker* Now?: Social Anthropological Reflections on the German-American Tradition

Christopher M. Hann

Both inside and outside anthropology, culture has long been an "essentially contested concept."[1] Its history can be grasped only when culture is set alongside other key terms, which range from civilization, race, and society to nature, reason, and structure. The wider context must include long-term changes in global social organization and their consequences for different intellectual traditions. In this chapter, I do not attempt a comprehensive review of the culture concept but focus on what I take to be the most problematical aspects of currently pervasive usages.[2]

I begin with a definition. According to Karl Marx's version of the labor theory of value, capital can be viewed as "congealed labor."[3] By analogy, I define culture as *congealed sociality*. The range of animals exhibiting patterns of behavior that they acquire socially is broader than formerly suspected (Box and Gibson 1999). It is useful to have a word for this patterning, but the concept of culture derives from a primary concept of sociality and must be used with care. Nearer to my own subfield, social anthropology, the word has had a richly muddled trajectory. In many disciplines, concern with "high" culture, in Matthew Arnold's sense, has been partly or wholly displaced by culture in Raymond Williams's more popular sense (see Eagleton 2000). In many parts of the world, these two kinds of culture are hard to disentangle. For example, many small towns and even villages in Eastern Europe still have a "house of culture," with a museum devoted to the local or regional culture close by.

So far so good: conceptual conflicts may be creative, and contestation is no reason for abandoning the term culture. The major problem is that it is also frequently used, even within anthropology, as a rough equivalent and sometimes even as a synonym for *people* or *nation(ality)* or *ethnic group*. A similar slippage can be found among primatologists. I find Christophe Boesch and Hedwige Boesch-Achermann more persuasive when they argue that "chimpanzees possess cultural behaviours" than when they write of "the notion of a culture in chimpanzees" (2000: 256). As I see it, neither chimp nor human populations are endowed with "a culture," understood as a corpus of traits that differentiate group members from the members of other cultures.[4] According to this perspective, humanity, too, can be carved up into a finite number of bounded cultures, often imagined territorially as a "mosaic" (most modern diasporas retain some notion of a "homeland," and "globalization" seems, if anything, to be strengthening the basic assumptions). This way of thinking has far-reaching implications. For example, advocates of "multiculturalism" argue that the prior claims of cultural "communities" should form the basis of rights in a democratic society. Anthropologists cannot step aside when political philosophers and others link rights to culture in this way (see Barry 2001). I think we must face up to our responsibilities for illusions that we have helped to disseminate (cf. Trouillot, this volume).

I term the basic illusion the "totalitarian" concept of culture. By this I mean the notion of "a culture" as a bounded, integrated whole, analogous to an evolving organism. Such a view of culture is totalitarian in a double sense: a culture is postulated to be a more or less unified totality, and it exercises total determining power over the identity of its members. The culture either *is* the identity or, if it does not determine every detail, it nonetheless permeates the whole and provides all the essential features. Paradoxically, it is with a shift to the plural usage of the term—"cultures"—that culture acquires this totalitarian character. This characterization is of course a straw man, inasmuch as few anthropologists would defend such a caricature. I argue, however, that the plural use of culture, which dominated twentieth-century anthropology, carried insidious implications in the way it classified people into separate cultural capsules.

In the first part of this chapter I touch on some of the intellectual origins of this habit in Central Europe. I attribute its dissemination to the context of modern nationalism as much as to individual thinkers or national schools. The concept of "a culture" received an emphatic idealist and relativist stamp in American anthropology, which strengthened the implicit totalitarianism. This concept now enjoys wide currency both inside and outside the discipline. I then return to Central Europe to explore the construction of "a culture" in one instructive case. Finally, I address the dilemma of whether anthropologists today should struggle to hold onto those meanings of culture that have scientific validity or whether, given that the word has been brought into disrepute, they would do better to seek out new terms for the usages we wish to retain. It is naive to imagine that anthropologists alone can determine the wider public usages of culture, but we can contribute by decisively rejecting the totalitarian view and by clearly subordinating the concept of culture to that of sociality.

A German-American Tradition

It is common to trace understandings of culture as an integrated, organic whole back to the writings of Johann Gottfried Herder, who criticized approaching the ideas and "mythology" of other peoples by reference to one's own.[5] Herder's rejection of what later came to be termed ethnocentrism was an important element in the German Romantic response to the universalist ideas gaining ground contemporaneously in France. He was particularly sympathetic to the Slavic world. In spite of his vision of a pluralist world of evolving, organic collectivities, however, Herder was no more a cultural relativist than his teacher Kant, and his status as ancestor turns out, on closer inspection, to be ambiguous. Herder used *Nation* and *Volk* as synonyms, and he sometimes added *Cultur* (sic) with an implication of congruence— but he did not actually use this last term in the plural (see Zimmerman 1998: 102–114).[6] Fichte and Engels later developed a dichotomy between the *Kulturnation* or *Kulturvolk* and the *Kleinvolk,* groups such as Slovaks and Estonians who had no history of statehood, though linguistic differences qualified them as a separate people (*Volk*). Though Wilhelm von Humboldt and other nineteenth-century scholars speculated about different "national characters," nothing resembling the later concept of culture was institutionalized in German scholarship in the nineteenth century. On the contrary, German anthropologists continued to operate with an anti-Darwinian dichotomy between *Kulturvölker* and *Naturvölker* that denied the latter any history at all. In this period an evolutionist conception of culture (used only in the singular) dominated in Great Britain.[7]

According to Andrew Zimmerman (1998), it is therefore a myth to seek the charter statement of modern cultural anthropology in Herder.[8]

This myth has acquired some of its international currency through the work of George Stocking on the German roots of Franz Boas (Stocking 1968, 1996). Yet none of Boas's teachers used culture in the modern relativist sense. The *Kulturvölker/Naturvölker* distinction broke down only in the twentieth century, when a younger generation that included Leo Frobenius attacked the universalist idealism of Adolf Bastian and Rudolf Virchow. It therefore seems unwarranted to view Boas as the heir of Herder and Kant. We need to consider alternative explanations for the demise of universalist definitions and the rise of the modern relativist concept of culture.

There are several possibilities. One is that Boas's German background was indeed decisive, but that he was influenced by other, nonanthropological voices. The term culture was sometimes used in the plural, relativist way by Nietzsche; moreover, as Stocking has convincingly shown, the broader idealist milieu of neo-Kantian scholarship ensured that even the physical geographer Franz Boas would be sensitive to "cosmological" questions. An alternative explanation would be that the modern American concept of culture was largely "made in America" or, more precisely, that it was pupils of Boas such as Edward Sapir, Margaret Mead, and Ruth Benedict who forged the relativist schema in the interwar decades. A third possibility is that we need to unravel a complicated tangle of European and American influences in this period. It is important to ask *why* a plural conception of culture should have become popular at this time; I postulate a connection with the dissolution of Europe's continental empires at the end of the First World War and the Wilsonian celebration of self-determination for nations. Poland was a major beneficiary of this doctrine, and Bronislaw Malinowski was influential in promoting the new view of culture in the Anglo-Saxon world in the interwar decades.[9]

At any rate, it seems clear that a new era opened after the Second World War. In Adam Kuper's account (1999: 16), Talcott Parsons is the key figure who persuaded anthropologists to concentrate on a definition of culture as "collective symbolic discourse." The most influential figure in the ensuing elaboration of this concept was Clifford Geertz, for whom the totality of culture consisted of "webs of meaning," to be interpreted through "thick description" (1973). Geertz paid little attention to Boas, though he did acknowledge a debt to German traditions in the person of Max Weber (Geertz 1973: 5).

In his recent book *Available Light* (2000), Geertz provides many further nuances, seeking a balance between, on the one hand, respect for cultural difference and for Charles Taylor's "deep diversity" and, on the other, the necessary rejection of what he terms the "configurational," "pointillist" view of culture (Geertz 2000: 224, 248, 257). He does not acknowledge that much of his own work has popularized the latter view (the title of his most influential book [1973] features "cultures" in the plural). The tone of the recent essays remains consistently relativist and idealist, as when Geertz explains that when he writes "culture" he means "the *mot,* not the *chose*—there is no *chose*" (2000: 12). According to Geertz, the ethnographer's job is to document "levels and dimensions of difference and integration" and then to cross-index these isolated identities, since they obtain their meanings only through interaction. At the end of the day, the culture resulting from complex processes of "cross-indexing" is a unified conglomerate. It is not, of course, a cozy frozen consensus but an *ad hoc* style or approach: "An enormous number of intersections of outlook, style or disposition, are the bases on which cultural complexity is ordered into at least something of an irregular, rickety, and indefinite whole" (Geertz 2000: 254–255). When all the caveats have been entered, the world according to Geertz is still to be understood in terms of bounded entities called cultures.

The work of Eric Wolf is much less dependent on a concept of culture, but his last monograph was an attempt to overcome "a situation of complementary naiveté, whereby anthropology has emphasized culture and discounted power, while 'culture' was long discounted among the other social sciences, until it came to be a slogan in movements to achieve ethnic recognition" (Wolf 1999: 19; see also Wolf 2001). According to Wolf, other social sciences have drawn an unhelpful contrast between culture and ideology: "In this contrast 'culture' was used to suggest a realm of intimate communitarian ties that bind, while 'ideology' conjured up scenarios of factional strife among self-seeking interest groups" (1999: 21). Though he rejected this contrast, Wolf retained a distinction between ideology and the wider ideational domain, and culture for him remained "idea-dependent." Unlike Geertz, Wolf highlighted material factors and insisted on the diversity of social actors and the ambiguities of the situations they must negotiate. Culture for him was not a "reified and animated 'thing'" but a process that depended critically on the exercise of power by particular agents: "Culture is not a shared stock of cultural content. Any coherence that it may possess must be the outcome of social processes through which people are organized into convergent action or into which they organize themselves .... There may be no inner drive at the core of a culture, but assuredly there are people who drive it on, as well as others who are driven" (1999: 66–67). But what is the "it" here, and does this formulation not reintroduce "thingness"?

Wolf's new, more "serviceable" concept of culture shifts effortlessly from culture in the singular to cultures in the plural: "It is precisely the shapeless, all-encompassing quality of the concept that allows us to draw together—synoptically and synthetically—material relations to the world, societal organization, and configurations of ideas.... If we want to understand how humans seek stability or organize themselves to manage change, we need a concept that allows us to capture patterned social flow in its multiple interdependent dimensions and to assess how idea-dependent power steers these flows over time. 'Culture' is such a concept" (1999: 288–289). A critic might question whether such a totalizing concept adds analytic purchase to the other terms Wolf deployed in his case studies, terms such as cosmology, ideology, and "patterned social flow."

The discussion can be extended to other leading contemporaries.[10] An extreme position can be found in the work of the mature Marshall Sahlins.[11] Culture, which was opposed to structure in the work of British structural-functionalists, is in Sahlins's work firmly allied with structure to form the basis of idealist history (in contrast to the materialist history of Wolf). This leads Sahlins to express romantic sympathy with those "peoples" (*Kulturnationen* such as Japan as well as myriad *Kleinnationen*) all over the world, including in the United States, who are currently asserting their cultures. He pours scorn on anthropologists who debunk these efforts—for example, in diagnosing the "invention of traditions." According to Sahlins, this is no improvement on Malinowski's "charter" theory of myth and leads only to *déjà-vu* functionalist investigations that reduce the cultural order to utilitarian considerations. Hapless political correctness among academics and "succumbing to powerism" (Sahlins 1999: 406) should be replaced by recognition of "the inventiveness of tradition," which always resonates with established customs and culture that are outside real historical time. "From what I know about culture, then, traditions are invented in the specific terms of the people who construct them. Fundamentally they are atemporal, being for the people conditions of their form of life as constituted, and considered coeval with it.... Analytically to fix their historical appearance at some time short of the origin of things is always possible, and always falls short of understanding them, even as reducing them to current interests is likewise comprehension by subtraction. In all cases, the missing part is a comparative sense of cultures as meaningful orders" (1999: 409).[12]

Culture, Ethnicity, Identity: A Case from the Polish Carpathians

Having drawn attention to influential academic usages of the culture concept, I turn now to the deployment of these ideas outside the academy. The term "culture" or a close cognate is now used all over the world, often to mobilize a group in a conflict situation, in order to accentuate the sense of common identity. It is particularly interesting to examine cases in which the group culture is still *in statu nascendi*—that is, where an ethnic or national identity is under construction by intellectual elites. Processes of ethnicity and nationalism, often covert principles of political legitimation under socialism, became overt and prominent in many parts of Eastern and Central Europe after the collapse of socialism in 1989–1991. The old dichotomy between the *Kulturvolk* and the *Kleinvolk* has reappeared in new guises, and some groups have taken advantage of new conditions to demand recognition on the basis of a cultural identity, that, for one reason or another, could not be openly proclaimed under socialism. The more recent linguistic imports "ethnicity" and "ethnic group" have been used synonymously with "nation" and "nationality," and all are grounded in the totalitarian concept of culture.

The case of the Lemkos in southeastern Poland highlights the malleability and ultimate contingency of all forms of collective identity. In this section I review the emergence of this identity and show how it can be professed nowadays at various levels. Whatever the level, the identity is closely tied to the group's territorial homeland in the Carpathians, where the allegedly shared culture developed over many centuries. Today this identity exists in the context of an emerging pluralism in Polish society, yet activists insist on a totalitarian concept of culture to deemphasize or deny this reality.

Many people in Eastern and Central Europe had no clearly developed sense of belonging to an ethnic or national group until well into the twentieth century. The "primordialist" view, according to which such collectivities have existed "since time immemorial," is clearly false. An alternative view, associated particularly with Fredrik Barth (1969b), emphasizes that ethnic identity is interactive, that individuals can cross ethnic boundaries, and that the cultural content of ethnic groups changes over time. Yet even when such points are acknowledged for "premodern" conditions outside Europe, the pertinence of the Barthian approach for regions such as Central Europe has seldom been recognized. It is only recently that Eastern European cases such as that of the Lemkos have come under external anthropological scrutiny.[13] The most important sources on these people are the works of the Eastern European "national ethnographers," the intellectuals who documented the customs of the folk more or less in the Herderian spirit of German *Volkskunde*. A critical reading of this work can yield valuable insights into social relations, including questions concerning group boundaries and identities.[14]

Almost every statement about the Lemkos, including the proposition that they constitute a group at all, can be contested. The term, however, is now widely used to describe a population that formerly occupied a one-hundred-kilometer-long section of the northern side of the Carpathians between the rivers Poprad and Oslawa, just east of the region in which Malinowski and Pope John Paul II grew up, each with his strong sense of Polish national identity. Their market centers were in towns to the north of their villages and were principally Polish in character.

The medieval settlement history of this territory is controversial, but politically it belonged to Poland until the first partition of the Polish state in 1772. From then until 1918 it was governed from Vienna as part of the Habsburg province of Galicia. Throughout this period the Lemko villages, with a total population exceeding one hundred thousand by the early twentieth century, were separated by a stable boundary to the north and west from neighbors who were overwhelmingly Roman Catholic and who spoke dialects of Polish. It is more difficult to specify a boundary to the south, across the ridge of the Carpathians, and to the east. The neighbors on those two sides, like the inhabitants of "Lemkovyna," followed the eastern Christian tradition, spoke East Slav dialects, and acknowledged a collective identity as Rusyn or Rusnak ("Ruthenian").

The term Lemko derives from a dialect word and was first applied by Polish ethnographers of the territory in the nineteenth century. It was not widely disseminated as an ethnonym until well into the twentieth century, under complex political conditions shaped by a diaspora in North America as well as by rising nationalist tensions in Central Europe (Magocsi 1993). Lemkos themselves attempted to influence these processes, notably in the turbulent years following the collapse of the Habsburg monarchy. Local agency, however, was highly constrained. The authorities in the new Polish republic were determined that the Lemkos not be enlisted by their East Slav neighbors for the cause of Ukrainian nationalism. Accordingly, in the interwar decades the culture of the Lemkos, previously "invisible" to its members, was given totalitarian treatment as a unique "folk culture."

No sooner had this Lemko culture become an object of study and identification than its bearers were forcibly removed from their homeland in the course of brutal acts of ethnic cleansing, which culminated in 1947. Following the Nazi atrocities and their aftermath, socialist Poland, in contrast to all previous mutations of the Polish state, was one of the most ethnically homogeneous in Europe. Some Lemkos were able to return to their Carpathian homeland after the political turning point of 1956, whereas others continued to cultivate a Lemko identity in a diaspora that now included communities in northern and western Poland as well as Ukraine and North America. For the remaining years of socialist rule, Lemkos in Poland had no official minority status but were classified as part of a stigmatized Ukrainian minority.

The assertion of a distinctive regional tradition increased markedly in the altered political climate of the 1980s, exemplified in the regular holding of the *Vatra* Festival from 1983 onward. The collapse of socialism gave "identity politics" a new salience, and it became possible for Lemkos to establish new formal associations such as the *Stovaryshynie Lemkiv*.[15] Among the descendants of the population dispersed in the 1940s, at least three groups with distinct orientations toward collective identity can be observed today: those who say they are Lemkos, those who say they are Ukrainians, and those who say they are both Lemkos and Ukrainians. Within each of these categories, it is probably the case that more members live outside the homeland than have returned to it. Of the population dispersed in the 1940s to other parts of Poland, many in the younger generations have no significant East Slav identification whatsoever. They have assimilated to a Polish identity (see Kwilecki 1974; Pudlo 1987).

Let us now look more closely at the construction of this Lemko identity, beginning with the outstanding Polish ethnographer Roman Reinfuss, who published scores of articles and several books on the topic over more than sixty years. The recent reissue of his most comprehensive study (Reinfuss 1998), first published in 1948 but written on the basis of his field research in the 1930s, is especially welcome.[16] Unlike some other Polish scholars in the interwar period (notably Pieradzka 1990), Reinfuss did not attempt to classify the Lemkos as a people entirely separate from their neighbors to the east, most of whom by the time of his work professed a national identity as Ukrainian. Nor did he claim that the members of this population had a strong collective identity as Lemkos. Instead he noted the widespread self-designation *Rusnak* and emphasized the local identities that villagers professed, identities typically encompassing a cluster of villages. For example, the Lemko villagers of Wislok Wielki, the location of my early fieldwork in 1979–1981 (Hann 1985), belonged to the cluster known as *Królewszczyzna*, an identity based on common allegiance to the Polish crown in the distant past. People were unaware of named groups of this or any other kind apart from those with whom they interacted at the marketplace. Reinfuss did not specify the importance of these "subjective" identifications in social life, because his prime concern was the meticulous documentation of a shared Lemko folk culture (*kultura ludowa*). He is to be seen not as a pioneering student of ethnicity in the Barthian sense but rather as a national ethnographer whose job was to delineate bounded units according to "objective" ethnographic criteria. In this way a folk culture could be created irrespective of the identifications of local people.

Reinfuss used the material-culture criteria that he investigated through his fieldwork in the interwar years to argue that Wislok Wielki and its neighbors fell within Lemkovyna, even though the local population was politically more firmly oriented eastward, toward the Ukrainian national movement, than westward, toward any developing sense of a distinct Lemko identity. Thus he sought to pin down the precise traits that would enable the observing scientist to distinguish Lemkos from neighboring Boikos at the eastern extremity of their territory (see Reinfuss 1938; compare Falkowski and Pasznycki 1991 [1935]). That neither of these terms was used by villagers in this fuzzy border area around the valley of the Oslawa River did not prevent his classifying those villagers as within the Lemko "ethnographic group" (*grupa etnograficzna*). In this respect, Reinfuss can be seen as the scholarly culmination of a process of constructing a new collective identity based on a common culture, a process that had begun about a century earlier with the coining of the term Lemko. Reinfuss and other national ethnographers all over Eastern Europe were still perfecting the scholarly art of ethnic cartography until the rules and conditions of the game were dramatically altered by the events of the 1940s.

Reinfuss's pioneering work has been continued by younger generations of Polish ethnographers and sociologists. Jerzy Czajkowski (1992, 1999), Ewa Michna (1995), and Elżbieta Slys-Janusz (1998) have all provided professional confirmation that the Lemkos indeed constitute a "separate culture." Czajkowski, the long-serving head of the region's principal open-air museum at Sanok, in his afterword to his recent reissue of Reinfuss's key text (1998), explicitly encouraged "root-seeking" and the (re)discovery of Lemko culture. He complimented Reinfuss on his intuitive prescience in establishing that the people of this region were "subconsciously" moving toward the level of national consciousness as Lemkos in the 1930s, even though this was not expressed by informants and, at the time, it was much easier to point to intraregional differences than to see the "threads" that unified. Such scholarly work continues to contribute to the development of the "culture," which it purports to find as a "given." As a result, there is nowadays a fairly widespread sense of Lemko identity even in districts where Reinfuss conceded that it did not exist subjectively when he did his fieldwork.[17]

This is not ethnicity of the sort that interested Barth, based on local maintenance of boundaries. It is an ethnicity designed largely by outsiders, mostly Polish ethnographers, according to the totalitarian model of what "a culture" is and what it should be. Ironically, its effective dissemination occurred only after the reference points in the homeland were largely destroyed with the deportations of the 1940s. This Lemko culture is not, however, the *invention* of outsiders. Though there is room to dispute the way in which the eastern boundary was drawn, the project to "construct" a Lemko identity was far from arbitrary. It is clear that the villagers on whom much of Reinfuss's work concentrated, in the central Lemko districts, were unattracted to the Ukrainian national identity that was being cultivated in cities hundreds of miles to the east. Some of their ethnographic traits and above all their long history of Russophilism distinguished them from the villagers of Wislok Wielki and facilitated the task of those who shaped Lemko identity, both at home and in North America. The collective identity as Lemko was new, but it could be promoted and adopted only because of differences that existed objectively and historically.

The Lemkos have recently begun to produce their own intellectuals, as every *Kulturvolk* must, to codify their language, collect the folk literature, and write the group's history (see, e.g., Duc'-Fajfer 1993; Horbal 1997; Zięba 1997). These efforts are being supported from afar by the Toronto-based historian Paul Robert Magocsi, who has helped make the Carpatho-Rusyns a well-established ethnic group in "multicultural" North America (see Magocsi 1978).[18] The collapse of socialism enabled him to expand his activities for the first time to the Carpathian homeland. His argument is that the Lemkos are a regional variant of the people known as Rusyns or Ruthenians. The Rusyns form a distinct East Slav nationality, fully on a par as a *Kulturvolk* with the dominant nationalities in the countries where they live—that is, with Ukrainians, Poles, Slovaks, Hungarians, and Romanians.[19] His recent attempts to consolidate this identity show many parallels with nineteenth-century nation building, notably in his encouragement of the standardization of a fourth East Slavic language (successfully achieved in Slovakia in 1995). In comparison with Reinfuss, Magocsi attaches greater weight to subjective identifications and historical contingencies. Whereas Reinfuss's cartography emphasized the objective delineation of cultural traits in separating Lemkos from Boikos, Magocsi knows that "Rusyns" may come to see themselves as Ukrainians if political circumstances conspire to suppress other options. He prefers the terms "nationality" and "ethnic group" to culture, though he does not avoid this term altogether. He is not a primordialist but a moderate constructivist, fully conscious of the intellectual's role in the shaping of collective identities.[20]

In some respects, recent strides in the construction of Lemko identity have been impressive. In addition to the codification of Rusyn, significant work has taken place in Cracow on the standardization of a Lemko language that diverges both from Rusyn and Ukrainian. This Lemko language is now taught in a number of Polish schools, with full state recognition. The number of conferences, publications, theatrical and musical groups, and festivals at which the culture is put on display continues to increase.

But uncertainties remain, above all the basic question, who exactly are the Lemkos? Neither Lemko nor Rusyn is a term acknowledged by all of the people to whom the activists apply it, any more than Reinfuss found the term Lemko enjoying general acknowledgment in the 1930s. In distinguishing Rusyns from the much larger nationality of Ukrainians, Magocsi faces the same difficult task that Reinfuss faced in distinguishing Lemkos from Boikos, because there is no sharp, objective ethnographic boundary. Although there is now more contact across state borders than was possible in the communist period, the Rusyn movement has not taken off; in Ukraine, the state where most Rusyns live, the leadership has lost credibility. No one should rule out the possibility, however, that the activist groups will succeed in persuading larger constituencies of the strength of distinct regional traditions, thus bringing about a *subjective* ethnogenesis. External factors may succeed where internal agitation has so far failed: if a committee of the European Union were to follow the lead of the postcommunist state and decide that the Lemkos or Rusyns, or possibly both, constitute *cultures,* it might have sufficient impact to make the members of that culture finally aware of their destiny.

Whatever the future may hold for these people (and although the debates are sometimes fierce, they seem unlikely to lead to further violence), the Lemko case reaffirms the anthropological commonplace that ethnicity is neither primordial nor invented but is shaped by particular actors in historical contexts. Long-term processes of settlement and migration contributed to the shaping of contemporary Lemko identity. The tragedies of the First World War and, above all, the ethnic cleansing of 1947, which apparently threatened the group's destruction, are now objects of intensive research and debate, which may serve to create a new charter for common identity. Lemkoness seems nowadays to be felt at different levels by different people. For some, it may be the powerful feeling of collective belonging that Barth (1969b: 15) called the individual's "basic, most general identity." For others, this powerful sentiment is experienced primarily at the level of Ukrainian ethnicity, and identification as Lemko is of a lower order. Yet others view Lemko as a lower order within a general Rusyn identity that precludes a Ukrainian affiliation.[21]

Of the various options available to these people in the current Polish context, it is the notion of a Rusyn *Kulturvolk* that faces the most practical difficulties. Most of the people with whom I have discussed this in Poland make either a clear assertion of the preeminence of Ukrainian identity or an equally clear declaration of the preeminence of Lemko identity. The basic social and institutional framework within which most Lemkos live is Poland, and the boundaries of this state continue to play a decisive role. Whichever ethnic option they choose, we might interpret their choice as an expression of cultural identity by people who are geographically dispersed but believe they have something important in common. Yet no matter how often they attend festivals and other cultural performances, this feeling is not necessarily of much social significance. It opens up positive ties of sentiment to a picturesque territory and to other people who share origins there, but it cannot warrant special recognition and constitutional protection as "a culture."

Conclusion

The concept of culture shifted during the twentieth century from the singular to the plural to become the foundational concept of anthropology. In the first part of this chapter I explored some of the intellectual context surrounding this shift, particularly the transplanting of a German intellectual heritage to the United States. The Boasian usage of culture was in many ways progressive and emancipatory. The term became relativized and distinguished from civilization in an age when distinctive customs, beliefs, and practices could be tied to territory more easily than they can today. For Malinowski, culture was not to be studied in terms of separable traits but as an integrated whole, as a "reality sui generis." He himself paid close attention to material artifacts, to "instrumental reality" and biological needs, but he pointed also to knowledge and "mental habits" as an ultimate source. Since his day, the culture concept has become prone to essentialist and idealist biases, which I summarize as the totalitarian usage. Examples range from political scientists who argue that many peoples all over the world need to change their cultures if they want to hasten economic development (Huntington and Harrison 2000) to philosophers such as Charles Taylor (1992) who call for a new politics of culture-based "recognition."

In the second part of the chapter I illustrated some of the ways in which the term culture has been applied over the last century or so to a small population in Central Europe. My purpose in choosing this example was not to insinuate that "Lemko culture" is less authentic than other ethnic or national cultures all over the world, but to question the conflation of culture, ethnicity, and identity by highlighting a case in which the "groupness" of a population is still in the formative phase of construction, a construction in which both insiders and outsiders are active participants.

If it is correct to link this concept of culture to the rise of modern nationalism, then in an age when the nation-state seems to many observers to be a fading force, we should not be surprised that critical voices have begun to make themselves heard. Adam Kuper (1999) concluded his survey by arguing *against* recognizing culture as a distinct sphere and *for* the disaggregation of its components. Cultural identities, he argued, are always multiple and not simple causes of behavior. Culture is all too often used as a shorthand or substitute for the complex processual, differentiated social phenomena that anthropologists describe and explain. Roger Keesing (1994) issued similar warnings about the way in which this culture concept leads anthropologists to exaggerate the otherness of the people they study. Like Eric Wolf, Kuper and Keesing have called for the study of culture to be tied more closely to the study of material and political forces. In a similar vein, Jack Goody (1992: 30) defined "the cultural" as "the social viewed from another perspective, not a distinct analytic entity." This hardly differs from Malinowski's assertion some eighty years earlier that "all achievements of culture exist in society and through society" (Thornton and Skalnik 1993: 164). Unfortunately, in the interim a number of leading figures accepted the Parsonian settlement that restricted them to culture in the idealist sense.

Accelerating globalization and the reintegration of studies of the ideational with studies of material social organization might gradually be expected to undermine the habit of referring to populations as cultures, and with it the embarrassing overlap between the anthropological usages and the nationalists' usages. At present, however, there are no grounds for complacency. Anthropologists have little control over the word "culture," which in its "thinglike" sense remains a potent force in contemporary identity politics. It is myopic to deny this problem. Virtually all anthropologists agree that culture is not a thing. Geertz tells us that there is *only* the word, but this is unhelpful, given what others are now doing with this word. Despite my sympathy with Wolf's project, I have become pessimistic not only about getting wider audiences to see the problem but even about conveying a defensible, "serviceable" concept of culture to our own students and to colleagues in other disciplines. Even so, I do not argue for a rejection of the culture concept on political grounds. Rather, I conclude that it is time to demote culture from its quasi-mystical status as the discipline's master concept. To return to my starting definition, culture is best understood as *congealed sociality*, a transient patterning of clusters of behaviors and ideas. Contrary to nationalist rhetoric and to the main thrust of so much of twentieth-century anthropology, human sociality has rarely, if ever, become so congealed as to form discontinuous blocks congruent with entire populations.[22]

Notes

For stimulating discussion on the themes of this chapter, I am grateful to all the participants in the Mexico symposium, and also to Steven P. Reyna, Han F. Vermeulen, and Paul Robert Magocsi, genial guests at the Max Planck Institute for Social Anthropology in 2000–2001.

1. I use the term "essentially contested concept" in the sense defined by W. B. Gallie (1956) and applied by Krishan Kumar (2000) to the concept of "civil society." Like civil society, culture has become deeply rooted outside as well as inside the academy. Close attention to the history of the concept may reveal new opportunities for constructive reinterpretation, but that is not the task of this chapter.

2. The classic review of the culture concept in anthropology remains that of Kroeber and Kluckhohn (1952). I am not aware of any work covering the last half century in comparable detail, but I find Kuper (1999) lucid and persuasive.

3. For several anthropological studies exploring the Marxist approach, see Wallman 1979.

4. The data that may support such a diagnosis for chimpanzees derive from encapsulated groups living in conditions that must differ substantially from those of their ancestors. It seems unlikely that many human groups have lived in conditions comparable to those of contemporary "wild" chimps.

5. "Jede Nation hat ihren Mittelpunkt der Glückseligkeit in sich wie jede Kugel ihren Schwerpunkt" (Every nation has its own center of happiness, just as every sphere has its own center of gravity; Herder 1997 [1774]: 163, cited in Berg 1984: 92).

6. Herder did not need to pluralize the term *Cultur* to make his basic point about the diversity of human groups: it was enough to pluralize *Volk*.

7. The most famous definition from this era remains that of Edward Tylor (1871: 1): "Culture or Civilization, taken in its wide ethnographic sense, is that complex whole which includes knowledge, belief, art, morals, law, custom, and any other capabilities and habits acquired by man as a member of society."

8. Zimmerman (1998) attributes the propagation of this myth to Wilhelm Mühlmann.

9. There is little doubt that Malinowski was raised as a Polish cultural nationalist (Gellner 1998). His comprehensive *Encyclopaedia of the Social Sciences* article on culture (1931) ranged as widely as Tylor's definition, but unlike Tylor, Malinowski frequently endorsed the plural, totalitarian usage. It would be interesting to discover whether he acquired this habit while still in Poland, during his studies in Leipzig, or only after his arrival in Britain. For assessments of Malinowski's writings on culture, see Paluch 1988; Richards 1957.

10. For usages by a nonanthropologist, see John Paul II's message to open the United Nations' year of "dialogue between cultures" (2001). He asserted (in article 5): "In any event, *a person necessarily lives within a specific culture*. People are marked by the culture whose very air they breathe" (emphasis in original).

11. See Sahlins 1976, in which his debt to Boas is made clear.

12. Sahlins (1999: 416, n. 4) argues that it is an oxymoron to use the adjective "cultural" while rejecting the noun "culture." The problem arises out of the "ordering" assumptions that he builds into his notion of "substantial" culture.

13. For studies by Western anthropologists, see Hann 1997; Lehmann 1999. For wide-ranging introductions, see Best and Moklak 2001; Magocsi 1999: 113–137. For a detailed investigation of how Lemko ethnic identity is being

constructed and reproduced in the postsocialist years, see Nowak 2000. Nowak's work suggests that the distinction between the native ethnographer and the Western anthropologist is now becoming obsolete.

14. Some of these ethnographers played a significant role in standardizing the new national cultures, which makes them immediately suspect to later ethnographers. Others, however, were aware of complications, especially if they worked in regions where the new national identities were slow to emerge. Józef Obrębski, a student and friend of Malinowski's who worked in the interwar period in Polesie, was an outstanding example (see Obrebski 1974).

15. This organization is based in Legnica, a formerly German city in western Poland where rival Lemko festivals are now organized far from the homeland. Lemkos who see themselves as Ukrainian at some higher level of identity formed their own organization within the Ukrainian community (see Majewicz 1999).

16. In the preface he wrote for this book not long before his death, Reinfuss showed his continuing concern with the genetic origins of the population. It has long been important to Poles to be able to establish a stream of migrants from the Balkans preceding the main waves of East Slav immigration to these hills, though no one now disputes that it is the latter immigrants who have had the most decisive influence on the region over more than half a millennium.

17. For example, Komańcza, a village east of Wislok Wielki that attracts some tourists, has a newly established Lemko Museum.

18. A bibliography of Magocsi's work up to 2000 has been compiled by Gabriele Scardellato (2000). Much pertinent material is collected in Magocsi 1999.

19. Since the eighteenth century there has also been a significant Rusyn group in Vojvodina, so Serbs may be added to this list. Like Reinfuss, Magocsi has refrained from taking any overt political stance, though he has been an active participant (as a representative of the United States) in the activities of the World Rusyn Congress.

20. For an expanded assessment of Magocsi's work, see my introduction to his collected Rusyn essays (Magocsi 1999).

21. In principle, Rusyn might in turn be classified as a subgroup of Ukrainian, opening up the possibility of a triple Lemko-Rusyn-Ukrainian alternative to the Lemko-Rusyn that Magocsi encourages. Indeed, one might move higher still, to embrace all East Slavs, and so on. There are good grounds for insisting on such moves, to highlight the contingency of identifying "culture" with "ethnic group" or "nation."

22. Stimulated by colleagues at the Mexico conference, I elaborated this definition at the last session as the CRIMES approach. It defines culture as *C*ongealed, *R*econstituted (in preference to "learned," as argued by C. Toren),

*I*ntersubjectively *M*eaningful (stressed particularly by F. Barth and S. Wright), *E*volving (C. Boesch, W. Durham, etc.) *S*ociality. Anthropological insistence on a specification of this sort, however clumsy, should help to counter the pervasive simplicity of the totalitarian concept and the "crimes" to which it has contributed in the past and to which it continues to contribute.

References

Abu-Lughod, Lila. 1991. Writing against culture. In *Recapturing anthropology: Working in the present,* edited by Richard G. Fox, 137–162. Santa Fe, N.M.: School of American Research Press.

Adam, Heribert. 1994. Ethnic versus civic nationalism: South Africa's non-racialism in comparative perspective. *South African Sociological Review* 7 (1): 15–31.

Alcoff, Linda. 1991. The problem of speaking for others. *Cultural Critique* 20: 5–32.

Almeida, José, ed. 1999. *El racismo en las Américas y el Caribe.* Quito: PUCE and Abya-Yala.

Althusser, Louis. 1971. *Lenin and philosophy.* Translated by Ben Brewster. New York: Monthly Review Press.

Andrade, Xavier. 2001. Machismo and politics in Ecuador: The case of Pancho Jaime. *Men and Masculinities* 3 (3): 299–315.

Arakawa, Akira. 1987 [1978]. *Shin nantō fudoki* [A new human geography of the southern islands]. Tokyo: Asahi Bunko.

Arias, Arturo, ed. 2001. *The Rigoberta Menchú controversy.* Minneapolis: University of Minnesota Press.

Armstrong, David, William Stokoe, and Sherman Wilcox. 1995. *Gesture and the nature of language.* Cambridge: Cambridge University Press.

Asquith, Pamela. 2000. Negotiating science: Internationalization and Japanese primatology. In *Primate encounters,* edited by S. C. Strum and L. M. Fedigan, 165–183. Chicago: University of Chicago Press.

Baker, Houston A. 1987. *Modernism and the Harlem renaissance.* Chicago: University of Chicago Press.

Baker, Lee D. 1998. *From savage to Negro: Anthropology and the construction of race.* Berkeley: University of California Press.

Balibar, Etienne. 1991. Racism and nationalism. In *Race, nation, class: Ambiguous identities,* edited by Etienne Balibar and Immanuel Wallerstein, 37–68. London: Verso.

Balibar, Etienne, and Immanuel Wallerstein. 1995. *Race, nation, class: Ambiguous identities.* London: Verso.

Banfield, Edward C. 1990. *Unheavenly city revisited.* New York: Waveland Press.

Barrett, Martyn. 1999. *The development of language.* Hove, East Sussex: Psychology Press.

Barry, Brian. 2001. *Culture and equality: An egalitarian critique of multiculturalism.* Cambridge: Polity.

Barth, Fredrik. 1966. *Models of social organization.* Occasional Paper 23. London: Royal Anthropological Institute of Great Britain and Ireland.

———, ed. 1969a. *Ethnic groups and boundaries: The social organization of culture difference.* London: George Allen and Unwin.

———. 1969b. Introduction. In *Ethnic groups and boundaries,* edited by F. Barth, 9–38. London: George Allen and Unwin.

———. 1975. *Ritual and knowledge among the Baktaman of New Guinea.* New Haven, Conn.: Yale University Press.

———. 1983. *Sohar: Culture and society in an Omani town.* Baltimore, Md.: Johns Hopkins University Press.

———. 1987. *Cosmologies in the making: A generative approach to cultural variation in inner New Guinea.* Cambridge: Cambridge University Press.

———. 1992. Towards greater naturalism in conceptualizing societies. In *Conceptualizing society,* edited by Adam Kuper. London: Routledge.

———. 1993. *Balinese worlds.* Chicago: University of Chicago Press.

Barwick, M., N. Cohen, N. Horodezky, and M. Lojkasek. n.d. *Language and communication in relation to the mother-infant attachment relationship in clinic and community infants.* Manuscript in preparation.

Basalla, Susan. 1997. Family resemblances. Ph.D. dissertation, Princeton University.

Basso, Keith. 1988. "Speaking names": Language and landscape among the Western Apache. *Cultural Anthropology* 3: 99–130.

Bateson, Gregory. 1972. *Steps to an ecology of mind.* New York: Ballantine.

Bayart, Jean-Francois. 1993. *The state in Africa: The politics of the belly.* London: Longman.

Bederman, Gail. 1995. *Manliness and civilization: A cultural history of gender and race in the United States, 1880–1917.* Chicago: University of Chicago Press.

Benedict, Ruth. 1934. *Patterns of culture.* Boston: Houghton Mifflin.

———. 1946. *The chrysanthemum and the sword.* New York: Meridian Books.

Benedict, Ruth, and Gene Weltfish. 1943. *The races of mankind.* New York: Public Affairs Committee, Inc.

Benomar, Jamal. 1993. Confronting the past: Justice after transitions. *Journal of Democracy* 4 (1): 3–14.

Berg, Eberhard. 1984. Die Nachwirkungen des Bildes vom "Homme naturel" auf den ethnologischen Kulturbegriff: Überlegungen zu Herders Kulturanthropologie." In *Ethnologie als Sozialwissenschaft*, edited by Ernst Wilhelm Müller, René König, Klaus-Peter Koepping, and Paul Drechsel, 85–100. Opladen: Westdeutscher Verlag.

Berlin, Isaiah. 2000. *The roots of Romanticism.* London: Pimlico.

Best, Paul J., and Jaroslaw Moklak, eds. 2001. The Lemkos of Poland: Articles and essays. New Haven, Conn.: Inter-Ed.

Beverley, John. 1999. *Subalternity and representation.* Durham, N.C.: Duke University Press.

———. 2001. What happens when the subaltern speaks. In *The Rigoberta Menchú controversy,* edited by Arturo Arias, 219–236. Minneapolis: University of Minnesota Press.

Blackmore, Susan. 1999. *The meme machine.* Oxford: Oxford University Press.

Bloch, Maurice. 1986. *From blessing to violence.* Cambridge: Cambridge University Press.

Boas, Franz. 1932. *Anthropology and modern life.* New York: W. W. Norton.

———. 1940. *Race, language, and culture.* New York: Macmillan.

———. 1945. *Race and democratic society.* New York: J. J. Augustin.

———. 1974. *A Franz Boas reader: The shaping of American anthropology, 1883–1911.* Edited by George W. Stocking, Jr. Chicago: University of Chicago Press.

———. 1990 [1935]. Preface. In *Mules and men,* by Zora Neale Hurston, xiii–xiv. New York: Harper and Row.

Boesch, Christophe. 2000. Cultural complexity in chimpanzees. Paper presented at a Wenner-Gren Foundation International Symposium, Morelia, Mexico.

Boesch, Christophe, and Hedwige Boesch-Achermann. 2000. *The chimpanzees of the Tai forest: Behavioural ecology and evolution.* Oxford: Oxford University Press.

Boesch, Christophe, and Michael Tomasello. 1998. Chimpanzee and human cultures. *Current Anthropology* 39 (1): 591–634.

Bonner, John Tyler. 2001. Review of Frans de Waal's *The ape and the sushi master* (New York: Basic Books, 2001). *Times Literary Supplement* 5128 (13 July): 8.

Boonzaier, Emile. 1988. Race and the race paradigm. In *South African keywords: The uses and abuses of political concepts,* edited by Emile Boonzaier and John Sharp, 58–67. Cape Town: David Philip.

Boraine, Alex. 1994. *The healing of a nation?* Cape Town: Justice in Transition.

———. 2000. *A country unmasked.* Oxford: Oxford University Press.

Borofsky, Robert. 1994. On the knowledge and knowing of cultural activities. In *Assessing cultural anthropology,* edited by R. Borofsky, 331–348. New York: McGraw-Hill.

Bourdieu, Pierre. 1977. *Outline of a theory of practice.* Translated by Richard Nice. Cambridge: Cambridge University Press.

Bowerman, Melissa. 1982. Reorganizational processes in lexical and syntactic development. In *Language acquisition: The state of the art,* edited by E. Wanner and L. P. Gleitman, 319–346. Cambridge: Cambridge University Press.

———. 1996. The origins of children's spatial semantic categories: Cognitive versus linguistic determinants. In *Rethinking linguistic relativity,* edited by John J. Gumperz and Stephen C. Levinson, 145–176. Cambridge: Cambridge University Press.

Bowerman, Melissa, and Stephen C. Levinson, eds. 2001. *Language acquisition and conceptual development.* Cambridge: Cambridge University Press.

Box, Hilary O., and Kathleen R. Gibson, eds. 1999. *Social learning in mammals: Comparative and ecological perspectives.* Cambridge: Cambridge University Press.

Boyd, Robert, and Peter J. Richerson. 1985. *Culture and the evolutionary process.* Chicago: University of Chicago Press.

Bray, Francesca. 1997. *Technology and gender: Fabrics of power in late imperial China.* Berkeley: University of California Press.

Briggs, Jean. 1998. *Inuit morality play: The emotional education of a three-year-old.* New Haven, Conn.: Yale University Press.

Brightman, Robert. 1995. Forget culture: Replacement, transcendence, relexification. *Cultural Anthropology* 10 (4): 509–546.

Brodie, Richard. 1996. *Virus of the mind: The new science of the meme.* Seattle: Integral Press.

Brown, Penelope. 1997. Isolating the CUC root in Tzeltal Mayan: A study of children's first verbs. *Proceedings of the Twenty-eighth Annual Child Language Research Forum,* 41–52. Stanford, Calif.: CSLI.

———. 1998a. Children's first verbs in Tzeltal: Evidence for an early verb category. *Linguistics* 36 (4): 713–753.

———. 1998b. Conversational structure and language acquisition: The role of repetition in Tzeltal adult and child speech. *Journal of Linguistic Anthropology* 8 (2): 1–25.

———. 2001a. Learning to talk about motion UP and DOWN in Tzeltal: Is there a language-specific bias for verb learning? In *Language acquisition and conceptual development,* edited by M. Bowerman and S. C. Levinson, 512–543. Cambridge: Cambridge University Press.

———. 2001b. Everyone has to lie in Tzeltal. In *Talking to adults,* edited by Shoshana Blum-Kulka and Catherine Snow, 241–275. Mahwah, N.J.: Erlbaum.

———. n.d. Verb semantics and argument realization in Tzeltal. In *Cross-linguistic perspectives on argument structure: issues of learnability,* edited by M. Bowerman and P. Brown. Manuscript in preparation.

Brown, Penelope, and Stephen C. Levinson. 1993a. *Linguistic and non-linguistic coding of spatial arrays: Explorations in Mayan cognition.* Working Paper 24, Cognitive Anthropology Research Group, Max Planck Institute, Nijmegen, Netherlands.

———. 1993b. "Uphill" and "downhill" in Tzeltal. *Journal of Linguistic Anthropology* 3 (1): 46–74.

———. 2000. Frames of spatial reference and their acquisition in Tenejapan Tzeltal. In *Culture, thought, and development,* edited by L. Nucci, G. Saxe, and E. Turiel, 167–197. Mahwah, N.J.: Erlbaum.

Brumann, Christoph. 1999. Writing for culture: Why a successful concept should not be discarded. *Current Anthropology* 40 (supplement): s1–s28.

Brumfiel, Elizabeth. 1996. Figurines and the Aztec state: Testing the effectiveness of ideological domination. In *Gender and archaeology,* edited by R. P. Wright, 143–166. Philadelphia: University of Pennsylvania Press.

Bruner, Jerome S. 1983. *Child's talk.* Oxford: Oxford University Press.

Buchanan, James M. 1995. Economic science and cultural diversity. *Kyklos* 48 (2): 193–200.

Bulmer, Martin, and John Solomos, eds. 1999. *Ethnic and racial studies today.* London: Routledge.

Burgos-Dobray, Elizabeth. 1984. *I, Rigoberta Menchú: An Indian woman in Guatemala.* Translated by Ann Wright. London: Verso.

Burling, Robbins. 1999. Motivation, conventionalization, and arbitrariness in the origin of language. In *The origins of language: What nonhuman primates can tell us,* edited by Barbara J. King, 307–350. Santa Fe, N.M.: School of American Research Press.

Campbell, Donald T. 1965. Variation and selective retention in sociocultural evolution. In *Social change in developing areas: A reinterpretation of evolutionary theory,* edited by H. R. Barringer, G. I. Blanksten, and R. W. Mack, 19–49. Cambridge, Mass: Schenkman.

Carr, David. 1970. Introduction. In *The crisis of European sciences and transcendental phenomenology: An introduction to phenomenological philosophy,* by Edmund Husserl [1954]. Evanston, Ill.: Northwestern University Press.

Carrier, Joseph. 1996. *De los otros: Intimacy and homosexuality among Mexican men.* New York: Columbia University Press.

Carrithers, Michael. 1992. *Why humans have cultures: Explaining anthropology and social diversity.* Oxford: Oxford University Press.

Cavalli-Sforza, Luigi L., and Marc W. Feldman. 1981. *Cultural transmission and evolution: A quantitative approach.* Princeton, N.J.: Princeton University Press.

Cervone, Emma, and Fredy Rivera, eds. 1999. *Ecuador racista: Imágenes e identidades.* Quito: FLACSO.

Childe, V. Gordon. 1956. *Piecing together the past.* New York: Praeger.

Chomsky, Noam. 1966. *Cartesian linguistics.* New York: Harper and Row.

———. 1980. *Rules and representations.* New York: Columbia University Press.

Clark, H. H. 1973. Space, time, semantics, and the child. In *Cognitive development and the acquisition of language,* edited by Timothy E. Moore, 28–64. New York: Academic Press.

Clarke, David. 1968. *Analytical archaeology.* London: Metheun.

Clifford, James. 1988. *The predicament of culture.* Cambridge, Mass.: Harvard University Press.

Cohen, Lawrence. 1995. Holy in Banaras and the Mahaland of modernity. *Gay and Lesbian Quarterly* 2: 399–424.

Cohn, Bernard S. 1987. *An anthropologist among the historians and other essays.* Delhi and New York: Oxford University Press.

Cojtí-Cuxil, Demetrio. 1990. Lingüística e idioma en Guatemala. In *Lecturas sobre la lingüística Maya,* edited by N. England and S. Elliot, 1–25. Antigua: CIRMA.

Cole, Douglas. 1999. *Franz Boas: The early years, 1858–1906.* Vancouver and Seattle: Douglas and McIntyre and University of Washington Press.

Conkey, Margaret, and Janet Spector. 1984. Archaeology and the study of gender. In *Advances in archaeological method and theory,* vol. 7, edited by M. Schiffer, 1–38. New York: Academic Press.

Coronil, Fernando. 1992. Can postcoloniality be decolonized? Imperial banality and postcolonial power. *Public Culture* 5 (1): 89–108.

Cowan, Jane, Marie-Bénédicte Dembour, and Richard A. Wilson, eds. 2001. *Culture and rights: Anthropological perspectives.* Cambridge: Cambridge University Press.

Cusick, James G. 1998. *Studies in culture contact: Interaction, culture change, and archaeology.* Center for Archaeological Investigations, Occasional Paper 25. Carbondale: Southern Illinois University.

Czajkowski, Jerzy. 1992. Dzieje osadnictwa historycznego na Podkarpaciu i jego odzwierciedlenie w grupach etnicznych. In *Lemkowie w Historii i Kulturze Karpat* 1, edited by Jerzy Czajkowski, 27–166. Warsaw-Sanok: Spotkania.

———. 1999. *Studia nad Lemkowszczyzna*. Sanok: Muzeum Budownictwa Ludowego.

D'Andrade, Roy. 1995. *The development of cognitive anthropology*. Cambridge: Cambridge University Press.

Darnell, Regna. 1997. The anthropological concept of culture at the end of the Boasian century. *Social Analysis* 41: 42–54.

———. 1998. *And along came Boas: Continuity and revolution in Americanist anthropology*. Amsterdam: John Benjamins.

Darwin, Charles. 1859. *On the origin of species*. Facsimile of the first edition, 1964. Cambridge, Mass.: Harvard University Press.

Davenport, Charles B., Ales Hrdlicka, Louis I. Newman, Melville J. Herskovits, Frank H. Hankins, and C. M. Goethe. 1930. Eugenics and racial intermarriage: A symposium. *Eugenics: A Journal of Race Betterment* 3 (2): 58–62.

Dawkins, Richard. 1976. *The selfish gene*. Oxford: Oxford University Press.

Deacon, Terrence. 1997. *The symbolic species: The co-evolution of language and the human brain*. London: Penguin.

De la Torre, Carlos. 1996. *El racismo en el Ecuador: Experiencias de los indios de clase media*. Quito: CAAP.

———. 2000. *Populist seduction in Latin America: The Ecuadorian experience*. Athens, Ohio: Ohio University Press.

de León, Lourdes. 1994. Exploration in the acquisition of geocentric location by Tzotzil children. *Linguistics* 32 (4–5): 857–885.

Dennett, Daniel. 1991. *Consciousness explained*. Boston: Little Brown.

de Waal, Frans B. M. 2001. *The ape and the sushi master*. New York: Basic Books.

di Leonardo, Micaela. 1998. *Exotics at home: Anthropologies, others, American modernity*. Chicago: University of Chicago Press.

Dobres, Marcia-Anne. 2000. *Technology and social agency*. Oxford: Blackwell.

Donald, J., and A. Rattansi, eds. 1992. *"Race," culture and difference*. London: Sage.

Dubois, W. E. B. 1986 [1903]. *W. E. B. DuBois: Writings*. Edited by N. Huggins. New York: Modern Library.

Dubow, Saul. 1994. Ethnic euphemisms and racial echoes. *Journal of Southern African Studies* (special issue, "Ethnicity and Identity in Southern Africa") 20 (3): 355–370.

———. 1995. *Scientific racism in modern South Africa.* Cambridge: Cambridge University Press.

Duc'-Fajfer, Olena. 1993. The Lemkos in Poland. In *The persistence of regional cultures: Rusyns and Ukrainians in their Carpathian homeland and abroad,* edited by Paul Robert Magocsi, 83–104. New York: East European Monographs.

Dugatkin, Lee A. 2000. *The imitation factor: Evolution beyond the gene.* New York: Free Press.

Duranti, Alessandro. 1997. *Linguistic anthropology.* Cambridge: Cambridge University Press.

Durham, William H. 1990. Advances in evolutionary culture theory. *Annual Review of Anthropology* 19: 187–210.

———. 1991. *Coevolution: Genes, culture, and human diversity.* Stanford, Calif.: Stanford University Press.

Durham, William H., Robert Boyd, and Peter J. Richerson. 1997. Models and forces of cultural evolution. In *Human by nature: Between biology and the social sciences,* edited by Peter Weingart, Sandra D. Mitchell, Peter J. Richerson, and Sabine Maasen, 327–353. Mahwah, N.J.: Erlbaum.

Durham, William H., and Peter Weingart. 1997. Units of culture. In *Human by nature: Between biology and the social sciences,* edited by Peter Weingart, Sandra D. Mitchell, Peter J. Richerson, and Sabine Maasen, 300–313. Mahwah, N.J.: Erlbaum.

Eagleton, Terry. 2000. *The idea of culture.* London: Blackwell.

Eisenstadt, S. 1986. *The origins and diversity of axial age civilizations.* SUNY Series in Near Eastern Studies. Albany: State University of New York Press.

Ellison, Ralph. 1995. "The little man at Chehaw Station." In *The collected essays of Ralph Ellison,* 511. New York: Modern Library.

Elman, Jeffrey L., Elizabeth A. Bates, Mark H. Turner, Annette Karmilov-Smith, Dominico Parisi, and Kim Plunkett, eds. 1996. *Rethinking innateness.* Cambridge, Mass.: MIT Press.

Engelstad, Ericka. 1991. Feminist theory and post-processual archaeology. In *The archaeology of gender,* edited by D. Walde and N. D. Willows, 116–120. Calgary: Archaeological Association of the University of Calgary.

English, Rosalind. 1997. Cases and comments: *Ubuntu,* the quest for an indigenous jurisprudence. *South African Journal of Human Rights* 13 (4): 641–648.

Ensalaco, Mark. 1994. Truth commissions for Chile and El Salvador: A report and assessment. *Human Rights Quarterly* 16: 656–675.

Evans-Pritchard, E. E. 1940. *The Nuer.* Oxford: Oxford University Press.
———. 1956. *Nuer religion.* Oxford: Oxford University Press.
Falkowski, Jerzy, and Bazyli Pasznycki. 1991 [1935]. *Na Pograniczu Lemkowsko-Bojkowskiem.* Warsaw: Stanislaw Krycinski.
Fanon, Frantz. 1963. *The wretched of the earth.* Edited by C. Farrington. New York: Grove Press.
Farnell, Brenda. 1999. Moving bodies, acting selves. *Annual Review of Anthropology* 28: 341–373.
Fischer, Edward, and R. M. Brown, eds. 1996. *Maya cultural activism in Guatemala.* Austin: University of Texas Press.
Fodor, Jerry A. 1983. *The modularity of mind.* Cambridge, Mass.: MIT Press.
Fogel, Alan. 1993. *Developing through relationships: Origin of communication, self, and culture.* Chicago: University of Chicago Press.
———. n.d. Beyond individuals: A relational-historical approach to theory and research on communication. In *Il rapporto madre-bambino,* edited by M. L. Genta. Rome: Carocci Editore. In press.
Foley, William. 1997. *Anthropological linguistics: An introduction.* Oxford: Blackwell.
Fortes, Meyer. 1953. The structure of unilineal descent groups. *American Anthropologist* 55: 17–41.
Fox, Richard G. 1985. *Lions of the Punjab: Culture in the making.* Berkeley: University of California Press.
———. 1991. For a nearly new culture history. In *Recapturing anthropology: Working in the present,* edited by Richard G. Fox, 93–113. Santa Fe, N.M.: School of American Research Press.
———. 1995. Cultural dis-integration and the invention of new peacefares. In *Articulating hidden histories,* edited by Rayna Rapp and Jane Schneider, 275–287. Berkeley: University of California Press.
Fracchia, Joseph, and R. C. Lewontin. 1999. Does culture evolve? *History and Theory* 38 (4): 52–78.
Gallie, W. B. 1956. Essentially contested concepts. *Proceedings of the Aristotelian Society* (n.s.) 56: 167–198.
Gardiner, Howard. 1989. *The mind's new science.* New York: Basic Books.
Gardner, Alan, and Beatrix Gardner. 1969. Teaching sign language to a chimpanzee. *Science* 165: 664–672.
Geertz, Clifford. 1973. *The interpretation of cultures.* New York: Basic Books.
———. 1995. *After the fact.* Cambridge, Mass.: Harvard University Press.
———. 2000. *Available light: Anthropological reflections on philosophical topics.* Princeton, N.J.: Princeton University Press.

Gellner, Ernest. 1983. *Nations and nationalism.* Oxford: Blackwell.
———. 1997. *Nationalism.* London: Wiedenfeld and Nicholson.
———. 1998. *Language and solitude: Wittgenstein, Malinowski, and the Habsburg dilemma.* Cambridge: Cambridge University Press.
Gewirth, Alan. 1978. *Reason and morality.* Chicago: University of Chicago Press.
Gilroy, Paul. 1987. *"There ain't no black in the Union Jack": The cultural politics of race and nation.* London: Hutchinson.
———. 2000. *Against race: Imagining political culture beyond the color line.* Cambridge, Mass: Harvard University Press.
Gleitman, Lila. 1990. The structural sources of verb meanings. *Language Acquisition* 1: 3–55.
Gluckman, Max. 1975. Anthropology and apartheid: The work of South African anthropologists. In *Studies in African social anthropology,* edited by Meyer Fortes and Sheila Patterson, 21–39. London: Academic Press.
Goldstein, Howard, and Elaine Hockenberger. 1991. Significant progress in child language intervention: An 11-year retrospective. *Research in Developmental Disabilities* 12 (4): 401–424.
Golinkoff, R. M., K. Hirsh-Pasek, C. B. Mervis, W. B. Frawley, and M. Parillo. 1995. Lexical principles can be extended to the acquisition of verbs. In *Beyond names for things,* edited by M. Tomasello and W. E. Merriman, 185–221. Mahwah, N.J.: Erlbaum.
Goodall, Jane. 1990. *Through a window: Thirty years with the chimpanzees of Gombe.* London: Weidenfeld and Nicolson.
Goodenough, Ward H. 1964 [1957]. Cultural anthropology and linguistics. In *Language in culture and society: A reader in linguistics and anthropology,* edited by Dell Hymes, 36–39. New York: Harper and Row.
Goody, Esther, ed. 1995. *Social intelligence and interaction.* Cambridge: Cambridge University Press.
Goody, Jack. 1992. Culture and its boundaries: A European view. *Social Anthropology* 1 (1): 9–33.
Gopnik, Myrna, Jenny Dalalakis, Suzy Fukuda, and Shinji Fukuda. 1997. Familial language impairment. In *The inheritance and innateness of grammars,* edited by M. Gopnik, 111–140. New York: Oxford University Press.
Gordon, R. J., and A. D. Spiegel. 1993. Southern Africa revisited. *Annual Review of Anthropology* 22: 83–105.
Gow, Peter. 1989. The perverse child: Desire in a native Amazonian subsistence economy. *Man* (n.s.) 24: 299–314.

———. 2001. *An Amazonian myth and its history.* Oxford: Oxford University Press.

Greenspan, Stanley I. 1997. *The growth of the mind.* New York: Addison-Wesley.

Gregory, Steven. 1998. *Black corona: Race and the politics of place in an urban community.* Princeton, N.J.: Princeton University Press.

Gregory, Steven, and Roger Sanjek, eds. 1994. *Race.* New Brunswick, N.J.: Rutgers University Press.

Gumperz, John J. 1992. Contextualization and understanding. In *Rethinking context: Language as an interactive phenomenon,* edited by A. Duranti and C. Goodwin, 229–252. New York: Cambridge University Press.

Gumperz, John J., and Stephen C. Levinson, eds. 1996. *Rethinking linguistic relativity.* Cambridge: Cambridge University Press.

Gutmann, Matthew C. 1996. *The meanings of macho: Being a man in Mexico City.* Berkeley: University of California Press.

Habermas, Jürgen. 1992. Citizenship and national identity: Some reflections on the future of Europe. *Praxis International* 12 (2): 1–19.

Hale, Charles. 1996. *Mestizaje,* hybridity, and the cultural politics of difference in post-revolutionary Central America. *Journal of Latin American Anthropology* 2 (1): 35–61.

Hall, Stuart. 1993. For Allon White: Metaphors of transformation. In *Stuart Hall: Critical dialogues in cultural studies,* edited by D. Morley and K-H. Chen, 287–305. London: Routledge.

Hanks, W. 1995. *Language and communicative practice.* Boulder, Colo.: Westview Press.

Hann, Christopher M. 1985. *A village without solidarity: Polish peasants in years of crisis.* New Haven, Conn.: Yale University Press.

———. 1997. Ethnicity in the new civil society: Lemko-Ukrainians in Poland. In *Beyond borders: Remaking cultural identities in the new East and Central Europe,* edited by László Kürti and Juliet Langman, 17–38. Boulder, Colo.: Westview Press.

Harris, Marvin. 1964. *Patterns of race in the Americas.* New York: Walker.

Harrison, Lawrence E., and Samuel P. Huttington, eds. 2000. *Culture matters: How values shape human progress.* New York: Basic Books.

Hayner, Priscilla B. 1994. Fifteen truth commissions, 1974 to 1994: A comparative study. *Human Rights Quarterly* 16: 597–655.

———. 2001. *Unspeakable truths: Confronting state terror and atrocity.* London: Routledge.

Hegeman, Susan. 1999. *Patterns for America.* Princeton, N.J.: Princeton University Press.

Hemenway, Robert. 1980. *Zora Neale Hurston.* Urbana: University of Illinois Press.

Hendricks, Fred. 1999. Amnesty and justice in post-apartheid South Africa: How not to construct a democratic normative framework. Paper presented at the conference "The TRC: Commissioning the Past," 11–14 June 1999, History Workshop, University of the Witwatersrand.

Herbert, Christopher. 1991. *Culture and anomie.* Chicago: University of Chicago Press.

Herder, Johann Gottfried. 1997 [1774]. *Auch eine Philosophie der Geschichte zur Bildung der Menschheit.* Stuttgart: Reclam.

Herskovits, Melville J. 1958. *The myth of the Negro past.* Boston: Beacon Press.

Hiyane, Teruo. 1981. *Kindai nihon to Ifa Fuyū* [Modern Japan and Fuyū Ifa]. Tokyo: Dai'ichi Shobō.

Hodder, Ian. 1986. *Reading the past.* Cambridge: Cambridge University Press.

Holland, Dorothy, and Naomi Quinn. 1987. *Cultural models in language and thought.* Cambridge: Cambridge University Press.

Hollinger, David A. 1995. *Postethnic America.* New York: Basic Books.

Horbal, Bogdan. 1997. *Dzialalnosc Polityczna Lemkow na Lemkowszczyznie 1918–21.* Wroclaw: Arboretum.

Howe, Michael J. A. 1999. *A teacher's guide to the psychology of learning.* Oxford: Blackwell.

Huffmann, Michael. 1996. Acquisition of innovative cultural behaviors in nonhuman primates: A case study of stone handling, a socially transmitted behavior in Japanese macaques. In *Social learning in animals: The roots of culture,* edited by C. M. Heyes and B. G. Galef, Jr., 267–289. San Diego: Academic Press.

Hunt, Lynn, ed. 1993. *The invention of pornography: Obscenity and the origins of modernity, 1500–1800.* New York: Zone Books.

Huntington, Samuel P., and Lawrence E. Harrison. 2000. *Culture matters: How values shape human progress.* New York: Basic Books.

Hurston, Zora Neale. 1990 [1935]. *Mules and men.* New York: Harper and Row.

Husserl, Edmund. 1965. *Phenomenology and the crisis of philosophy.* Translated with notes and introduction by Quentin Lauer. New York: Harper and Row.

Hutchins, Edwin. 1995. *Cognition in the wild.* Cambridge, Mass.: MIT Press.

Hutchinson, Sharon. 1985. Changing concepts of incest among the Nuer. *American Ethnologist* 12 (4): 625–641.

———. 1996. *Nuer dilemmas: Coping with money, war, and the state.* Berkeley: University of California Press.

Huyse, Luc. 1995. Justice after transition: On the choices successor elites make in dealing with the past. *Law and Social Enquiry* 1: 51–78.

Hyatt, Marshall. 1990. *Franz Boas, social activist: The dynamics of ethnicity.* New York: Greenwood Press.

Hymes, Dell. 1974. *Foundations in sociolinguistics.* Philadelphia: University of Pennsylvania Press.

Ifa, Fuyū. 1974 [1914] *Ifa Fuyū zenshū* 1 [Collected works of Fuyū Ifa]. Tokyo: Heibonsha.

Ingold, Tim. 1996. Situated action V: The history and evolution of bodily skills. *Ecological Psychology* 8 (2): 171–182.

———. 1998. From complementarity to obviation: On dissolving the boundaries between social and biological anthropology, archaeology and psychology. *Zeitschrift fur Ethnologie* 123: 21–52.

Ishida, Eiichirō. 1960. Nihon no kenkyūkikan ni okeru bunkajinruigaku [Cultural anthropology in Japanese academic institutions]. In *Ishida Ei'ichirō zenshū* 1 [Collected works of Ei'ichiro Ishida 1], 207–220. Tokyo: Chikuma Shobō.

Jackendoff, Ray. 1992. *Languages of the mind.* Cambridge, Mass.: MIT Press.

Jacobsen, Thorkild. 1987. *The harps that once—: Sumerian poetry in translation.* Translated and edited by Thorkild Jacobsen. New Haven, Conn.: Yale University Press.

Jacobson, Matthew Frye. 1998. *Whiteness of a different color: European immigrants and the alchemy of race.* Cambridge, Mass.: Harvard University Press.

Jaime, Pancho. 1984–1989. *Comentarios de Pancho Jaime* 1–20. Guayaquil: Publicitaria Pancho Jaime y Asociados.

Jarrige, Catherine, J-F. Jarrige, R. H. Meadow, and G. Quivron. 1995. *Mehrgarh: Field reports 1974–1985. From Neolithic times to the Indus civilization.* Department of Culture and Tourism, Government of Sindh, Pakistan.

Jeffery, Anthea. 1999. *The truth about the truth commission.* Spotlight Series. Johannesburg: South African Institute of Race Relations.

John Paul II, Pope (Karol Wojtyla). 2001. Dialogue between cultures: For a civilization of love and peace. Message for the Celebration of the World Day of Peace, 1 January 2001. The Vatican: available at www.vatican.va/holy_father/john_...xxxiv-world-day-for-peace_en.html.

Johnson, Christine. 2001. Distributed primate cognition: A review. *Animal Cognition* 4: 167–183.

Johnson, Mark. 1987. *The body in the mind: The bodily basis of meaning, imagination, and reason.* Chicago: University of Chicago Press.

Jolly, Alison. 2000. The bad old days of primatology? In *Primate encounters,* edited by S. C. Strum and L. M. Fedigan, 71–84. Chicago: University of Chicago Press.

Jomo K. Sundaram. 2001. Asian values and the East Asian crisis. Paper presented at the conference "Identidade e diferenca na era global." Candido Mendes University, Rio de Janeiro, 21–23 May.

Kahn, Joel S. 1989. Culture, demise, or resurrection. *Critique of Anthropology* 9: 5–26.

———. 1995. *Culture, multiculture, postculture.* London: Sage.

Kano, Masanao. 1983. *Kindai nihon no minkangaku* [Scholars outside of academic institutions in modern Japan]. Tokyo: Iwanami Shoten.

———. 1993. *Okinawa no fuchi* [The edges of Okinawa]. Tokyo: Iwanami Shoten.

Kawai, Masao. 1965. Newly acquired pre-cultural behavior of the natural troop of Japanese monkeys on Koshima islet. *Primates* 6 (1): 1–30.

Kawamura, Syunzo. 1959. The process of sub-culture propagation among Japanese macaques. *Primates* 2 (1): 32–60.

Keesing, Roger M. 1976. *Cultural anthropology: A contemporary perspective.* New York: Holt Rinehart and Winston.

———. 1994. Theories of culture revisited. In *Assessing cultural anthropology,* edited by R. Borofsky, 301–310. New York: McGraw Hill.

Keller, Charles M., and Janet Dixon Keller. 1996. *Cognition and tool use: The blacksmith at work.* Cambridge: Cambridge University Press.

King, Barbara J. 1994. *The information continuum: Social information transfer in monkeys, apes, and hominids.* Santa Fe, N.M.: School of American Research Press.

King, Barbara J., and Stuart G. Shanker. n.d. The dancer and the dance: Co-regulated communication in primates. Manuscript in preparation.

Kinjō, Seitoku, and Kurayoshi Takara. 1972. *Ifa Fuyū* [Fuyū Ifa]. Tokyo: Shimizu Shoin.

Knauft, Bruce M. 1996. *Genealogies for the present in cultural anthropology: A critical humanist perspective.* New York: Routledge.

Kohl, Philip L. 1993. Limits to a post-processual archaeology (or, The dangers of a new scholasticism). In *Archaeological theory: Who sets the agenda?* edited by Norman Yoffee and Andrew Sherratt, 13–19. Cambridge: Cambridge University Press.

Kopytoff, Igor. 1987. The cultural biography of things: Commoditization as process. In *The social life of things,* edited by A. Appadurai, 64–91. Cambridge: Cambridge University Press.

Kroeber, Alfred L. 1916. Zuni potsherds. *Anthropological Papers of the American Museum of Natural History* 18 (1): 7–37.

———. 1928. Sub-human culture beginnings. *Quarterly Review of Biology* 3:325–342.

———. 1952. *The nature of culture*. Chicago: University of Chicago Press.

Kroeber, A. L., and Clyde Kluckhohn. 1952. *Culture: A critical review of concepts and definitions*. Cambridge, Mass.: Peabody Museum of American Archaeology and Ethnology, Harvard University.

Kroeber, A. L., and Talcott Parsons. 1958. The concept of culture and of social system. *American Sociological Review* 23: 582–583.

Krog, Antjie. 1998. *Country of my skull*. Johannesburg: Random House.

Kumar, Krishan. 2000. A further note on civil society. *European Journal of Sociology* 41: 167–180.

Kuper, Adam. 1986. Anthropology and apartheid. In *South Africa in question*, edited by John Lonsdale, 33–51. Cambridge: African Studies Centre, University of Cambridge.

———. 1994. Culture, identity and the project of a cosmopolitan anthropology. *Journal of the Royal Anthropological Institute* 29: 537–54.

———. 1999. *Culture: The anthropologists' account*. Cambridge, Mass.: Harvard University Press.

Kwilecki, Andrzej. 1974. *Lemkowie: Zagadnienie mygracji i asymilacji*. Warsaw: PWN.

Lakoff, George. 1987. *Women, fire and dangerous things: What categories reveal about the mind*. Chicago: University of Chicago Press.

Lamar, Howard, and Leonard Thompson. 1981. *The frontier in history: North America and southern Africa compared*. New Haven, Conn.: Yale University Press.

Lamberg-Karlovsky, C. C., and M. Tosi. 1973. Shahri-i Sokhta and Tepe Yahya: Tracks on the earliest history of the Iranian plateau. *East and West* (n.s.) 23 (1–2): 21–53. Rome: IsMEO.

Lancaster, Roger N. 1992. *Life is hard: Machismo, danger, and the intimacy of power in Nicaragua*. Berkeley: University of California Press.

Langacker, Ronald W. 1986. *An introduction to cognitive grammar*. Amsterdam: Benjamins.

Laurendeau, Monique, and Adrien Pinard. 1970. *The development of the concept of space in the child*. New York: International Universities Press.

Lave, Jean. 1988. *Cognition in practice*. Cambridge: Cambridge University Press.

Lave, Jean, and E. Wenger. 1991. *Situated learning: Legitimate peripheral participation*. Cambridge: Cambridge University Press.

Lechtman, Heather. 1977. Style in technology: Some early thoughts. In *Material culture: Styles, organization and dynamics of technology,* edited by H. Lechtman and R. S. Merrill, 3–20. St. Paul, Minn.: American Ethnological Society.

Lechtman, Heather, and Arthur Steinberg. 1979. The history of technology: An anthropological perspective. In *History and philosophy of technology,* edited by G. Bugliarello and D. B. Doner, 135–60. Urbana: University of Illinois Press.

Lehmann, Rosa. 1999. Ethno-nationalism and the socialist heritage: The case of the Lemkos in Poland. *Focaal* 33: 59–73.

Lemmonier, Pierre. 1992. *Technical choices: Transformation in material cultures since the Neolithic.* London: Routledge.

Lenneberg, Eric H. 1967. *Biological foundations of language.* New York: Wiley.

Leonard, Laurence. 1987. Is specific language impairment a useful construct? In *Advances in applied psycholinguistics,* vol. 1, *Disorders of first-language development,* edited by S. Rosenberg, 1–39. New York: Cambridge University Press.

Leroi-Gourhan, A. 1943. *Evolution et techniques: L'homme et la matière.* Paris: Albin Michel.

Lesser, Alexander. 1961. Social fields and the evolution of society. *Southwestern Journal of Anthropology* 17: 40–48.

Levinson, Stephen C. 1996a. Relativity in spatial conception and description. In *Rethinking linguistic relativity,* edited by John J. Gumperz and Stephen C. Levinson, 177–202. Cambridge: Cambridge University Press.

———. 1996b. Frames of reference and Molyneux's question: Cross-linguistic evidence. In *Language and space,* edited by Paul Bloom, Mary A. Peterson, Lynn Nadell, and Merrill F. Garrett, 109–169. Cambridge, Mass.: MIT Press.

———. 1996c. Language and space. *Annual Review of Anthropology* 25: 353–382.

———. 1997. From outer to inner space: Linguistic categories and non-linguistic thinking. In *Language and conceptual representation,* edited by J. Nuyts and E. Pederson, 13–45. Cambridge: Cambridge University Press.

———. 1998. Studying spatial conceptualization across cultures: Anthropology and cognitive science. *Ethos* 26 (1): 7–24.

———. 2000. Language as nature and language as art. In *Changing concepts of nature at the turn of the millennium,* edited by R. Hide, J. Mittelstrass, and W. Singer, 257–287. Vatican City: Pontifical Academy of Science.

Levinson, Stephen C., and Penelope Brown. 1994. Immanuel Kant among the Tenejapans: Anthropology as empirical philosophy. *Ethos* 22 (1): 3–41.

Levinson, Stephen C., and David Wilkins, eds. n.d. *Grammars of space.* Cambridge: Cambridge University Press. Manuscript in preparation.

Lewontin, Richard C. 1970. The units of selection. *Annual Review of Ecology and Systematics* 1: 1–18.

Lieberman, Leonard, Blaine W. Stevenson, and Larry T. Reynolds. 1989. Race and anthropology: A core concept without consensus. *Anthropology and Education Quarterly* 20: 67–73.

Lieberman, Leonard, et al. 1992. Race in biology and anthropology: A study of college texts and professors. *Journal of Research of Science Teaching* 29: 301–321.

Lightfoot, Kent G., and Antoinette Martinez. 1995. Frontiers and boundaries in archaeological perspective. *Annual Review of Anthropology* 24: 471–492.

Linton, Ralph. 1955. *The tree of culture.* New York: Knopf.

Lomnitz-Adler, Claudio. 1992. Concepts for the study of regional culture. In *Mexico's regions: Comparative history and development,* edited by E. Van Young, 60–89. San Diego: Center for U.S.–Mexican Studies.

Lucy, John A. 1992a. *Grammatical categories and cognition: A case study of the linguistic relativity hypothesis.* Cambridge: Cambridge University Press.

———. 1992b. *Language diversity and thought.* Cambridge: Cambridge University Press.

———. 1996. The scope of linguistic relativity: An analysis and review of empirical research. In *Rethinking linguistic relativity,* edited by John J. Gumperz and Stephen C. Levinson, 37–69. Cambridge: Cambridge University Press.

Luhmann, Niklas. 1990. *Essays on self-reference.* New York: Columbia University Press.

Lumsden, Charles J., and Edward O. Wilson. 1981. *Genes, mind, and culture: The coevolutionary process.* Cambridge, Mass.: Harvard University Press.

Lynch, Aaron. 1996. *Thought contagion: How belief spreads through society.* New York: Basic Books.

Macdonald, Margaret. 1984. Natural rights. In *Theories of rights,* edited by Jeremy Waldron, 21–40. Oxford: Oxford University Press.

Magocsi, Paul Robert. 1978. *The shaping of a national identity: Sub-Carpathian Rus, 1848–1948.* Cambridge, Mass.: Harvard University Press.

———. 1993. Made or re-made in America? Nationality and identity formation among Carpatho-Rusyn immigrants and their descendants. In *The persistence of regional cultures: Rusyns and Ukrainians in their Carpathian homeland and abroad,* edited by Paul Robert Magocsi, 163–78. New York: East European Monographs.

———. 1999. *Of the making of nationalities there is no end.* 2 vols. New York: East European Monographs.

Majewicz, Alfred F. 1999. Minority situation attitudes and developments after the return to power of "post-communists" in Poland. *Nationalities Papers* 27 (1): 115–137.

Malik, K. 1996. *The meaning of race: Race, history and culture.* Basingstoke, U.K.: Macmillan.

Malinowski, Bronislaw. 1931. "Culture." *Encyclopaedia of the Social Sciences* 4: 621–645.

Marcus, G. F., S. Vijayan, S. Bandi Rao, and P. M. Vishton. 1999. Rule learning by seven-month-old infants. *Science* 283: 77–80.

Maturana, Humberto P., and Francisco J. Varela. 1980. *Autopoiesis and cognition: The realisation of the living.* Boston: D. Reidel.

———. 1987. *The tree of knowledge: The biological roots of human understanding.* Boston: New Science Library.

Mauss, M. 1935. Les techniques du corps. *Journal de Psycologie* 32: 271–293.

Mayhew, Anne. 1987. Culture: Core concept under attack. *Journal of Economic Issues* 21 (2): 587–603.

Mayr, Ernst. 1982. *The growth of biological thought: Diversity, evolution, and inheritance.* Cambridge, Mass.: Harvard University Press.

———. 1991. *One long argument: Charles Darwin and the genesis of modern evolutionary thought.* London: Penguin.

Mbembe, Achille. 1992. The banality of power and the aesthetics of vulgarity in the postcolony. *Public Culture* 4 (2): 1–30.

McGrew, William C. 1992. *Chimpanzee material culture: Implications for Human evolution.* Cambridge: Cambridge University Press.

———. 1998. Culture in nonhuman primates? *Annual Review of Anthropology* 27: 301–328.

Mehler, Jacques, and Emmanuel Dupoux. 1990. *What infants know.* Cambridge: Blackwell.

Memmi, Albert. 2000 [1982]. *Racism.* Translated by Steve Martinot. Minneapolis: University of Minnesota Press.

Merleau-Ponty, Maurice. 1962 [1945]. *The phenomenology of perception.* London: Routledge and Kegan Paul.

Méry, Sophie. 2000. *Les ceramiques d'Oman et l'Asie moyenne: Une archeologie des echanges a l'age du Bronze.* Paris: CRA23 Monographies, CNRS Editions.

Michna, Ewa. 1995. *Lemkowie: grupa etniczna czy Naród?* Kraków: Nomos.

Miller, George A., and Philip N. Johnson-Laird. 1976. *Language and perception.* Cambridge, Mass.: Harvard University Press.

Mimica, Jadran. 1988. *Intimations of infinity: The cultural meanings of the Iqwaye counting system and number.* Oxford: Berg.

Minow, Martha. 1998. *Between vengeance and forgiveness: Facing history after genocide and mass violence.* Boston: Beacon Press.

Mintz, Sidney W. 1971. Le rouge et le noir. *Les Temps Modernes* 299–300: 2354–2361.

———. 1990. Introduction. In *Myth of the Negro past,* by Melville Herskovits [1958], ix–xxi. Boston: Beacon Press.

Montagu, Ashley. 1946. What every child and adult should know about "race." *Education* (January): 262–264.

———. 1964. The concept of race. In *The concept of race,* edited by Ashley Montagu, 12–28. New York: Free Press.

Montejo, Victor. 1993. The dynamics of cultural resistance and transformations. Ph.D. dissertation, University of Connecticut.

Morales, Mario Roberto. 1998. *La articulación de las diferencias, ó el síndrome de Maximón.* Guatemala City: FLACSO.

Muratorio, Blanca, ed. 1994. *Imágenes e imagineros: Representaciones de los indígenas ecuatorianos, siglos XIX y XX.* Quito: FLACSO.

Murdoch, George P. 1949. *Social structure.* New York: Macmillan.

Murray, Charles, and Richard J. Herrnstein. 1994. *The bell curve: Intelligence and class structure in American life.* New York: Free Press.

Myrdal, Gunnar. 1962. *An American dilemma: The Negro problem and modern democracy.* New York: Harper and Row.

Nelson, Diane. 1999. *A finger in the wound.* Berkeley: University of California Press.

Niehaus, Isak. 2001. *Witchcraft, power and politics: Exploring the occult in the South African lowveld.* London: Pluto Press.

North, Michael. 1994. *The dialect of modernism.* New York: Oxford University Press.

Nowak, Jacek. 2000. *Zaginivny swiat? Nazywaja, ich Łemkami.* Kraków: Universitas.

Obrebski, Józef. 1974 [1936]. *The changing peasantry of eastern Europe.* Cambridge: Schenkman.

Ochs, Elinor. 1988. *Culture and language development: Language acquisition and language socialization in a Samoan village.* Cambridge: Cambridge University Press.

Ochs, Elinor, and Bambi Schieffelin. 1986. *Language socialization across cultures*. Cambridge: Cambridge University Press.

Olaniyan, Tejumola. 1992. Narrativizing postcoloniality: Responsibilities. *Public Culture* 5 (1): 47–55.

Ortner, Sherry B. 1981. Gender and sexuality in hierarchical societies: The case of Polynesia and some comparative implications. In *Sexual meanings,* edited by Sherry B. Ortner and Harriet Whitehead. Cambridge: Cambridge University Press.

———. 1984. Theory in anthropology since the sixties. *Comparative Studies in Society and History* 26: 126–166.

———. 1999. Introduction. In *The fate of "culture": Geertz and beyond,* edited by Sherry B. Ortner, 1–13. Berkeley: University of California Press.

Ōshiro, Tatsuhiro. 1960. *Kakuteru pātī* [Cocktail party]. Tokyo: Shinchōsha.

———. 1992 [1970]. Okinawa de nihonjin ni narukoto [Becoming Japanese in Okinawa]. *Okinawa bungaku zenshū* [Collected Works of Okinawan Literature] 18: 31–60. Tokyo: KokushoKankōkai.

Ota, Yoshinobu. 1997a. Appropriating media, resisting power. In *Between resistance and revolution,* edited by R. G. Fox and O. Starn, 145–170. New Brunswick, N.J.: Rutgers University Press.

———. 1997b *Toransupojishon no shisō* [Transposition]. Kyoto: Sekaishisōsha.

———. 2001 *Minzokushiteki kindai heno kainyū* [Refashioning culture under the condition of ethnographic modernity]. Kyoto: Jinbun Shoin.

Owens, Robert E. 1996. *Language development: An introduction*. Boston: Allyn and Bacon.

Paluch, A. 1988. Malinowski's theory of culture. In *Malinowski between two worlds: The Polish roots of an anthropological tradition,* edited by Roy Ellen, Ernest Gellner, Grazyna Kubica, and Janusz Mucha, 65–88. Cambridge: Cambridge University Press.

Pederson, Eric, Eve Danziger, Stephen Levinson, Sotaro Kita, Gunter Senft, and David Wilkins. 1998. Semantic typology and spatial conceptualization. *Language* 74: 557–589.

Peters, A., and S. T. Boggs. 1986. Interactional routines as cultural influences upon language acquisition. In *Language socialization across cultures,* edited by E. Ochs and B. Schieffelin, 80–96. Cambridge: Cambridge University Press.

Piaget, Jean. 1971. *Structuralism*. Translated and edited by Chaninah Maschler. London: Routledge and Kegan Paul.

Piaget, Jean, and Barbel Inhelder. 1967 [1948]. *The child's conception of space*. New York: Norton.

Pieradzka, Krystyna. 1990 [1939]. *Na Szlakach Lemkowszczyzny*. Warsaw: Stanislaw Krycinski.

Pinker, Steven. 1991. "Rules of language." *Science* 253: 530–535.

———. 1994. *The language instinct*. New York: William Morrow.

———. 1997. *How the mind works*. New York: Norton.

Poole, Deborah. 1997. *Vision, race and modernity: A visual economy of the Andean image world*. Princeton, N.J.: Princeton University Press.

Posel, Deborah. 2001. Racial classification in twentieth-century South Africa. *African Studies Review*. September 44(2): 87–113.

Postgate, J. N. 1992. *Early Mesopotamia: Society and economy in the dawn of history*. London: Routledge.

Premack, David. 1976. *Intelligence in ape and man*. Hillsdale, N.J.: Erlbaum.

Premack, David, and Ann James Premack. 1994. Why animals have neither culture nor history. In *Companion encyclopedia of anthropology*, edited by Tim Ingold, 350–365. London: Routledge.

Preucel, Robert. 1991. *Processual and post-processual archaeologies: Multiple ways of knowing the past*. Carbondale: Southern Illinois University Press.

Price, Robert. 1997. Race and reconciliation in the new South Africa. *Politics and Society* 25 (2): 149–178.

Pudło, Kazimierz. 1987. *Łemkowie: Proces wrastania w środowisko Dolnego Śląska, 1947–1985*. Wroclaw: PTL.

Quine, W. V. O. 1960. *Word and object*. Cambridge, Mass.: MIT Press.

Quintero, Rafael, ed. 1991. *La cuestión regional y el poder*. Quito: Corporación Editora Nacional.

Radcliffe-Brown, A. R. 1952. *Structure and function in primitive society*. London: Cohen and West.

Rahier, Jean. 1998. Blackness, the "racial"/spatial order, migrations, and Miss Ecuador 1995–1996. *American Anthropologist* 100 (2): 421–430.

Reinfuss, Roman. 1938. *Problem wschodniego zasiegu etnograficznego Lemkowszczyzny*. Kraków-Warsaw: Komisja Naukowych Badan Ziem Wschodnich.

———. 1998 [1948]. *Lemkowie jako Grupa Etnograficzna*. Sanok: Muzeum Budownictwa Ludowego.

Rex, John. 1982. *Race relations in sociological theory*. Second edition. London: Routledge.

Rex, John, and David Mason, eds. 1986. *Theories of race and ethnic relations*. Cambridge: Cambridge University Press.

Richards, Audrey. 1957. The concept of culture in Malinowski's work. In *Man and culture: An evaluation of the work of Bronislaw Malinowski*, edited by Raymond Firth, 15–31. London: Routledge and Kegan Paul.

Richardson, Ken. 1998. *The origins of human potential: Evolution, development and psychology.* London: Routledge.

Rodseth, Lars. 1998. Distributive models of culture: A Sapirian alternative to essentialism. *American Anthropologist* 100 (1): 55–69.

Rogoff, B. 1990. *Apprenticeship in thinking.* New York: Oxford University Press.

Roht-Arriaza, Naomi. 1995. *Impunity and human rights in International law and practice.* Oxford: Oxford University Press.

Rosaldo, Renato. 1989. *Culture and truth.* Boston: Beacon Press.

Ross, Dorothy. 1991. *The origins of American social science.* New York: Cambridge University Press.

Rumbaugh, Duane, ed. 1977. *Language learning by a chimpanzee.* New York: Academic Press.

Sahlins, Marshall. 1976. *Culture and practical reason.* Chicago: University of Chicago Press.

———. 1985. *Islands of history.* Chicago: University of Chicago Press.

———. 1999. Two or three things that I know about culture. *Journal of the Royal Anthropological Institute* (n.s.) 5 (3): 399–421.

Said, Edward. 1989. Representing the colonized. *Critical Inquiry* 15 (2): 205–225.

Sampson, Geoffrey. 1999. *Educating Eve: The "language instinct" debate.* Continuum International Publishing Group.

Sanderon, A., B. Dugoni, T. Hoffer, and S. Myers. 2000. *Doctorate recipients from United States universities: Summary report 1999.* Chicago: National Opinion Research Center.

Sanderon, A., B. Dugoni, T. Hoffer, and L. Selfa. 1999. *Doctorate recipients from United States universities: Summary report 1998.* Chicago: National Opinion Research Center.

Sanjek, Roger. 1998. *The future of us all: Race and neighborhood politics in New York City.* Ithaca, N.Y.: Cornell University Press.

Sarkin, Jeremy. 1998. The development of a human rights culture in South Africa. *Human Rights Quarterly* 20 (3): 628–665.

Savage-Rumbaugh, Sue, and Roger Lewin. 1994. *Kanzi: The ape at the brink of the human mind.* New York: John Wiley and Sons.

Savage-Rumbaugh, Sue, Jeannine Murphy, Rose Sevcik, Karen Brakke, Shelley Williams, and Duane Rumbaugh. 1993. *Language comprehension in ape and child.* Monographs of the Society for Research in Child Development, serial no. 233, vol. 58, nos. 3–4.

Savage-Rumbaugh, Sue, Stuart G. Shanker, and Talbot J. Taylor. 1998. *Apes, language, and the human mind.* New York: Oxford University Press.

Savage-Rumbaugh, Sue, B. J. Wilkerson, and Roger Bakeman. 1977. Spontaneous gestural communication among conspecifics in the pygmy chimpanzee (*Pan paniscus*). In *Progress in ape research*, edited by G. H. Bourne, 97–116.

Scardellato, Gabriele. 2000. *Paul Robert Magocsi: A bibliography 1964–2000*. Toronto: Chair of Ukrainian Studies.

Schieffelin, Bambi. 1990. *The give and take of everyday life: Language socialization of Kaluli children*. Cambridge: Cambridge University Press.

Schortman, Edward, and Seiichi Nakamura. 1991. A crisis of identity: Late classic competition and interaction on the southeast Maya periphery. *Latin American Antiquity* 2 (4): 311–336.

Shanker, Stuart G. 1998. *Wittgenstein's remarks on the foundations of artificial intelligence*. London: Routledge.

———. 2001. What a child knows when she knows what a name is: The non-Cartesian view of language acquisition. *Current Anthropology* 42(4): 481–513.

Shanker, Stuart G., Sue Savage-Rumbaugh, and Talbot J. Taylor. 1999. Kanzi: A new beginning. *Animal Learning and Behavior* 27 (1): 24–25.

Shanker, Stuart G., and Talbot J. Taylor. 2001. The house that Bruner built. In *Language, culture, self: The philosophical psychology of Jerome Bruner*, edited by D. Bakhurst and S. Shanker, 50–70. London: Sage.

Shanklin, Eugenia. 2000. Representations of race and racism in American anthropology. *Current Anthropology* 41 (1): 99–103.

Sharp, John. 1981. The roots and development of *volkekunde* in South Africa. *Journal of Southern African Studies* 8: 16–36.

Shatz, Marilyn. 1994. *A toddler's life*. Oxford: Oxford University Press.

Shennan, S. J. 1989. *Archaeological approaches to cultural identity*. London: Unwin Hyman.

Shivji, Issa G. 1991. *State and constitutionalism: An African debate on democracy*. Harare, Zimbabwe: Southern African Political Economy Series Trust.

Shore, Bradd. 1996. *Culture in mind: Cognition, culture, and the problem of meaning*. New York: Oxford University Press.

Shryock, Andrew. 1997. *Nationalism and the genealogical imagination: Oral history and textual authority in tribal Jordan*. Berkeley: University of California Press.

Shweder, Richard A. n.d. Culture: Contemporary views. In *International encyclopedia of the social and behavioral sciences*. Forthcoming.

Silverstein, Michael. 2000. Languages/cultures are dead! Long live the linguistic-cultural! Paper presented at the annual meeting of the American Anthropological Association, San Francisco.

Slobin, Dan I. 1996. From "thought and language" to "thinking for speaking." In *Rethinking linguistic relativity,* edited by John J. Gumperz and Stephen C. Levinson, 70–96. Cambridge: Cambridge University Press.

Slyś-Janusz, Elzbieta. 1998. *Nad Rzeką Panną.* Krosno: Muzeum Okręgowe.

Smith, Carol. 1991. Mayan nationalism. *NACLA Report on Americas* 25 (3): 29–33.

Smith, Linda B., Maria Sera, and Bea Gattuso. 1988. The development of thinking. In *The psychology of human thought,* edited by Robert J. Sternberg and Edward E. Smith, 366–391. Cambridge: Cambridge University Press.

Spencer, Jonathan. 1990. Writing within: Anthropology, nationalism, and culture in Sri Lanka. *Current Anthropology* 31: 283–300.

Sperber, Dan. 1996. *Explaining culture: A naturalistic approach.* Oxford: Blackwell.

Spivak, Gayatri C. 1988. Can the subaltern speak? In *Marxism and the interpretation of culture,* edited by C. Nelson and L. Grossberg, 271–313. Urbana: University of Illinois Press.

Stallybrass, Peter, and Allon White. 1986. *The politics and poetics of transgression.* Ithaca, N.Y.: Cornell University Press.

Stanford, Craig B. 2000. The cultured ape? *The Sciences,* May–June: 38–43.

Stein, Sir Aurel. 1929. *An archaeological tour in Waziristan and northern Baluchistan.* Memoirs of the Archaeological Survey of India, no. 37.

———. 1931. *An archaeological tour in Gedrosia.* Memoirs of the Archaeological Survey of India, no. 43.

———. 1937. *Archaeological reconnaissances in northwestern India and southeastern Iran.* London: Macmillan.

Stein, Gil J. 1999. *Rethinking world-systems: Diasporas, colonies, and interaction in Uruk Mesopotamia.* Tucson: University of Arizona Press.

Stocking, George W., Jr. 1968. Franz Boas and the culture concept in historical perspective. In *Race, culture, and evolution: Essays in the history of anthropology,* 195–233. New York: Free Press.

———. 1974. The basic assumptions of Boasian anthropology. In *A Franz Boas reader,* edited by G. Stocking, 1–20. Chicago: University of Chicago Press.

———, ed. 1996. *Volksgeist as method and ethic: Essays on Boasian ethnography and the German anthropological tradition.* History of Anthropology 8. Madison: University of Wisconsin Press.

———. 2000. "Do good, young men." In *Excluded ancestors, inventible traditions,* edited by R. Handler, 171–264. Chicago: University of Chicago Press.

Stolcke, Verena. 1995. Talking culture: New boundaries, new rhetorics of exclusion in Europe. *Current Anthropology* 36: 1–24.

Stoll, David. 1998. *Rigoberta Menchú and the story of all poor Guatemalans.* Boulder, Colo.: Westview Press.

Stone, Elizabeth. 1999. City-states and their centers: The Mesopotamian example. In *The archaeology of city-states: Cross-cultural approaches,* edited by D. L. Nichols and T. H. Charlton. Washington, D.C.: Smithsonian Institution Press.

Strauss, Claudia, and Naomi Quinn. 1997. *A cognitive theory of cultural meaning.* Cambridge: Cambridge University Press.

Suchman, Lucy. 1987. *Plans and situated actions: The problem of human-machine interaction.* Cambridge: Cambridge University Press.

Susman, Warren. 1970. The thirties. In *The development of American culture,* edited by S. Coben and L. Ratner, 179–218. Englewood Cliffs, N.J.: Prentice-Hall.

Takasaki, Hiroyuki. 2000. Traditions of the Kyoto school of field primatology in Japan. In *Primate encounters,* edited by S. C. Strum and L. M. Fedigan, 151–183. Chicago: University of Chicago Press.

Tallal, Paula, and Rachel Stark. 1981. Speech acoustic cue discrimination abilities of normally developing and language-impaired children. *Journal of the Acoustical Society of America* 69: 568–574.

Talmy, Leonard. 1983. How language structures space. In *Spatial orientation: Theory, research, and application,* edited by H. Pick and L. Acredolo, 225–282. New York: Plenum.

———. 2000. The cognitive culture system. In L. Talmy, *Towards a cognitive semantics,* vol. 2, 373–415. Cambridge, Mass.: MIT Press.

Tanaka, I. 1995. Matrilineal distribution of louse egg handling techniques during grooming in free-ranging Japanese macaques. *American Journal of Physical Anthropology* 98:197–201.

Tanner, Joanne, and Richard W. Byrne. 1999. The development of spontaneous gestural communication in a group of zoo-living lowland gorillas. In *The mentalities of gorillas and orangutans,* edited by S. T. Parker, R. W. Mitchell, and H. L. Miles, 211–239. Cambridge: Cambridge University Press.

Taylor, Charles. 1992. *Multiculturalism and the politics of recognition.* Princeton, N.J.: Princeton University Press.

Taylor, Talbot J. 1992. *Mutual misunderstanding.* London: Routledge.

Taylor, W. W. 1948. *A study of archaeology.* Memoirs of the American Anthropological Association, no. 69. Menasha, Wis.

Terrace, H. S. 1979. *Nim: A chimpanzee who learned sign language.* New York: Knopf.

Thornton, Robert, and Peter Skalnik, eds. 1993. *The early writings of Bronislaw Malinowski.* Cambridge: Cambridge University Press.

Tobin, Jeffrey. 1994. Cultural construction and native nationalism. *Boundary 2* 21 (1): 111–133.

Tomasello, Michael. 1995. Language is not an instinct. *Cognitive Development* 10: 131–156.

———. 1999. *The cultural origins of human cognition.* Cambridge, Mass.: Harvard University Press.

Tomasello, Michael, Josep Call, J. Warren, G. T. Frost, M. Carpenter, and K. Nagell. 1997. The ontogeny of chimpanzee gestural signals: A comparison across groups and generations. *Evolution of Communication* 1 (2): 223–259.

Tooby, John, and Leda Cosmides. 1992. The psychological foundations of culture. In *The adapted mind: Evolutionary psychology and the generation of culture,* edited by J. H. Barkow, L. Cosmides, and J. Tooby, 19–136. Oxford: Oxford University Press.

Toren, Christina. 1990. *Making sense of hierarchy: Cognition as social process in Fiji.* London School of Economics, Monographs in Social Anthropology 61. London: Athlone Press.

———. 1999a. *Mind, materiality and history: Explorations in Fijian ethnography.* London: Routledge.

———. 1999b. Compassion for one another: Constituting kinship as intentionality in Fiji. *Journal of the Royal Anthropological Institute* (n.s.) 5: 265–280.

———. n.d. Becoming a Christian in Fiji. In *Power and transformation in local Christianities,* edited by Fenella Cannell. London. Forthcoming.

Tosi, Maurizio. 1983. *Prehistoric Sistan I.* Rome: IsMEO.

TRC (Truth and Reconciliation Commission of South Africa). 1998. *Report.* 5 vols. Cape Town: Juta and Co. Also at http://www.struth.org.za/.

Trigger, Bruce. 1989. *A history of archaeological thought.* Cambridge: Cambridge University Press.

Trinkaus, Kathryn M. 1987. *Polities and partitions: Human boundaries and the growth of complex societies.* Arizona State University Anthropological Research Papers 37. Tempe.

Trouillot, Michel-Rolph. 1991. Anthropology and the savage slot: The poetics and politics of otherness. In *Recapturing anthropology: Working in the present,* edited by Richard G. Fox, 17–44. Santa Fe, N.M.: School of American Research Press.

———. 1992a. The Caribbean region: An open frontier in anthropological theory. *Annual Review of Anthropology* 21: 19–42.

———. 1992b. The vulgarity of power. *Public Culture* 5 (1): 75–81.
———. 1995. *Silencing the past: Power and the production of history.* Boston: Beacon Press.
———. 2000. Abortive rituals: Historical apologies in a global era. *Interventions: The International Journal of Post-Colonial Studies* 2 (2): 171–186.
———. 2001. The anthropology of the state in the age of globalization: Close encounters of the deceptive kind. *Current Anthropology* 42 (1): 125–138.
Tsing, Anna L. 1993. *In the realm of the diamond queen.* Princeton, N.J.: Princeton University Press.
Tutu, Desmond. 1999. *No future without forgiveness.* London: Rider.
Tylor, Edward Burnett. 1871. *Primitive culture: Researches into the development of mythology, philosophy, religion, art and custom.* 2 vols. London: Murray.
Ulland, Amy. 1999. The patterned interactions of *Pan paniscus:* Contextual descriptions and implications for the originals of language. Undergradate senior thesis, on file, Anthropology Department, College of William and Mary, Williamsburg, Va.
van de Ritj-Plooij, H. H. C., and F. X. Plooij. 1987. Growing independence, conflict and learning in mother-infant relations in free-ranging chimpanzees. *Behaviour* 101 (1–3): 1–86.
van Huyssteen, Elsa. 1996. The South African Constitutional Court and the death penalty: Whose values? *International Journal of the Sociology of Law* 24: 291–311.
van Lawick-Goodall, Jane. 1973. Cultural elements in a chimpanzee community. In *Symposium IVth International Congress of Primatology,* edited by E. W. Menzel, 124–143. Basel: Karger.
Vayda, Andrew P. 1994. Actions, variations, and change: The emerging anti-essentialist view in anthropology. In *Assessing cultural anthropology,* edited by R. Borofsky, 320–330. New York: McGraw-Hill.
Veit, Ulrich. 1986. Ethnic concepts in German prehistory: A case study on the relationship between cultural identity and archaeological objectivity. In *Archaeological approaches to cultural identity,* edited by S. Shennan, 33–56. London: Unwin Hyman.
Vygotsky, Lev S. 1986 [1934]. *Thought and language.* Cambridge, Mass.: Harvard University Press.
Waetzoldt, Hartmut. 1972. *Untersuchungen zur neosumerischen Textilindustrie.* Studi economici e tecnologici 1. Rome: Centro per le Antichita e la Storia dell'a Vicino Oriente.
———. 1987. Compensation of craft workers and officials in the Ur III period. In *Labor in the ancient Near East,* edited by M. A. Powell, 117–142. New Haven, Conn.: American Oriental Society.

Wallerstein, Immanuel, et al. 1996. *Open the social sciences: A report of the Gulbenkian Commission for the Restructuring of the Social Sciences.* Stanford, Calif.: Stanford University Press.

Wallman, Joel. 1992. *Aping language.* Cambridge: Cambridge University Press.

Wallman, Sandra, ed. 1979. *Social anthropology of work.* London: Academic Press.

Warren, Kay. 1998. *Indigenous movements and their critics.* Princeton, N.J.: Princeton University Press.

Wassman, Jürg, and Pierre R. Dasen. 1998. Balinese spatial orientation: Some empirical evidence for moderate linguistic relativity. *Journal of the Royal Anthropological Institute* (n.s.) 4: 689–711.

Watanabe, John. 1995. Unimagining the Maya. *Bulletin of Latin American Research* 14: 25–45.

Weber, Kendra. 2001. The significance of play in the sensorimotor and social development of a captive infant lowland gorilla (*Gorilla gorilla gorilla*). Undergraduate senior thesis, on file, Anthropology Department, College of William and Mary, Williamsburg, Va.

Welsch, Robert L., and John E. Terrell. 1999. Material culture, social fields, and social boundaries on the Sepik coast of New Guinea. In *The archaeology of social boundaries,* edited by M. Stark. Washington, D.C.: Smithsonian Institution Press.

Whiten, Andrew. 1999. Parental encouragement in *Gorilla* in comparative perspective: Implications for social cognition and the evolution of teaching. In *The mentalities of gorillas and orangutans,* edited by S. T. Parker, R. W. Mitchell, and H. L. Miles, 342–366. Cambridge: Cambridge University Press.

―――. 2001. Primate culture and social learning. *Cognitive Science* 24 (3): 477–508.

Whiten, Andrew, Jane Goodall, William C. McGrew, Toshisada Nishida, Vernon Reynolds, Yukimaru Sugiyama, Caroline E. G. Tutin, Richard W. Wrangham, and Christophe Boesch. 1999. Cultures in chimpanzees. *Nature* 399: 682–685.

Whitten, Norman, Jr. 1999. Los paradigmas mentales de la conquista y el nacionalismo: La formación de los conceptos de las "razas" y las transformaciones del racismo. In *Ecuador racista: Imágenes e identidades,* edited by Emma Cervone and Fredy Rivera, 45–70. Quito: FLACSO.

Wierzbicka, Anna. 1992. *Semantics, culture, and cognition: Universal human concepts in culture-specific configurations.* Oxford: Oxford University Press.

Wikan, Unni. 1990. *Managing turbulent hearts: A Balinese formula for living.* Chicago: University of Chicago Press.
Williams, Brackette F. 1989. A class act: Anthropology and the race to nation across ethnic terrain. *Annual Review of Anthropology* 18: 401–444.
Williams, Thomas R. 1972. *Introduction to socialization: Human culture transmitted.* St. Louis, Mo.: C. V. Mosby.
Williams, Vernon. 1996. *Rethinking race.* Lexington: University of Kentucky Press.
Wilson, Richard A. 1996. The *Sizwe* will not go away: The Truth and Reconciliation Commission, human rights and nation-building in South Africa. *African Studies* 55 (2): 1–20.
———, ed. 1997. *Human rights, culture and context: Anthropological approaches.* London: Pluto Press.
———. 2000. Reconciliation and revenge in post-apartheid South Africa: Rethinking legal pluralism and human rights. *Current Anthropology* 41 (1): 75–98.
———. 2001. *The politics of truth and reconciliation in South Africa: Legitimizing the post-apartheid state.* Cambridge: Cambridge University Press.
Wissler, Clark. 1923. *Man and culture.* New York: Thomas Y. Crowell.
Wolf, Eric R. 1982. *Europe and the people without history.* Berkeley: University of California Press.
———. 1999. *Envisioning power: Ideologies of dominance and crisis.* Berkeley: University of California Press.
———. 2001. *Pathways of power: Building an anthropology of the modern world.* Berkeley: University of California Press.
Wrangham, Richard, W. C. McGrew, Frans B. M. de Waal, and Paul G. Heltne, eds. 1994. *Chimpanzee cultures.* Cambridge, Mass.: Harvard University Press.
Wright, Rita P. 1987. The frontier of prehistoric Baluchistan and the development of the Indus civilization. In *Polities and partitions: Human boundaries and the growth of complex societies,* edited by Kathryn M. Trinkaus, 61–82. Arizona State University Anthropological Research Papers 37. Tempe.
———. 1989. New tracks on ancient frontiers: Ceramic technology on the Indo-Iranian borderlands. In *Archaeological thought in America,* edited by C. C. Lamberg-Karlovsky, 268–279. Cambridge: Cambridge University Press.
———. 1996. Technology, gender and class: Worlds of difference in Ur III Mesopotamia. In *Gender and archaeology,* edited by R. P. Wright, 79–110. Philadelphia: University of Pennsylvania Press.

———. 1998. Crafting social identity in Ur III southern Mesopotamia. In *Craft and social identity,* edited by C. Costin and R. P. Wright, 57–70. Archaeological Papers of the American Anthropological Association, no. 8. Washington, D.C.

———. 2000. Gender, workplace, and society: Institutional interventions in textile production in Lagash and Lowell. *Knowledge and Society* 12: 31–51.

Wright, Susan. 1998. The politicization of culture. *Anthropology Today* 14 (1): 7–14.

Yamanokuchi, Baku. 1999. *Yamanokuchi baku shibunshū* [Poems and essays by Baku Yamanokuchi]. Tokyo: Kōdansha.

Yoffee, Norman, and Andrew Sherratt. 1993. *Archaeological theory: Who sets the agenda?* Cambridge: Cambridge University Press.

Zagarell, Allen. 1986. Trade, women, class, and society in ancient Western Asia. *Current Anthropology* 27 (5): 415–430.

Zięba, Andrzej, ed. 1997. Łemkowie i Łemkoznowstwo w Polsce. Kraków: Polska Akademia Umiejętności.

Zimmerman, Andrew. 1998. Anthropology and the place of knowledge in imperial Berlin. Ph.D. dissertation, University of California, San Diego.

Index

Significant information in endnotes is indicated in the form 65n4, ie. note 4 on page 65

academic studies, culture concept 39–58, 65–70, 261–4, 271–3, 274n2
Adam, Heribert 218
Afrikaner Weerstandsbeweging (AWB) organization 222–5
afterologists 3
American Anthropological Association (AAA) 46, 47, 48–9
Andrade, Xavier 18, 235–57
anthropologists, "native" 14, 61–4, 68–70
anthropology
　academic study of 39–58, 64–70, 261–4, 271–3
　culture concept 2–11, 19, 23, 274n2
　disciplinary emergence 41–5
　as human definition 105–24
　in Japan 64–5
　North America 44–5, 48–58, 59n4, 262–4
　and race and racism 40–1, 46–58, 59nn3,4
　subjectivity 61–4
ape language research (ALR) 126–7, 129–34, 141–2

archaeology
　and culture concept 147–68
　gender analysis 151–7
　patterns 16
　social interaction 157–65
　technological developments 158–61
Arnold, Matthew 259
Asquith, Pamela 10
Australia, Aboriginal languages 184
autopoiesis 111, 115, 123n3
Aztecs, gender analysis 151–2, 167n2

Bali 30, 192n12
Balibar, Etienne 52, 237
Barth, Fredrik 13, 23–36, 160–1, 265
Bastian, Adolf 262
Bayart, Jean-Francois 254
Bederman, Gail 242
Benedict, Ruth 44, 59–60n5, 63, 64–70, 262
Binford, Lewis 150
biological anthropology 54, 58, 60n8
Bloch, Maurice 120
Boas, Franz
　culture concept 41, 44, 53, 67–9, 149, 262

307

kulturbrille 65
　on race 40, 46, 49–50
Boesch, Christophe 85, 260
Boesch-Achermann, Hedwige 260
bonobos
　language research 129–34
　patterned interactions 15, 89–96
Boonzaier, Emile 231n4
Bray, Francesca 167n3
Brightman, Robert 37, 56
Brown, Penelope 14, 16, 157, 169–92
Brown, Roger 191n5
Brumfiel, Elizabeth 151–2, 167n2
Bruner, Jerome 191n5

Campbell, Donald 198–9
capital punishment, South Africa 217, 232n15
caricatures, politicians 247–53
carnivalesque 257n10
Cartesian theory 110, 127–8
categories, theory of 26
ceramics *see* pottery
chaine operatoire 158–9
Childe, V. Gordon 149, 153
children
　language acquisition 15–16, 125–44, 176, 185–6, 189
　Piaget's study of 114–18, 124n4
　study of 113–14
　understanding of ritual 119–22
　see also infants
chimpanzees, culture of 7–11, 83–5, 260, 274n4
China, gender divisions 167n3
cholo 251–3, 257n11
Chomsky, Noam 117, 127–8, 176
civil society 273n1
Clarke, David 166–7n1
Clifford, James 67
Coertze, P.J. 213

Coetzee, Robbie 223
coevolutionary theory 193–4, 204
cognitive science, and culture concept 169–92
colonialism 42
communication
　patterns 88–103
　social interactions 86–7
complex category 26
conceptualization 38–9
congealed sociality 259, 273
contestation, culture concept 205–6
coregulation, great apes 88
Cosmides, Leda 108–10, 174
CRIMES approach, culture concept 275–6n22
cultural anthropology *see* anthropology
cultural entanglement 168n8
cultural evolution 198–200
cultural identity
　Guatemala 75–9
　Japan 70–5
　Poland 265–71
cultural interactions, archaeological studies 157–65
cultural politics
　Ecuador 18, 235–57
　South Africa 17–18, 222–31
cultural studies 38, 59n1
cultural systems, terminology 196
cultural virus 196
culture
　as context 179
　and Culture 172, 181, 187–8
　as ethnic or linguistic group 173–4, 194–5, 265–71
　globalization 57
　and human rights 227–31
　as knowledge 178–9
　as mental module 174–8

nature of 24–7, 32–6
as process 179–81, 191n5
social transmission 194–8, 204–6
terminology 14
use of 189–91
culture concept
  academic studies 39–45, 55–8, 65–70, 261–4, 271–3, 274n2
  and archaeology 147–68
  authencity discourse 63
  and cognitive science 169–92
  CRIMES approach 275–6n22
  and Culture 172, 181, 187–8
  definition 1–5, 23–4, 259–61
  kernels of 14, 16, 37–9, 47, 160
  and language 126, 142–4, 173–4
  populational 193–206
  primatology 1–2, 7–11, 83, 103, 260, 274n4
  public uses 235–57
  totalitarian 18, 260–1
  worry about 1–11, 13–15, 19
culturgen 196
Czajkowski, Jerzy 268–9

D'Andrade, Roy 183
Darwin, Charles 193
Davis, Allison 59n5
Dawkins, Richard 196
de Waal, Frans 8
Deacon, Terrence 191
Dennett, Daniel 191
Drake, St. Clair 59n5
dual mechanism hypothesis, language development 135–6
DuBois, W.E.B. 70
Dubow, Saul 232n5
Duranti, Alessandro 180
Durham, William 14, 17, 193–206

Eatonville 67–8

Ecuador
  cholo 251–3, 257n11
  cultural stereotypes 18, 235–57
  Febres Cordero, Leon 239–44, 255–6n2
  Jaime, Pancho (PJ) 247–53, 256n7, 257nn9,10
  Mahuad, Jamil 243–7, 256nn5,6
Elikya (bonobo), gestural interactions 89–96
ethnicity, and culture 173–4, 194–5, 265–71
ethnographic modernity 64, 67
ethnolinguistic groups, as culture 194–5
ethnomethodology 29
Eugenics 51, 60n6
Europe, nationalism 18, 265–71
Evans-Pritchard, E.E. 202
evolution, cultural 198–200, 204
evolutionary psychology 108–10
exceptionalism 60n7
exchange systems 163, 167n6

Fanon, Frantz 70
Febres Cordero, León (LFC) 18, 239–44, 255–6n2
Fiji, children's understanding 119–20
Fogel, Alan 87–8
Foley, William 180
Fortes, Meyer 27
Fox, Richard 1–19
Fracchia, Joseph 195
Frobenius, Leo 262

Gallie, W.B. 273n1
Gardner, Alan and Beatrix 129
Geertz, Clifford 6, 23, 44, 174, 262–3, 273
Gellner, Ernest 230–1
gender, stereotypes 239–55

gender analysis
　Aztecs 151–2, 167n2
　China 167n3
　Mesopotamia 152–7
generativist theory, language acquisition 127–9, 130–1, 134–41
genetic epistemology 115, 116
Germany, culture concept 261–4
gestures, ape interaction 87–103
Gilroy, Paul 229
Gleitman, Lila 186
globalization 57
Gluckman, Max 229
Goodall, Jane 10
Goodenough, Ward 178
Goody, Jack 272
gorillas
　culture 9
　patterned interactions 15, 97–103
Guatemala, cultural identity 75–9
Gumperz, John 180
Gutmann, Matthew 241
Guugu Yimithirr language 184

Hanks, William 180
Hann, Christopher 18, 143–4, 259–76
Harrison, Lawrence E. 38
Hendricks, Fred 232n17
Herder, Johann Gottfried 209, 261
Herskovits, Melville 59n3, 60n6
hierarchy, children's understanding of 119
historicity 123n1
history, and human nature 110–13
Hobbes, Thomas 209
Hollinger, David 63
homosexuality, stereotypes 247–53
human behavior, patterns 39–40
human beings
　and history 110–13
　mind of 105–10
human rights 209–11
　South Africa 211–31
Hurston, Zora Neale 63, 67–70
Husserl, Edmund 105, 123n1
Hutchinson, Sharon 200–3
Huttington, Samuel P. 38
Hymes, Dell 179

identity, cultural *see* cultural identity
Ifa, Fuyû 73–4
Imanishi, Kinji 10
incest taboos, Nuer, Sudan 17, 200–3
indigenous people
　as anthropologists 14, 61–4, 68–70
　Guatemala 77–8
Indo-Iranian borderlands, archaeology 161–5, 167–8n7
infants
　primates 86, 87–103
　see also children
interaction, social *see* social interaction
interactionism, language development 136–8, 142–3
Internet 38
Ishida, Eiichiro 64

Jackendoff, Ray 175–7, 186
Jaime, Pancho (PJ) 18, 247–53, 256n7, 257nn9,10
James Premack, Ann 9
Japan
　academic anthropology 64–5
　cultural identity 70–5
　Ryukyu Islands 70–5
John Paul II, Pope 266, 274n10
Johnson, Mark 115

Kahn, Joel 63
Kanzi (bonobo), language development of 129–34, 141–2

Kawakami, Hajime 73
Keesing, Roger 272
kernels, of culture 14, 16, 37–9, 47, 160
King, Barbara 1–19, 15, 83–104
King, Eugene 59n5
Klineberg, Otto 59n5
Kluckhohn, Clyde 5, 274n2
knowledge, and culture 178–9
Kossinna, Gustaf 149
Kroeber, Alfred 5, 32–4, 149, 274n2
kulturbrille 65
Kulturvölker 261–2, 269–71
Kumar, Krishan 273n1
Kuper, Adam 7, 213, 262, 272, 274n2
Kwame (gorilla), patterned interactions of 97–102

Lakoff, George 26, 27
Lamar, Howard 161
language
   acquisition 15–16, 123n2, 125–44
   ape language research (ALR) 126–7, 129–34, 141–2
   and culture concept 126, 142–4, 173–4
   dual mechanism hypothesis 135–6
   generativist theory 127–9, 130–1, 134–41
   skills, nature of 138–41
   spatial relations 170–2, 183–9
   Specific Language Impairment 15–16, 126–7, 134–8, 141–2, 144n2
   see also linguistics
Language Acquisition Device (LAD) 128
Lave, Jean 180
law, South Africa 216–18
Leach, Edmund 229
Leakey, Louis 10

Lechtman, Heather 159
Lemkos, Poland, ethnic identity 18, 265–71
Lemmonier, Pierre 158–9
Leroi-Gourhan, Andre 158
Lesser, Alexander 161
Levinson, Stephen 183, 186, 191n1
Lewontin, Richard C. 195
lexigrams 130
Lieberman, Leonard 46, 47
Lightfoot, Ken 157
linguistics
   and cognitive science 172–82
   see also language
Linton, Ralph 44
Locke, John 209
Lucy, John 181
Luhmann, Niklas 123n3
Lumsden, Charles 196

macaques, Japanese 8–9
McGrew, William 8–9
machismo 18, 241–2
Magocsi, Paul Robert 269, 275nn18–21
Mahuad, Jamil 18, 243–7, 256nn5,6
Malan, D.F. 212
Malinowski, Bronislaw 262, 266, 272, 274n9
Mall, Hassen 224–5
Mandela, Nelson 214
Martinez, Antoinette 157
Marx, Karl 259
masculinity, political stereotypes 239–55
material culture 157, 160–1
Maturana, Humberto 123n3
Max Planck Institute for Psycholinguistics 183–4
Mayan Indians
   Guatemala 75–80

Mexico 16–17, 170–2, 184–6
Mayr, Ernst 197
Mbembe, Achille 254
Mead, Margaret 262
meaning, and understanding 111–12
Mehrgarh 164, 167–8n7
meme 196
Memmi, Albert 52
memory, spatial 184, 191–2n7
Menchú, Rigoberta 75–6
mental modules 174–8
mental representations 196
Mesopotamia, social organization 152–7, 158
metaculture 108–9
Mexico, Mayan Indians 16–17, 170–2, 184–6
Michna, Ewa 268
microhistories 15, 122–3
mind, human 105–10, 122–3
Mintz, Sidney W. 48
monkeys 8–9
Montagu, Ashley 49, 58
Morales, Roberto 78
Moses, Yolanda 49
Murray, Charles 54
Myrdal, Gunnar 50

Nakamura, Seiichi 158
nationalism 18, 265–71
Native Americans, contact with Europeans 157–8
Naturvölker 261–2
Ngoepe, Bernard 224, 225
North America
 academic anthropology 44–5, 48–58, 59n4, 262–4
 cultural concept 39–45
 Native Americans 157–8
 racial issues 45–8

Nowak, Jacek 274n13
Nuer, Sudan, incest taboos 17, 200–3

Obrebski, Józef 275n14
Ochs, Elinor 180
Okinawa, cultural identity 71–5
ontogenetic ritualization (OR) 88–9
Ortner, Sherry 6–7, 119
Ôshiro, Tatsuhiro 74–5
Ota, Yoshinobu 14, 61–80

Pakistan, archaeology 161–5
Parsons, Talcott 262
patterns
 ape interactions 87–103
 continuity of 16–17
 human behavior 39–40
Piaget, Jean 114–18, 124nn4,5
Pinker, Steven 172, 174–5, 191
Poland, Lemkos 18, 265–71
politics
 cultural 14–15, 17–18
 racial 222–31
 satire 247–53
Poole, Deborah 255n1
populational culture 193–206
Posel, Deborah 212
postmodern critique, anthropology 62–4
pottery, as social exchange indicator 163–5, 167–8n7
Premack, David 9, 129
Price, Robert 218, 225
primatology
 ape language research (ALR) 126–7, 129–34, 141–2
 culture concept 1–2, 7–11, 103, 260, 274n4
 patterned interactions 15, 83–103

Quine, W.V.O. 186

race and racism
  and anthropology 40–1, 46–58, 59nn3,4
  Ecuador 236–9
  South Africa 211–15, 222–7
Radcliffe-Brown, A.R. 28
regional stereotypes, Ecuador 236–9, 255n1
Reinfuss, Roman 267–9, 270, 275n16
restorative justice, South Africa 216, 232n11
ritual, children's understanding of 119–22
Romanticism 209
Ross, Dorothy 60n7
rual 201–2
Rumbaugh, Duane 129
Rusyns 269–71, 275nn19,21
Ryukyu Islands 70–5

Sahlins, Marshall 3, 119, 121–2, 264
Said, Edward 61
Sapir, Edward 44, 193, 262
Sarich, Vincent 54
Savage-Rumbaugh, Sue 129–33
Schieffelin, Bambi 180
Schortman, Edward 158
selective systems 198–9
sexuality
  homosexuality 247–53
  machismo 18, 241–2
  stereotypes 239–55
Shahr-i Sokhta 162–3, 167–8n7
Shanker, Stuart 15–16, 125–44
Shanklin, Eugenia 46–7
Shennan, Stephen 148–9
Shweder, Richard 37
Silverman, Sydel 11
Slys-Janusz, Elzbieta 268
social action 35
social anthropology
  culture concept 259–61
  see also anthropology
social cognition module 176
social interaction
  dynamic 86–7
  patterns 88–103
  studies of 15–16
  and technological developments 157–65
social transmission, of culture 194–8, 204–6
South Africa
  Amnesty Committee 220, 222–7
  apartheid 212–15
  Constitutional Court 211, 215, 217–18
  cultural politics 17–18, 222–31
  human rights 211–31
  Truth and Reconciliation Commission (TRC) 211, 215, 219–22
  ubuntu 215–19
spatial language 170–2, 183–9
spatial memory 184, 191–2n7
species society 10
Specific Language Impairment 15–16, 126–7, 134–8, 141–2, 144n2
Sperber, Dan 196–7
Spivak, Gayatri 76
Stallybrass, Peter 257n10
standard social science model (SSSM) 110
Stanford, Craig 84
Stein, Aurel 161, 163
Stein, Gil 158
Steinberg, Arthur 159
Steinen, Karl von den 65
stereotypes
  cultural 236–9
  gender 239–55

Steward, Julian 150
Stocking, George 262
Stoll, David 76
Stone, Elizabeth 153
Stovaryshynie Lemkiv 267, 275n15
structural-functionalism 28, 31
Suchman, Lucy 180
Sudan, Nuer incest taboos 17, 200–3

taboos, social transmission of 200–3
Talmy, Leonard 178
Taylor, Charles 272
Taylor, W.W. 150
technology, and social interaction 157–65
Tenejapa, Mexico 170–2, 184–6
Tepe Yahya 167–8n7
terminology 14, 196
Terrace, H.S. 129
Thompson, Leonard 161
Tomasello, Michael 9, 86, 88–9, 191n2
Tooby, John 108–10, 174
Toren, Christina 15, 87, 105–24, 190
totalitarian culture 18, 260–1
Trouillot, Michel-Rolph 14, 37–60, 63, 143–4, 150
Tutu, Desmond 215, 222, 228, 232n10
Tylor, Edward B. 24, 25, 26, 274n7
Tzeltal language, Mayan Indians 170–2, 184–6, 189
Tzotzil language 192n12

ubuntu 215–19
Ukrainians, ethnic identity 266–71, 275n15
understanding, and meaning 111–12
United States *see* North America
Universal Grammar (UG) 174, 187

van Huyssteen, Elsa 218
van Straaten brothers 222–7
Varela, Francisco 123n3
variation 13, 27–32, 196–7
Verwoerd, H.F. 212
Virchow, Rudolf 262
volkekunde 213, 232n7
von Humboldt, Wilhelm 261
vulgarity, codes of 243, 256n3

Wallerstein, Immanuel 237
Washburn, Sherwood 10
Washington, Booker T. 73
Weber, Kendra 101
Webster, David 213, 232n6
Weltfish, Gene 59–60n5
Wenner-Gren Foundation, international symposium on culture (2000) 3, 11–13
White, Allon 257n10
White, Leslie 150
Whiten, Andrew 102
Whitten, Norman 257n11
Whorfianism 180
Wilkins, David 186
Williams, Raymond 259
Wilson, Edward O. 196
Wilson, Richard 17–18, 209–33
Wissler, Clark 51–2, 60n6
Wolf, Eric 60n10, 161, 263–4, 273
women *see* gender analysis
words, and concepts 37–9
World Archaeological Congress, Southampton (1986) 148
worldliness 61
Wright, Rita 14, 16, 147–68

Yamanokuchi, Baku 74
yaqona ceremony, Fiji 119, 121

Zimmerman, Andrew 261, 274n8